McGraw-Hill's Compound Interest and Annuity Tables

McGraw-Hill's
Compound Interest
and
Annuity Tables

Second Edition

Jack C. Estes

Dennis R. Kelley

McGraw-Hill, Inc.

New York   St. Louis   San Francisco   Auckland   Bogotá
Caracas   Lisbon   London   Madrid   Mexico   Milan
Montreal   New Delhi   Paris   San Juan   São Paulo
Singapore   Sydney   Tokyo   Toronto

Library of Congress Cataloging-in-Publication Data

Estes, Jack C., 1922-1975
    McGraw-Hill's compound interest and annuity tables / Jack C.
Estes, Dennis R. Kelley. — 2nd ed.
    p.   cm.
    Previously published under title: Compound interest and annuity
tables
    Includes index.
    ISBN 0-07-019686-9
    1. Interest — Tables. 2. Annuities — Tables. I. Kelley, Dennis R.
II. Estes, Jack C., 1922-1975. Compound interest and annuity
tables. III. Title.
HG1626.E82 1992
332.8'2'0212 — dc20   92-25142
                                                        CIP

1 2 3 4 5 6 7 8 9 0 DOC/DOC 9 8 7 6 3 2

ISBN   0-07-019686-9

*The sponsoring editor for this book was David Conti, the
editing supervisor was Kimberly A. Goff, and the produc-
tion supervisor was Pamela A. Pelton.*

Composed by Realty Computing Company, Ltd.

Printed and bound by R. R. Donnelly & Sons Company.

Contents

Preface to the Second Edition

Financial analysts, mortgage lenders, bond dealers, bankers, appraisers and students all need correct, easy-to-use financial tables. In his original text, the late Jack C. Estes provided a wide array of just such financial tables in a convenient form. In this revision, his tables have been expanded to include more interest rates and compounding periods. New and augmented examples explain each table. A smaller page size improves portability, and larger type adds to legibility.

Estes' original aim has guided the presentation throughout: to avoid complicated formulas, while presenting simple, straightforward descriptions. No knowledge of higher math or of annuity theory is presupposed. With only simple arithmetic and these tables, anyone can solve the most complex financial problems.

The book provides the **six financial functions of $1** for interest rates from 5 percent to 16 percent, from 1 month to 50 years. Each two-page spread presents all six functions for a given interest rate. Monthly, quarterly, semiannual and annual compounding periods are shown for each function, as are continuous and daily compounding for the future value of 1, future value of 1 per period and sinking fund payments.

Examples demonstrate each use of the financial functions in practical applications, whether finding the balance in a deposit account or on a mortgage loan, figuring mortgage payments, or setting up a fund for college education costs.

Acknowledgments

I am grateful to David J. Conti, Editorial Director of Business McGraw-Hill. His insight and direction improved the text, while retaining all the elements of its lasting popularity.

Section 1
Introduction

Compound interest and annuity functions surround us in everyday life. Advertising posters in banks set out the compound interest rates offered on deposits. Educators point out that university costs are rising at a ten percent compounded growth rate. The consumer price index shows that only five loaves of bread can be had today with the dollars that paid for ten just a few years ago. An annuity from an insurance company may offer to return $16,000 after seven years from a $10,000 deposit. In each case, the mathematics of compound growth and discount presented in this book are the base for all required calculations.

Growth at an increasing rate (compound amount) and its reciprocal, decline at a decreasing rate (compound discount) are common concepts. But finding the right path to describe daily events in actual numbers and solving them mathematically can be frustrating, even for experienced business persons and educators.

For a small-scale exercise, we can quickly find the interest earned on a loan; for example, 5 percent interest on $100 due in one year is $5. But when the problem becomes interest compounded quarterly for 80 periods, time is seldom available for the laborious calculations needed. Financial calculators can handle one such problem well, but to see the entire range of probable answers or to search for the terms that best fit a given case, it is faster and more certain to use these tables.

Studying the explanations and examples in the pages that follow is the best means to ensure that you know where to turn when you encounter a compound interest or annuity problem. With these tables, you will be able to solve it quickly, without having to search for the right formula or the right words to express the answer.

Explanation of the Tables

The mathematics of finance has evolved to a point where today six formulas are accepted as standard. They are often called the **six financial functions of $1**. Deriving the functions of compound interest and annuities from their formulas is not simple. But with the financial tables in this book, it is only necessary to know the category of problem, since the tricky part of the math has been preprinted. Used alone or in combination, the six financial functions of $1 permit the answer to virtually every financial problem to be computed.

Compounding is what makes financial functions complex. Compounding assumes that, at certain time intervals called the compounding periods, interest earned up to that point is added to the base amount, or principal. The added interest itself then begins to earn interest for the next period. At the next compounding period, interest is added again and is now called compound interest. The monthly mortgage payment of a 30-year loan has 360 such compoundings calculated into it.

Compounding is always associated with the interest rate. When using tables, it is as important to know one as the other. In this book, the compounding period is shown on every page, just below the interest rate.

At the head of each column in the tables, there is a reference to 1. It means that the answers in the columns have been solved using $1 (or 1 peso or 1 franc; the unit of currency will not make any difference). With the answer for 1 of something, it only remains to multiply or divide by the number of somethings in the specific case. So the first step in solving a problem using the tables is to look for the 1 involved, which will always be the known quantity. This will tell you the correct column to use. The number of years or months in your problem tell which line on the page to use. With these known factors, the unknown given by the tables can be found. Multiplying or dividing to bring the scale in line completes the problem.

The following description of the six financial functions of $1 gives the quantity that is known at the start, and the unknown, which is the answer found in the tables.

Future Value of 1

In this case, 1 is the amount on hand now; for example, $1 in a bank deposit. The answer given in the column is the sum in the future that 1 will grow to, including accumulated interest.

To find the future value of 1 without tables, it would be possible to multiply the balance for each year times the interest ratio, or 1 plus the interest rate. So for 6 percent and three years, you would calculate

1	×	1.06	=	1.06
1.06	×	1.06	=	1.1236
1.1236	×	1.06	=	1.191015

This says that $1 deposited for three years at 6 percent, compounded annually, has a future value of $1.19. The simple case here would soon become clumsy, however, if the desired terms were 0.667 percent interest per month for 180 months. But there is no need for such labor, since the tables will do the work for you.

Future Value of 1 per Period

In this column, 1 is a payment or deposit to be made in a series every compounding period (day, month, year or whatever). Examples are a savings deposit program, such as an IRA account, or the regular premiums on a life insurance policy. The answer given in this column is the accumulation of the deposits, plus the interest on them.

Deposits in a series can be looked on as many separate calculations of the future value of 1. In a 10-year series, the first deposit would be made at the end of 1 year, and interest compounded for the next nine years; another deposit made at the end of the second year would earn interest for the 8 years after that, and so on through the series. Totalling the values gives the future value of 1 per period. But in the column, future value of 1 per period, the sum is already there. The column is a running total of the figures under future value of 1 next to it.

Payment for a Sinking Fund of 1

For this case, 1 is the amount desired to be on hand at some future date. The future amount might be needed a fund to pay off a bond issue, to replace a roof or provide a retirement fund. The answer in the column is the payment or deposit that has to be made each period, so that at term, with interest, the desired amount will be on hand.

The payment for a sinking fund of 1 is the inverse of the future value of 1 per period. There, the amount of the deposit was known, but the eventual total had to be found from the tables. Here, the future value at the end of the series is a given, 1, but the deposit to reach it is to be found in the tables. Not surprisingly, the payment for a sinking fund of 1 is also the mathematical inverse, the reciprocal, of the future value of 1 per period. You could divide 1 by either factor and get the other, but the tables have done it for you.

Present Value of 1

Here, 1 is the amount you will get, once, at some date in the future after the initial, unknown amount has earned interest for a period. The payment of 1 will only arrive at a time in the future, so it must be worth less than 1 now, since interest could be earned on it until payment.

If 6 percent interest could be earned, $100 one year from now is only worth $94.34 today. A 1-year deposit of $94.34 at 6 percent interest will earn $5.66 interest, or $94.34 $\times$ 0.06 = $5.66, for a total value in a year of $100. So $94.34 is the present value of $100 in 1 year at 6 percent simple interest. "Simple" means "without compounding."

The starting value, $94.34, was found by dividing $100 by the interest ratio, 1 plus the interest rate or 1.06. And that is the construction of the column, present value of 1. Each entry in the column (for yearly compounding) is the entry above it divided by the interest ratio, 1 plus the interest rate.

Another way to look at the present value of 1 is this: It is the one-time deposit needed now in order to have 1 on hand at a future date. It is a one-time sinking fund payment, while the sinking fund column gives figures for a series of deposits.

Present Value of 1 per Period

The name of this function implies a series; 1 is each payment or deposit in the series to be paid in the future at regular intervals. They might be annual receipts from a winning lottery ticket, payments that will fall due on a mortgage, rent payments, anything that is paid in level (equal) amounts at intervals (the compounding period).

Here again, the series of payments that make up the per-period column could be broken into individual values. The present value of 1 for the first payment can be added to that for the second and so on. In fact, the column, present value of 1 per period, is a running total of present value of 1 figures in the column next to it.

Payment to Pay off a Loan of 1

Under this heading, 1 is the amount of a loan received now that will be repaid in installments over time. The unknown is the installment.

The figures in the column are the portion of the loan amount, 1, to be paid each month, quarter or other period. Multiplying the actual loan amount by the factor gives the amount to be paid every period.

It is often desirable to know the annual debt service and the annual mortgage constant. To find annual debt service, multiply the loan amount by the periodic factor and by the number of payments per year. For a $10,000 loan with monthly payment factor .008, the results would be

$$\$10,000 \quad \times \quad .00800 \times \quad 12 \quad = \quad \$960$$

annual debt service.

The annual mortgage constant is found by dividing the payments in 1 year by the loan amount. For a loan of $10,000 with $80 monthly payments, the result would be

$$\$80 \quad \times \quad 12 \quad \div \quad \$10,000 \quad = \quad 0.0960$$

or 9.60 percent, the annual mortgage constant.

Examples and Solved Problems

Future Value of 1

Example 1.   Balance of a Bank Deposit

Smithson deposited $21,000 in a bank certificate of deposit (CD) at 5.75 percent interest per year, compounded monthly. What will be the value of the CD at its maturity three years from now?

Enter the page for 5.75 percent interest, monthly compounding. On the line for 3 years, read in the future value of 1 column, 1.18778239. Multiply the initial deposit by the factor to get

$$\$21,000 \quad \times \quad 1.18778239 \quad = \quad \$24,943.43$$

the total balance of the certificate in 3 years with 5.75 percent interest compounded monthly.

Example 2.   Cost of Replacing a Machine

The Aquilo Corporation has installed new machinery expected to last 7 years. Equipment of this type has been increasing in cost at the rate of 8 percent per year. Assuming this rate of increase continues, what will replacement machinery cost in 7 years?

The interest rate will represent the inflation rate in this case. Enter the page for 8.00 percent, yearly compounding. On the line for 7 years, find under future value of 1 the factor, 1.71382427. With these assumptions, the replacement machine will cost 1.71 times what the current machine did.

Future Value of 1 per Period

Example 3.   Balance of a Savings Program

Through the 401(k) program at her office, Elaine Gelson may make deposits to an investment account that under present law will earn interest free of tax until withdrawal. The fund has averaged a yield of 6.50 percent per year over the past several years. If she makes regular deposits of $1200 per quarter, what will the account balance total, when she is eligible for retirement in 11 years?

Enter the page for 6.50 percent, quarterly compounding. Find the factor on the line for 11 years, under future value of 1 per period; it is 63.53674053. Multiply the deposits in one quarter by this factor to get

$$\$1,200 \ \times \ 63.53674053 \ = \ \$76,244.09$$

the accumulated total of principal and interest in the account 11 years in the future, if an average interest rate of 6.50 percent per year is earned.

Example 4.   Amount of a Past Due Loan

Sarwood Corporation holds a loan which the debtor has fallen behind on; eleven monthly payments of $688 have not been made. The loan states that payments not paid when due will bear interest at 15 percent per year.

To find the principal and interest due, enter the page for 15.00 percent, monthly compounding. On the line for 11 months, the factor in the column, future value of 1 per period, is given as 11.71393720. Multiply the monthly payment by the factor to get

$688 × 11.71393720 = $8,059.19

the balance with interest at 15 percent per year.

Payment for a Sinking Fund of 1

Example 5.   Building a College Tuition Fund

College education costs for the Sodan children are estimated to be $150,000, beginning 15 years from now. To have this amount on hand, their parents intend to establish a fund that will be invested in tax-exempt bonds. Twice each year they will add to the fund's holdings at a constant rate. If the bonds earn an average 7.50 percent per year interest with semiannual compounding, what amount added each half-year period will achieve the target?

Enter the page with 7.50 percent, semiannual compounding. On the 15-year line, take the factor under payment for sinking fund of 1, which is 0.01858762. Next, multiply the desired future fund by the factor to get

$150,000 × 0.01858762 = $2,788.14

the amount of bonds earning 7.50% interest, compounded semiannually, that, if added to the fund twice a year, will build the desired total.

Example 6.   Reserve for Replacements

Deborah Prenill will need to renovate her office building when the present tenant moves out in 6 years, at an expected cost of $21 per square foot of rented space. She is considering putting a a part of the monthly rentals from the tenant aside to build a fund for this cost. Bank money market accounts are currently paying 8 percent interest, compounded monthly.

To find the necessary deposit to build the fund for future renovations, enter the tables at 8 percent monthly compounding. On the line for 6 years, find the factor under payment for a sinking fund of 1, 0.01086657. Multiply the renovation cost by the factor to get

$21 per s.f. $\times$ 0.01086657 $=$ $0.228

per square foot, the monthly deposit she would make to build a renovation fund of $21 per square foot in 6 years.

Present Value of 1

Example 7.   Present Value of a Note

Storheld & Company paid for its building partially by a cash payment and partially with a promissory note to the builder. The note calls for a single payment of $360,000 in two years without interest. The accountants for the builder are valuing the promissory note as of today. They have determined that banks currently charge 10.50 percent, compounded monthly, on loans of this type.

Enter the tables at 10.50 percent, monthly compounding. Under the column present value of 1, find the factor, 0.81132499. Multiplying the face amount of the note by the factor gives

$$\$360,000 \quad \times \quad 0.81132499 \quad = \quad \$292,077$$

The accountants will record the note on the books of the builder at its present value, $292,077. They will probably round it to the next lower multiple of $5,000 or $290,000.

Example 8.   Single Deposit to Build a Fund

Kim Fallingby has a major commission due in the near future. To assure that at least $500,000 will be on hand at retirement age in 22 years, she plans to place part of the commission in a deposit account. Based on interest rates over the past few years, she expects the account can earn interest of 7 percent, compounded quarterly.

To find the single deposit, enter the tables on the page for 7 percent, quarterly compounding. On the 22-year line, find under present value of 1, the factor 0.21725572. Multiply the desired future fund by the factor to get

$$\$500,000 \quad \times \quad 0.21725572 \quad = \quad \$108,628$$

the deposit that will grow, with 7 percent interest, compounded quarterly, to $500,000 in 22 years.

Present Value of 1 per Period

Example 9.   Value of Future Receipts

The Mondrian Partnership have receivables from various well-established companies that will bring in an average of $61,000 per month over the next 36 months. A bank will lend the partnership fifty percent of the present value of the receivables. The valuation will be made using the interest rate of 12 percent per year, compounded monthly.

To find the potential amount the bank will lend, enter the tables at the page for 12 percent interest, monthly compounding. On the line for 36 months, find the factor under present value of 1 per period. It is 30.10750504. Multiply the average receivables for a month by the factor and by 50 percent to get

$$\$61,000 \times 30.10750504 \times 0.50 = \$918,279$$

The bank will advance up to $918,000, which is one-half the present value of the receivables.

Example 10.   Valuing a Lease with Concessions

Palgrave & Garrick have been offered a lease for 5 years with monthly rental of $5600. The landlord will waive the rent during the first year. Bank loans at present require 10 percent interest.

To find the value of the lease, enter the page for 10 percent, monthly compounding. On the line for 48 months, take the factor in the column present value of 1 per period, 39.42816009. Multiply the monthly rental paid during 48 months by the factor to get

$$\$5,600 \times 39.42816009 = \$220,799$$

the present value of the payments once they start to flow to the landlord in one year. Now, under present value of 1, take the factor on the line for 12 months, 0.90521243. Next, discount the present value of the payments for 12 months, the free rent period, by multiplying it by this new factor, to get

$$\$220,799 \quad \times \quad 0.90521243 \quad = \quad \$199,869$$

the present value of the lease with free rent for 12 months followed by 48 months at $5600 monthly. (This value is calculated with end of month factors, while rents are paid at the beginning of the month. The small error is within acceptable trade practice.)

Example 11.   Balance on a Mortgage Loan

Jan Squires has a loan that requires payments of $1355 monthly. It bears interest at 10.75 percent and has 216 payments until it will be fully paid off. What is the balance on the loan?

Enter the page with 10.75 percent interest with monthly compounding. Read down to the line for 216 months and take the factor under present value of 1 per period, 95.36662649. Multiply the monthly payment by the factor to get

$$\$1,355 \quad \times \quad 95.36662649 \quad = \quad \$129,222$$

the remaining balance on the mortgage loan (and also the present value of all remaining payments).

Payment to Pay Off a Loan of 1

Example 12.   Payment on a Mortgage Loan

Terry Greatspan has applied for a $160,000 loan mortgage loan. The interest rate will be 11 percent, with payments to amortize the loan over 30 years.

To find the mortgage payments, enter the tables at 11 percent, monthly compounding. On the line for 30 years, read the periodic payment factor, .00952323. Multiply the loan amount by this factor to get the monthly payment, or

$$\$160{,}000 \quad \times \quad 0.00952323 \quad = \quad \$1{,}523.72$$

the monthly payment. Multiplying the monthly payment by 12 gives

$$\$1{,}523.72 \quad \times \quad 12 \quad = \quad \$18{,}284.64$$

the annual debt service on the loan.

Example 13.   Regular Withdrawal from Account

The Cassidys have established a money market account of $350,000 that currently earns interest at 9 percent per year, with compounding monthly. They would like to have the bank issue a monthly check to them out of the principal and interest. The checks are to be in equal monthly payments over the next 10 years, in an amount that will exhaust the account in that time. What monthly payment can they receive from this fund?

Enter the tables at 9 percent interest, monthly compounding. On the line for 10 years, take the factor under the column, payment to pay off a loan of 1; it is 0.01266758. This is the monthly portion of 1 that can be withdrawn. Multiplying the initial deposit by this factor gives

$$\$350{,}000 \quad \times \quad 0.01266758 \quad = \quad \$4433.65$$

the monthly payment that, if interest averages 9 percent, can be received each month and retire the account in 10 years.

Section 2

Compound Interest and Annuity Tables

5.00%
Monthly

	Present Value of 1	Present Value of 1 per Period	Payment to Pay Off a Loan of 1	Months
	0.99585062	0.99585062	1.00416667	1
	0.99171846	1.98756908	0.50312717	2
	0.98760345	2.97517253	0.33611496	3
	0.98350551	3.95867804	0.25260958	4
	0.97942457	4.93810261	0.20250693	5
	0.97536057	5.91346318	0.16910564	6
	0.97131343	6.88477661	0.14524800	7
	0.96728308	7.85205970	0.12735512	8
	0.96326946	8.81532916	0.11343876	9
	0.95927249	9.77460165	0.10230596	10
Years	0.95529211	10.72989376	0.09319757	11
1	0.95132824	11.68122200	0.08560748	12
2	0.90502542	22.79389839	0.04387139	24
3	0.86097624	33.36570128	0.02997090	36
4	0.81907102	43.42295594	0.02302929	48
5	0.77920539	52.99070632	0.01887123	60
6	0.74128009	62.09277748	0.01610493	72
7	0.70520069	70.75183482	0.01413391	84
8	0.67087733	78.98944062	0.01265992	96
9	0.63822455	86.82610765	0.01151727	108
10	0.60716104	94.28135033	0.01060655	120
11	0.57760944	101.37373323	0.00986449	132
12	0.54949618	108.12091739	0.00924890	144
13	0.52275123	114.53970423	0.00873060	156
14	0.49730801	120.64607743	0.00828871	168
15	0.47310316	126.45524271	0.00790794	180
16	0.45007639	131.98166570	0.00757681	192
17	0.42817038	137.23910796	0.00728655	204
18	0.40733058	142.24066127	0.00703034	216
19	0.38750508	146.99878018	0.00680278	228
20	0.36864453	151.52531307	0.00659956	240
21	0.35070195	155.83153166	0.00641719	252
22	0.33363267	159.92815901	0.00625281	264
23	0.31739418	163.82539630	0.00610406	276
24	0.30194605	167.53294821	0.00596898	288
25	0.28724980	171.06004704	0.00584590	300
26	0.27326885	174.41547577	0.00573344	312
27	0.25996838	177.60758989	0.00563039	324
28	0.24731526	180.64433819	0.00553574	336
29	0.23527799	183.53328262	0.00544860	348
30	0.22382660	186.28161705	0.00536822	360
31	0.21293256	188.89618520	0.00529391	372
32	0.20256876	191.38349772	0.00522511	384
33	0.19270938	193.74974838	0.00516130	396
34	0.18332988	196.00082945	0.00510202	408
35	0.17440689	198.14234644	0.00504688	420
36	0.16591820	200.17963204	0.00499551	432
37	0.15784267	202.11775903	0.00494761	444
38	0.15016019	203.96155463	0.00490288	456
39	0.14285163	205.71560914	0.00486108	468
40	0.13589879	207.38429072	0.00482197	480
41	0.12928436	208.97175464	0.00478534	492
42	0.12299186	210.48195390	0.00475100	504
43	0.11700563	211.91864911	0.00471879	516
44	0.11131076	213.28541783	0.00468855	528
45	0.10589307	214.58566352	0.00466014	540
46	0.10073907	215.82262397	0.00463343	552
47	0.09583592	216.99937937	0.00460831	564
48	0.09117142	218.11886002	0.00458466	576
49	0.08673394	219.18583358	0.00456238	588
50	0.08251245	220.19701202	0.00454139	600

	Future Value of 1	Future Value of 1 per Period	Payment for Sinking Fund of 1	**5.00%** Monthly
Months				
1	1.00416667	1.00000000	1.00000000	
2	1.00835069	2.00416667	0.49896050	
3	1.01255216	3.01251736	0.33194829	
4	1.01677112	4.02506952	0.24844291	
5	1.02100767	5.04184064	0.19834026	
6	1.02526187	6.06284831	0.16493898	
7	1.02953379	7.08811018	0.14108133	
8	1.03382352	8.11764397	0.12318845	
9	1.03813111	9.15146749	0.10927209	
10	1.04245666	10.18959860	0.09813929	
11	1.04680023	11.23205526	0.08903090	Years
12	1.05116190	12.27885549	0.08144082	1
24	1.10494134	25.18592053	0.03970472	2
36	1.16147223	38.75333552	0.02580423	3
48	1.22089536	53.01488521	0.01886263	4
60	1.28335868	68.00608284	0.01470457	5
72	1.34901774	83.76425860	0.01193827	6
84	1.41803605	100.32865253	0.00996724	7
96	1.49058547	117.74051230	0.00849325	8
108	1.56684665	136.04319586	0.00735061	9
120	1.64700950	155.28227945	0.00643988	10
132	1.73127363	175.50567106	0.00569782	11
144	1.81984887	196.76372977	0.00508224	12
156	1.91295580	219.10939111	0.00456393	13
168	2.01082625	242.59829890	0.00412204	14
180	2.11370393	267.28894379	0.00374127	15
192	2.22184504	293.24280892	0.00341014	16
204	2.33551885	320.52452306	0.00311989	17
216	2.45500842	349.20202147	0.00286367	18
228	2.58061131	379.34671512	0.00263611	19
240	2.71264029	411.03366852	0.00243289	20
252	2.85142411	444.34178658	0.00225052	21
264	2.99730838	479.35401118	0.00208614	22
276	3.15065637	516.15752764	0.00193739	23
288	3.31184992	554.84398186	0.00180231	24
300	3.48129045	595.50970849	0.00167923	25
312	3.65939988	638.25597087	0.00156677	26
324	3.84662172	683.18921317	0.00146372	27
336	4.04342219	730.42132542	0.00136907	28
348	4.25029134	780.06992217	0.00128194	29
360	4.46774431	832.25863536	0.00120155	30
372	4.69632259	887.11742217	0.00112725	31
384	4.93659537	944.78288862	0.00105844	32
396	5.18916096	1005.39862978	0.00099463	33
408	5.45464828	1069.11558730	0.00093535	34
420	5.73371844	1136.09242529	0.00088021	35
432	6.02706636	1206.49592543	0.00082885	36
444	6.33542251	1280.50140225	0.00078094	37
456	6.65955475	1358.29313972	0.00073622	38
468	7.00027021	1440.06485012	0.00069441	39
480	7.35841732	1526.02015642	0.00065530	40
492	7.73488791	1616.37309932	0.00061867	41
504	8.13061946	1711.34867026	0.00058433	42
516	8.54659738	1811.18337166	0.00055213	43
528	8.98385752	1916.12580586	0.00052189	44
540	9.44348873	2026.43729415	0.00049348	45
552	9.92663553	2142.39252755	0.00046677	46
564	10.43450104	2264.28025076	0.00044164	47
576	10.96834942	2392.40398122	0.00041799	48
588	11.52951152	2527.08276489	0.00039571	49
600	12.11938321	2668.65197074	0.00037472	50

5.25% Monthly	Present Value of 1	Present Value of 1 per Period	Payment to Pay Off a Loan of 1	Months
	0.99543758	0.99543758	1.00458333	1
	0.99089597	1.98633355	0.50344012	2
	0.98637509	2.97270863	0.33639355	3
	0.98187483	3.95458346	0.25287113	4
	0.97739510	4.93197856	0.20275838	5
	0.97293581	5.90491437	0.16935047	6
	0.96849687	6.87341123	0.14548817	7
	0.96407817	7.83748941	0.12759188	8
	0.95967964	8.79716905	0.11367293	9
	0.95530118	9.75247023	0.10253812	10
Years	0.95094269	10.70341292	0.09342814	11
1	0.94660409	11.65001701	0.08583678	12
2	0.89605930	22.67797074	0.04409566	24
3	0.84821340	33.11707683	0.03019590	36
4	0.80292227	42.99877734	0.02325648	48
5	0.76004950	52.35283545	0.01910116	60
6	0.71946597	61.20742509	0.01633789	72
7	0.68104943	69.58921586	0.01437004	84
8	0.64468417	77.52345327	0.01289932	96
9	0.61026067	85.03403484	0.01176000	108
10	0.57767525	92.14358207	0.01085263	120
11	0.54682975	98.87350854	0.01011393	132
12	0.51763128	105.24408446	0.00950172	144
13	0.48999189	111.27449767	0.00898679	156
14	0.46382832	116.98291147	0.00854826	168
15	0.43906179	122.38651931	0.00817083	180
16	0.41561768	127.50159659	0.00784304	192
17	0.39342540	132.34354966	0.00755609	204
18	0.37241809	136.92696223	0.00730316	216
19	0.35253249	141.26563931	0.00707886	228
20	0.33370869	145.37264877	0.00687887	240
21	0.31589001	149.26036072	0.00669970	252
22	0.29902278	152.94048475	0.00653849	264
23	0.28305618	156.42410520	0.00639288	276
24	0.26794214	159.72711456	0.00626089	288
25	0.25363513	162.84324507	0.00614087	300
26	0.24009205	165.79809861	0.00603143	312
27	0.22727211	168.59517505	0.00593137	324
28	0.21513671	171.24289905	0.00583966	336
29	0.20364929	173.74924541	0.00575542	348
30	0.19277525	176.12176312	0.00567789	360
31	0.18248184	178.36759809	0.00560640	372
32	0.17273806	180.49351466	0.00554037	384
33	0.16351455	182.50591597	0.00547927	396
34	0.15478354	184.41086328	0.00542267	408
35	0.14651873	186.21409419	0.00537016	420
36	0.13869523	187.92103984	0.00532138	432
37	0.13128948	189.53684177	0.00527602	444
38	0.12427915	191.06636639	0.00523378	456
39	0.11764316	192.51422065	0.00519442	468
40	0.11136149	193.88476541	0.00515770	480
41	0.10541524	195.18212868	0.00512342	492
42	0.09978650	196.41021806	0.00509138	504
43	0.09445831	197.57273249	0.00506143	516
44	0.08941462	198.67317340	0.00503339	528
45	0.08464025	199.71485527	0.00500714	540
46	0.08012080	200.70091558	0.00498254	552
47	0.07584268	201.63432431	0.00495947	564
48	0.07179299	202.51789282	0.00493784	576
49	0.06795954	203.35428239	0.00491753	588
50	0.06433078	204.14601218	0.00489845	600

Months	Future Value of 1	Future Value of 1 per Period	Payment for Sinking Fund of 1	
1	1.00437500	1.00000000	1.00000000	
2	1.00876914	2.00437500	0.49890864	
3	1.01318251	3.01314414	0.33187924	
4	1.01761518	4.02632665	0.24836534	
5	1.02206725	5.04394183	0.19825764	
6	1.02653879	6.06600907	0.16485303	
7	1.03102990	7.09254786	0.14099306	
8	1.03554065	8.12357776	0.12309847	
9	1.04007114	9.15911841	0.10918081	
10	1.04462145	10.19918955	0.09804701	
11	1.04919167	11.24381101	0.08893782	Years
12	1.05378189	12.29300268	0.08134709	1
24	1.11045626	25.24714624	0.03960844	2
36	1.17017870	38.89798808	0.02570827	3
48	1.23311312	53.28299795	0.01876771	4
60	1.29943227	68.44166079	0.01461098	5
72	1.36931818	84.41558512	0.01184615	6
84	1.44296270	101.24861723	0.00987668	7
96	1.52056796	118.98696158	0.00840428	8
108	1.60234697	137.67930755	0.00726326	9
120	1.68852421	157.37696315	0.00635417	10
132	1.77933623	178.13399584	0.00561375	11
144	1.87503229	200.00738091	0.00499982	12
156	1.97587507	223.05715789	0.00448316	13
168	2.08214135	247.34659537	0.00404291	14
180	2.19412285	272.94236463	0.00366378	15
192	2.31212691	299.91472264	0.00333428	16
204	2.43647746	328.33770497	0.00304564	17
216	2.56751581	358.28932890	0.00279104	18
228	2.70560166	389.85180769	0.00256508	19
240	2.85111402	423.11177613	0.00236344	20
252	3.00445231	458.16052843	0.00218264	21
264	3.16603743	495.09426875	0.00201982	22
276	3.33631289	534.01437531	0.00187261	23
288	3.51574609	575.02767864	0.00173905	24
300	3.70482955	618.24675479	0.00161748	25
312	3.90408228	663.79023441	0.00150650	26
324	4.11405119	711.78312829	0.00140492	27
336	4.33531262	762.35717055	0.00131172	28
348	4.56847391	815.65118022	0.00122601	29
360	4.81417506	871.81144229	0.00114704	30
372	5.07309048	930.99210920	0.00107412	31
384	5.34593086	993.35562405	0.00100669	32
396	5.63344510	1059.07316638	0.00094422	33
408	5.93642241	1128.32512213	0.00088627	34
420	6.25569441	1201.30157872	0.00083243	35
432	6.59213745	1278.20284683	0.00078235	36
444	6.94667504	1359.24001024	0.00073571	37
456	7.32028034	1444.63550518	0.00069222	38
468	7.71397882	1534.62373097	0.00065163	39
480	8.12885116	1629.45169332	0.00061370	40
492	8.56603611	1729.37968239	0.00057824	41
504	9.02673369	1834.68198726	0.00054505	42
516	9.51220846	1945.64764876	0.00051397	43
528	10.02379298	2062.58125290	0.00048483	44
540	10.56289148	2185.80376669	0.00045750	45
552	11.13098371	2315.65342017	0.00043184	46
564	11.72962902	2452.48663279	0.00040775	47
576	12.36047060	2596.67899376	0.00038511	48
588	13.02524003	2748.62629195	0.00036382	49
600	13.72576201	2908.74560252	0.00034379	50

5.50% Monthly	Present Value of 1	Present Value of 1 per Period	Payment to Pay Off a Loan of 1	Months
	0.99543758	0.99543758	1.00458333	1
	0.99089597	1.98633355	0.50344012	2
	0.98637509	2.97270863	0.33639355	3
	0.98187483	3.95458346	0.25287113	4
	0.97739510	4.93197856	0.20275838	5
	0.97293581	5.90491437	0.16935047	6
	0.96849687	6.87341123	0.14548817	7
	0.96407817	7.83748941	0.12759188	8
	0.95967964	8.79716905	0.11367293	9
	0.95530118	9.75247023	0.10253812	10
Years	0.95094269	10.70341292	0.09342814	11
1	0.94660409	11.65001701	0.08583678	12
2	0.89605930	22.67797074	0.04409566	24
3	0.84821340	33.11707683	0.03019590	36
4	0.80292227	42.99877734	0.02325648	48
5	0.76004950	52.35283545	0.01910116	60
6	0.71946597	61.20742509	0.01633789	72
7	0.68104943	69.58921586	0.01437004	84
8	0.64468417	77.52345327	0.01289932	96
9	0.61026067	85.03403484	0.01176000	108
10	0.57767525	92.14358207	0.01085263	120
11	0.54682975	98.87350854	0.01011393	132
12	0.51763128	105.24408446	0.00950172	144
13	0.48999189	111.27449767	0.00898679	156
14	0.46382832	116.98291147	0.00854826	168
15	0.43906179	122.38651931	0.00817083	180
16	0.41561768	127.50159659	0.00784304	192
17	0.39342540	132.34354966	0.00755609	204
18	0.37241809	136.92696223	0.00730316	216
19	0.35253249	141.26563931	0.00707886	228
20	0.33370869	145.37264877	0.00687887	240
21	0.31589001	149.26036072	0.00669970	252
22	0.29902278	152.94048475	0.00653849	264
23	0.28305618	156.42410520	0.00639288	276
24	0.26794214	159.72171456	0.00626089	288
25	0.25363513	162.84324507	0.00614087	300
26	0.24009205	165.79809861	0.00603143	312
27	0.22727211	168.59517505	0.00593137	324
28	0.21513671	171.24289905	0.00583966	336
29	0.20364929	173.74924541	0.00575542	348
30	0.19277525	176.12176312	0.00567789	360
31	0.18248184	178.36759809	0.00560640	372
32	0.17273806	180.49351466	0.00554037	384
33	0.16351455	182.50591597	0.00547927	396
34	0.15478354	184.41086328	0.00542267	408
35	0.14651873	186.21409419	0.00537016	420
36	0.13869523	187.92103994	0.00532138	432
37	0.13128948	189.53684177	0.00527602	444
38	0.12427915	191.06636639	0.00523378	456
39	0.11764316	192.51422065	0.00519442	468
40	0.11136149	193.88476541	0.00515770	480
41	0.10541524	195.18212868	0.00512342	492
42	0.09978650	196.41021806	0.00509138	504
43	0.09445831	197.57273249	0.00506143	516
44	0.08941462	198.67317340	0.00503339	528
45	0.08464025	199.71485527	0.00500714	540
46	0.08012080	200.70091558	0.00498254	552
47	0.07584268	201.63432431	0.00495947	564
48	0.07179299	202.51789282	0.00493784	576
49	0.06795954	203.35428239	0.00491753	588
50	0.06433078	204.14601218	0.00489845	600

	Future Value of 1	Future Value of 1 per Period	Payment for Sinking Fund of 1	**5.50%** Monthly
Months				
1	1.00458333	1.00000000	1.00000000	
2	1.00918767	2.00458333	0.49885679	
3	1.01381312	3.01377101	0.33181021	
4	1.01845976	4.02758412	0.24828780	
5	1.02312770	5.04604388	0.19817505	
6	1.02781704	6.06917159	0.16476713	
7	1.03252786	7.09698862	0.14090483	
8	1.03726028	8.12951649	0.12300855	
9	1.04201439	9.16677677	0.10908960	
10	1.04679029	10.20879116	0.09795479	
11	1.05158808	11.25558146	0.08884841	Years
12	1.05640786	12.30716954	0.08125345	1
24	1.11599757	25.30856018	0.03951232	2
36	1.17894860	39.04333145	0.02561257	3
48	1.24545057	53.55285177	0.01867314	4
60	1.31570377	68.88082310	0.01451783	5
72	1.38991981	85.07341249	0.01175455	6
84	1.46832221	102.17939120	0.00978671	7
96	1.55114712	120.25028157	0.00831599	8
108	1.63864401	139.34051221	0.00717666	9
120	1.73107642	159.50758191	0.00626929	10
132	1.82872273	180.81223285	0.00553060	11
144	1.93187707	203.31863358	0.00491839	12
156	2.04085012	227.09457222	0.00440345	13
168	2.15597011	252.21166068	0.00396492	14
180	2.27758377	278.74555036	0.00358750	15
192	2.40605740	306.77615999	0.00325971	16
204	2.54177795	336.38791633	0.00297276	17
216	2.68515421	367.67000849	0.00271983	18
228	2.83661801	400.71665653	0.00249553	19
240	2.99662556	435.62739528	0.00229554	20
252	3.16565880	472.50737412	0.00211637	21
264	3.34422684	511.46767365	0.00195516	22
276	3.53286752	552.62564031	0.00180954	23
288	3.73214902	596.10523981	0.00167756	24
300	3.94267156	642.03743050	0.00155754	25
312	4.16506922	690.56055778	0.00144810	26
324	4.40001187	741.82077084	0.00134803	27
336	4.64820712	795.97246286	0.00125632	28
348	4.91040254	853.17873595	0.00117209	29
360	5.18738784	913.61189251	0.00109456	30
372	5.47999729	977.45395413	0.00102307	31
384	5.78911221	1044.89720985	0.00095703	32
396	6.11566365	1116.14479531	0.00089594	33
408	6.46063515	1191.41130464	0.00083934	34
420	6.82506575	1270.92343671	0.00078683	35
432	7.21005311	1354.92067803	0.00073805	36
444	7.61675678	1443.65602400	0.00069269	37
456	8.04640173	1537.39674099	0.00065045	38
468	8.50028203	1636.42517125	0.00061109	39
480	8.97976476	1741.03958338	0.00057437	40
492	9.48629407	1851.55507067	0.00054009	41
504	10.02139563	1968.30450013	0.00050805	42
516	10.58668111	2091.63951510	0.00047809	43
528	11.18385314	2221.93159439	0.00045006	44
540	11.81471037	2359.57377109	0.00042381	45
552	12.48115290	2504.97881463	0.00039920	46
564	13.18518803	2658.58647942	0.00037614	47
576	13.92893628	2820.85882391	0.00035450	48
588	14.71463777	2992.28460415	0.00033419	49
600	15.54465900	3173.38014588	0.00031512	50

5.75% Monthly	Present Value of 1	Present Value of 1 per Period	Payment to Pay Off a Loan of 1	
				Months
	0.99523118	0.99523118	1.00479167	1
	0.99048511	1.98571629	0.50359661	2
	0.98576167	2.97147796	0.33653287	3
	0.98106075	3.95253871	0.25300195	4
	0.97638225	4.92892097	0.20288416	5
	0.97172607	5.90064703	0.16947294	6
	0.96709208	6.86773912	0.14560833	7
	0.96248020	7.83021932	0.12771034	8
	0.95789031	8.78810962	0.11379011	9
	0.95332231	9.74143193	0.10265431	10
Years	0.94877609	10.69020802	0.09354355	11
1	0.94425155	11.63445956	0.08595156	12
2	0.89161099	22.62031602	0.04420805	24
3	0.84190505	32.99372798	0.03030879	36
4	0.79497015	42.78883828	0.02337058	48
5	0.75065179	52.03788634	0.01921677	60
6	0.70880412	60.77131429	0.01645513	72
7	0.66928939	69.01786715	0.01448900	84
8	0.63197754	76.80468746	0.01302004	96
9	0.59674577	84.15740458	0.01188250	108
10	0.56347812	91.10021911	0.01097692	120
11	0.53206508	97.65598248	0.01024003	132
12	0.50240328	103.84627218	0.00962962	144
13	0.47439507	109.69146282	0.00911648	156
14	0.44794828	115.21079312	0.00867974	168
15	0.42297586	120.42242931	0.00830410	180
16	0.39939561	125.34352484	0.00797807	192
17	0.37712992	129.99027692	0.00769288	204
18	0.35610551	134.37797976	0.00744170	216
19	0.33625318	138.52107496	0.00721912	228
20	0.31750759	142.43319901	0.00702084	240
21	0.29980703	146.12722821	0.00684335	252
22	0.28309325	149.61532099	0.00668381	264
23	0.26731124	152.90915800	0.00653984	276
24	0.25240905	156.01897985	0.00640948	288
25	0.23833764	158.95562279	0.00629106	300
26	0.22505069	161.72855244	0.00618320	312
27	0.21250446	164.34689555	0.00608469	324
28	0.20065766	166.81927008	0.00599451	336
29	0.18947131	169.15381356	0.00591178	348
30	0.17890858	171.35820985	0.00583573	360
31	0.16893470	173.43971447	0.00576569	372
32	0.15951685	175.40517842	0.00570109	384
33	0.15062404	177.26107080	0.00564140	396
34	0.14222698	179.01350006	0.00558617	408
35	0.13429804	180.66823409	0.00553501	420
36	0.12681114	182.23071926	0.00548755	432
37	0.11974161	183.70609831	0.00544348	444
38	0.11306620	185.09922725	0.00540251	456
39	0.10676294	186.41469142	0.00536438	468
40	0.10081107	187.65682049	0.00532888	480
41	0.09519101	188.82970279	0.00529578	492
42	0.08988426	189.93719872	0.00526490	504
43	0.08487335	190.98295346	0.00523607	516
44	0.08014179	191.97040900	0.00520914	528
45	0.07567401	192.90281541	0.00518396	540
46	0.07145530	193.78324162	0.00516040	552
47	0.06747178	194.61458542	0.00513836	564
48	0.06371033	195.39958310	0.00511772	576
49	0.06015858	196.14081837	0.00509838	588
50	0.05680483	196.84073092	0.00508025	600

	Future Value of 1	Future Value of 1 per Period	Payment for Sinking Fund of 1	**5.75%** Monthly
Months				
1	1.00479167	1.00000000	1.00000000	
2	1.00960629	2.00479167	0.49880495	
3	1.01444399	3.01439796	0.33174120	
4	1.01930487	4.02884195	0.24821028	
5	1.02418904	5.04814682	0.19809250	
6	1.02909661	6.07233585	0.16468127	
7	1.03402770	7.10143246	0.14081666	
8	1.03898241	8.13546016	0.12291868	
9	1.04396087	9.17444257	0.10899845	
10	1.04896318	10.21840345	0.09786265	
11	1.05398947	11.26736663	0.08875188	Years
12	1.05903983	12.32135609	0.08115990	1
24	1.12156536	25.37016297	0.03941638	2
36	1.18778239	39.18936921	0.02551712	3
48	1.25790887	53.82445905	0.01857891	4
60	1.33217559	69.32360212	0.01442510	5
72	1.41082702	85.73781199	0.01166347	6
84	1.49412200	103.12111404	0.00969734	7
96	1.58233472	121.53072330	0.00822837	8
108	1.67575549	141.02723280	0.00709083	9
120	1.77469181	161.67481292	0.00618526	10
132	1.87946932	183.54142269	0.00544836	11
144	1.99043287	206.69903341	0.00483795	12
156	2.10794769	231.22386557	0.00432481	13
168	2.23240057	257.19663967	0.00388808	14
180	2.36420112	284.70284198	0.00351243	15
192	2.50378315	313.83300583	0.00318641	16
204	2.65160609	344.68300963	0.00290122	17
216	2.80815646	377.35439246	0.00265003	18
228	2.97394955	411.95468822	0.00242745	19
240	3.14953103	448.59777960	0.00222917	20
252	3.33547881	487.40427292	0.00205168	21
264	3.53240491	528.50189505	0.00189214	22
276	3.74095750	572.02591386	0.00174817	23
288	3.96182300	618.11958339	0.00161781	24
300	4.19572837	666.93461540	0.00149940	25
312	4.44344346	718.63167867	0.00139153	26
324	4.70578361	773.38092782	0.00129302	27
336	4.98361228	831.36256341	0.00120284	28
348	5.27784391	892.76742498	0.00112021	29
360	5.58944693	957.79761922	0.00104406	30
372	5.91944693	1026.66718515	0.00097403	31
384	6.26893008	1099.60279864	0.00090942	32
396	6.63904665	1176.84451844	0.00084973	33
408	7.03101485	1258.64657635	0.00079450	34
420	7.44612478	1345.27821395	0.00074334	35
432	7.88574273	1437.02456883	0.00069588	36
444	8.35131565	1534.18761301	0.00065181	37
456	8.84437591	1637.08714693	0.00061084	38
468	9.36654637	1746.06185197	0.00057272	39
480	9.91954569	1861.47040521	0.00053721	40
492	10.50519400	1983.69265997	0.00050411	41
504	11.12541888	2113.13089602	0.00047323	42
516	11.78226173	2250.21114369	0.00044440	43
528	12.47788447	2395.38458605	0.00041747	44
540	13.21457667	2549.12904396	0.00039229	45
552	13.99476305	2711.95054873	0.00036874	46
564	14.82101150	2884.38500766	0.00034669	47
576	15.69604151	3066.99996796	0.00032605	48
588	16.62273316	3260.39648470	0.00030671	49
600	17.60413652	3465.21109916	0.00028858	50

23

	Present Value of 1	Present Value of 1 per Period	Payment to Pay Off a Loan of 1	
6.00% Monthly				Months
	0.99502488	0.99502488	1.00500000	1
	0.99007450	1.98509938	0.50375312	2
	0.98514876	2.97024814	0.33667221	3
	0.98024752	3.95049566	0.25313279	4
	0.97537067	4.92586633	0.20300997	5
	0.97051808	5.89638441	0.16959546	6
	0.96568963	6.86207404	0.14572854	7
	0.96088520	7.82295924	0.12782866	8
	0.95610468	8.77906392	0.11390736	9
	0.95134794	9.73041186	0.10277057	10
Years	0.94661487	10.67702673	0.09365903	11
1	0.94190534	11.61893207	0.08606643	12
2	0.88718567	22.56286622	0.04432061	24
3	0.83564492	32.87101624	0.03042194	36
4	0.78709841	42.58031778	0.02348503	48
5	0.74137220	51.72556075	0.01933280	60
6	0.69830243	60.33951394	0.01657289	72
7	0.65773479	68.45304244	0.01460855	84
8	0.61952391	76.09521825	0.01314143	96
9	0.58353288	83.29342446	0.01200575	108
10	0.54963273	90.07345333	0.01110205	120
11	0.51770201	96.45959872	0.01036703	132
12	0.48762628	102.47474316	0.00975850	144
13	0.45929780	108.14043983	0.00924723	156
14	0.43261505	113.47698978	0.00881236	168
15	0.40748243	118.50351467	0.00843857	180
16	0.38380987	123.23802530	0.00811438	192
17	0.36151257	127.69748615	0.00783101	204
18	0.34051062	131.89787613	0.00758162	216
19	0.32072877	135.85424589	0.00736083	228
20	0.30209614	139.58077168	0.00716431	240
21	0.28454597	143.09080623	0.00698857	252
22	0.26801537	146.39692651	0.00683074	264
23	0.25244511	149.51097886	0.00668847	276
24	0.23777939	152.44412139	0.00655978	288
25	0.22396568	155.20686401	0.00644301	300
26	0.21095447	157.80910603	0.00633677	312
27	0.19869914	160.26017168	0.00623985	324
28	0.18715578	162.56884351	0.00615124	336
29	0.17628303	164.74339383	0.00607005	348
30	0.16604193	166.79161439	0.00599551	360
31	0.15639578	168.72084427	0.00592695	372
32	0.14731002	170.53799620	0.00586380	384
33	0.13875209	172.24958131	0.00580553	396
34	0.13069134	173.86173245	0.00575170	408
35	0.12309887	175.38022623	0.00570190	420
36	0.11594748	176.81050362	0.00565577	432
37	0.10921155	178.15768954	0.00561300	444
38	0.10286694	179.42661115	0.00557331	456
39	0.09689092	180.62181518	0.00553643	468
40	0.09126208	181.74758425	0.00550214	480
41	0.08596024	182.80795214	0.00547022	492
42	0.08096641	183.80671832	0.00544050	504
43	0.07626269	184.74746152	0.00541279	516
44	0.07183224	185.63355256	0.00538696	528
45	0.06765917	186.46816645	0.00536285	540
46	0.06372853	187.25429372	0.00534033	552
47	0.06002624	187.99475120	0.00531930	564
48	0.05653904	188.69219205	0.00529964	576
49	0.05325442	189.34911531	0.00528125	588
50	0.05016063	189.96787484	0.00526405	600

	Future Value of 1	Future Value of 1 per Period	Payment for Sinking Fund of 1	**6.00%** Monthly
Months				
1	1.00500000	1.00000000	1.00000000	
2	1.01002500	2.00500000	0.49875312	
3	1.01507513	3.01502500	0.33167221	
4	1.02015050	4.03010013	0.24813279	
5	1.02525125	5.05025063	0.19800997	
6	1.03037751	6.07550188	0.16459546	
7	1.03552940	7.10587939	0.14072854	
8	1.04070704	8.14140879	0.12282886	
9	1.04591058	9.18211583	0.10890736	
10	1.05114013	10.22802641	0.09777057	
11	1.05639583	11.27916654	0.08865903	Years
12	1.06167781	12.33556237	0.08106643	1
24	1.12715978	25.43195524	0.03932061	2
36	1.19668052	39.33610496	0.02542194	3
48	1.27048916	54.09783222	0.01848503	4
60	1.34885015	69.77003051	0.01433280	5
72	1.43204428	86.40885570	0.01157289	6
84	1.52036964	104.07392722	0.00960855	7
96	1.61414271	122.82854169	0.00814143	8
108	1.71369950	142.73989975	0.00700575	9
120	1.81939673	163.87934681	0.00610205	10
132	1.93161314	186.32262870	0.00536703	11
144	2.05075082	210.15016311	0.00475850	12
156	2.17723664	235.44732771	0.00424723	13
168	2.31152383	262.30476606	0.00381236	14
180	2.45409356	290.81871245	0.00343857	15
192	2.60545668	321.09133666	0.00311438	16
204	2.76615555	353.23111008	0.00283101	17
216	2.93676597	387.35319441	0.00258162	18
228	3.11789927	423.57985423	0.00236083	19
240	3.31020448	462.04089516	0.00216431	20
252	3.51437064	502.87412894	0.00198857	21
264	3.73112926	546.22586723	0.00183074	22
276	3.96125723	592.25144588	0.00168847	23
288	4.20557891	641.11578150	0.00155978	24
300	4.46496981	692.99396243	0.00144301	25
312	4.74035938	748.07187604	0.00133677	26
324	5.03273437	806.54687494	0.00123985	27
336	5.34314242	868.62848363	0.00115124	28
348	5.67269575	934.53915019	0.00107005	29
360	6.02257521	1004.51504245	0.00099551	30
372	6.39403447	1078.80689463	0.00092695	31
384	6.78840453	1157.68090569	0.00086380	32
396	7.20709847	1241.41969316	0.00080553	33
408	7.65161653	1330.32330581	0.00075170	34
420	8.12355149	1424.71029876	0.00070190	35
432	8.62459437	1524.91887490	0.00065577	36
444	9.15654048	1631.30809675	0.00061300	37
456	9.72129587	1744.25917301	0.00057331	38
468	10.32088412	1864.17682449	0.00053643	39
480	10.95745367	1991.49073433	0.00050214	40
492	11.63328544	2126.65708755	0.00047022	41
504	12.35080103	2270.16020566	0.00044050	42
516	13.11257141	2422.51428211	0.00041279	43
528	13.92132612	2584.26522461	0.00038696	44
540	14.77996306	2755.99261131	0.00036285	45
552	15.69155884	2938.31176747	0.00034033	46
564	16.65937985	3131.87597023	0.00031930	47
576	17.68689395	3337.37878948	0.00029964	48
588	18.77778286	3555.55657295	0.00028125	49
600	19.93595542	3787.19108470	0.00026405	50

6.25% Monthly	Present Value of 1	Present Value of 1 per Period	Payment to Pay Off a Loan of 1	
				Months
	0.99481865	0.99481865	1.00520833	1
	0.98966415	1.98448280	0.50390963	2
	0.98453636	2.96901916	0.33681157	3
	0.97943513	3.94845430	0.25326366	4
	0.97436034	4.92281464	0.20313582	5
	0.96931184	5.89212648	0.16971801	6
	0.96428950	6.85641598	0.14584879	7
	0.95929318	7.81570916	0.12794744	8
	0.95432275	8.77003191	0.11402467	9
	0.94937807	9.71940998	0.10288690	10
Years	0.94445902	10.66386900	0.09377660	11
1	0.93956545	11.60343445	0.08618138	12
2	0.88278323	22.50562050	0.04443334	24
3	0.82943262	32.74893780	0.03053534	36
4	0.77930623	42.37320478	0.02359982	48
5	0.73220920	51.41583348	0.01944926	60
6	0.68795846	59.91197494	0.01669115	72
7	0.64638200	67.89465587	0.01472870	84
8	0.60731819	75.39490704	0.01326350	96
9	0.57061519	82.44188388	0.01212976	108
10	0.53613031	89.06297981	0.01122801	120
11	0.50372952	95.28393275	0.01049495	132
12	0.47328685	101.12892518	0.00988837	144
13	0.44468397	106.62067810	0.00937904	156
14	0.41780969	111.78053937	0.00894610	168
15	0.39255955	116.62856673	0.00857423	180
16	0.36883539	121.18306571	0.00825194	192
17	0.34654498	125.46336295	0.00797045	204
18	0.32560169	129.48447496	0.00772293	216
19	0.30592410	133.26457286	0.00750398	228
20	0.28743571	136.81234309	0.00730928	240
21	0.27006466	140.14758455	0.00713534	252
22	0.25374343	143.28126217	0.00697928	264
23	0.23840856	146.22555738	0.00683875	276
24	0.22400044	148.99691542	0.00671177	288
25	0.21046307	151.59108985	0.00659669	300
26	0.19774383	154.03318433	0.00649211	312
27	0.18579327	156.32769192	0.00639682	324
28	0.17456494	158.48353196	0.00630980	336
29	0.16401518	160.50908477	0.00623018	348
30	0.15410300	162.41222420	0.00615717	360
31	0.14478985	164.20034825	0.00609012	372
32	0.13603954	165.88040781	0.00602844	384
33	0.12781805	167.45893373	0.00597161	396
34	0.12009343	168.94206213	0.00591919	408
35	0.11283563	170.33555833	0.00587076	420
36	0.10601646	171.64483921	0.00582598	432
37	0.09960940	172.87499428	0.00578453	444
38	0.09358955	174.03080548	0.00574611	456
39	0.08793351	175.11676575	0.00571048	468
40	0.08261929	176.13709648	0.00567740	480
41	0.07762623	177.09576399	0.00564666	492
42	0.07293492	177.99649485	0.00561809	504
43	0.06852713	178.84279045	0.00559150	516
44	0.06438573	179.63794054	0.00556675	528
45	0.06049460	180.38503610	0.00554370	540
46	0.05683864	181.08698127	0.00552221	552
47	0.05340362	181.74650469	0.00550217	564
48	0.05017620	182.36617011	0.00548347	576
49	0.04714382	182.94838633	0.00546602	588
50	0.04429471	183.49541657	0.00544973	600

	Future Value of 1	Future Value of 1 per Period	Payment for Sinking Fund of 1	**6.25%** Monthly
Months				
1	1.00520833	1.00000000	1.00000000	
2	1.01044379	2.00520833	0.49870130	
3	1.01570652	3.01565213	0.33160323	
4	1.02099666	4.03135865	0.24805533	
5	1.02631435	5.05235531	0.19792749	
6	1.03165974	6.07866966	0.16450968	
7	1.03703297	7.11032940	0.14064046	
8	1.04243418	8.14736236	0.12273911	
9	1.04786352	9.18979654	0.10881634	
10	1.05332115	10.23766006	0.09767857	
11	1.05880719	11.29098121	0.08856626	Years
12	1.06432181	12.34978840	0.08097305	1
24	1.13278093	25.49393761	0.03922501	2
36	1.20564345	39.48354234	0.02532701	3
48	1.28319262	54.37298384	0.01839149	4
60	1.36572990	70.22014123	0.01424093	5
72	1.45357613	87.08661654	0.01148282	6
84	1.54707278	105.03797415	0.00952037	7
96	1.64658331	124.14399565	0.00805516	8
108	1.75249454	144.47895113	0.00692142	9
120	1.86521817	166.12188784	0.00601968	10
132	1.98519238	189.15693752	0.00528662	11
144	2.11288356	213.67364339	0.00468003	12
156	2.24878806	239.76730827	0.00417071	13
168	2.39343419	267.53936502	0.00373777	14
180	2.54738422	297.09777086	0.00336590	15
192	2.71123660	328.55742701	0.00304361	16
204	2.88562826	362.04062532	0.00276212	17
216	3.07123710	397.67752370	0.00251460	18
228	3.26878465	435.60665206	0.00229565	19
240	3.47903881	475.97545078	0.00210095	20
252	3.70281690	518.94084389	0.00192700	21
264	3.94098880	564.66984904	0.00177095	22
276	4.19448035	613.34022679	0.00163042	23
288	4.46427694	665.14117155	0.00150344	24
300	4.75142733	720.27404708	0.00138836	25
312	5.05704776	778.95316921	0.00128377	26
324	5.38232624	841.40663895	0.00118849	27
336	5.72852724	907.87722919	0.00110147	28
348	6.09699650	978.62332842	0.00102184	29
360	6.48916638	1053.91994513	0.00094884	30
372	6.90656134	1134.05977685	0.00088179	31
384	7.35080390	1219.35434797	0.00082011	32
396	7.82362094	1310.13522069	0.00076328	33
408	8.32685044	1406.75528387	0.00071086	34
420	8.86244857	1509.59012484	0.00066243	35
432	9.43249734	1619.03984938	0.00061765	36
444	10.03921269	1735.52883566	0.00057619	37
456	10.68495306	1859.51098808	0.00053778	38
468	11.37222863	1991.46789752	0.00050214	39
480	12.10371101	2131.91251482	0.00046906	40
492	12.88224367	2281.39078476	0.00043833	41
504	13.71085296	2440.48376827	0.00040975	42
516	14.59275990	2609.80990116	0.00038317	43
528	15.53139270	2790.02739819	0.00035842	44
540	16.53040006	2981.83681164	0.00033536	45
552	17.59366539	3185.98375463	0.00031387	46
564	18.72532187	3403.26179944	0.00029384	47
576	19.92976855	3634.51556237	0.00027514	48
588	21.21168743	3880.64398696	0.00025769	49
600	22.57606166	4142.60383845	0.00024139	50

6.50% Monthly	Present Value of 1	Present Value of 1 per Period	Payment to Pay Off a Loan of 1	Months
	0.99461252	0.99461252	1.00541667	1
	0.98925406	1.98386657	0.50406616	2
	0.98392447	2.96779104	0.33695095	3
	0.97862359	3.94641462	0.25339456	4
	0.97335127	4.91976589	0.20326170	5
	0.96810735	5.88787325	0.16984061	6
	0.96289169	6.85076494	0.14596910	7
	0.95770413	7.80846906	0.12806608	8
	0.95254451	8.76101357	0.11414204	9
	0.94741269	9.70842626	0.10300331	10
Years	0.94230852	10.65073478	0.09389024	11
1	0.93723185	11.58796663	0.08629642	12
2	0.87840354	22.44857800	0.04454625	24
3	0.82326777	32.62748886	0.03064900	36
4	0.77159277	42.16748829	0.02371495	48
5	0.72316132	51.10867958	0.01956615	60
6	0.67776982	59.48864882	0.01680993	72
7	0.63522746	67.34262286	0.01484944	84
8	0.59535541	74.70361746	0.01338623	96
9	0.55798605	81.60257603	0.01225452	108
10	0.52296229	88.06849972	0.01135480	120
11	0.49013692	94.12856932	0.01062377	132
12	0.45937193	99.80825955	0.01001921	144
13	0.43053800	105.13144612	0.00951190	156
14	0.40351393	110.12050610	0.00908096	168
15	0.37818610	114.79641200	0.00871107	180
16	0.35444806	119.17881992	0.00839075	192
17	0.33220001	123.28615220	0.00811121	204
18	0.31134843	127.13567482	0.00786561	216
19	0.29180566	130.74357001	0.00764856	228
20	0.27348956	134.12500429	0.00745573	240
21	0.25632313	137.29419219	0.00728363	252
22	0.24023420	140.26445601	0.00712939	264
23	0.22515514	143.04828187	0.00699065	276
24	0.21102257	145.65737211	0.00686543	288
25	0.19777707	148.10269459	0.00675207	300
26	0.18536297	150.39452869	0.00664918	312
27	0.17372808	152.54250859	0.00655555	324
28	0.16282349	154.55566377	0.00647016	336
29	0.15260336	156.44245691	0.00639213	348
30	0.14302473	158.21081954	0.00632068	360
31	0.13404733	159.86818531	0.00625515	372
32	0.12563343	161.42152129	0.00619496	384
33	0.11774765	162.87735724	0.00613959	396
34	0.11035685	164.24181306	0.00608858	408
35	0.10342995	165.52062451	0.00604154	420
36	0.09693784	166.71916732	0.00599811	432
37	0.09085323	167.84247982	0.00595797	444
38	0.08515054	168.89528407	0.00592083	456
39	0.07980580	169.88200574	0.00588644	468
40	0.07479654	170.80679271	0.00585457	480
41	0.07010170	171.67353252	0.00582501	492
42	0.06570154	172.48586866	0.00579758	504
43	0.06157758	173.24721597	0.00577210	516
44	0.05771247	173.96077491	0.00574842	528
45	0.05408996	174.62954508	0.00572641	540
46	0.05069484	175.25633778	0.00570593	552
47	0.04751282	175.84378786	0.00568687	564
48	0.04453042	176.39436478	0.00566912	576
49	0.04173543	176.91038301	0.00565258	588
50	0.03911577	177.39401173	0.00563717	600

	Future Value of 1	Future Value of 1 per Period	Payment for Sinking Fund of 1	**6.50%** Monthly
Months				
1	1.00541667	1.00000000	1.00000000	
2	1.01086267	2.00541667	0.49864949	
3	1.01633818	3.01627934	0.33153428	
4	1.02184334	4.03261752	0.24797789	
5	1.02737833	5.05446086	0.19784504	
6	1.03294330	6.08183919	0.16442395	
7	1.03853841	7.11478249	0.14055243	
8	1.04416382	8.15332090	0.12264941	
9	1.04981971	9.19748472	0.10872538	
10	1.05550623	10.24730443	0.09758664	
11	1.06122356	11.30281066	0.08847357	Years
12	1.06697185	12.36403422	0.08087975	1
24	1.13842893	25.55611070	0.03912958	2
36	1.21467163	39.63168498	0.02523234	3
48	1.29602044	54.64992654	0.01829829	4
60	1.38281732	70.67396755	0.01414948	5
72	1.47542716	87.77116826	0.01139326	6
84	1.57423925	106.01340016	0.00943277	7
96	1.67966897	125.47734812	0.00796957	8
108	1.79215951	146.24483273	0.00683785	9
120	1.91218375	168.40315424	0.00593813	10
132	2.04024624	192.04545958	0.00520710	11
144	2.17688531	217.27113389	0.00460254	12
156	2.32267535	244.18621833	0.00409524	13
168	2.47822922	272.90385582	0.00366429	14
180	2.64420082	303.54477608	0.00329441	15
192	2.82128785	336.23775608	0.00297409	16
204	3.01023472	371.12025554	0.00269454	17
216	3.21183571	408.33890058	0.00244895	18
228	3.42693830	448.05014722	0.00223189	19
240	3.65644670	490.42092958	0.00203906	20
252	3.90132571	535.62936171	0.00186696	21
264	4.16260472	583.86548627	0.00171272	22
276	4.44138206	635.33207342	0.00157398	23
288	4.73882965	690.24547323	0.00144876	24
300	5.05619784	748.83652512	0.00133540	25
312	5.39482078	811.35152827	0.00123251	26
324	5.75612192	878.05327696	0.00113888	27
336	6.14162006	949.22216529	0.00105349	28
348	6.55293573	1025.15736588	0.00097546	29
360	6.99179797	1106.17808748	0.00090401	30
372	7.46005163	1192.62491686	0.00083849	31
384	7.95966511	1284.86125050	0.00077829	32
396	8.49273862	1383.27482223	0.00072292	33
408	9.06151305	1488.27933312	0.00067192	34
420	9.66837937	1600.31619057	0.00062488	35
432	10.31588864	1719.85636386	0.00058144	36
444	11.00676280	1847.40236395	0.00054130	37
456	11.74390609	1983.49035587	0.00050416	38
468	12.53041724	2128.69241265	0.00046977	39
480	13.36960248	2283.61892008	0.00043790	40
492	14.26498952	2448.92114264	0.00040834	41
504	15.22034229	2625.29396119	0.00038091	42
516	16.23967680	2813.47879404	0.00035543	43
528	17.32277803	3014.26671366	0.00033176	44
540	18.48771793	3228.50177212	0.00030974	45
552	19.72587464	3457.08454921	0.00028926	46
564	21.04695300	3700.97593821	0.00027020	47
576	22.45650642	3961.20118523	0.00025245	48
588	23.96046024	4238.85419897	0.00023591	49
600	25.56513664	4535.10214926	0.00022050	50

6.75% Monthly	Present Value of 1	Present Value of 1 per Period	Payment to Pay Off a Loan of 1	
				Months
	0.99440646	0.99440646	1.00562500	1
	0.98884421	1.98325068	0.50422269	2
	0.98331308	2.96656376	0.33709034	3
	0.97781288	3.94437664	0.25352548	4
	0.97234345	4.91672009	0.20338762	5
	0.96690461	5.88362470	0.16996325	6
	0.96149619	6.84512089	0.14608946	7
	0.95611803	7.80123893	0.12818477	8
	0.95076995	8.75200888	0.11425948	9
	0.94545178	9.69746066	0.10311978	10
Years	0.94016336	10.63762402	0.09400595	11
1	0.93490453	11.57252855	0.08641154	12
2	0.87404647	22.39173788	0.04465933	24
3	0.81715001	32.50666566	0.03076292	36
4	0.76395724	41.96315743	0.02383043	48
5	0.71422708	50.80407440	0,01968346	60
6	0.66773413	59.06948769	0.01692921	72
7	0.62426766	66.79685999	0.01497076	84
8	0.58363066	74.02121534	0.01350964	96
9	0.54563895	80.77529786	0.01238002	108
10	0.51012032	87.08972018	0.01148241	120
11	0.47691380	92.99310220	0.01075349	132
12	0.44586887	98.51220077	0.01015103	144
13	0.41684483	103.67203100	0.00964580	156
14	0.38971011	108.49597965	0.00921693	168
15	0.36434175	113.00591107	0.00884909	180
16	0.34062475	117.22226638	0.00853080	192
17	0.31845162	121.16415604	0.00825327	204
18	0.29772186	124.84944653	0.00800965	216
19	0.27834152	128.29484130	0.00779455	228
20	0.26022274	131.51595646	0.00760364	240
21	0.24328342	134.52739160	0.00743343	252
22	0.22744677	137.34279595	0.00728105	264
23	0.21264102	139.97493022	0.00714414	276
24	0.19879905	142.43572447	0.00702071	288
25	0.18585813	144.73633215	0.00690912	300
26	0.17375961	146.88718069	0.00680795	312
27	0.16244864	148.89801872	0.00671601	324
28	0.15187397	150.77796030	0.00663227	336
29	0.14198767	152.53552619	0.00655585	348
30	0.13274491	154.18780250	0.00648598	360
31	0.12410382	155.71487677	0.00642199	372
32	0.11602522	157.15107175	0.00636330	384
33	0.10847250	158.49377694	0.00630940	396
34	0.10141144	159.74907809	0.00625982	408
35	0.09481001	160.92266483	0.00621417	420
36	0.08863831	162.01985638	0.00617208	432
37	0.08286836	163.04562573	0.00613325	444
38	0.07747400	164.00462214	0.00609739	456
39	0.07243079	164.90119222	0.00606424	468
40	0.06771588	165.73939965	0.00603357	480
41	0.06330788	166.52304357	0.00600517	492
42	0.05918682	167.25567582	0.00597887	504
43	0.05533403	167.94061702	0.00595449	516
44	0.05173203	168.58097165	0.00593187	528
45	0.04836451	169.17964210	0.00591088	540
46	0.04521620	169.73934181	0.00589139	552
47	0.04227283	170.26260760	0.00587328	564
48	0.03952106	170.75181116	0.00585645	576
49	0.03694842	171.20916978	0.00584081	588
50	0.03454325	171.63675643	0.00582626	600

	Future Value of 1	Future Value of 1 per Period	Payment for Sinking Fund of 1	**6.75%** Monthly
Months				
1	1.00562500	1.00000000	1.00000000	
2	1.01128164	2.00562500	0.49859769	
3	1.01697010	3.01690664	0.33146534	
4	1.02269056	4.03387674	0.24790048	
5	1.02844319	5.05656730	0.19776262	
6	1.03422818	6.08501049	0.16433825	
7	1.04004572	7.11923867	0.14046446	
8	1.04589597	8.15928439	0.12255977	
9	1.05177914	9.20518036	0.10863448	
10	1.05769540	10.25695950	0.09749478	
11	1.06364493	11.31465490	0.08838095	Years
12	1.06962794	12.37829983	0.08078654	1
24	1.14410392	25.61847515	0.03903433	2
36	1.22376552	39.78053654	0.02513792	3
48	1.30897379	54.92867305	0.01820543	4
60	1.40011493	71.13154305	0.01405846	5
72	1.49760204	88.46258545	0.01130421	6
84	1.60187698	107.00035258	0.00934576	7
96	1.71341237	126.82886618	0.00788464	8
108	1.83271374	148.03799826	0.00675502	9
120	1.96032182	170.72387845	0.00585741	10
132	2.09681498	194.98932966	0.00512849	11
144	2.24281188	220.94433418	0.00452603	12
156	2.39897424	248.70653210	0.00402080	13
168	2.56600987	278.40175457	0.00359193	14
180	2.74467584	310.16345491	0.00322409	15
192	2.93578196	344.13901464	0.00290580	16
204	3.14019440	380.47900396	0.00262827	17
216	3.35883965	419.34927175	0.00238465	18
228	3.59270873	460.92599608	0.00216955	19
240	3.84286162	505.39762193	0.00197864	20
252	4.11043215	552.96571533	0.00180843	21
264	4.39663306	603.84587692	0.00165605	22
276	4.70276155	658.26871917	0.00151914	23
288	5.03020513	716.48091163	0.00139571	24
300	5.38044793	778.74629894	0.00128412	25
312	5.75507742	845.34709668	0.00118295	26
324	6.15579158	916.58511554	0.00109101	27
336	6.58440665	992.78340449	0.00100727	28
348	7.04286530	1074.28716425	0.00093085	29
360	7.53324548	1161.46586261	0.00086098	30
372	8.05776982	1254.71463386	0.00079699	31
384	8.61881570	1354.45612464	0.00073830	32
396	9.21892605	1461.14240961	0.00068440	33
408	9.86082085	1575.25704046	0.00063482	34
420	10.54740946	1697.31723760	0.00058917	35
432	11.28180382	1827.87623439	0.00054708	36
444	12.06733254	1967.52578474	0.00050825	37
456	12.90755600	2116.89884511	0.00047239	38
468	13.80628249	2276.67244347	0.00043924	39
480	14.76758546	2447.57074779	0.00040857	40
492	15.79582196	2630.36834841	0.00038017	41
504	16.89565245	2825.89376876	0.00035387	42
516	18.07206187	3035.03322069	0.00032949	43
528	19.33038224	3258.73462111	0.00030687	44
540	20.67631687	3498.01188845	0.00028588	45
552	22.11596615	3753.94953818	0.00026639	46
564	23.65585524	4027.70759835	0.00024828	47
576	25.30296363	4320.52686737	0.00023145	48
588	27.06475678	4633.73453789	0.00021581	49
600	28.94921994	4968.75021221	0.00020126	50

7.00% Monthly	Present Value of 1	Present Value of 1 per Period	Payment to Pay Off a Loan of 1	
				Months
	0.99420050	0.99420050	1.00583333	1
	0.98843463	1.98263513	0.50437924	2
	0.98270220	2.96533732	0.33722976	3
	0.97700301	3.94234034	0.25365644	4
	0.97133688	4.91367722	0.20351357	5
	0.96570361	5.87938083	0.17008594	6
	0.96010301	6.83948384	0.14620986	7
	0.95453489	7.79401874	0.12830352	8
	0.94899906	8.74301780	0.11437698	9
	0.94349534	9.68651314	0.10323632	10
Years	0.93802354	10.62453667	0.09412175	11
1	0.93258347	11.55712014	0.08652675	12
2	0.86971192	22.33509930	0.04477258	24
3	0.81107896	32.38646445	0.03087710	36
4	0.75639883	41.76020141	0.02394624	48
5	0.70540504	50.50199350	0.01980120	60
6	0.65784908	58.65444427	0.01704901	72
7	0.61349917	66.25728507	0.01509268	84
8	0.57213918	73.34756869	0.01363372	96
9	0.53356754	79.95984996	0.01250628	108
10	0.49759627	86.12635414	0.01161085	120
11	0.46405005	91.87713399	0.01088410	132
12	0.43276541	97.24021619	0.01028381	144
13	0.40358986	102.24173797	0.00978074	156
14	0.37638123	106.90607449	0.00935401	168
15	0.35100691	111.25595761	0.00898828	180
16	0.32734324	115.31258668	0.00867208	192
17	0.30527490	119.09573189	0.00839661	204
18	0.28469432	122.62383055	0.00815502	216
19	0.26550122	125.91407703	0.00794192	228
20	0.24760205	128.98250650	0.00775299	240
21	0.23090957	131.84407308	0.00758472	252
22	0.21534245	134.51272277	0.00743424	264
23	0.20082481	137.00146134	0.00729919	276
24	0.18728590	139.32241778	0.00717760	288
25	0.17465973	141.48690339	0.00706779	300
26	0.16288478	143.50546687	0.00696838	312
27	0.15190365	145.38794580	0.00687815	324
28	0.14166283	147.14351453	0.00679609	336
29	0.13211241	148.78072890	0.00672130	348
30	0.12320585	150.30756795	0.00665302	360
31	0.11489974	151.73147280	0.00659059	372
32	0.10715360	153.05938292	0.00653341	384
33	0.09992968	154.29776995	0.00648098	396
34	0.09319276	155.45266921	0.00643283	408
35	0.08691003	156.52970917	0.00638856	420
36	0.08105046	157.53413882	0.00634783	432
37	0.07558669	158.47085331	0.00631031	444
38	0.07049090	159.34441776	0.00627571	456
39	0.06573864	160.15908952	0.00624379	468
40	0.06130677	160.91883893	0.00621431	480
41	0.05717368	161.62736867	0.00618707	492
42	0.05331923	162.28813179	0.00616188	504
43	0.04972463	162.90434855	0.00613857	516
44	0.04637237	163.47902211	0.00611699	528
45	0.04324611	164.01495318	0.00609701	540
46	0.04033060	164.51475363	0.00607848	552
47	0.03761165	164.98085926	0.00606131	564
48	0.03507601	165.41554167	0.00604538	576
49	0.03271130	165.82091929	0.00603060	588
50	0.03050602	166.19896777	0.00601688	600

	Future Value of 1	Future Value of 1 per Period	Payment for Sinking Fund of 1	**7.00%** Monthly
Months				
1	1.00583333	1.00000000	1.00000000	
2	1.01170069	2.00583333	0.49854591	
3	1.01760228	3.01753403	0.33139643	
4	1.02353830	4.03513631	0.24782310	
5	1.02950894	5.05867460	0.19768024	
6	1.03551440	6.08818354	0.16425260	
7	1.04155490	7.12369794	0.14037653	
8	1.04763064	8.16525285	0.12247018	
9	1.05374182	9.21288349	0.10854365	
10	1.05988865	10.26662531	0.09740299	
11	1.06607133	11.32651396	0.08828842	Years
12	1.07229008	12.39258529	0.08069341	1
24	1.14980602	25.68103157	0.03893925	2
36	1.23292559	39.93010071	0.02504376	3
48	1.32205388	55.20923621	0.01811291	4
60	1.41762526	71.59290165	0.01396787	5
72	1.52010550	89.16094359	0.01121567	6
84	1.62999405	107.99898070	0.00925935	7
96	1.74782646	128.19882103	0.00780038	8
108	1.87417697	149.85890946	0.00667294	9
120	2.00966138	173.08480743	0.00577751	10
132	2.15493996	197.98970745	0.00505077	11
144	2.31072074	224.69498470	0.00445048	12
156	2.47776293	253.33078860	0.00394741	13
168	2.65688062	284.03667708	0.00352067	14
180	2.84894673	316.96229672	0.00315495	15
192	3.05489732	352.26811207	0.00283875	16
204	3.27573609	390.12618766	0.00256327	17
216	3.51253932	430.72102660	0.00232169	18
228	3.76646107	474.25046973	0.00210859	19
240	4.03873885	520.92665983	0.00191966	20
252	4.33069961	570.97707547	0.00175138	21
264	4.64376623	624.64563972	0.00160091	22
276	4.97946447	682.19390881	0.00146586	23
288	5.33943036	743.90234693	0.00134426	24
300	5.72541821	810.07169302	0.00123446	25
312	6.13930915	881.02442650	0.00113504	26
324	6.58312031	957.10633882	0.00104482	27
336	7.05901461	1038.68821873	0.00096275	28
348	7.56931135	1126.16765934	0.00088797	29
360	8.11649748	1219.97099578	0.00081969	30
372	8.70323973	1320.55538299	0.00075726	31
384	9.33239764	1428.41102369	0.00070008	32
396	10.00703742	1544.06355738	0.00064764	33
408	10.73044696	1668.07662208	0.00059949	34
420	11.50615184	1801.05460126	0.00055523	35
432	12.33793249	1943.64556930	0.00051450	36
444	13.22984262	2096.54444995	0.00047698	37
456	14.18622902	2260.49640304	0.00044238	38
468	15.21175266	2436.30045608	0.00041046	39
480	16.31141149	2624.81339833	0.00038098	40
492	17.49056475	2826.95395642	0.00035374	41
504	18.75495909	3043.70727180	0.00032855	42
516	20.11075659	3276.12970187	0.00030524	43
528	21.56456481	3525.35396820	0.00028366	44
540	23.12346895	3792.59467690	0.00026367	45
552	24.79506639	4079.15423804	0.00024515	46
564	26.58750374	4386.42921302	0.00022797	47
576	28.50951654	4715.91712079	0.00021205	48
588	30.57047179	5069.22373605	0.00019727	49
600	32.78041367	5448.07091510	0.00018355	50

7.25% Monthly	Present Value of 1	Present Value of 1 per Period	Payment to Pay Off a Loan of 1	
				Months
	0.99399462	0.99399462	1.00604167	1
	0.98802530	1.98201991	0.50453580	2
	0.98209182	2.96411174	0.33736920	3
	0.97619399	3.94030572	0.25378741	4
	0.97033157	4.91063729	0.20363956	5
	0.96450435	5.87514164	0.17020866	6
	0.95871213	6.83385378	0.14633032	7
	0.95295470	7.78680847	0.12842232	8
	0.94723184	8.73404031	0.11449455	9
	0.94154335	9.67558366	0.10335294	10
Years	0.93588902	10.61147268	0.09423763	11
1	0.93026865	11.54174133	0.08664204	12
2	0.86539975	22.27866141	0.04488600	24
3	0.80505426	32.26688151	0.03099153	36
4	0.74891673	41.55860951	0.02406240	48
5	0.69669376	50.20241273	0.01991936	60
6	0.64811236	58.24347185	0.01716931	72
7	0.60291861	65.72381704	0.01521518	84
8	0.56087627	72.68254762	0.01375846	96
9	0.52176561	79.15603560	0.01263328	108
10	0.48538219	85.17812024	0.01174010	120
11	0.45153583	90.78027593	0.01101561	132
12	0.42004963	95.99178571	0.01041756	144
13	0.39075900	100.83988986	0.00991671	156
14	0.36351084	105.34992915	0.00949218	168
15	0.33816274	109.54547729	0.00912863	180
16	0.31458220	113.44846417	0.00881448	192
17	0.29264595	117.07929050	0.00854122	204
18	0.27223935	120.45693440	0.00830172	216
19	0.25325574	123.59905061	0.00809068	228
20	0.23559587	126.52206280	0.00790376	240
21	0.21916745	129.24124940	0.00773747	252
22	0.20388461	131.77082343	0.00758893	264
23	0.18966746	134.12400684	0.00745579	276
24	0.17644169	136.31309959	0.00733605	288
25	0.16413817	138.34954393	0.00722807	300
26	0.15269260	140.24398426	0.00713043	312
27	0.14204513	142.00632269	0.00704194	324
28	0.13214013	143.64577088	0.00696157	336
29	0.12292582	145.17089813	0.00688843	348
30	0.11435404	146.58967619	0.00682176	360
31	0.10637998	147.90952094	0.00676089	372
32	0.09896196	149.13733112	0.00670523	384
33	0.09206121	150.27952444	0.00665427	396
34	0.08564165	151.34207107	0.00660755	408
35	0.07966975	152.33052489	0.00656467	420
36	0.07411427	153.25005248	0.00652528	432
37	0.06894618	154.10546017	0.00648906	444
38	0.06413847	154.90121913	0.00645573	456
39	0.05966601	155.64148873	0.00642502	468
40	0.05550541	156.33013833	0.00639672	480
41	0.05163495	156.97076747	0.00637061	492
42	0.04803437	157.56672466	0.00634652	504
43	0.04468487	158.12112496	0.00632427	516
44	0.04156893	158.63686617	0.00630370	528
45	0.03867028	159.11664405	0.00628470	540
46	0.03597374	159.56296637	0.00626712	552
47	0.03346525	159.97816602	0.00625085	564
48	0.03113167	160.36441325	0.00623580	576
49	0.02896082	160.72372693	0.00622186	588
50	0.02694134	161.05798518	0.00620894	600

	Future Value of 1	Future Value of 1 per Period	Payment for Sinking Fund of 1	**7.25%** Monthly
Months				
1	1.00604167	1.00000000	1.00000000	
2	1.01211984	2.00604167	0.49849413	
3	1.01823473	3.01816150	0.33132753	
4	1.02438656	4.03639623	0.24774575	
5	1.03057556	5.06078279	0.19759789	
6	1.03680196	6.09135835	0.16416700	
7	1.04306597	7.12816031	0.14028865	
8	1.04936783	8.17122628	0.12238065	
9	1.05570776	9.22059410	0.10845288	
10	1.06208599	10.27630186	0.09731127	
11	1.06850276	11.33838785	0.08819596	Years
12	1.07495830	12.40689061	0.08060037	1
24	1.15553534	25.74378061	0.03884433	2
36	1.24215230	40.08038118	0.02494986	3
48	1.33526192	55.49162892	0.01802074	4
60	1.43535089	72.05807756	0.01387769	5
72	1.54294234	89.86631897	0.01112764	6
84	1.65859867	109.00943585	0.00917352	7
96	1.78292441	129.58748817	0.00771679	8
108	1.91656939	151.70803626	0.00659161	9
120	2.06023216	175.48670297	0.00569844	10
132	2.21466366	201.04777805	0.00497394	11
144	2.38067108	228.52486780	0.00437589	12
156	2.55912213	258.06159342	0.00387504	13
168	2.75094956	289.81234170	0.00345051	14
180	2.95715606	323.94307201	0.00308696	15
192	3.17881944	360.63218376	0.00277291	16
204	3.41709834	400.07144885	0.00249955	17
216	3.67323821	442.46701412	0.00226006	18
228	3.94857789	488.04047877	0.00204901	19
240	4.24455657	537.03005273	0.00186209	20
252	4.56272130	589.69180176	0.00169580	21
264	4.90473512	646.30098583	0.00154727	22
276	5.27238572	707.15349796	0.00141412	23
288	5.66759477	772.56741079	0.00129439	24
300	6.09242803	842.88463915	0.00118640	25
312	6.54910606	918.47272723	0.00108876	26
324	7.04001590	999.72676970	0.00100027	27
336	7.56772351	1087.07147685	0.00091990	28
348	8.13498718	1180.96339454	0.00084677	29
360	8.74477196	1281.89329052	0.00078010	30
372	9.40026518	1390.38871966	0.00071922	31
384	10.10489305	1507.01678145	0.00066356	32
396	10.86233863	1632.38708418	0.00061260	33
408	11.67656104	1767.15493135	0.00056588	34
420	12.55181618	1912.02474689	0.00052301	35
432	13.49267895	2067.75375715	0.00048362	36
444	14.50406719	2235.15594888	0.00044740	37
456	15.59126737	2415.10632389	0.00041406	38
468	16.75996223	2608.54547263	0.00038336	39
480	18.01626046	2816.48449061	0.00035505	40
492	19.36672867	3040.01026334	0.00032895	41
504	20.81842568	3280.29114744	0.00030485	42
516	22.37893943	3538.58307750	0.00028260	43
528	24.05642662	3816.23613088	0.00026204	44
540	25.85965541	4114.70158442	0.00024303	45
552	27.79805115	4435.53950019	0.00022545	46
564	29.88174573	4780.42687988	0.00020919	47
576	32.12163052	5151.16643035	0.00019413	48
588	34.52941325	5549.69598631	0.00018019	49
600	37.11767928	5978.09863926	0.00016728	50

7.50% Monthly	Present Value of 1	Present Value of 1 per Period	Payment to Pay Off a Loan of 1	Months
	0.99378882	0.99378882	1.00625000	1
	0.98761622	1.98140504	0.50469237	2
	0.98148196	2.96288699	0.33750865	3
	0.97538580	3.93827279	0.25391842	4
	0.96932750	4.90760029	0.20376558	5
	0.96330683	5.87090712	0.17033143	6
	0.95732356	6.82823068	0.14645082	7
	0.95137745	7.77960813	0.12854118	8
	0.94546827	8.72507640	0.11461218	9
	0.93959580	9.66467220	0.10346962	10
Years	0.93375980	10.59843200	0.09435358	11
1	0.92796005	11.52639205	0.08675742	12
2	0.86110985	22.22242338	0.04499959	24
3	0.79907554	32.14791315	0.03110622	36
4	0.74151018	41.35837114	0.02417890	48
5	0.68809182	49.90530818	0.02003795	60
6	0.63852172	57.83652431	0.01729011	72
7	0.59252265	65.19637602	0.01533828	84
8	0.54983735	72.02602438	0.01388387	96
9	0.51022709	78.36366521	0.01276102	108
10	0.47347036	84.24474271	0.01187018	120
11	0.43936158	89.70214768	0.01114801	132
12	0.40770999	94.76640147	0.01055226	144
13	0.37833858	99.46586664	0.01005370	156
14	0.35108309	103.82670550	0.00963143	168
15	0.32579108	107.87342684	0.00927012	180
16	0.30232111	111.62862258	0.00895828	192
17	0.28054191	115.11329421	0.00868709	204
18	0.26033169	118.34693026	0.00844973	216
19	0.24157740	121.34761534	0.00824079	228
20	0.22417418	124.13213121	0.00805593	240
21	0.20802468	126.71605069	0.00789166	252
22	0.19303860	129.11382474	0.00774510	264
23	0.17913210	131.33886327	0.00761389	276
24	0.16622744	133.40361014	0.00749605	288
25	0.15425242	135.31961274	0.00738991	300
26	0.14314008	137.09758661	0.00729407	312
27	0.13282828	138.74747534	0.00720734	324
28	0.12325934	140.27850616	0.00712868	336
29	0.11437974	141.69924159	0.00705720	348
30	0.10613983	143.01762732	0.00699215	360
31	0.09849352	144.24103660	0.00693284	372
32	0.09139805	145.37631154	0.00687870	384
33	0.08481374	146.42980133	0.00682921	396
34	0.07870376	147.40739777	0.00678392	408
35	0.07303395	148.31456821	0.00674243	420
36	0.06777259	149.15638613	0.00670437	432
37	0.06289025	149.93755954	0.00666944	444
38	0.05835964	150.66245725	0.00663735	456
39	0.05415542	151.33513336	0.00660785	468
40	0.05025406	151.95934993	0.00658071	480
41	0.04663376	152.53859796	0.00655572	492
42	0.04327427	153.07611699	0.00653270	504
43	0.04015679	153.57491318	0.00651148	516
44	0.03726390	154.03777611	0.00649191	528
45	0.03457941	154.46729443	0.00647386	540
46	0.03208831	154.86587026	0.00645720	552
47	0.02977667	155.23573271	0.00644182	564
48	0.02763156	155.57895329	0.00642760	576
49	0.02564098	155.89744249	0.00641447	588
50	0.02379381	156.19299053	0.00640234	600

	Future Value of 1	Future Value of 1 per Period	Payment for Sinking Fund of 1	**7.50%** Monthly
Months				
1	1.00625000	1.00000000	1.00000000	
2	1.01253906	2.00625000	0.49844237	
3	1.01886743	3.01878906	0.33125865	
4	1.02523535	4.03765649	0.24766842	
5	1.03164307	5.06289185	0.19751558	
6	1.03809084	6.09453492	0.16408143	
7	1.04457891	7.13262576	0.14020082	
8	1.05110753	8.17720468	0.12229118	
9	1.05767695	9.22831220	0.10836218	
10	1.06428743	10.28598916	0.09721962	
11	1.07093923	11.35027659	0.08810358	Years
12	1.07763260	12.42121582	0.08050742	1
24	1.16129202	25.80672290	0.03874959	2
36	1.25144614	40.23138168	0.02485622	3
48	1.34859915	55.77586421	0.01792890	4
60	1.45329441	72.52710532	0.01378795	5
72	1.56611743	90.57878882	0.01104011	6
84	1.68769920	110.03187141	0.00908828	7
96	1.81871967	130.99514736	0.00763387	8
108	1.95991161	153.58585690	0.00651102	9
120	2.11206464	177.93034194	0.00562018	10
132	2.27602970	204.16475262	0.00489801	11
144	2.45272380	232.43580878	0.00430226	12
156	2.64313513	262.90162049	0.00380370	13
168	2.84832858	295.73257235	0.00338143	14
180	3.06945173	331.11227633	0.00302012	15
192	3.30774124	369.23859867	0.00270828	16
204	3.56452979	410.32476650	0.00243709	17
216	3.84125350	454.60056032	0.00219973	18
228	4.13945999	502.31359907	0.00199079	19
240	4.46081703	553.73072502	0.00180593	20
252	4.80712185	609.13949609	0.00164166	21
264	5.18031121	668.84979406	0.00149510	22
276	5.58247224	733.19555763	0.00136389	23
288	6.01585406	802.53665006	0.00124605	24
300	6.48288045	877.26087169	0.00113991	25
312	6.98616331	957.78612886	0.00104407	26
324	7.52851732	1044.56277100	0.00095734	27
336	8.11297568	1138.07610940	0.00087868	28
348	8.74280707	1238.84913129	0.00080720	29
360	9.42153390	1347.44542476	0.00074215	30
372	10.15295207	1464.47233071	0.00068284	31
384	10.94115212	1590.58433952	0.00062870	32
396	11.79054220	1726.48675131	0.00057921	33
408	12.70587263	1872.93962052	0.00053392	34
420	13.69226254	2030.76200658	0.00049243	35
432	14.75522847	2200.83655463	0.00045437	36
444	15.90071520	2384.11443184	0.00041944	37
456	17.13512904	2581.62064697	0.00038735	38
468	18.46537364	2794.45978287	0.00035785	39
480	19.89888859	3023.82217403	0.00033071	40
492	21.44369102	3270.99056369	0.00030572	41
504	23.10842049	3537.34727780	0.00028270	42
516	24.90238722	3824.38195585	0.00026148	43
528	26.83562426	4133.69988192	0.00024191	44
540	28.91894352	4467.03096246	0.00022386	45
552	31.16399626	4826.23940107	0.00020720	46
564	33.58333828	5213.33412429	0.00019182	47
576	36.19050101	5630.48001688	0.00017760	48
588	39.00006268	6080.01002921	0.00016447	49
600	42.02773890	6564.43822467	0.00015234	50

7.75% Monthly	Present Value of 1	Present Value of 1 per Period	Payment to Pay Off a Loan of 1	Months
	0.99358311	0.99358311	1.00645833	1
	0.98720739	1.98079050	0.50484895	2
	0.98087259	2.96166310	0.33764813	3
	0.97457844	3.93624154	0.25404945	4
	0.96832468	4.90456621	0.20389163	5
	0.96211104	5.86667726	0.17045424	6
	0.95593728	6.82261454	0.14657138	7
	0.94980314	7.77241767	0.12866010	8
	0.94370835	8.71612603	0.11472987	9
	0.93765268	9.65377870	0.10358638	10
Years	0.93163586	10.58541457	0.09446961	11
1	0.92565766	11.51107223	0.08687288	12
2	0.85684210	22.16638439	0.04511336	24
3	0.79314245	32.02955570	0.03122116	36
4	0.73417839	41.15947576	0.02429574	48
5	0.67959785	49.61065619	0.02015696	60
6	0.62907495	57.43355607	0.01741142	72
7	0.58230805	64.67488326	0.01546195	84
8	0.53901790	71.37787323	0.01400994	96
9	0.49894605	77.58254724	0.01288950	108
10	0.46185323	83.32595124	0.01200106	120
11	0.42751798	88.64237715	0.01128129	132
12	0.39573529	93.56356751	0.01068792	144
13	0.36631540	98.11890505	0.01019172	156
14	0.33908266	102.33558813	0.00977177	168
15	0.31387446	106.23879312	0.00941276	180
16	0.29054030	109.85182472	0.00910317	192
17	0.26894085	113.19625508	0.00883421	204
18	0.24894716	116.29205266	0.00859904	216
19	0.23043985	119.15770140	0.00839224	228
20	0.21330841	121.81031110	0.00820949	240
21	0.19745056	124.26571958	0.00804727	252
22	0.18277162	126.53858725	0.00790273	264
23	0.16918395	128.64248462	0.00777348	276
24	0.15660642	130.58997333	0.00765756	288
25	0.14496393	132.39268116	0.00755329	300
26	0.13418698	134.06137148	0.00745927	312
27	0.12421120	135.60600745	0.00737430	324
28	0.11497705	137.03581157	0.00729736	336
29	0.10642939	138.35932070	0.00722756	348
30	0.09851718	139.58443706	0.00716412	360
31	0.09119318	140.71847540	0.00710639	372
32	0.08441367	141.76820668	0.00705377	384
33	0.07813816	142.73989848	0.00700575	396
34	0.07232918	143.63953243	0.00696188	408
35	0.06695206	144.47193887	0.00692176	420
36	0.06197469	145.24262889	0.00688503	432
37	0.05736734	145.95602400	0.00685138	444
38	0.05310252	146.61638365	0.00682052	456
39	0.04915476	147.22765062	0.00679220	468
40	0.04550048	147.79347457	0.00676620	480
41	0.04211786	148.31723385	0.00674230	492
42	0.03898672	148.80205563	0.00672034	504
43	0.03608836	149.25083463	0.00670013	516
44	0.03340547	149.66625034	0.00668153	528
45	0.03092203	150.05078308	0.00666441	540
46	0.02862321	150.40672875	0.00664864	552
47	0.02649529	150.73621259	0.00663411	564
48	0.02452557	151.04120183	0.00662071	576
49	0.02270228	151.32351746	0.00660836	588
50	0.02101454	151.58484508	0.00659697	600

	Future Value of 1	Future Value of 1 per Period	Payment for Sinking Fund of 1	
Months				
1	1.00645833	1.00000000	1.00000000	
2	1.01295838	2.00645833	0.49839061	
3	1.01950040	3.01941671	0.33118979	
4	1.02608467	4.03891711	0.24759112	
5	1.03271147	5.06500178	0.19743330	
6	1.03938106	6.09771325	0.16399590	
7	1.04609373	7.13709432	0.14011304	
8	1.05284976	8.18318805	0.12220176	
9	1.05964941	9.23603781	0.10827154	
10	1.06649298	10.29568722	0.09712805	
11	1.07338075	11.36218020	0.08801128	Years
12	1.08031300	12.43556095	0.08041455	1
24	1.16707617	25.86985907	0.03865502	2
36	1.26080756	40.38310595	0.02476283	3
48	1.36206679	56.06195519	0.01783741	4
60	1.47145846	73.00001982	0.01369863	5
72	1.58963570	91.29843119	0.01095309	6
84	1.71730411	111.06644284	0.00900362	7
96	1.85522595	132.42208276	0.00755161	8
108	2.00422471	155.49285815	0.00643116	9
120	2.16519000	180.41651666	0.00554273	10
132	2.33908290	207.34186891	0.00482295	11
144	2.52694166	236.42967691	0.00422959	12
156	2.72988792	267.85361397	0.00373338	13
168	2.94913341	301.80130162	0.00331344	14
180	3.18598715	338.47542983	0.00295442	15
192	3.44186333	378.09496722	0.00264484	16
204	3.71828969	420.89646842	0.00237588	17
216	4.01691668	467.13548650	0.00214071	18
228	4.33952730	517.08809873	0.00193391	19
240	4.68804775	571.05255500	0.00175115	20
252	5.06455892	629.35105852	0.00158894	21
264	5.47130883	692.33168963	0.00144439	22
276	5.91072604	760.37048402	0.00131515	23
288	6.38543417	833.87367795	0.00119922	24
300	6.89826753	913.28013374	0.00109495	25
312	7.45228808	999.06396003	0.00100094	26
324	8.05080367	1091.73734258	0.00091597	27
336	8.69738785	1191.85360228	0.00083903	28
348	9.39590114	1300.01049894	0.00076922	29
360	10.15051413	1416.85380019	0.00070579	30
372	10.96573234	1543.08113723	0.00064805	31
384	11.84642318	1679.44617011	0.00059543	32
396	12.79784494	1826.76308758	0.00054742	33
408	13.82567823	1985.91146831	0.00050355	34
420	14.93605990	2157.84153258	0.00046343	35
432	16.13561964	2343.57981573	0.00042670	36
444	17.43151963	2544.23529720	0.00039305	37
456	18.83149722	2761.00602190	0.00036219	38
468	20.34391122	2995.08809873	0.00033387	39
480	21.97779172	3248.17420117	0.00030787	40
492	23.74289405	3521.48036950	0.00028397	41
504	25.64975705	3816.73657552	0.00026200	42
516	27.70976593	4135.70569255	0.00024180	43
528	29.93522030	4480.29217557	0.00022320	44
540	32.33940758	4852.55343204	0.00020608	45
552	34.93668235	5254.71210596	0.00019031	46
564	37.74255204	5689.16934857	0.00017577	47
576	40.77376954	6158.51915474	0.00016238	48
588	44.04843320	6665.56385084	0.00015002	49
600	47.58609492	7213.33082649	0.00013863	50

8.00% Monthly	Present Value of 1	Present Value of 1 per Period	Payment to Pay Off a Loan of 1	
				Months
	0.99337748	0.99337748	1.00666667	1
	0.98679882	1.98017631	0.50500554	2
	0.98026373	2.96044004	0.33778762	3
	0.97377192	3.93421196	0.25418051	4
	0.96732310	4.90153506	0.20401772	5
	0.96091699	5.86245205	0.17057709	6
	0.95455330	6.81700535	0.14669198	7
	0.94823175	7.76523710	0.12877907	8
	0.94195207	8.70718917	0.11484763	9
	0.93571398	9.64290315	0.10370321	10
Years	0.92951720	10.57242035	0.09458572	11
1	0.92336145	11.49578180	0.08698843	12
2	0.85259638	22.11054361	0.04522729	24
3	0.78725463	31.91180551	0.03133637	36
4	0.72692058	40.96191296	0.02441292	48
5	0.67121044	49.31843334	0.02027639	60
6	0.61976985	57.03452215	0.01753324	72
7	0.57227159	64.15926114	0.01558621	84
8	0.52841353	70.73797049	0.01413668	96
9	0.48791669	76.81249714	0.01301871	108
10	0.45052346	82.42148089	0.01213276	120
11	0.41599600	87.60060029	0.01141545	132
12	0.38411467	92.38279952	0.01082453	144
13	0.35467668	96.79849795	0.01033074	156
14	0.32749478	100.87578368	0.00991318	168
15	0.30239605	104.64059216	0.00955652	180
16	0.27922086	108.11687119	0.00924925	192
17	0.25782178	111.32673326	0.00898257	204
18	0.23806269	114.29059616	0.00874963	216
19	0.21981791	117.02731293	0.00854501	228
20	0.20297139	119.55429170	0.00836440	240
21	0.18741596	121.88760650	0.00820428	252
22	0.17305267	124.04209944	0.00806178	264
23	0.15979017	126.03147518	0.00793453	276
24	0.14754408	127.86838806	0.00782054	288
25	0.13623652	129.56452260	0.00771816	300
26	0.12579555	131.13066786	0.00762598	312
27	0.11615476	132.57678603	0.00754280	324
28	0.10725283	133.91207580	0.00746759	336
29	0.09903313	135.14503091	0.00739946	348
30	0.09144337	136.28349413	0.00733765	360
31	0.08443529	137.33470719	0.00728148	372
32	0.07796429	138.30535681	0.00723038	384
33	0.07198922	139.20161725	0.00718382	396
34	0.06647207	140.02918960	0.00714137	408
35	0.06137775	140.79333800	0.00710261	420
36	0.05667385	141.49892318	0.00706719	432
37	0.05233044	142.15043335	0.00703480	444
38	0.04831992	142.75201272	0.00700516	456
39	0.04461675	143.30748792	0.00697800	468
40	0.04119738	143.82039231	0.00695312	480
41	0.03804008	144.29398845	0.00693030	492
42	0.03512474	144.73128888	0.00690936	504
43	0.03243283	145.13507523	0.00689013	516
44	0.02994723	145.50791599	0.00687248	528
45	0.02765211	145.85218277	0.00685626	540
46	0.02553290	146.17006545	0.00684135	552
47	0.02357609	146.46358607	0.00682764	564
48	0.02176926	146.73461169	0.00681502	576
49	0.02010089	146.98486630	0.00680342	588
50	0.01856039	147.21594176	0.00679274	600

	Future Value of 1	Future Value of 1 per Period	Payment for Sinking Fund of 1	**8.00%** Monthly
Months				
1	1.00666667	1.00000000	1.00000000	
2	1.01337778	2.00666667	0.49833887	
3	1.02013363	3.02004444	0.33112095	
4	1.02693452	4.04017807	0.24751384	
5	1.03378075	5.06711259	0.19735105	
6	1.04067262	6.10089335	0.16391042	
7	1.04761044	7.14156597	0.14002531	
8	1.05459451	8.18917641	0.12211240	
9	1.06162514	9.24377092	0.10818096	
10	1.06870264	10.30539606	0.09703654	
11	1.07582732	11.37409870	0.08791905	Years
12	1.08299951	12.44992602	0.08032176	1
24	1.17288793	25.93318976	0.03856062	2
36	1.27023705	40.53555774	0.02466970	3
48	1.37566610	56.34991507	0.01774626	4
60	1.48984571	73.47685625	0.01360973	5
72	1.61350217	92.02532510	0.01086657	6
84	1.74742205	112.11330771	0.00891955	7
96	1.89245722	133.86858298	0.00747001	8
108	2.04953024	157.42953537	0.00635205	9
120	2.21964023	182.94603518	0.00546609	10
132	2.40386928	210.58039190	0.00474878	11
144	2.60338924	240.50838659	0.00415786	12
156	2.81946927	272.92039008	0.00366407	13
168	3.05348383	308.02257387	0.00324652	14
180	3.30692148	346.03822161	0.00288985	15
192	3.58139433	387.20914936	0.00258258	16
204	3.87864829	431.79724381	0.00231590	17
216	4.20057419	480.08612811	0.00208296	18
228	4.54921977	532.38296599	0.00187835	19
240	4.92680277	589.02041562	0.00169773	20
252	5.33572497	650.35874564	0.00153761	21
264	5.77858751	716.78812680	0.00139511	22
276	6.25820743	788.73111383	0.00126786	23
288	6.77763556	866.64533330	0.00115387	24
300	7.34017596	951.02639456	0.00105150	25
312	7.94940695	1042.41104229	0.00095931	26
324	8.60920380	1141.38057071	0.00087613	27
336	9.32376347	1248.56452118	0.00080092	28
348	10.09763124	1364.64468668	0.00073279	29
360	10.93572966	1490.35944866	0.00067098	30
372	11.84338983	1626.50847389	0.00061481	31
384	12.82638534	1773.95780106	0.00056371	32
396	13.89096900	1933.64534967	0.00051716	33
408	15.04391257	2106.58688605	0.00047470	34
420	16.29254990	2293.88248466	0.00043594	35
432	17.64482350	2496.72352559	0.00040052	36
444	19.10933515	2716.40027287	0.00036813	37
456	20.69540055	2954.31008183	0.00033849	38
468	22.41310858	3211.96628759	0.00031134	39
480	24.27338554	3491.00783137	0.00028645	40
492	26.28806457	3793.20968565	0.00026363	41
504	28.46996097	4120.49414480	0.00024269	42
516	30.83295368	4474.94305265	0.00022347	43
528	33.39207363	4858.81104503	0.00020581	44
540	36.16359928	5274.53989146	0.00018959	45
552	39.16516018	5724.77402711	0.00017468	46
564	42.41584916	6212.37737396	0.00016097	47
576	45.93634372	6740.45155812	0.00014836	48
588	49.74903759	7312.35563913	0.00013675	49
600	53.87818318	7931.72747680	0.00012608	50

8.25% Monthly	Present Value of 1	Present Value of 1 per Period	Payment to Pay Off a Loan of 1	Months
	0.99317194	0.99317194	1.00687500	1
	0.98639051	1.97956245	0.50516214	2
	0.97965538	2.95921783	0.33792713	3
	0.97296623	3.93218406	0.25431159	4
	0.96632277	4.89850683	0.20414384	5
	0.95972466	5.85823149	0.17069998	6
	0.95317160	6.81140309	0.14681263	7
	0.94666329	7.75806638	0.12889810	8
	0.94019942	8.69826581	0.11496545	9
	0.93377969	9.63204549	0.10382011	10
Years	0.92740379	10.55944928	0.09470191	11
1	0.92107142	11.48052070	0.08710406	12
2	0.84837256	22.05490021	0.04534140	24
3	0.78141172	31.79465896	0.03145182	36
4	0.71973600	40.76567238	0.02453044	48
5	0.66292826	49.02861645	0.02039625	60
6	0.61060428	56.63937809	0.01765556	72
7	0.56241015	63.64943311	0.01571106	84
8	0.51801991	70.10619445	0.01426407	96
9	0.47713334	76.05333294	0.01314867	108
10	0.43947388	81.53107194	0.01226526	120
11	0.40478683	86.57646092	0.01155048	132
12	0.37283758	91.22362452	0.01096207	144
13	0.34341004	95.50399409	0.01047077	156
14	0.31630517	99.44652017	0.01005566	168
15	0.29133966	103.07786827	0.00970140	180
16	0.26834463	106.42259921	0.00939650	192
17	0.24716457	109.50333530	0.00913214	204
18	0.22765622	112.34091326	0.00890148	216
19	0.20968764	114.95452522	0.00869909	228
20	0.19313729	117.36184850	0.00852066	240
21	0.17789324	119.57916518	0.00836266	252
22	0.16385238	121.62147219	0.00822223	264
23	0.15091974	123.50258282	0.00809700	276
24	0.13900786	125.23522005	0.00798497	288
25	0.12803617	126.83110269	0.00788450	300
26	0.11793046	128.30102458	0.00779417	312
27	0.10862237	129.65492762	0.00771278	324
28	0.10004896	130.90196902	0.00763930	336
29	0.09215224	132.05058321	0.00757286	348
30	0.08487879	133.10853891	0.00751267	360
31	0.07817943	134.08299168	0.00745807	372
32	0.07200884	134.98053227	0.00740848	384
33	0.06632529	135.80723125	0.00736338	396
34	0.06109032	136.56868006	0.00732232	408
35	0.05626855	137.27002880	0.00728491	420
36	0.05182736	137.91602107	0.00725079	432
37	0.04773670	138.51102610	0.00721964	444
38	0.04396891	139.05906822	0.00719119	456
39	0.04049850	139.56385415	0.00716518	468
40	0.03730201	140.02879805	0.00714139	480
41	0.03435782	140.45704459	0.00711961	492
42	0.03164600	140.85149024	0.00709968	504
43	0.02914823	141.21480285	0.00708141	516
44	0.02684760	141.54943971	0.00706467	528
45	0.02472856	141.85766416	0.00704932	540
46	0.02277677	142.14156089	0.00703524	552
47	0.02097903	142.40305006	0.00702232	564
48	0.01932319	142.64390026	0.00701046	576
49	0.01779803	142.86574049	0.00699958	588
50	0.01639326	143.07007119	0.00698958	600

	Future Value of 1	Future Value of 1 per Period	Payment for Sinking Fund of 1	**8.25%** Monthly
Months				
1	1.00687500	1.00000000	1.00000000	
2	1.01379727	2.00687500	0.49828714	
3	1.02076712	3.02067227	0.33105213	
4	1.02778490	4.04143939	0.24743659	
5	1.03485092	5.06922428	0.19726884	
6	1.04196552	6.10407520	0.16382498	
7	1.04912903	7.14604072	0.13993763	
8	1.05634179	8.19516975	0.12202310	
9	1.06360414	9.25151154	0.10809045	
10	1.07091642	10.31511568	0.09694511	
11	1.07827897	11.38603210	0.08782691	Years
12	1.08569214	12.46431107	0.08022906	1
24	1.17872742	25.99671562	0.03846640	2
36	1.27973509	40.68874085	0.02457682	3
48	1.38939833	56.63975714	0.01765544	4
60	1.50845884	73.95765013	0.01352125	5
72	1.63772191	92.75955041	0.01078056	6
84	1.77806180	113.17262573	0.00883606	7
96	1.93042772	135.33494114	0.00738907	8
108	2.09585020	159.39639275	0.00627367	9
120	2.27544809	185.51972160	0.00539026	10
132	2.47043610	213.88161437	0.00467548	11
144	2.68213305	244.67389839	0.00408707	12
156	2.91197077	278.10483908	0.00359577	13
168	3.16150377	314.40054858	0.00318066	14
180	3.43241979	353.80651504	0.00282640	15
192	3.72655118	396.58926304	0.00252150	16
204	4.04588732	443.03815622	0.00225714	17
216	4.39258806	493.46735439	0.00202648	18
228	4.76899833	548.21793839	0.00182409	19
240	5.17766399	607.66021704	0.00164566	20
252	5.62134909	672.19623166	0.00148766	21
264	6.10305452	742.26247540	0.00134723	22
276	6.62603831	818.33284540	0.00122200	23
288	7.19383771	900.92184810	0.00110997	24
300	7.81029304	990.58807906	0.00100950	25
312	8.47957376	1087.93800112	0.00091917	26
324	9.20620657	1193.63004620	0.00083778	27
336	9.99510610	1308.37906865	0.00076430	28
348	10.85160811	1432.96118024	0.00069786	29
360	11.78150562	1568.21899940	0.00063767	30
372	12.79108803	1715.06735036	0.00058307	31
384	13.88718372	1874.49945056	0.00053348	32
396	15.07720620	2047.59362839	0.00048838	33
408	16.36920424	2235.52061650	0.00044732	34
420	17.77191636	2439.55147013	0.00040991	35
432	19.29482988	2661.06616395	0.00037579	36
444	20.94824511	2901.56292562	0.00034464	37
456	22.74334504	3162.66836913	0.00031619	38
468	24.69227091	3446.14849650	0.00029018	39
480	26.80820442	3753.92064224	0.00026639	40
492	29.10545678	4088.06644135	0.00024461	41
504	31.59956562	4450.84590860	0.00022468	42
516	34.30739998	4844.71272425	0.00020641	43
528	37.24727445	5272.33082966	0.00018967	44
540	40.43907306	5736.59244503	0.00017432	45
552	43.90438371	6240.63763111	0.00016024	46
564	47.66664425	6787.87552714	0.00014732	47
576	51.75130094	7382.00740882	0.00013546	48
588	56.18598059	8027.05172206	0.00012458	49
600	61.00067743	8727.37126201	0.00011458	50

8.50% Monthly	Present Value of 1	Present Value of 1 per Period	Payment to Pay Off a Loan of 1	
				Months
	0.99296649	0.99296649	1.00708333	1
	0.98598245	1.97894893	0.50531875	2
	0.97904753	2.95799646	0.33806667	3
	0.97216138	3.93015784	0.25444271	4
	0.96532367	4.89548151	0.20427000	5
	0.95853406	5.85401557	0.17082291	6
	0.95179220	6.80580776	0.14693333	7
	0.94509775	7.75090552	0.12901718	8
	0.93845040	8.68935591	0.11508333	9
	0.93184979	9.62120570	0.10393708	10
Years	0.92529562	10.54650132	0.09481817	11
1	0.91878754	11.46528886	0.08721978	12
2	0.84417054	21.99945337	0.04545567	24
3	0.77561337	31.67811244	0.03156754	36
4	0.71262390	40.57074377	0.02464830	48
5	0.65474996	48.71118261	0.02051650	60
6	0.60157610	56.24807999	0.01777838	72
7	0.55272062	63.14532375	0.01583649	84
8	0.50783282	69.48242536	0.01439213	96
9	0.46659047	75.30487533	0.01327935	108
10	0.42869751	80.65446981	0.01239857	120
11	0.39388193	85.56961054	0.01168639	132
12	0.36189380	90.08558059	0.01110056	144
13	0.33250352	94.23479759	0.01061179	156
14	0.30550009	98.04704646	0.01019919	168
15	0.28068967	101.54969321	0.00984740	180
16	0.25789417	104.76788139	0.00954491	192
17	0.23694995	107.72471259	0.00928292	204
18	0.21770666	110.44141224	0.00905457	216
19	0.20002617	112.93748202	0.00885446	228
20	0.18378155	115.23083982	0.00867823	240
21	0.16885620	117.33794840	0.00852239	252
22	0.15514297	119.27393349	0.00838406	264
23	0.14254343	121.05269247	0.00826087	276
24	0.13096713	122.68699405	0.00815082	288
25	0.12033096	124.18856997	0.00805227	300
26	0.11055859	125.56819922	0.00796380	312
27	0.10157985	126.83578538	0.00788421	324
28	0.09333030	128.00042704	0.00781247	336
29	0.08575072	129.07048663	0.00774770	348
30	0.07878669	130.05364340	0.00768913	360
31	0.07238823	130.95695559	0.00763610	372
32	0.06650940	131.78690757	0.00758801	384
33	0.06110801	132.54945711	0.00754435	396
34	0.05614528	133.25007812	0.00750469	408
35	0.05158558	133.89379997	0.00746861	420
36	0.04739619	134.48524359	0.00743576	432
37	0.04354703	135.02865461	0.00740584	444
38	0.04001047	135.52793389	0.00737855	456
39	0.03676112	135.98666546	0.00735366	468
40	0.03377566	136.40814232	0.00733094	480
41	0.03103265	136.79539000	0.00731019	492
42	0.02851242	137.15118834	0.00729122	504
43	0.02619685	137.47809143	0.00727389	516
44	0.02406934	137.77844591	0.00725803	528
45	0.02211461	138.05440786	0.00724352	540
46	0.02031863	138.30795826	0.00723024	552
47	0.01866850	138.54091721	0.00721808	564
48	0.01715239	138.75495699	0.00720695	576
49	0.01575940	138.95161408	0.00719675	588
50	0.01447954	139.13230015	0.00718740	600

	Future Value of 1	Future Value of 1 per Period	Payment for Sinking Fund of 1	**8.50%** Monthly
Months				
1	1.00708333	1.00000000	1.00000000	
2	1.01421684	2.00708333	0.49823542	
3	1.02140088	3.02130017	0.33098333	
4	1.02863580	4.04270105	0.24735937	
5	1.03592197	5.07133685	0.19718666	
6	1.04325975	6.10725882	0.16373958	
7	1.05064951	7.15051857	0.13985000	
8	1.05809161	8.20116807	0.12193385	
9	1.06558642	9.25925968	0.10800002	
10	1.07313433	10.32484610	0.09685374	
11	1.08073569	11.39798043	0.08773484	Years
12	1.08839091	12.47871613	0.08013645	1
24	1.18459476	26.06043727	0.03837234	2
36	1.28930217	40.84265906	0.02448420	3
48	1.40326475	56.93149462	0.01756497	4
60	1.52730060	74.44243735	0.01343320	5
72	1.66230008	93.50118795	0.01069505	6
84	1.80923229	114.24455878	0.00875315	7
96	1.96915197	136.82145495	0.00730880	8
108	2.14320710	161.39394342	0.00619602	9
120	2.33264712	188.13841641	0.00531524	10
132	2.53883191	217.24685760	0.00460306	11
144	2.76324156	248.92822027	0.00401722	12
156	3.00748698	283.40992729	0.00352846	13
168	3.27332148	320.93950362	0.00311585	14
180	3.56265334	361.78635321	0.00276406	15
192	3.87755949	406.24369284	0.00246158	16
204	4.22030049	454.63065699	0.00219959	17
216	4.59333667	507.29458873	0.00197124	18
228	4.99934586	564.61353311	0.00177112	19
240	5.44124257	626.99895090	0.00159490	20
252	5.92219893	694.89867229	0.00143906	21
264	6.44566746	768.80011157	0.00130073	22
276	7.01540584	849.23376601	0.00117753	23
288	7.63550392	936.77702402	0.00106749	24
300	8.31041303	1032.05830992	0.00096894	25
312	9.04497796	1135.76159500	0.00088047	26
324	9.84447176	1248.63130738	0.00080088	27
336	10.71463354	1371.47767589	0.00072914	28
348	11.66170970	1505.18254620	0.00066437	29
360	12.69249879	1650.70571112	0.00060580	30
372	13.81440025	1809.09180042	0.00055276	31
384	15.03546761	1981.47777962	0.00050467	32
396	16.36446621	2169.10111170	0.00046102	33
408	17.81093620	2373.30864006	0.00042135	34
420	19.38526099	2595.56625684	0.00038527	35
432	21.09874177	2837.46942572	0.00035243	36
444	22.96367866	3100.75463482	0.00032250	37
456	24.99345902	3387.31186207	0.00029522	38
468	27.20265351	3699.19814223	0.00027033	39
480	29.60712069	4038.65233322	0.00024761	40
492	32.22412091	4408.11118767	0.00022685	41
504	35.07244015	4810.22684495	0.00020789	42
516	38.17252491	5247.88586945	0.00019055	43
528	41.54662897	5724.22997159	0.00017470	44
540	45.21897314	6242.67856045	0.00016019	45
552	49.21591914	6806.95328973	0.00014691	46
564	53.56615881	7421.10477350	0.00013475	47
576	58.30092011	8089.54166338	0.00012362	48
588	63.45419126	8817.06229528	0.00011342	49
600	69.06296471	9608.88913500	0.00010407	50

8.75% Monthly	Present Value of 1	Present Value of 1 per Period	Payment to Pay Off a Loan of 1	Months
	0.99276112	0.99276112	1.00729167	1
	0.98557464	1.97833575	0.50547537	2
	0.97844018	2.95677593	0.33820622	3
	0.97135736	3.92813324	0.25457385	4
	0.96432582	4.89245911	0.20439619	5
	0.95734518	5.84980429	0.17094589	6
	0.95041507	6.80021935	0.14705408	7
	0.94353512	7.74375448	0.12913633	8
	0.93670498	8.68045946	0.11520128	9
	0.92992429	9.61038374	0.10405412	10
Years	0.92319267	10.53357642	0.09493452	11
1	0.91650979	11.45008620	0.08733559	12
2	0.83999019	21.94420228	0.04557012	24
3	0.76985923	31.56216239	0.03168351	36
4	0.70558352	40.37711697	0.02476650	48
5	0.64667420	48.45610912	0.02063723	60
6	0.59268324	55.86058451	0.01790171	72
7	0.54319999	62.64685867	0.01596249	84
8	0.49784811	68.86654537	0.01452084	96
9	0.45628266	74.56694911	0.01341077	108
10	0.41818753	79.79142493	0.01253268	120
11	0.38327296	84.57970816	0.01182317	132
12	0.35127342	88.96821661	0.01123997	144
13	0.32194553	92.99032755	0.01075381	156
14	0.29506623	96.67663161	0.01034376	168
15	0.27043109	100.05516535	0.00999449	180
16	0.24785274	103.15162460	0.00969447	192
17	0.22715946	105.98955981	0.00943489	204
18	0.20819387	108.59055520	0.00920890	216
19	0.19081172	110.97439294	0.00901109	228
20	0.17488081	113.15920356	0.00883711	240
21	0.16027997	115.16160388	0.00868345	252
22	0.14689816	116.99682338	0.00854724	264
23	0.13463360	118.67882000	0.00842610	276
24	0.12339302	120.22038638	0.00831806	288
25	0.11309091	121.63324705	0.00822144	300
26	0.10364892	122.92814768	0.00813483	312
27	0.09499525	124.11493679	0.00805705	324
28	0.08706408	125.20264062	0.00798705	336
29	0.07979508	126.19953182	0.00792396	348
30	0.07313297	127.11319237	0.00786700	360
31	0.06702708	127.95057121	0.00781552	372
32	0.06143098	128.71803711	0.00776892	384
33	0.05630209	129.42142712	0.00772670	396
34	0.05160142	130.06609095	0.00768840	408
35	0.04729321	130.65693166	0.00765363	420
36	0.04334469	131.19844295	0.00762204	432
37	0.03972583	131.69474335	0.00759332	444
38	0.03640911	132.14960753	0.00756718	456
39	0.03336931	132.56649500	0.00754338	468
40	0.03058330	132.94857644	0.00752171	480
41	0.02802989	133.29875783	0.00750195	492
42	0.02568967	133.61970249	0.00748393	504
43	0.02354483	133.91385142	0.00746749	516
44	0.02157907	134.18344179	0.00745248	528
45	0.01977743	134.43052401	0.00743879	540
46	0.01812621	134.65697728	0.00742628	552
47	0.01661285	134.86452391	0.00741485	564
48	0.01522584	135.05474244	0.00740440	576
49	0.01395463	135.22907958	0.00739486	588
50	0.01278955	135.38886127	0.00738613	600

	Future Value of 1	Future Value of 1 per Period	Payment for Sinking Fund of 1	**8.75%** Monthly
Months				
1	1.00729167	1.00000000	1.00000000	
2	1.01463650	2.00729167	0.49818371	
3	1.02203489	3.02192817	0.33091455	
4	1.02948723	4.04396306	0.24728218	
5	1.03699391	5.07345029	0.19710452	
6	1.04455532	6.11044420	0.16365422	
7	1.05217187	7.15499952	0.13976241	
8	1.05984396	8.20717139	0.12184466	
9	1.06757199	9.26701535	0.10790961	
10	1.07535637	10.33458734	0.09676245	
11	1.08319751	11.40994371	0.08764285	Years
12	1.09109582	12.49314121	0.08004392	1
24	1.19049009	26.12435538	0.03827846	2
36	1.29893876	40.99731620	0.02439184	3
48	1.41726666	57.22514161	0.01747484	4
60	1.54637373	74.93125409	0.01334557	5
72	1.68724191	94.25031944	0.01061004	6
84	1.84094260	115.32927091	0.00867083	7
96	2.00864478	138.32842678	0.00722917	8
108	2.19162392	163.42270964	0.00611910	9
120	2.39127171	190.80297682	0.00524101	10
132	2.60910657	220.67747191	0.00453150	11
144	2.84678527	253.27340868	0.00394830	12
156	3.10611551	288.83869907	0.00346214	13
168	3.38906966	327.64383881	0.00305209	14
180	3.69779974	369.98396462	0.00270282	15
192	4.03465385	416.18109897	0.00240280	16
204	4.40219395	466.58659922	0.00214322	17
216	4.80321543	521.58382991	0.00191724	18
228	5.24076828	581.59107850	0.00171942	19
240	5.71818037	647.06473668	0.00154544	20
252	6.23908271	718.50277154	0.00139178	21
264	6.80743707	796.44851285	0.00125557	22
276	7.42756614	881.49478549	0.00113444	23
288	8.10418638	974.28841819	0.00102639	24
300	8.84244390	1075.53516307	0.00092977	25
312	9.64795359	1186.00506334	0.00084317	26
324	10.52684184	1306.53830990	0.00076538	27
336	11.48579315	1438.05163155	0.00069539	28
348	12.53210091	1581.54526726	0.00063229	29
360	13.67372293	1738.11057357	0.00057534	30
372	14.91934195	1908.93832504	0.00052385	31
384	16.27843166	2095.32777085	0.00047725	32
396	17.76132876	2298.69651631	0.00043503	33
408	19.37931160	2520.59130467	0.00039673	34
420	21.14468590	2762.69978102	0.00036196	35
432	23.07087843	3026.86332788	0.00033038	36
444	25.17253905	3315.09107001	0.00030165	37
456	27.46565217	3629.57515503	0.00027551	38
468	29.96765832	3972.70742608	0.00025172	39
480	32.69758676	4347.09761319	0.00023004	40
492	35.67620028	4755.59318189	0.00021028	41
504	38.92615305	5201.30098993	0.00019226	42
516	42.47216294	5687.61091682	0.00017582	43
528	46.34119950	6218.22164592	0.00016082	44
540	50.56268913	6797.16879519	0.00014712	45
552	55.16873883	7428.85561054	0.00013461	46
564	60.19438040	8118.08645516	0.00012318	47
576	65.67783692	8870.10334965	0.00011274	48
588	71.66081342	9690.62584081	0.00010319	49
600	78.18881408	10585.89450222	0.00009447	50

9.00% Monthly	Present Value of 1	Present Value of 1 per Period	Payment to Pay Off a Loan of 1	Months
	0.99255583	0.99255583	1.00750000	1
	0.98516708	1.97772291	0.50563200	2
	0.97783333	2.95555624	0.33834579	3
	0.97055417	3.92611041	0.25470501	4
	0.96332920	4.88943961	0.20452242	5
	0.95615802	5.84559763	0.17106891	6
	0.94904022	6.79463785	0.14717488	7
	0.94197540	7.73661325	0.12925552	8
	0.93496318	8.67157642	0.11531929	9
	0.92800315	9.59957958	0.10417123	10
Years	0.92109494	10.52067452	0.09505094	11
1	0.91423815	11.43491267	0.08745148	12
2	0.83583140	21.88914614	0.04568474	24
3	0.76414896	31.44680525	0.03179973	36
4	0.69861414	40.18478189	0.02488504	48
5	0.63869970	48.17337352	0.02075836	60
6	0.58392363	55.47684880	0.01802554	72
7	0.53384527	62.15396456	0.01608908	84
8	0.48806171	68.25843856	0.01465020	96
9	0.44620464	73.83938160	0.01354291	108
10	0.40793730	78.94169267	0.01266758	120
11	0.37295185	83.60642013	0.01196080	132
12	0.34096681	87.87109195	0.01138031	144
13	0.31172487	91.77001765	0.01089681	156
14	0.28499077	95.33456429	0.01048938	168
15	0.26054943	98.59340884	0.01014267	180
16	0.23820423	101.57276886	0.00984516	192
17	0.21777540	104.29661347	0.00958804	204
18	0.19909858	106.78685614	0.00936445	216
19	0.18202352	109.06353100	0.00916901	228
20	0.16641284	111.14495403	0.00899726	240
21	0.15214097	113.04787038	0.00884581	252
22	0.13909308	114.78758911	0.00871174	264
23	0.12716420	116.37810635	0.00859268	276
24	0.11625837	117.83221790	0.00848664	288
25	0.10628783	119.16162216	0.00839196	300
26	0.09717239	120.37701426	0.00830723	312
27	0.08883871	121.48817209	0.00823125	324
28	0.08121974	122.50403497	0.00816300	336
29	0.07425418	123.43277558	0.00810158	348
30	0.06788601	124.28186568	0.00804623	360
31	0.06206398	125.05813624	0.00799628	372
32	0.05674126	125.76783241	0.00795116	384
33	0.05187502	126.41666373	0.00791035	396
34	0.04742612	127.00985008	0.00787341	408
35	0.04335877	127.55216367	0.00783994	420
36	0.03964024	128.04796745	0.00780957	432
37	0.03624062	128.50125018	0.00778203	444
38	0.03313256	128.91565854	0.00775701	456
39	0.03029105	129.29452648	0.00773428	468
40	0.02769323	129.64090201	0.00771361	480
41	0.02531821	129.95757173	0.00769482	492
42	0.02314688	130.24708328	0.00767772	504
43	0.02116176	130.51176578	0.00766214	516
44	0.01934689	130.75374862	0.00764796	528
45	0.01768766	130.97497856	0.00763505	540
46	0.01617073	131.17723542	0.00762327	552
47	0.01478390	131.36214635	0.00761254	564
48	0.01351601	131.53119899	0.00760276	576
49	0.01235685	131.68575335	0.00759384	588
50	0.01129710	131.82705285	0.00758570	600

	Future Value of 1	Future Value of 1 per Period	Payment for Sinking Fund of 1	**9.00%** Monthly
Months				
1	1.00750000	1.00000000	1.00000000	
2	1.01505625	2.00750000	0.49813200	
3	1.02266917	3.02255625	0.33084579	
4	1.03033919	4.04522542	0.24720501	
5	1.03806673	5.07556461	0.19702242	
6	1.04585224	6.11363135	0.16356891	
7	1.05369613	7.15948358	0.13967488	
8	1.06159885	8.21317971	0.12175552	
9	1.06956084	9.27477856	0.10781929	
10	1.07758255	10.34433940	0.09667123	
11	1.08566441	11.42192194	0.08755094	Years
12	1.09380690	12.50758636	0.07995148	1
24	1.19641353	26.18847059	0.03818474	2
36	1.30864537	41.15271612	0.02429973	3
48	1.43140533	57.52071111	0.01738504	4
60	1.56568103	75.42413693	0.01325836	5
72	1.71255271	95.00702758	0.01052554	6
84	1.87320196	116.42692845	0.00858908	7
96	2.04892123	139.85616377	0.00715020	8
108	2.24112417	165.48322296	0.00604291	9
120	2.45135708	193.51427708	0.00516758	10
132	2.68131128	224.17483743	0.00446080	11
144	2.93283677	257.71156982	0.00388031	12
156	3.20795709	294.39427903	0.00339681	13
168	3.50888560	334.51807940	0.00298938	14
180	3.83804327	378.40576900	0.00264267	15
192	4.19807820	426.41042660	0.00234516	16
204	4.59188689	478.91825221	0.00208804	17
216	5.02263756	536.35167405	0.00186445	18
228	5.49379560	599.17274701	0.00166897	19
240	6.00915152	667.88686993	0.00149726	20
252	6.57285139	743.04685155	0.00134581	21
264	7.18943018	825.25735787	0.00121174	22
276	7.86384833	915.17977675	0.00109268	23
288	8.60153154	1013.53753878	0.00098664	24
300	9.40841453	1121.12193732	0.00089196	25
312	10.29098871	1238.79849452	0.00080723	26
324	11.25635443	1367.51392449	0.00073125	27
336	12.31227812	1508.30374963	0.00066300	28
348	13.46725474	1662.30063148	0.00060158	29
360	14.73057612	1830.74348307	0.00054623	30
372	16.11240577	2014.98743601	0.00049628	31
384	17.62386057	2216.51474258	0.00045116	32
396	19.27710025	2436.94670058	0.00041035	33
408	21.08542523	2678.05669651	0.00037341	34
420	23.06338355	2941.78447357	0.00033993	35
432	25.22688801	3230.25173501	0.00030957	36
444	27.59334411	3545.77921532	0.00028203	37
456	30.18179012	3890.90534969	0.00025701	38
468	33.01305022	4268.40669603	0.00023428	39
480	36.10990204	4681.32027254	0.00021361	40
492	39.49725993	5132.96799067	0.00019482	41
504	43.20237535	5626.98338008	0.00017772	42
516	47.25505615	6167.34082056	0.00016214	43
528	51.68790637	6758.38751618	0.00014796	44
540	56.53658852	7404.87846868	0.00013505	45
552	61.84011049	8112.01473182	0.00012327	46
564	67.64113941	8885.48525403	0.00011254	47
576	73.98634485	9731.51264636	0.00010276	48
588	80.92677433	10656.90324372	0.00009384	49
600	88.51826397	11669.10186215	0.00008570	50

9.25% Monthly	Present Value of 1	Present Value of 1 per Period	Payment to Pay Off a Loan of 1	Months
	0.99235063	0.99235063	1.00770833	1
	0.98475977	1.97711040	0.50578865	2
	0.97722698	2.95433739	0.33848538	3
	0.96975181	3.92408920	0.25483621	4
	0.96233382	4.88642302	0.20464868	5
	0.95497258	5.84139560	0.17119197	6
	0.94766764	6.78906324	0.14729573	7
	0.94041858	7.72948181	0.12937478	8
	0.93322497	8.66270678	0.11543736	9
	0.92608639	9.58879317	0.10428841	10
Years	0.91900241	10.50779558	0.09516744	11
1	0.91197262	11.41976820	0.08756745	12
2	0.83169406	21.83428412	0.04579953	24
3	0.75848221	31.33203750	0.03191621	36
4	0.69171501	39.99347853	0.02500392	48
5	0.63082515	47.89295359	0.02087090	60
6	0.57529526	55.09683057	0.01814986	72
7	0.52465353	61.66656913	0.01621624	84
8	0.47846965	67.65799082	0.01478022	96
9	0.43635122	73.12000336	0.01367577	108
10	0.39794037	78.10503319	0.01280327	120
11	0.36291072	82.64941997	0.01209930	132
12	0.33096464	86.79377628	0.01152156	144
13	0.30183069	90.57331576	0.01104078	156
14	0.27526133	94.02015229	0.01063602	168
15	0.25103079	97.16357282	0.01029192	180
16	0.22893321	100.03028629	0.00999697	192
17	0.20878082	102.64465048	0.00974235	204
18	0.19040239	105.02887904	0.00952119	216
19	0.17364177	107.20723020	0.00932808	228
20	0.15835654	109.18617893	0.00915867	240
21	0.14441683	110.99457388	0.00900945	252
22	0.13170419	112.64378056	0.00887754	264
23	0.12011062	114.14781190	0.00876057	276
24	0.10953759	115.51944730	0.00865655	288
25	0.09989529	116.77034123	0.00856382	300
26	0.09110177	117.91112224	0.00848096	312
27	0.08308232	118.95148329	0.00840679	324
28	0.07576880	119.90026409	0.00834027	336
29	0.06909907	120.76552619	0.00828051	348
30	0.06301646	121.55462154	0.00822675	360
31	0.05746929	122.27425490	0.00817834	372
32	0.05241041	122.93054081	0.00813468	384
33	0.04779686	123.52905560	0.00809526	396
34	0.04358943	124.07488469	0.00805965	408
35	0.03975237	124.57266589	0.00802744	420
36	0.03625307	125.02662870	0.00799830	432
37	0.03306181	125.44063036	0.00797190	444
38	0.03015146	125.81818854	0.00794798	456
39	0.02749731	126.16251127	0.00792628	468
40	0.02507679	126.47652416	0.00790661	480
41	0.02286935	126.76289532	0.00788874	492
42	0.02085622	127.02405798	0.00787252	504
43	0.01902030	127.26223118	0.00785779	516
44	0.01734599	127.47943861	0.00784440	528
45	0.01581907	127.67752584	0.00783223	540
46	0.01442656	127.85817597	0.00782117	552
47	0.01315663	128.02292395	0.00781110	564
48	0.01199848	128.17316959	0.00780194	576
49	0.01094229	128.31018950	0.00779361	588
50	0.00997907	128.43514790	0.00778603	600

	Future Value of 1	Future Value of 1 per Period	Payment for Sinking Fund of 1	**9.25%** Monthly
Months				
1	1.00770833	1.00000000	1.00000000	
2	1.01547609	2.00770833	0.49808032	
3	1.02330371	3.02318442	0.33077704	
4	1.03119168	4.04648813	0.24712787	
5	1.03914045	5.07767981	0.19694034	
6	1.04715049	6.11682026	0.16348363	
7	1.05522227	7.16397075	0.13958739	
8	1.06335628	8.21919302	0.12166645	
9	1.07155298	9.28254930	0.10772903	
10	1.07981287	10.35410229	0.09658008	
11	1.08813643	11.43391516	0.08745911	Years
12	1.09652415	12.52205159	0.07985912	1
24	1.20236521	26.25278353	0.03809120	2
36	1.31842248	41.30886268	0.02420788	3
48	1.44568209	57.81821703	0.01729559	4
60	1.58522532	75.92112273	0.01317156	5
72	1.73823784	95.77139598	0.01044153	6
84	1.90601977	117.53769994	0.00850791	7
96	2.08999670	141.40497783	0.00707189	8
108	2.29173185	167.57602438	0.00596744	9
120	2.51293932	196.27320889	0.00509494	10
132	2.75549864	227.74036467	0.00439097	11
144	3.02147080	262.24486085	0.00381323	12
156	3.31311570	300.07987411	0.00333245	13
168	3.63291136	341.56687978	0.00292768	14
180	3.98357504	387.05838331	0.00258359	15
192	4.36808622	436.94091544	0.00228864	16
204	4.78971202	491.63831647	0.00203402	17
216	5.25203489	551.61533751	0.00181286	18
228	5.75898308	617.38158939	0.00161974	19
240	6.31486402	689.49587267	0.00145034	20
252	6.92440089	768.57092569	0.00130112	21
264	7.59277278	855.27863080	0.00116921	22
276	8.32565870	950.35572324	0.00105224	23
288	9.12928581	1054.61005098	0.00094822	24
300	10.01048234	1168.92743886	0.00085549	25
312	10.97673562	1294.27921516	0.00077263	26
324	12.03625567	1431.73046483	0.00069846	27
336	13.19804499	1582.44907921	0.00063193	28
348	14.47197503	1747.71567939	0.00057218	29
360	15.86887008	1928.93449729	0.00051842	30
372	17.40059924	2127.64530712	0.00047000	31
384	19.08017725	2345.53650850	0.00042634	32
396	20.92187510	2584.45947238	0.00038693	33
408	22.94134126	2846.44427171	0.00035132	34
420	25.15573467	3133.71693049	0.00031911	35
432	27.58387052	3448.71833780	0.00028996	36
444	30.24638011	3794.12498747	0.00026357	37
456	33.16588617	4172.87171959	0.00023964	38
468	36.36719507	4588.17665721	0.00021795	39
480	39.87750757	5043.56854996	0.00019827	40
492	43.72665000	5542.91675700	0.00018041	41
504	47.94732762	6090.46412411	0.00016419	42
516	52.57540255	6690.86303414	0.00014946	43
528	57.65019847	7349.21493722	0.00013607	44
540	63.21483474	8071.11369660	0.00012390	45
552	69.31659279	8862.69311843	0.00011283	46
564	76.00731783	9730.67906925	0.00010277	47
576	83.34385939	10682.44662416	0.00009361	48
588	91.38855439	11726.08273108	0.00008528	49
600	100.20975670	12870.45492369	0.00007770	50

9.50%
Monthly

	Present Value of 1	Present Value of 1 per Period	Payment to Pay Off a Loan of 1	Months
	0.99214551	0.99214551	1.00791667	1
	0.98435272	1.97649824	0.50594530	2
	0.97662114	2.95311938	0.33862498	3
	0.96895028	3.92206966	0.25496742	4
	0.96133968	4.88340933	0.20477497	5
	0.95378885	5.83719818	0.17131507	6
	0.94629733	6.78349551	0.14741662	7
	0.93886465	7.72236016	0.12949409	8
	0.93149035	8.65385051	0.11555550	9
	0.92417397	9.57802448	0.10440566	10
Years	0.91691506	10.49493954	0.09528402	11
1	0.90971317	11.40465271	0.08768351	12
2	0.82757804	21.77961543	0.04591449	24
3	0.75285864	31.21785562	0.03203295	36
4	0.68488542	39.80394698	0.02512314	48
5	0.62304928	47.61482734	0.02100186	60
6	0.56679614	54.72048804	0.01827469	72
7	0.51562191	61.18460113	0.01634398	84
8	0.46906804	67.06508991	0.01491089	96
9	0.42671737	72.41464799	0.01380936	108
10	0.38819041	77.28121140	0.01293976	120
11	0.35314193	81.70838820	0.01223865	132
12	0.32125786	85.73584924	0.01166373	144
13	0.29225251	89.39968356	0.01118572	156
14	0.26586595	92.73272188	0.01078368	168
15	0.24186176	95.76483073	0.01044225	180
16	0.22002482	98.52318007	0.01014990	192
17	0.20015948	101.03248678	0.00989781	204
18	0.18208771	103.31523613	0.00967911	216
19	0.16564759	105.39188327	0.00948840	228
20	0.15069179	107.28103652	0.00932131	240
21	0.13708631	108.99962410	0.00917434	252
22	0.12470922	110.56304584	0.00904461	264
23	0.11344962	111.98531119	0.00892974	276
24	0.10320661	113.27916470	0.00882775	288
25	0.09388841	114.45620028	0.00873697	300
26	0.08541153	115.52696504	0.00865599	312
27	0.07769999	116.50105384	0.00858361	324
28	0.07068470	117.38719525	0.00851882	336
29	0.06430281	118.19332975	0.00846071	348
30	0.05849711	118.92668092	0.00840854	360
31	0.05321559	119.59382014	0.00836164	372
32	0.04841092	120.20072547	0.00831942	384
33	0.04404005	120.75283524	0.00828138	396
34	0.04006382	121.25590676	0.00824708	408
35	0.03644658	121.71201068	0.00821612	420
36	0.03315594	122.12767130	0.00818815	432
37	0.03016239	122.50580323	0.00816288	444
38	0.02743912	122.84979482	0.00814002	456
39	0.02496173	123.16272851	0.00811934	468
40	0.02270802	123.44740840	0.00810062	480
41	0.02065778	123.70638544	0.00808366	492
42	0.01879266	123.94198027	0.00806829	504
43	0.01709593	124.15630399	0.00805436	516
44	0.01555239	124.35127710	0.00804173	528
45	0.01414821	124.52864670	0.00803028	540
46	0.01287082	124.69000216	0.00801989	552
47	0.01170875	124.83678935	0.00801046	564
48	0.01065160	124.97032359	0.00800190	576
49	0.00968991	125.09180144	0.00799413	588
50	0.00881503	125.20231145	0.00798707	600

	Future Value of 1	Future Value of 1 per Period	Payment for Sinking Fund of 1	**9.50%** Monthly
Months				
1	1.00791667	1.00000000	1.00000000	
2	1.01589601	2.00791667	0.49802864	
3	1.02393852	3.02381267	0.33070832	
4	1.03204470	4.04775119	0.24705076	
5	1.04021505	5.07979589	0.19685830	
6	1.04845009	6.12001094	0.16339840	
7	1.05675032	7.16846102	0.13949996	
8	1.06511626	8.22521134	0.12157742	
9	1.07354843	9.29032760	0.10763883	
10	1.08204735	10.36387602	0.09648900	
11	1.09061356	11.44592338	0.08736735	Years
12	1.09924758	12.53653694	0.07976685	1
24	1.20834525	26.31729488	0.03799783	2
36	1.32827060	41.46575975	0.02411628	3
48	1.46009825	58.11767316	0.01720647	4
60	1.60500947	76.42224875	0.01308519	5
72	1.76430278	96.54350925	0.01035802	6
84	1.93940557	118.66175624	0.00842732	7
96	2.13188689	142.97518580	0.00699422	8
108	2.34347151	169.70166451	0.00589269	9
120	2.57605540	199.08068167	0.00502309	10
132	2.83172267	231.37549530	0.00432198	11
144	3.11276430	266.87549116	0.00374707	12
156	3.42169864	305.89877584	0.00326906	13
168	3.76129397	348.79502725	0.00286701	14
180	4.13549330	395.94862799	0.00252558	15
192	4.54494170	447.78210967	0.00223323	16
204	4.99601619	504.75993919	0.00198114	17
216	5.49185872	567.39268063	0.00176245	18
228	6.03691243	636.24157034	0.00157173	19
240	6.63606141	711.92354603	0.00140465	20
252	7.29467447	795.11677496	0.00125768	21
264	8.01865329	886.56673087	0.00112795	22
276	8.81448525	987.09287397	0.00101308	23
288	9.68930162	1097.59599391	0.00091108	24
300	10.65094140	1219.06628154	0.00082030	25
312	11.70802160	1352.59220176	0.00073932	26
324	12.87001446	1499.37024696	0.00066695	27
336	14.14733230	1660.71565856	0.00060215	28
348	15.55142085	1838.07421245	0.00054405	29
360	17.09486180	2033.03517433	0.00049188	30
372	18.79148553	2247.34554067	0.00044497	31
384	20.65649507	2482.92569312	0.00040275	32
396	22.70660230	2741.88660655	0.00036471	33
408	24.96017772	3026.54876501	0.00033041	34
420	27.43741506	3339.46295498	0.00029945	35
432	30.16051222	3683.43312284	0.00027149	36
444	33.15387019	4061.54149777	0.00024621	37
456	36.44431171	4477.17621601	0.00022336	38
468	40.06132160	4934.06167589	0.00020267	39
480	44.03731098	5436.29191386	0.00018395	40
492	48.40790771	5988.36728961	0.00016699	41
504	53.21227560	6595.23481263	0.00015162	42
516	58.49346540	7262.33247117	0.00013770	43
528	64.29880052	7995.63796066	0.00012507	44
540	70.68030113	8801.72224838	0.00011361	45
552	77.69515026	9687.80845422	0.00010322	46
564	85.40620622	10661.83657528	0.00009379	47
576	93.88256585	11732.53463418	0.00008523	48
588	103.20018370	12909.49688870	0.00007746	49
600	113.44255261	14203.26980354	0.00007041	50

9.75% Monthly	Present Value of 1	Present Value of 1 per Period	Payment to Pay Off a Loan of 1
			Months
	0.99194048	0.99194048	1.00812500	1
	0.98394592	1.97588641	0.50610197	2
	0.97601579	2.95190220	0.33876461	3
	0.96814958	3.92005178	0.25509867	4
	0.96034676	4.88039854	0.20490130	5
	0.95260683	5.83300537	0.17143821	6
	0.94492928	6.77793465	0.14753757	7
	0.93731361	7.71524826	0.12961346	8
	0.92975931	8.64500758	0.11567370	9
	0.92226590	9.56727348	0.10452299	10
Years	0.91483289	10.48210636	0.09540067	11
1	0.90745978	11.38956614	0.08779966	12
2	0.82348324	21.72513927	0.04602962	24
3	0.74727792	31.10425613	0.03214994	36
4	0.67812465	39.61542742	0.02524269	48
5	0.61537084	47.33897299	0.02112424	60
6	0.55842429	54.34777993	0.01840002	72
7	0.50674758	60.70799029	0.01647230	84
8	0.45985304	66.47962536	0.01504220	96
9	0.41729814	71.71715202	0.01394367	108
10	0.37868128	76.46999678	0.01307702	120
11	0.34363803	80.78301222	0.01237884	132
12	0.31183769	84.69690024	0.01180681	144
13	0.28298016	88.24859619	0.01133163	156
14	0.25679311	91.47161739	0.01093235	168
15	0.23302942	94.39637948	0.01059363	180
16	0.21146482	97.05048344	0.01030392	192
17	0.19189582	99.45897602	0.01005440	204
18	0.17413774	101.64458615	0.00983820	216
19	0.15802299	103.62793943	0.00964991	228
20	0.14339951	105.42775275	0.00948517	240
21	0.13012929	107.06101094	0.00934047	252
22	0.11808709	108.54312705	0.00921293	264
23	0.10715929	109.88808780	0.00910017	276
24	0.09724274	111.10858559	0.00900020	288
25	0.08824388	112.21613823	0.00891124	300
26	0.08007777	113.22119770	0.00883227	312
27	0.07266735	114.13324874	0.00876169	324
28	0.06594270	114.96089838	0.00869861	336
29	0.05984035	115.71195713	0.00864215	348
30	0.05430271	116.39351273	0.00859154	360
31	0.04927752	117.01199703	0.00854613	372
32	0.04471737	117.57324665	0.00850534	384
33	0.04057922	118.08255810	0.00846865	396
34	0.03682401	118.54473776	0.00843563	408
35	0.03341630	118.96414721	0.00840589	420
36	0.03032395	119.34474441	0.00837909	432
37	0.02751777	119.69012107	0.00835491	444
38	0.02497127	120.00353649	0.00833309	456
39	0.02266042	120.28794837	0.00831338	468
40	0.02056342	120.54604072	0.00829559	480
41	0.01866048	120.78024914	0.00827950	492
42	0.01693363	120.99278386	0.00826496	504
43	0.01536659	121.18565058	0.00825180	516
44	0.01394456	121.36066936	0.00823990	528
45	0.01265413	121.51949186	0.00822913	540
46	0.01148311	121.66361690	0.00821938	552
47	0.01042046	121.79440457	0.00821056	564
48	0.00945615	121.91308912	0.00820256	576
49	0.00858108	122.02079058	0.00819532	588
50	0.00778698	122.11852532	0.00818877	600

	Future Value of 1	Future Value of 1 per Period	Payment for Sinking Fund of 1	**9.75%** Monthly
Months				
1	1.00812500	1.00000000	1.00000000	
2	1.01631602	2.00812500	0.49797697	
3	1.02457358	3.02444102	0.33063961	
4	1.03289824	4.04901460	0.24697367	
5	1.04129054	5.08191284	0.19677630	
6	1.04975103	6.12320338	0.16331321	
7	1.05828025	7.17295441	0.13941257	
8	1.06687878	8.23123467	0.12148846	
9	1.07554717	9.29811345	0.10754870	
10	1.08428599	10.37366062	0.09639799	
11	1.09309582	11.45794661	0.08727567	Years
12	1.10197722	12.55104243	0.07967466	1
24	1.21435379	26.38200527	0.03790462	2
36	1.33819022	41.62341125	0.02402494	3
48	1.47465513	58.41909343	0.01711769	4
60	1.62503636	76.92755258	0.01299924	5
72	1.79075306	97.32345295	0.01027502	6
84	1.97336907	119.79927052	0.00834730	7
96	2.17460776	144.56710948	0.00691720	8
108	2.39636822	171.86070380	0.00581867	9
120	2.64074319	201.93762299	0.00495202	10
132	2.91003883	235.08170277	0.00425384	11
144	3.20679650	271.60572365	0.00368181	12
156	3.53381670	311.85436264	0.00320663	13
168	3.89418550	356.20744594	0.00280735	14
180	4.29130371	405.08353035	0.00246863	15
192	4.72891893	458.94386827	0.00217892	16
204	5.21116093	518.29673040	0.00192940	17
216	5.74258064	583.70223239	0.00171320	18
228	6.32819305	655.77760563	0.00152491	19
240	6.97352458	735.20302504	0.00136017	20
252	7.68466523	822.72802790	0.00121547	21
264	8.46832602	919.17858721	0.00108793	22
276	9.33190236	1025.46490640	0.00097517	23
288	10.28343482	1142.58000892	0.00087520	24
300	11.33223103	1271.65920375	0.00078637	25
312	12.48786044	1413.89051623	0.00070727	26
324	13.76133773	1570.62618250	0.00063669	27
336	15.16468069	1743.34531626	0.00057361	28
348	16.71113267	1933.67786708	0.00051715	29
360	18.41528752	2143.42000225	0.00046654	30
372	20.29322734	2374.55105723	0.00042113	31
384	22.36267424	2629.25221459	0.00038034	32
396	24.64315759	2909.92708783	0.00034365	33
408	27.15619828	3219.22440430	0.00031063	34
420	29.92551188	3560.06300118	0.00028089	35
432	32.97723239	3935.65937054	0.00025409	36
444	36.34015886	4349.55801339	0.00022991	37
456	40.04602722	4805.66488909	0.00020809	38
468	44.12980974	5308.28427588	0.00018838	39
480	48.63004505	5862.15939031	0.00017059	40
492	53.58920184	6472.51714899	0.00015450	41
504	59.05407965	7145.11749495	0.00013996	42
516	65.07625050	7886.30775417	0.00012680	43
528	71.71254560	8703.08253533	0.00011490	44
540	79.02559162	9603.14973781	0.00010413	45
552	87.08440174	10595.00329118	0.00009438	46
564	95.96502691	11688.00331230	0.00008556	47
576	105.75127355	12892.46443674	0.00007756	48
588	116.53549441	14219.75315793	0.00007032	49
600	128.41946013	15682.39509268	0.00006377	50

10.00% Monthly	Present Value of 1	Present Value of 1 per Period	Payment to Pay Off a Loan of 1	
				Months
	0.99173554	0.99173554	1.00833333	1
	0.98353938	1.97527491	0.50625864	2
	0.97541095	2.95068586	0.33890426	3
	0.96734970	3.91803557	0.25522994	4
	0.95935508	4.87739065	0.20502766	5
	0.95142652	5.82881717	0.17156139	6
	0.94356349	6.77238066	0.14765856	7
	0.93576545	7.70814611	0.12973288	8
	0.92803185	8.63617796	0.11579196	9
	0.92036217	9.55654013	0.10464038	10
Years	0.91275587	10.46929600	0.09551741	11
1	0.90521243	11.37450843	0.08791589	12
2	0.81940954	21.67085483	0.04614493	24
3	0.74173970	30.99123559	0.03226719	36
4	0.67143200	39.42816009	0.02536258	48
5	0.60778859	47.06536902	0.02124704	60
6	0.55017779	53.97866548	0.01852584	72
7	0.49802777	60.23666736	0.01660118	84
8	0.45082093	65.90148845	0.01517416	96
9	0.40808871	71.02935491	0.01407869	108
10	0.36940697	75.67116337	0.01321507	120
11	0.33439178	79.87298608	0.01251988	132
12	0.30269560	83.67652823	0.01195078	144
13	0.27400382	87.11954186	0.01147848	156
14	0.24803166	90.23620060	0.01108203	168
15	0.22452134	93.05743882	0.01074605	180
16	0.20323951	95.61125873	0.01045902	192
17	0.18397493	97.92300826	0.01021210	204
18	0.16653639	100.01563266	0.00999844	216
19	0.15075081	101.90990228	0.00981259	228
20	0.13646151	103.62461869	0.00965022	240
21	0.12352666	105.17680130	0.00950780	252
22	0.11181786	106.58185628	0.00938246	264
23	0.10121892	107.85372952	0.00927182	276
24	0.09162463	109.00504499	0.00917389	288
25	0.08293975	110.04723006	0.00908701	300
26	0.07507809	110.99062894	0.00900977	312
27	0.06796162	111.84460533	0.00894094	324
28	0.06151971	112.61763538	0.00887960	336
29	0.05568840	113.31739178	0.00882477	348
30	0.05040983	113.95081998	0.00877572	360
31	0.04563161	114.52420705	0.00873178	372
32	0.04130630	115.04324416	0.00869238	384
33	0.03739097	115.51308300	0.00865703	396
34	0.03384678	115.93838696	0.00862527	408
35	0.03063852	116.32337739	0.00859672	420
36	0.02773437	116.67187552	0.00857105	432
37	0.02510550	116.98734035	0.00854793	444
38	0.02272581	117.27290304	0.00852712	456
39	0.02057168	117.53139793	0.00850836	468
40	0.01862174	117.76539073	0.00849146	480
41	0.01685663	117.97720391	0.00847621	492
42	0.01525883	118.16893984	0.00846246	504
43	0.01381249	118.34250158	0.00845005	516
44	0.01250323	118.49961183	0.00843885	528
45	0.01131808	118.64182998	0.00842873	540
46	0.01024527	118.77056761	0.00841959	552
47	0.00927415	118.88710252	0.00841134	564
48	0.00839507	118.99259137	0.00840388	576
49	0.00759932	119.08808119	0.00839715	588
50	0.00687900	119.17451975	0.00839106	600

Months	Future Value of 1	Future Value of 1 per Period	Payment for Sinking Fund of 1	**10.00%** Monthly
1	1.00833333	1.00000000	1.00000000	
2	1.01673611	2.00833333	0.49792531	
3	1.02520891	3.02506944	0.33057092	
4	1.03375232	4.05027836	0.24689661	
5	1.04236692	5.08403068	0.19669433	
6	1.05105331	6.12639760	0.16322806	
7	1.05981209	7.17745091	0.13932523	
8	1.06864386	8.23726300	0.12139955	
9	1.07754922	9.30590686	0.10745863	
10	1.08652880	10.38345608	0.09630705	
11	1.09558321	11.46998489	0.08718407	Years
12	1.10471307	12.56556809	0.07958255	1
24	1.22039096	26.44691537	0.03781159	2
36	1.34818184	41.78182109	0.02393385	3
48	1.48935410	58.72249183	0.01702925	4
60	1.64530893	77.43707217	0.01291371	5
72	1.81759428	98.11121363	0.01019250	6
84	2.00792015	120.95041832	0.00826785	7
96	2.21817563	146.18107572	0.00684083	8
108	2.45044761	174.05371266	0.00574535	9
120	2.70704149	204.84497890	0.00488174	10
132	2.99050411	238.86049309	0.00418654	11
144	3.30364897	276.43787610	0.00361745	12
156	3.64958418	317.95010216	0.00314515	13
168	4.03174334	363.80920074	0.00274869	14
180	4.45391955	414.47034621	0.00241272	15
192	4.92030313	470.43637562	0.00212569	16
204	5.43552316	532.26277964	0.00187877	17
216	6.00469347	600.56321607	0.00166510	18
228	6.63346334	676.01560071	0.00147926	19
240	7.32807363	759.36883599	0.00131688	20
252	8.09541870	851.45024422	0.00117447	21
264	8.94311483	953.17377916	0.00104913	22
276	9.87957581	1065.54909747	0.00093848	23
288	10.91409650	1189.69158007	0.00084055	24
300	12.05694502	1326.83340282	0.00075367	25
312	13.31946472	1478.33576651	0.00067644	26
324	14.71418673	1645.70240742	0.00060764	27
336	16.25495436	1830.59452269	0.00054627	28
348	17.95706049	2034.84725849	0.00049144	29
360	19.83739937	2260.48792480	0.00044238	30
372	21.91463431	2509.75611741	0.00039845	31
384	24.20938289	2785.12594708	0.00035905	32
396	26.74442164	3089.33059631	0.00032369	33
408	29.54491206	3425.38944748	0.00029194	34
420	32.63865043	3796.63805180	0.00026339	35
432	36.05634364	4206.76123626	0.00023771	36
444	39.83191398	4659.82967740	0.00021460	37
456	44.00283587	5160.34030476	0.00019379	38
468	48.61050779	5713.26093521	0.00017503	39
480	53.70066317	6324.07958092	0.00015813	40
492	59.32382434	6998.85892067	0.00014288	41
504	65.53580396	7744.29647494	0.00012913	42
516	72.39825902	8567.79108210	0.00011672	43
528	79.97930280	9477.51633559	0.00010551	44
540	88.35418092	10482.50177091	0.00009540	45
552	97.60601823	11592.72218761	0.00008626	46
564	107.82664380	12819.19725596	0.00007801	47
576	119.11750242	14174.10029087	0.00007055	48
588	131.59066149	15670.87937864	0.00006381	49
600	145.36992330	17324.39079597	0.00005772	50

57

	Present Value of 1	Present Value of 1 per Period	Payment to Pay Off a Loan of 1	
10.25% Monthly				Months
	0.99153068	0.99153068	1.00854167	1
	0.98313308	1.97466376	0.50641533	2
	0.97480661	2.94947036	0.33904392	3
	0.96655065	3.91602102	0.25536124	4
	0.95836462	4.87438564	0.20515406	5
	0.95024792	5.82463356	0.17168462	6
	0.94219996	6.76683352	0.14777961	7
	0.93422017	7.70105369	0.12985236	8
	0.92630795	8.62736164	0.11591029	9
	0.91846275	9.54582439	0.10475785	10
Years	0.91068399	10.45650838	0.09563422	11
1	0.90297111	11.35947950	0.08803220	12
2	0.81535683	21.61676134	0.04626040	24
3	0.73624366	30.87879053	0.03238469	36
4	0.66480676	39.24213534	0.02548281	48
5	0.60030130	46.79399411	0.02137026	60
6	0.54205473	53.61310442	0.01865216	72
7	0.48945977	59.77056405	0.01673064	84
8	0.44196803	65.33057222	0.01530677	96
9	0.39908436	70.35109898	0.01421442	108
10	0.36036165	74.88448962	0.01335390	120
11	0.32539616	78.97801041	0.01266175	132
12	0.29382333	82.67434143	0.01209565	144
13	0.26531398	86.01202156	0.01162628	156
14	0.23957086	89.02585031	0.01123269	168
15	0.21632557	91.74725060	0.01089951	180
16	0.19533574	94.20459645	0.01061519	192
17	0.17638253	96.42350877	0.01037091	204
18	0.15926833	98.42712250	0.01015980	216
19	0.14381470	100.23632781	0.00997642	228
20	0.12986052	101.86998795	0.00981643	240
21	0.11726030	103.34513586	0.00967631	252
22	0.10588266	104.67715181	0.00955318	264
23	0.09560898	105.87992373	0.00944466	276
24	0.08633215	106.96599203	0.00934877	288
25	0.07795544	107.94668034	0.00926383	300
26	0.07039151	108.83221355	0.00918846	312
27	0.06356150	109.63182445	0.00912144	324
28	0.05739420	110.35385000	0.00906176	336
29	0.05182530	111.00581822	0.00900854	348
30	0.04679675	111.59452668	0.00896101	360
31	0.04225611	112.12611342	0.00891853	372
32	0.03815605	112.60612088	0.00888051	384
33	0.03445381	113.03955376	0.00884646	396
34	0.03111080	113.43093113	0.00881594	408
35	0.02809215	113.78433358	0.00878856	420
36	0.02536640	114.10344579	0.00876398	432
37	0.02290513	114.39159490	0.00874190	444
38	0.02068267	114.65178522	0.00872206	456
39	0.01867585	114.88672956	0.00870423	468
40	0.01686375	115.09887752	0.00868818	480
41	0.01522748	115.29044099	0.00867375	492
42	0.01374998	115.46341727	0.00866075	504
43	0.01241583	115.61960986	0.00864905	516
44	0.01121114	115.76064725	0.00863851	528
45	0.01012333	115.88799995	0.00862902	540
46	0.00914108	116.00299575	0.00862047	552
47	0.00825413	116.10683364	0.00861276	564
48	0.00745324	116.20059625	0.00860581	576
49	0.00673006	116.28526118	0.00859954	588
50	0.00607705	116.36171117	0.00859389	600

	Future Value of 1	Future Value of 1 per Period	Payment for Sinking Fund of 1	**10.25%** Monthly
Months				
1	1.00854167	1.00000000	1.00000000	
2	1.01715629	2.00854167	0.49787366	
3	1.02584450	3.02569796	0.33050226	
4	1.03460693	4.05154246	0.24681958	
5	1.04344419	5.08614939	0.19661239	
6	1.05235695	6.12959358	0.16314295	
7	1.06134583	7.18195053	0.13923794	
8	1.07041149	8.24329635	0.12131069	
9	1.07955459	9.31370784	0.10736862	
10	1.08877578	10.39326243	0.09621618	
11	1.09807574	11.48203821	0.08709255	Years
12	1.10745514	12.58011396	0.07949054	1
24	1.22645689	26.51202582	0.03771873	2
36	1.35824598	41.94099323	0.02384302	3
48	1.50419650	59.02788249	0.01694115	4
60	1.66583014	77.95084583	0.01282860	5
72	1.84483215	98.90717884	0.01011049	6
84	2.04306885	122.11537755	0.00818898	7
96	2.26260710	147.81741651	0.00676510	8
108	2.50573586	176.28127166	0.00567275	9
120	2.77499006	207.80371435	0.00481223	10
132	3.07317701	242.71340554	0.00412009	11
144	3.40340567	281.37432248	0.00355398	12
156	3.76911910	324.18955367	0.00308462	13
168	4.17413033	371.60550153	0.00269103	14
180	4.62266208	424.11653670	0.00235784	15
192	5.11939089	482.27015251	0.00207353	16
204	5.66949575	546.67267325	0.00182925	17
216	6.27871221	617.99557587	0.00161813	18
228	6.95339211	696.98249099	0.00143476	19
240	7.70056983	784.45695613	0.00127477	20
252	8.52803564	881.33100218	0.00113465	21
264	9.44441691	988.61466242	0.00101152	22
276	10.45926805	1107.42650338	0.00090299	23
288	11.58317016	1239.00528737	0.00080710	24
300	12.82784134	1384.72288801	0.00072217	25
312	14.20625882	1546.09859384	0.00064679	26
324	15.73279435	1724.81494874	0.00057977	27
336	17.42336397	1922.73529458	0.00052009	28
348	19.29559399	2141.92319901	0.00046687	29
360	21.36900475	2384.66397020	0.00041935	30
372	23.66521414	2653.48848506	0.00037686	31
384	26.20816304	2951.19957582	0.00033885	32
396	29.02436487	3280.90125354	0.00030479	33
408	32.14318207	3646.03107120	0.00027427	34
420	35.59713220	4050.39596457	0.00024689	35
432	39.42222702	4498.21194418	0.00022231	36
444	43.65834795	4994.14805261	0.00020023	37
456	48.34966184	5543.37504502	0.00018040	38
468	53.54508153	6151.61930083	0.00016256	39
480	59.29877576	6825.22252833	0.00014652	40
492	65.67073402	7571.20788499	0.00013208	41
504	72.72739194	8397.35320263	0.00011909	42
516	80.54232403	9312.27208108	0.00010739	43
528	89.19701073	10325.50369575	0.00009685	44
540	98.78168802	11447.61225549	0.00008735	45
552	109.39628814	12690.29714768	0.00007880	46
564	121.15148160	14066.51491900	0.00007109	47
576	134.16983102	15590.61436369	0.00006414	48
588	148.58706901	17278.48612766	0.00005788	49
600	164.55351332	19147.72838843	0.00005223	50

10.50% Monthly	Present Value of 1	Present Value of 1 per Period	Payment to Pay Off a Loan of 1	Months
	0.99132590	0.99132590	1.00875000	1
	0.98272704	1.97405294	0.50657203	2
	0.97420276	2.94825570	0.33918361	3
	0.96575243	3.91400813	0.25549257	4
	0.95737539	4.87138352	0.20528049	5
	0.94907102	5.82045454	0.17180789	6
	0.94083868	6.76129323	0.14790070	7
	0.93267775	7.69397098	0.12997190	8
	0.92458761	8.61855859	0.11602868	9
	0.91656765	9.53512624	0.10487538	10
Years	0.90861724	10.44374348	0.09575111	11
1	0.90073581	11.34447929	0.08814860	12
2	0.81132499	21.56285799	0.04637604	24
3	0.73078947	30.76691757	0.03250244	36
4	0.65824824	39.05734359	0.02560338	48
5	0.59290776	46.52482716	0.02149390	60
6	0.53405325	53.25105699	0.01877897	72
7	0.48104089	59.30961304	0.01686067	84
8	0.43329075	64.76677141	0.01544002	96
9	0.39028049	69.68222935	0.01435086	108
10	0.35153961	74.10975832	0.01349350	120
11	0.31664432	78.09779220	0.01280446	132
12	0.28521288	81.68995711	0.01224141	144
13	0.25690145	84.92554867	0.01177502	156
14	0.23140033	87.83996184	0.01138434	168
15	0.20843057	90.46507813	0.01105399	180
16	0.18774087	92.82961438	0.01077242	192
17	0.16910493	94.95943684	0.01053081	204
18	0.15231886	96.87784419	0.01032228	216
19	0.13719905	98.60582238	0.01014139	228
20	0.12358010	100.16227421	0.00998380	240
21	0.11131302	101.56422610	0.00984599	252
22	0.10026362	102.82701437	0.00972500	264
23	0.09031104	103.96445298	0.00961867	276
24	0.08134638	104.98898466	0.00952481	288
25	0.07327160	105.91181703	0.00944182	300
26	0.06599835	106.74304519	0.00936829	312
27	0.05944708	107.49176216	0.00930304	324
28	0.05354611	108.16615834	0.00924504	336
29	0.04823090	108.77361113	0.00919341	348
30	0.04344330	109.32076560	0.00914739	360
31	0.03913094	109.81360723	0.00910634	372
32	0.03524664	110.25752733	0.00906968	384
33	0.03174791	110.65738206	0.00903690	396
34	0.02859648	111.01754553	0.00900759	408
35	0.02575787	111.34195767	0.00898134	420
36	0.02320104	111.63416730	0.00895783	432
37	0.02089800	111.89737097	0.00893676	444
38	0.01882358	112.13444795	0.00891787	456
39	0.01695507	112.34799166	0.00890092	468
40	0.01527204	112.54033814	0.00888570	480
41	0.01375607	112.71359149	0.00887204	492
42	0.01239059	112.86964700	0.00885978	504
43	0.01116065	113.01021177	0.00884876	516
44	0.01005279	113.13682350	0.00883886	528
45	0.00905491	113.25086722	0.00882995	540
46	0.00815608	113.35359048	0.00882195	552
47	0.00734648	113.44611700	0.00881476	564
48	0.00661723	113.52945895	0.00880829	576
49	0.00596038	113.60452802	0.00880247	588
50	0.00536873	113.67214543	0.00879723	600

	Future Value of 1	Future Value of 1 per Period	Payment for Sinking Fund of 1	**10.50%** Monthly
Months				
1	1.00875000	1.00000000	1.00000000	
2	1.01757656	2.00875000	0.49782203	
3	1.02648036	3.02632656	0.33043361	
4	1.03546206	4.05280692	0.24674257	
5	1.04452235	5.08826898	0.19653049	
6	1.05366192	6.13279133	0.16305789	
7	1.06288147	7.18645326	0.13915070	
8	1.07218168	8.24933472	0.12122190	
9	1.08156327	9.32156640	0.10727868	
10	1.09102695	10.40307967	0.09612538	
11	1.10057343	11.49410662	0.08700111	Years
12	1.11020345	12.59468005	0.07939860	1
24	1.23255170	26.57733730	0.03762604	2
36	1.36838315	42.10093163	0.02375244	3
48	1.51918370	59.33527961	0.01685338	4
60	1.68660298	78.46891221	0.01274390	5
72	1.87247245	99.71113714	0.01002897	6
84	2.07882537	123.29432855	0.00811067	7
96	2.30791910	149.47646903	0.00669002	8
108	2.56225975	178.54397174	0.00560086	9
120	2.84462962	210.81481353	0.00474350	10
132	3.15811762	246.64201344	0.00405446	11
144	3.50615308	286.41749440	0.00349141	12
156	3.89254324	330.57637060	0.00302502	13
168	4.32151494	379.60170733	0.00263434	14
180	4.79776080	434.02980533	0.00230399	15
192	5.32649059	494.45606753	0.00202242	16
204	5.91348823	561.54151232	0.00178081	17
216	6.56517504	636.02000460	0.00157228	18
228	7.28867998	718.70628371	0.00139139	19
240	8.09191767	810.50487609	0.00123380	20
252	8.98367491	912.41999009	0.00109599	21
264	9.97370689	1025.56650131	0.00097507	22
276	11.07284380	1151.18214848	0.00086867	23
288	12.29310939	1290.64107339	0.00077481	24
300	13.64785246	1445.46885302	0.00069182	25
312	15.15189290	1617.35918820	0.00061829	26
324	16.82168377	1808.19243141	0.00055304	27
336	18.67549137	2020.05615649	0.00049504	28
348	20.73359496	2255.26799509	0.00044341	29
360	23.01850866	2516.40098989	0.00039739	30
372	25.55522774	2806.31174175	0.00035634	31
384	28.37150201	3128.17165879	0.00031968	32
396	31.49813943	3485.50164924	0.00028690	33
408	34.96934308	3882.21063760	0.00025759	34
420	38.82308535	4322.63832529	0.00023134	35
432	43.10152331	4811.60266385	0.00020783	36
444	47.85145990	5354.45255966	0.00018676	37
456	53.12485589	5957.12638706	0.00016787	38
468	58.97939831	6626.21694975	0.00015092	39
480	65.47913151	7369.04360110	0.00013570	40
492	72.69515773	8193.73231253	0.00012204	41
504	80.70641495	9109.30456550	0.00010978	42
516	89.60054035	10125.77603988	0.00009876	43
528	99.47482906	11254.26617803	0.00008886	44
540	110.43729845	12507.11982320	0.00007995	45
552	122.60786980	13898.04226299	0.00007195	46
564	136.11968011	15442.24915495	0.00006476	47
576	151.12053853	17156.63297461	0.00005829	48
588	167.77454331	19059.94780660	0.00005247	49
600	186.26387688	21173.01450037	0.00004723	50

10.75% Monthly	Present Value of 1	Present Value of 1 per Period	Payment to Pay Off a Loan of 1	Months
	0.99112121	0.99112121	1.00895833	1
	0.98232124	1.97344245	0.50672874	2
	0.97359942	2.94704187	0.33932331	3
	0.96495503	3.91199689	0.25562392	4
	0.95638739	4.86838429	0.20540696	5
	0.94789582	5.81628011	0.17193120	6
	0.93947965	6.75575976	0.14802184	7
	0.93113821	7.68689797	0.13009149	8
	0.92287082	8.60976879	0.11614714	9
	0.91467684	9.52444563	0.10499299	10
Years	0.90655561	10.43100124	0.09586807	11
1	0.89850649	11.32950774	0.08826509	12
2	0.80731392	21.50914400	0.04649185	24
3	0.72537680	30.65561329	0.03262045	36
4	0.65175576	38.87377533	0.02572428	48
5	0.58560678	46.25784728	0.02161795	60
6	0.52617150	52.89248388	0.01890628	72
7	0.47276851	58.85374795	0.01699127	84
8	0.42478557	64.20998242	0.01557390	96
9	0.38167260	69.02259387	0.01448801	108
10	0.34293531	73.34675650	0.01363387	120
11	0.30812960	77.23204471	0.01294799	132
12	0.27685645	80.72300139	0.01238804	144
13	0.24875731	83.85964864	0.01192469	156
14	0.22351006	86.67794655	0.01153696	168
15	0.20082524	89.21020553	0.01120948	180
16	0.18044278	91.48545667	0.01093070	192
17	0.16212901	93.52978458	0.01069178	204
18	0.14567397	95.36662649	0.01048585	216
19	0.13088901	97.01704087	0.01030747	228
20	0.11760462	98.49994891	0.01015229	240
21	0.10566852	99.83235141	0.01001679	252
22	0.09494385	101.02952371	0.00989810	264
23	0.08530767	102.10519080	0.00979382	276
24	0.07664949	103.07168466	0.00970199	288
25	0.06887007	103.94008566	0.00962093	300
26	0.06188020	104.72034961	0.00954924	312
27	0.05559976	105.42142183	0.00948574	324
28	0.04995675	106.05133977	0.00942940	336
29	0.04488646	106.61732513	0.00937934	348
30	0.04033078	107.12586666	0.00933481	360
31	0.03623747	107.58279452	0.00929517	372
32	0.03255960	107.99334717	0.00925983	384
33	0.02925501	108.36223139	0.00922831	396
34	0.02628582	108.69367625	0.00920017	408
35	0.02361798	108.99148162	0.00917503	420
36	0.02122091	109.25906167	0.00915256	432
37	0.01906712	109.49948409	0.00913246	444
38	0.01713193	109.71550519	0.00911448	456
39	0.01539315	109.90960156	0.00909839	468
40	0.01383085	110.08399840	0.00908397	480
41	0.01242711	110.24069510	0.00907106	492
42	0.01116584	110.38148809	0.00905949	504
43	0.01003258	110.50799152	0.00904912	516
44	0.00901433	110.62165566	0.00903982	528
45	0.00809944	110.72378364	0.00903148	540
46	0.00727740	110.81554629	0.00902400	552
47	0.00653879	110.89799562	0.00901730	564
48	0.00587514	110.97207689	0.00901128	576
49	0.00527886	111.03863938	0.00900587	588
50	0.00474309	111.09844622	0.00900103	600

	Future Value of 1	Future Value of 1 per Period	Payment for Sinking Fund of 1	**10.75%** Monthly
Months				
1	1.00895833	1.00000000	1.00000000	
2	1.01799692	2.00895833	0.49777040	
3	1.02711647	3.02695525	0.33036498	
4	1.03631773	4.05407173	0.24666559	
5	1.04560141	5.09038945	0.19644862	
6	1.05496825	6.13599086	0.16297286	
7	1.06441901	7.19095911	0.13906351	
8	1.07395443	8.25537812	0.12113316	
9	1.08357527	9.32933255	0.10718880	
10	1.09328230	10.41290782	0.09603465	
11	1.10307629	11.50619012	0.08690974	Years
12	1.11295801	12.60926640	0.07930675	1
24	1.23867554	26.64285047	0.03753352	2
36	1.37859386	42.26164028	0.02366212	3
48	1.53431708	59.64469753	0.01676595	4
60	1.70763049	78.99131036	0.01265962	5
72	1.90052103	100.52327811	0.00994794	6
84	2.11520011	124.48745412	0.00803294	7
96	2.35412891	151.15857580	0.00661557	8
108	2.62004663	180.84241435	0.00552968	9
120	2.91600189	213.87928028	0.00467553	10
132	3.24538766	250.64792489	0.00398966	11
144	3.61198020	291.56988248	0.00342971	12
156	4.01998230	337.11430303	0.00296635	13
168	4.47407150	387.80333076	0.00257863	14
180	4.97945373	444.21809027	0.00225115	15
192	5.54192292	507.00534883	0.00197237	16
204	6.16792751	576.88493127	0.00173345	17
216	6.86464434	654.65797238	0.00152752	18
228	7.64006091	741.21610158	0.00134913	19
240	8.50306700	837.55166492	0.00119396	20
252	9.46355654	944.76910194	0.00105846	21
264	10.53254107	1064.09760745	0.00093976	22
276	11.72227596	1196.90522366	0.00083549	23
288	13.04640095	1344.71452411	0.00074365	24
300	14.52009645	1509.22006922	0.00066259	25
312	16.16025768	1692.30783360	0.00059091	26
324	17.98568825	1896.07682777	0.00052740	27
336	20.01731583	2122.86316233	0.00047106	28
348	22.27843202	2375.26683029	0.00042101	29
360	24.79495940	2656.18151468	0.00037648	30
372	27.59574871	2968.82776323	0.00033683	31
384	30.71290961	3316.78991033	0.00030150	32
396	34.18217881	3704.05716965	0.00026997	33
408	38.04332976	4135.06936850	0.00024183	34
420	42.34062864	4614.76784829	0.00021670	35
432	47.12334186	5148.65211448	0.00019423	36
444	52.44630085	5742.84288576	0.00017413	37
456	58.37053071	6404.15226504	0.00015615	38
468	64.96394979	7140.16183680	0.00014005	39
480	72.30214838	7959.30958625	0.00012564	40
492	80.46925529	8870.98663662	0.00011273	41
504	89.55890235	9885.64491375	0.00010116	42
516	99.67529788	11014.91697225	0.00009079	43
528	110.93442132	12271.74935694	0.00008149	44
540	123.46535296	13670.55102863	0.00007315	45
552	137.41175373	15227.35855566	0.00006567	46
564	152.93351219	16960.01996528	0.00005896	47
576	170.20857762	18888.39936238	0.00005294	48
588	189.43500009	21034.60466163	0.00004754	49
600	210.83320102	23423.24104381	0.00004269	50

11.00% Monthly	Present Value of 1	Present Value of 1 per Period	Payment to Pay Off a Loan of 1	Months
	0.99091660	0.99091660	1.00916667	1
	0.98191570	1.97283230	0.50688546	2
	0.97299657	2.94582887	0.33946303	3
	0.96415845	3.90998732	0.25575531	4
	0.95540061	4.86538793	0.20553346	5
	0.94672232	5.81211025	0.17205455	6
	0.93812286	6.75023312	0.14814303	7
	0.92960152	7.67983463	0.13021114	8
	0.92115757	8.60099220	0.11626566	9
	0.91279033	9.51378253	0.10511066	10
Years	0.90449909	10.41828162	0.09598512	11
1	0.89628316	11.31456477	0.08838166	12
2	0.80332350	21.45561860	0.04660784	24
3	0.72000532	30.54487433	0.03273872	36
4	0.64532864	38.69142114	0.02584552	48
5	0.57839719	45.99303383	0.02174242	60
6	0.51840766	52.53734630	0.01903408	72
7	0.46464005	58.40290334	0.01712244	84
8	0.41644905	63.66010331	0.01570843	96
9	0.37325627	68.37204309	0.01462586	108
10	0.33454331	72.59527536	0.01377500	120
11	0.29984553	76.38048730	0.01309235	132
12	0.26874650	79.77310900	0.01253555	144
13	0.24087296	82.81385869	0.01207527	156
14	0.21589038	85.53923142	0.01169054	168
15	0.19349891	87.98193710	0.01136597	180
16	0.17342981	90.17129305	0.01109000	192
17	0.15544222	92.13357591	0.01085381	204
18	0.13932024	93.89233698	0.01065050	216
19	0.12487039	95.46868491	0.01047464	228
20	0.11191923	96.88153901	0.01032188	240
21	0.10031132	98.14785634	0.01018871	252
22	0.08990734	99.28283523	0.01007223	264
23	0.08058244	100.30009769	0.00997008	276
24	0.07222468	101.21185291	0.00988027	288
25	0.06473377	102.02904375	0.00980113	300
26	0.05801978	102.76147813	0.00973127	312
27	0.05200215	103.41794673	0.00966950	324
28	0.04660866	104.00632848	0.00961480	336
29	0.04177455	104.53368513	0.00956629	348
30	0.03744183	105.00634602	0.00952323	360
31	0.03355848	105.42998401	0.00948497	372
32	0.03007790	105.80968360	0.00945093	384
33	0.02695832	106.15000196	0.00942063	396
34	0.02416228	106.45502356	0.00939364	408
35	0.02165625	106.72840929	0.00936958	420
36	0.01941013	106.97344031	0.00934811	432
37	0.01739697	107.19305749	0.00932896	444
38	0.01559261	107.38989667	0.00931186	456
39	0.01397540	107.56632031	0.00929659	468
40	0.01252591	107.72444584	0.00928294	480
41	0.01122676	107.86617110	0.00927075	492
42	0.01006236	107.99319706	0.00925984	504
43	0.00901872	108.10704829	0.00925009	516
44	0.00808333	108.20909122	0.00924137	528
45	0.00724495	108.30055059	0.00923356	540
46	0.00649353	108.38252408	0.00922658	552
47	0.00582004	108.45599554	0.00922033	564
48	0.00521640	108.52184671	0.00921474	576
49	0.00467538	108.58068811	0.00920973	588
50	0.00419046	108.63376795	0.00920524	600

	Future Value of 1	Future Value of 1 per Period	Payment for Sinking Fund of 1	**11.00%** Monthly
Months				
1	1.00916667	1.00000000	1.00000000	
2	1.01841736	2.00916667	0.49771879	
3	1.02775285	3.02758403	0.33029637	
4	1.03717392	4.05533688	0.24658864	
5	1.04668135	5.09251080	0.19636679	
6	1.05627593	6.13919215	0.16288788	
7	1.06595846	7.19546808	0.13897637	
8	1.07572974	8.26142654	0.12104447	
9	1.08559060	9.33715628	0.10709899	
10	1.09554185	10.42274688	0.09594400	
11	1.10558431	11.51828873	0.08681845	Years
12	1.11571884	12.62387304	0.07921499	1
24	1.24482852	26.70856598	0.03744117	2
36	1.38887863	42.42312319	0.02357205	3
48	1.54959805	59.95615007	0.01667684	4
60	1.72891573	79.51807969	0.01257576	5
72	1.92898385	101.34369236	0.00986741	6
84	2.15220361	125.69493954	0.00795577	7
96	2.40125411	152.86408470	0.00654176	8
108	2.67912444	183.17721171	0.00545919	9
120	2.98914960	216.99813851	0.00460833	10
132	3.33505052	254.73278359	0.00392568	11
144	3.72097868	296.83403789	0.00336889	12
156	4.15156600	343.80720034	0.00290861	13
168	4.63198039	396.21604248	0.00252388	14
180	5.16798777	454.68957484	0.00219930	15
192	5.76602130	519.92959630	0.00192334	16
204	6.43325857	592.71911713	0.00168714	17
216	7.17770777	673.93175660	0.00148383	18
228	8.00830376	764.54222818	0.00130797	19
240	8.93501535	865.63803809	0.00115522	20
252	9.96896493	978.43253747	0.00102204	21
264	11.12256195	1104.27948504	0.00090557	22
276	12.40965187	1244.68929492	0.00080341	23
288	13.84568234	1401.34716459	0.00071360	24
300	15.44788859	1576.13330062	0.00063446	25
312	17.23550028	1771.14548490	0.00056461	26
324	19.22997231	1988.72425218	0.00050283	27
336	21.45524233	2231.48098120	0.00044813	28
348	23.93801800	2502.32923637	0.00039963	29
360	26.70809758	2804.51973642	0.00035657	30
372	29.79872755	3141.67936945	0.00031830	31
384	33.24700163	3517.85472282	0.00028426	32
396	37.09430596	3937.56065028	0.00025396	33
408	41.38681588	4405.83445922	0.00022697	34
420	46.17605004	4928.29636835	0.00020291	35
432	51.51948881	5511.21696156	0.00018145	36
444	57.48126410	6161.59244741	0.00016230	37
456	64.13292909	6887.22862757	0.00014520	38
468	71.55431700	7696.83458201	0.00012992	39
480	79.83449929	8600.12719526	0.00011628	40
492	89.07285464	9607.94777847	0.00010408	41
504	99.38026171	10732.39218666	0.00009318	42
516	110.88042994	11986.95599313	0.00008342	43
528	123.71138425	13386.69646321	0.00007470	44
540	138.02712166	14948.41327148	0.00006690	45
552	153.99945954	16690.85013126	0.00005991	46
564	171.82009777	18634.91975659	0.00005366	47
576	191.70291952	20803.95485646	0.00004807	48
588	213.88655826	23223.98817374	0.00004306	49
600	238.63726186	25924.06493006	0.00003857	50

11.25% Monthly	Present Value of 1	Present Value of 1 per Period	Payment to Pay Off a Loan of 1	Months
	0.99071207	0.99071207	1.00937500	1
	0.98151041	1.97222249	0.50704219	2
	0.97239422	2.94461671	0.33960277	3
	0.96336269	3.90797940	0.25588671	4
	0.95441505	4.86239445	0.20565999	5
	0.94555052	5.80794497	0.17217794	6
	0.93676831	6.74471328	0.14826427	7
	0.92806768	7.67278096	0.13033084	8
	0.91944785	8.59222881	0.11638424	9
	0.91090809	9.50313691	0.10522841	10
Years	0.90244764	10.40558455	0.09610224	11
1	0.89406578	11.29965033	0.08849831	12
2	0.79935362	21.40228099	0.04672399	24
3	0.71467471	30.43469734	0.03285723	36
4	0.63896620	38.51027169	0.02596710	48
5	0.57127782	45.73036635	0.02186731	60
6	0.51075994	52.18560591	0.01916237	72
7	0.45665299	57.95701468	0.01725417	84
8	0.40827781	63.11703376	0.01584358	96
9	0.36502722	67.73043024	0.01476441	108
10	0.32635834	71.85511014	0.01391668	120
11	0.29178583	75.54284529	0.01323752	132
12	0.26087572	78.83992309	0.01268393	144
13	0.23324005	81.78772752	0.01222677	156
14	0.20853195	84.42325858	0.01184540	168
15	0.18644128	86.77959670	0.01152345	180
16	0.16669077	88.88631799	0.01125033	192
17	0.14903251	90.76986539	0.01101687	204
18	0.13324487	92.45388066	0.01081620	216
19	0.11912968	93.95950109	0.01064288	228
20	0.10650977	95.30562478	0.01049256	240
21	0.09522674	96.50914791	0.01036171	252
22	0.08513897	97.58517676	0.01024746	264
23	0.07611984	98.54721733	0.01014742	276
24	0.06805614	99.40734487	0.01005962	288
25	0.06084667	100.17635548	0.00998240	300
26	0.05440092	100.86390154	0.00991435	312
27	0.04863800	101.47861295	0.00985429	324
28	0.04348557	102.02820538	0.00980121	336
29	0.03887896	102.51957717	0.00975423	348
30	0.03476035	102.95889587	0.00971261	360
31	0.03107804	103.35167568	0.00967570	372
32	0.02778581	103.70284667	0.00964294	384
33	0.02484234	104.01681664	0.00961383	396
34	0.02221069	104.29752644	0.00958796	408
35	0.01985782	104.54849947	0.00956494	420
36	0.01775420	104.77288586	0.00954445	432
37	0.01587342	104.97350206	0.00952621	444
38	0.01419188	105.15286613	0.00950996	456
39	0.01268847	105.31322941	0.00949548	468
40	0.01134433	105.45660474	0.00948257	480
41	0.01014258	105.58479170	0.00947106	492
42	0.00906813	105.69939929	0.00946079	504
43	0.00810751	105.80186600	0.00945163	516
44	0.00724864	105.89347799	0.00944345	528
45	0.00648076	105.97538513	0.00943615	540
46	0.00579423	106.04861550	0.00942964	552
47	0.00518042	106.11408827	0.00942382	564
48	0.00463164	106.17262523	0.00941862	576
49	0.00414099	106.22496113	0.00941398	588
50	0.00370232	106.27175286	0.00940984	600

	Future Value of 1	Future Value of 1 per Period	Payment for Sinking Fund of 1	**11.25%** Monthly
Months				
1	1.00937500	1.00000000	1.00000000	
2	1.01883789	2.00937500	0.49766719	
3	1.02838950	3.02821289	0.33022777	
4	1.03803065	4.05660239	0.24651171	
5	1.04776218	5.09463303	0.19628499	
6	1.05758496	6.14239522	0.16280294	
7	1.06749981	7.19998017	0.13888927	
8	1.07750762	8.26747999	0.12095584	
9	1.08760926	9.34498761	0.10700924	
10	1.09780560	10.43259687	0.09585341	
11	1.10809752	11.53040247	0.08672724	Years
12	1.11848594	12.63849999	0.07912331	1
24	1.25101079	26.77448450	0.03734899	2
36	1.39923798	42.58538438	0.02348223	3
48	1.56502800	60.26965356	0.01659210	4
60	1.75046181	80.04925995	0.01249231	5
72	1.95786692	102.17247155	0.00978737	6
84	2.18984662	126.91697261	0.00787917	7
96	2.44931265	154.59334907	0.00646858	8
108	2.73952175	185.54898694	0.00538941	9
120	3.06411656	220.17243259	0.00454189	10
132	3.42717128	258.89826965	0.00386252	11
144	3.83324288	302.21257381	0.00330893	12
156	4.28742826	350.65901390	0.00285177	13
168	4.79542821	404.84567587	0.00247008	14
180	5.36361902	465.45269527	0.00214845	15
192	5.99913245	533.24079418	0.00187533	16
204	6.70994528	609.06082953	0.00164187	17
216	7.50497943	693.86447285	0.00144120	18
228	8.39421396	788.71615534	0.00126788	19
240	9.38881027	894.80642835	0.00111756	20
252	10.50125225	1013.46690680	0.00098671	21
264	11.74550297	1146.18698328	0.00087246	22
276	13.13717990	1294.63252243	0.00077242	23
288	14.69375097	1460.66677044	0.00068462	24
300	16.43475383	1646.37374197	0.00060740	25
312	18.38204104	1854.08437811	0.00053935	26
324	20.56005441	2086.40580368	0.00047929	27
336	22.99613173	2346.25405113	0.00042621	28
348	25.72084995	2636.89066177	0.00037923	29
360	28.76840897	2961.96362367	0.00033761	30
372	32.17706088	3325.55316019	0.00030070	31
384	35.98959010	3732.22294377	0.00026794	32
396	40.25385042	4187.07737788	0.00023883	33
408	45.02336562	4695.82566599	0.00021296	34
420	50.35800130	5264.85347193	0.00018994	35
432	56.32471629	5901.30307087	0.00016945	36
444	62.99840310	6613.16299715	0.00015121	37
456	70.46282794	7409.36831411	0.00013496	38
468	78.81168217	8299.91276441	0.00012048	39
480	88.14975821	9295.97420871	0.00010757	40
492	98.59426494	10410.05492696	0.00009606	41
504	110.27629884	11656.13854346	0.00008579	42
516	123.34248949	13049.86554536	0.00007663	43
528	137.95683998	14608.72959756	0.00006845	44
540	154.30278548	16352.29711829	0.00006115	45
552	172.58549567	18302.45287115	0.00005464	46
564	193.03444990	20483.67465648	0.00004882	47
576	215.90631765	22923.34054975	0.00004362	48
588	241.48818009	25652.07254334	0.00003898	49
600	270.10113349	28704.12090514	0.00003484	50

11.50% Monthly	Present Value of 1	Present Value of 1 per Period	Payment to Pay Off a Loan of 1	
				Months
	0.99050764	0.99050764	1.00958333	1
	0.98110538	1.97161301	0.50719893	2
	0.97179237	2.94340538	0.33974253	3
	0.96256776	3.90597313	0.25601815	4
	0.95343071	4.85940385	0.20578656	5
	0.94438040	5.80378425	0.17230137	6
	0.93541600	6.73920024	0.14838556	7
	0.92653669	7.66573693	0.13045060	8
	0.91774166	8.58347860	0.11650288	9
	0.90903012	9.49250872	0.10534623	10
Years	0.90040128	10.39291000	0.09621944	11
1	0.89185434	11.28476434	0.08861505	12
2	0.79540417	21.34913042	0.04684032	24
3	0.70938466	30.32507899	0.03297601	36
4	0.63266779	38.33031771	0.02608901	48
5	0.56424751	45.46902461	0.02199261	60
6	0.50322660	51.83722484	0.01929116	72
7	0.44880482	57.51601837	0.01738646	84
8	0.40026853	62.58067505	0.01597937	96
9	0.35698123	67.09761109	0.01490366	108
10	0.31837526	71.12600011	0.01405954	120
11	0.28394436	74.71884986	0.01338350	132
12	0.25323701	77.92309500	0.01283317	144
13	0.22585052	80.78081494	0.01237918	156
14	0.20142577	83.32948487	0.01200055	168
15	0.17964245	85.60252722	0.01168190	180
16	0.16021490	87.62974900	0.01141165	192
17	0.14288835	89.43773726	0.01118096	204
18	0.12743560	91.05019863	0.01098295	216
19	0.11365399	92.48827930	0.01081218	228
20	0.10136280	93.77083780	0.01066430	240
21	0.09040086	94.91469316	0.01053578	252
22	0.08062440	95.93484553	0.01042374	264
23	0.07190522	96.84467285	0.01032581	276
24	0.06412898	97.65610630	0.01024002	288
25	0.05719371	98.37978674	0.01016469	300
26	0.05100846	99.02520428	0.01009844	312
27	0.04549212	99.60082272	0.01004008	324
28	0.04057234	100.11419052	0.00998859	336
29	0.03618462	100.57203983	0.00994312	348
30	0.03227141	100.98037472	0.00990291	360
31	0.02878140	101.34454996	0.00986733	372
32	0.02566881	101.66934124	0.00983345	384
33	0.02289284	101.95900774	0.00980786	396
34	0.02041708	102.21734808	0.00978304	408
35	0.01820906	102.44775002	0.00976107	420
36	0.01623983	102.65323500	0.00974153	432
37	0.01448356	102.83649767	0.00972417	444
38	0.01291723	102.99994128	0.00970874	456
39	0.01152029	103.14570917	0.00969502	468
40	0.01027442	103.27571289	0.00968282	480
41	0.00916328	103.39165728	0.00967196	492
42	0.00817231	103.49506278	0.00966230	504
43	0.00728851	103.58728543	0.00965369	516
44	0.00650029	103.66953460	0.00964604	528
45	0.00579731	103.74288888	0.00963921	540
46	0.00517036	103.80831021	0.00963314	552
47	0.00461121	103.86665651	0.00962773	564
48	0.00411253	103.91869291	0.00962291	576
49	0.00366777	103.96510180	0.00961861	588
50	0.00327112	104.00649177	0.00961478	600

	Future Value of 1	Future Value of 1 per Period	Payment for Sinking Fund of 1	**11.50%** Monthly
Months				
1	1.00958333	1.00000000	1.00000000	
2	1.01925851	2.00958333	0.49761559	
3	1.02902640	3.02884184	0.33015920	
4	1.03888790	4.05786640	0.24643481	
5	1.04884391	5.09675615	0.19620323	
6	1.05889533	6.14560006	0.16271804	
7	1.06904308	7.20449539	0.13880223	
8	1.07928808	8.27353847	0.12086727	
9	1.08963125	9.35282655	0.10691955	
10	1.10007355	10.44245780	0.09576290	
11	1.11061593	11.54253136	0.08663611	Years
12	1.12125933	12.65314728	0.07903172	1
24	1.25722248	26.84060671	0.03725698	2
36	1.40967243	42.74842793	0.02339267	3
48	1.58060837	60.58522086	0.01650568	4
60	1.77227188	80.58489132	0.01240927	5
72	1.98717637	103.00970838	0.00970782	6
84	2.22814004	128.15374370	0.00780313	7
96	2.49832281	156.34672784	0.00639604	8
108	2.80126775	187.95837430	0.00532033	9
120	3.14094760	223.40322777	0.00447621	10
132	3.52181680	263.14610036	0.00380017	11
144	3.94886993	307.70816697	0.00324983	12
156	4.42770725	357.67379985	0.00279584	13
168	4.96460805	413.69823179	0.00241722	14
180	5.56661309	476.51614871	0.00209856	15
192	6.24161686	546.95132404	0.00182838	16
204	6.99847112	625.92742140	0.00159763	17
216	7.84710103	714.48010726	0.00139962	18
228	8.79863523	813.77063232	0.00122885	19
240	9.86555182	925.10105974	0.00108096	20
252	11.06184201	1049.93133999	0.00095244	21
264	12.40319354	1189.89845615	0.00084041	22
276	13.90719645	1346.83789078	0.00074248	23
288	15.59357375	1522.80769581	0.00065668	24
300	17.48444003	1720.11548117	0.00058136	25
312	19.60459148	1941.34867602	0.00051511	26
324	21.98183107	2189.40845944	0.00045674	27
336	24.64733314	2467.54780554	0.00040526	28
348	27.63605219	2779.41414187	0.00035979	29
360	30.98718131	3129.09718062	0.00031958	30
372	34.74466610	3521.18254970	0.00028400	31
384	38.95778097	3960.81192721	0.00025247	32
396	43.68177532	4453.75046767	0.00022453	33
408	48.97859804	5006.46240436	0.00019974	34
420	54.91770993	5626.19581915	0.00017774	35
432	61.57699454	6321.07769143	0.00015820	36
444	69.04377953	7100.22047269	0.00014084	37
456	77.41598185	7973.84158412	0.00012541	38
468	86.80339179	8953.39740457	0.00011169	39
480	97.32911276	10051.73350569	0.00009949	40
492	109.13117558	11283.25310450	0.00008863	41
504	122.36434862	12664.10594244	0.00007896	42
516	137.20216732	14212.40006778	0.00007036	43
528	153.83920994	15948.43929851	0.00006270	44
540	172.49364918	17894.98947998	0.00005588	45
552	193.41011319	20077.57702864	0.00004981	46
564	216.86289357	22524.82367706	0.00004440	47
576	243.15954234	25268.82180985	0.00003957	48
588	272.64490508	28345.55531263	0.00003528	49
600	305.70564309	31795.37145283	0.00003145	50

11.75% Monthly	Present Value of 1	Present Value of 1 per Period	Payment to Pay Off a Loan of 1	Months
	0.99030328	0.99030328	1.00979167	1
	0.98070059	1.97100387	0.50735568	2
	0.97119101	2.94219488	0.33988231	3
	0.96177364	3.90396852	0.25614961	4
	0.95244759	4.85641611	0.20591316	5
	0.94321198	5.79962808	0.17242485	6
	0.93406591	6.73369400	0.14850690	7
	0.92500854	7.65870254	0.13057042	8
	0.91603899	8.57474152	0.11662159	9
	0.90715642	9.48189794	0.10546412	10
Years	0.89835997	10.38025792	0.09633672	11
1	0.88964883	11.26990675	0.08873188	12
2	0.79147504	21.29616609	0.04695681	24
3	0.70413484	30.21601599	0.03309503	36
4	0.62643274	38.15155001	0.02621125	48
5	0.55730515	45.24113885/	0.02211832	60
6	0.49580588	51.49216568	0.01942043	72
7	0.44109312	57.07985168	0.01751932	84
8	0.39241798	62.05093000	0.01611579	96
9	0.34911419	66.47344401	0.01504360	108
10	0.31058903	70.40792842	0.01420295	120
11	0.27631517	73.90823787	0.01353029	132
12	0.24582347	77.02228408	0.01298326	144
13	0.21869656	79.79269164	0.01253248	156
14	0.19456314	82.25738149	0.01215696	168
15	0.17309287	84.45008993	0.01184131	180
16	0.15399187	86.40083043	0.01157396	192
17	0.13699869	88.13630443	0.01134606	204
18	0.12188072	89.68026684	0.01115073	216
19	0.10843104	91.05385119	0.01098251	228
20	0.09646555	92.27585891	0.01083707	240
21	0.08582046	93.36301664	0.01071088	252
22	0.07635007	94.33020524	0.01060106	264
23	0.06792475	95.19066345	0.01050523	276
24	0.06042918	95.95616909	0.01042142	288
25	0.05376075	96.63720029	0.01034798	300
26	0.04782819	97.24307890	0.01028351	312
27	0.04255029	97.78209809	0.01022682	324
28	0.03785482	98.26163589	0.01017691	336
29	0.03367749	98.68825612	0.01013292	348
30	0.02996114	99.06779832	0.01009410	360
31	0.02665489	99.40545759	0.01005981	372
32	0.02371350	99.70585576	0.01002950	384
33	0.02109668	99.97310465	0.01000269	396
34	0.01876864	100.21086231	0.00997896	408
35	0.01669750	100.42238313	0.00995794	420
36	0.01485491	100.61056238	0.00993931	432
37	0.01321565	100.77797583	0.00992280	444
38	0.01175729	100.92691501	0.00990816	456
39	0.01045986	101.05941858	0.00989517	468
40	0.00930560	101.17730022	0.00988364	480
41	0.00827872	101.28217349	0.00987341	492
42	0.00736515	101.37547387	0.00986432	504
43	0.00655240	101.45847844	0.00985625	516
44	0.00582933	101.53232336	0.00984908	528
45	0.00518606	101.59801941	0.00984271	540
46	0.00461377	101.65646582	0.00983705	552
47	0.00410464	101.70846260	0.00983202	564
48	0.00365169	101.75472148	0.00982755	576
49	0.00324872	101.79587564	0.00982358	588
50	0.00289022	101.83248838	0.00982005	600

	Future Value of 1	Future Value of 1 per Period	Payment for Sinking Fund of 1	**11.75%** Monthly
Months				
1	1.00979167	1.00000000	1.00000000	
2	1.01967921	2.00979167	0.49756401	
3	1.02966357	3.02947088	0.33009065	
4	1.03974569	4.05913445	0.24635794	
5	1.04992653	5.09888014	0.19612150	
6	1.06020707	6.14880667	0.16263318	
7	1.07058826	7.20901374	0.13871523	
8	1.08107110	8.27960200	0.12077875	
9	1.09165659	9.36067310	0.10682992	
10	1.10234573	10.45232969	0.09567245	
11	1.11313953	11.55467542	0.08654505	Years
12	1.12403902	12.66781495	0.07894021	1
24	1.26346372	26.90693327	0.03716514	2
36	1.42018253	42.91225789	0.02330336	3
48	1.59634058	60.90286731	0.01641959	4
60	1.79434910	81.12501432	0.01232665	5
72	2.01691840	103.85549665	0.00962876	6
84	2.26709499	129.40544577	0.00772765	7
96	2.54830323	158.12458557	0.00632413	8
108	2.86439227	190.40601937	0.00525193	9
120	3.21968869	226.69161062	0.00441128	10
132	3.61905572	267.47803110	0.00373862	11
144	4.06795985	313.32355927	0.00319159	12
156	4.57254561	364.85572188	0.00274081	13
168	5.13971969	422.77988352	0.00236530	14
180	5.77724549	487.88090147	0.00204965	15
192	6.49384937	561.07397830	0.00178230	16
204	7.29934009	643.33686043	0.00155440	17
216	8.20474309	735.80354996	0.00135906	18
228	9.22245140	839.73971717	0.00119085	19
240	10.36639524	956.56802485	0.00104540	20
252	11.65223276	1087.88760147	0.00091921	21
264	13.09756431	1235.49592987	0.00080939	22
276	14.72217337	1401.41345087	0.00071357	23
288	16.54829735	1587.91121881	0.00062976	24
300	18.60093196	1797.54198736	0.00055632	25
312	20.90817336	2033.17515130	0.00049184	26
324	23.50160272	2298.03602230	0.00043515	27
336	26.41671852	2595.74997653	0.00038525	28
348	29.69342243	2930.39207829	0.00034125	29
360	33.37656549	3306.54285887	0.00030243	30
372	37.51656201	3729.35101416	0.00026814	31
384	42.17007965	4204.60387927	0.00023783	32
396	47.40081506	4738.80664466	0.00021102	33
408	53.28036577	5339.27139829	0.00018729	34
420	59.88921020	6014.21721232	0.00016627	35
432	67.31780923	6772.88264461	0.00014765	36
444	75.66784441	7625.63014734	0.00013114	37
456	85.05360978	8584.19844517	0.00011649	38
468	95.60357630	9661.64183453	0.00010350	39
480	107.46215034	10872.73024749	0.00009197	40
492	120.79165030	12234.04088199	0.00008174	41
504	135.77452840	13764.20715537	0.00007265	42
516	152.61586803	15484.17375584	0.00006458	43
528	171.54619094	17417.48333023	0.00005741	44
540	192.82461259	19590.59873224	0.00005104	45
552	216.74238883	22033.26524204	0.00004539	46
564	243.62690263	24778.91771526	0.00004036	47
576	273.84614521	27865.13823429	0.00003589	48
588	307.81375307	31334.17052624	0.00003191	49
600	345.99466977	35233.49818879	0.00002838	50

12.00% Monthly	Present Value of 1	Present Value of 1 per Period	Payment to Pay Off a Loan of 1	Months
	0.99009901	0.99009901	1.01000000	1
	0.98029605	1.97039506	0.50751244	2
	0.97059015	2.94098521	0.34002211	3
	0.96098034	3.90196555	0.25628109	4
	0.95146569	4.85343124	0.20603980	5
	0.94204524	5.79547647	0.17254837	6
	0.93271805	6.72819453	0.14862828	7
	0.92348322	7.65167775	0.13069029	8
	0.91433982	8.56601758	0.11674036	9
	0.90528695	9.47130453	0.10558208	10
Years	0.89632372	10.36762825	0.09645408	11
1	0.88744923	11.25507747	0.08884879	12
2	0.78756613	21.24338726	0.04707347	24
3	0.69892495	30.10750504	0.03321431	36
4	0.62026041	37.97395949	0.02633384	48
5	0.55044962	44.95503841	0.02224445	60
6	0.48849609	51.15039148	0.01955019	72
7	0.43351547	56.64845276	0.01765273	84
8	0.38472297	61.52770299	0.01625284	96
9	0.34142210	65.85778983	0.01518423	108
10	0.30299478	69.70052203	0.01434709	120
11	0.26889248	73.11075175	0.01367788	132
12	0.23862843	76.13715747	0.01313419	144
13	0.21177061	78.82293889	0.01268666	156
14	0.18793566	81.20643352	0.01231430	168
15	0.16678336	83.32166399	0.01200168	180
16	0.14801176	85.19882363	0.01173725	192
17	0.13135293	86.86470750	0.01151216	204
18	0.11656905	88.34309484	0.01131950	216
19	0.10344911	89.65508855	0.01115386	228
20	0.09180584	90.81941635	0.01101086	240
21	0.08147302	91.85269815	0.01088700	252
22	0.07230317	92.76968329	0.01077938	264
23	0.06416539	93.58346103	0.01068565	276
24	0.05694353	94.30564747	0.01060382	288
25	0.05053449	94.94651125	0.01053224	300
26	0.04484679	95.51532083	0.01046952	312
27	0.03979925	96.02007494	0.01041449	324
28	0.03531981	96.46801859	0.01036613	336
29	0.03134454	96.86554583	0.01032359	348
30	0.02781669	97.21833108	0.01028613	360
31	0.02468590	97.53141007	0.01025311	372
32	0.02190748	97.80925178	0.01022398	384
33	0.01944178	98.05582219	0.01019827	396
34	0.01725359	98.27464091	0.01017557	408
35	0.01531169	98.46883141	0.01015550	420
36	0.01358834	98.64116562	0.01013776	432
37	0.01205897	98.79410348	0.01012206	444
38	0.01070172	98.92982807	0.01010817	456
39	0.00949723	99.05027675	0.01009588	468
40	0.00842831	99.15716884	0.01008500	480
41	0.00747970	99.25203014	0.01007536	492
42	0.00663785	99.33621473	0.01006682	504
43	0.00589076	99.41092427	0.01005926	516
44	0.00522775	99.47722520	0.01005255	528
45	0.00463936	99.53606391	0.01004661	540
46	0.00411720	99.58828028	0.01004134	552
47	0.00365380	99.63461965	0.01003667	564
48	0.00324257	99.67574349	0.01003253	576
49	0.00287761	99.71223881	0.01002886	588
50	0.00255373	99.74462656	0.01002560	600

	Future Value of 1	Future Value of 1 per Period	Payment for Sinking Fund of 1	**12.00%** Monthly
Months				
1	1.01000000	1.00000000	1.00000000	
2	1.02010000	2.01000000	0.49751244	
3	1.03030100	3.03010000	0.33002211	
4	1.04060401	4.06040100	0.24628109	
5	1.05101005	5.10100501	0.19603980	
6	1.06152015	6.15201506	0.16254837	
7	1.07213535	7.21353521	0.13862828	
8	1.08285671	8.28567056	0.12069029	
9	1.09368527	9.36852727	0.10674036	
10	1.10462213	10.46221254	0.09558208	
11	1.11566835	11.56683467	0.08645408	Years
12	1.12682503	12.68250301	0.07884879	1
24	1.26973465	26.97346485	0.03707347	2
36	1.43076878	43.07687836	0.02321431	3
48	1.61222608	61.22260777	0.01633384	4
60	1.81669670	81.66966986	0.01224445	5
72	2.04709931	104.70993121	0.00955019	6
84	2.30672274	130.67227440	0.00765273	7
96	2.59927293	159.92729256	0.00625284	8
108	2.92892579	192.89257927	0.00518423	9
120	3.30038689	230.03868946	0.00434709	10
132	3.71895856	271.89585619	0.00367788	11
144	4.19061559	319.06155936	0.00313419	12
156	4.72209054	372.20905425	0.00268666	13
168	5.32096982	432.09698179	0.00231430	14
180	5.99580198	499.58019754	0.00200168	15
192	6.75621974	575.62197415	0.00173725	16
204	7.61307751	661.30775138	0.00151216	17
216	8.57860630	757.86062989	0.00131950	18
228	9.66658830	866.65883013	0.00115386	19
240	10.89255365	989.25536539	0.00101086	20
252	12.27400210	1127.40020992	0.00088700	21
264	13.83065279	1283.06527853	0.00077938	22
276	15.58472574	1458.47257416	0.00068565	23
288	17.56125905	1656.12590533	0.00060382	24
300	19.78846626	1878.84662619	0.00053224	25
312	22.29813909	2129.81390919	0.00046952	26
324	25.12610125	2412.61012541	0.00041449	27
336	28.31271980	2731.27198027	0.00036613	28
348	31.90348134	3090.34813448	0.00032359	29
360	35.94964133	3494.96413277	0.00028613	30
372	40.50895567	3950.89556723	0.00025311	31
384	45.64650520	4464.65051961	0.00022398	32
396	51.43562459	5043.56245930	0.00019827	33
408	57.95094923	5695.89492318	0.00017557	34
420	65.30959471	6430.95947146	0.00015550	35
432	73.59248603	7259.24860322	0.00013776	36
444	82.92585529	8192.58552907	0.00012206	37
456	93.44292939	9244.29293866	0.00010817	38
468	105.29383172	10429.38317217	0.00009588	39
480	118.64772510	11764.77251025	0.00008500	40
492	133.69522641	13269.52264137	0.00007536	41
504	150.65112753	14965.11275322	0.00006682	42
516	169.75746132	16875.74613208	0.00005926	43
528	191.28695647	19028.69564680	0.00005255	44
540	215.54693049	21454.69304859	0.00004661	45
552	242.88367644	24188.36764396	0.00004134	46
564	273.68740602	27268.74060226	0.00003667	-47
576	308.39781954	30739.78195382	0.00003253	48
588	347.51038229	34651.03822937	0.00002886	49
600	391.58339700	39058.33969993	0.00002560	50

12.25% Monthly	Present Value of 1	Present Value of 1 per Period	Payment to Pay Off a Loan of 1	Months
	0.98989482	0.98989482	1.01020833	1
	0.97989176	1.96978659	0.50766921	2
	0.96998978	2.93977637	0.34016193	3
	0.96018787	3.89996423	0.25641261	4
	0.95048500	4.85044923	0.20616647	5
	0.94088018	5.79132941	0.17267193	6
	0.93137242	6.72270183	0.14874972	7
	0.92196074	7.64466257	0.13081022	8
	0.91264416	8.55730673	0.11685920	9
	0.90342173	9.46072846	0.10570015	10
Years	0.89429249	10.35502095	0.09657151	11
1	0.88525551	11.24027646	0.08896578	12
2	0.78367732	21.19079315	0.04719031	24
3	0.69375467	29.99954288	0.03333384	36
4	0.61415014	37.79753713	0.02645675	48
5	0.54367980	44.70075451	0.02237099	60
6	0.48129554	50.81186574	0.01968044	72
7	0.42606953	56.22176064	0.01778671	84
8	0.37718040	61.01089991	0.01639051	96
9	0.33390102	65.25051185	0.01532555	108
10	0.29558772	69.00365168	0.01449199	120
11	0.26167066	72.32613940	0.01382626	132
12	0.23164539	75.26738996	0.01328597	144
13	0.20506536	77.87114823	0.01284173	156
14	0.18153524	80.17613959	0.01247254	168
15	0.16070507	82.21664590	0.01216299	180
16	0.14226505	84.02301535	0.01190150	192
17	0.12594092	85.62211386	0.01167923	204
18	0.11148989	87.03772463	0.01148927	216
19	0.09869704	88.29090186	0.01132620	228
20	0.08737210	89.40028392	0.01118565	240
21	0.07734663	90.38237050	0.01106410	252
22	0.06847153	91.25176805	0.01095869	264
23	0.06061480	92.01140703	0.01086704	276
24	0.05365959	92.70273418	0.01078717	288
25	0.04750245	93.30588279	0.01071744	300
26	0.04205180	93.83982342	0.01065646	312
27	0.03722659	94.31249731	0.01060305	324
28	0.03295504	94.73093447	0.01055621	336
29	0.02917363	95.10135827	0.01051510	348
30	0.02582612	95.42927799	0.01047896	360
31	0.02286272	95.71957072	0.01044718	372
32	0.02023934	95.97655397	0.01041921	384
33	0.01791699	96.20404980	0.01039457	396
34	0.01586112	96.40544174	0.01037286	408
35	0.01404114	96.58372506	0.01035371	420
36	0.01243000	96.74155136	0.01033682	432
37	0.01100372	96.88126796	0.01032191	444
38	0.00974111	97.00495284	0.01030875	456
39	0.00862337	97.11444557	0.01029713	468
40	0.00763388	97.21137461	0.01028686	480
41	0.00675794	97.29718158	0.01027779	492
42	0.00598250	97.37314267	0.01026977	504
43	0.00529604	97.44038765	0.01026268	516
44	0.00468835	97.49991663	0.01025642	528
45	0.00415039	97.55261500	0.01025088	540
46	0.00367415	97.59926651	0.01024598	552
47	0.00325257	97.64056502	0.01024164	564
48	0.00287935	97.67712476	0.01023781	576
49	0.00254896	97.70948946	0.01023442	588
50	0.00225648	97.73814050	0.01023142	600

	Future Value of 1	Future Value of 1 per Period	Payment for Sinking Fund of 1	**12.25%** Monthly
Months				
1	1.01020833	1.00000000	1.00000000	
2	1.02052088	2.01020833	0.49746088	
3	1.03093869	3.03072921	0.32995360	
4	1.04146286	4.06166790	0.24620427	
5	1.05209446	5.10313076	0.19595814	
6	1.06283459	6.15522522	0.16246359	
7	1.07368436	7.21805981	0.13854138	
8	1.08464489	8.29174418	0.12060189	
9	1.09571731	9.37638906	0.10665086	
10	1.10690275	10.47210637	0.09549177	
11	1.11820238	11.57900912	0.08636318	Years
12	1.12961737	12.69721151	0.07875745	1
24	1.27603540	27.04020214	0.03698197	2
36	1.44143175	43.24229346	0.02312551	3
48	1.62826633	61.54445721	0.01624842	4
60	1.83931793	82.21889924	0.01216265	5
72	2.07772548	105.57310803	0.00947211	6
84	2.34703478	131.95442787	0.00757837	7
96	2.65125125	161.75522494	0.00618218	8
108	2.99489946	195.41872287	0.00511722	9
120	3.38309045	233.44559479	0.00428365	10
132	3.82159772	276.40140974	0.00361793	11
144	4.31694316	324.92504434	0.00307763	12
156	4.87649397	379.73818471	0.00263339	13
168	5.50857228	441.65606004	0.00226421	14
180	6.22257892	511.59956737	0.00195465	15
192	7.02913321	590.60896799	0.00169317	16
204	7.94023096	679.85935912	0.00147089	17
216	8.96942279	780.67815100	0.00128094	18
228	10.13201576	894.56480927	0.00111786	19
240	11.44530097	1023.21315638	0.00097731	20
252	12.92881075	1168.53656356	0.00085577	21
264	14.60460917	1332.69640821	0.00075036	22
276	16.49762016	1518.13421977	0.00065870	23
288	18.63599825	1727.60799229	0.00057884	24
300	21.05154729	1964.23320376	0.00050910	25
312	23.78019343	2231.52915220	0.00044812	26
324	26.86251950	2533.47129782	0.00039472	27
336	30.34436856	2874.55038948	0.00034788	28
348	34.27752573	3259.83925510	0.00030676	29
360	38.72048838	3695.06824918	0.00027063	30
372	43.73933615	4186.71047972	0.00023885	31
384	49.40871375	4742.07808192	0.00021088	32
396	55.81294116	5369.43097068	0.00018624	33
408	63.04726766	6078.09968935	0.00016453	34
420	71.21928852	6878.62418173	0.00014538	35
432	80.45054521	7782.91055140	0.00012849	36
444	90.87833309	8804.40813974	0.00011358	37
456	102.65774339	9958.30955634	0.00010042	38
468	115.96396983	11261.77663687	0.00008880	39
480	130.99491432	12734.19568894	0.00007853	40
492	147.97413027	14397.46582233	0.00006946	41
504	167.15414749	16276.32465178	0.00006144	42
516	188.82022804	18398.71621654	0.00005435	43
528	213.29460893	20796.20658863	0.00004809	44
540	240.94129463	23504.45335125	0.00004255	45
552	272.17147095	26563.73592967	0.00003765	46
564	307.44962051	30019.55466222	0.00003331	47
576	347.30043095	33923.30752129	0.00002948	48
588	392.31659852	38333.05454915	0.00002609	49
600	443.16764323	43314.38137792	0.00002309	50

12.50% Monthly	Present Value of 1	Present Value of 1 per Period	Payment to Pay Off a Loan of 1	
				Months
	0.98969072	0.98969072	1.01041667	1
	0.97948772	1.96917845	0.50782599	2
	0.96938991	2.93856836	0.34030177	3
	0.95939620	3.89796456	0.25654415	4
	0.94950552	4.84747008	0.20629318	5
	0.93971680	5.78718688	0.17279553	6
	0.93002900	6.71721589	0.14887120	7
	0.92044107	7.63765696	0.13093021	8
	0.91095199	8.54860895	0.11697810	9
	0.90156073	9.45016968	0.10581821	10
Years	0.89226629	10.34243597	0.09668902	11
1	0.88306767	11.22550364	0.08908286	12
2	0.77980851	21.13838300	0.04730731	24
3	0.68862368	29.89212627	0.03345363	36
4	0.60810131	37.62227395	0.02658000	48
5	0.53699461	44.44851716	0.02249791	60
6	0.47420258	50.47655241	0.01981118	72
7	0.41875297	55.79971519	0.01792124	84
8	0.36978721	60.50042814	0.01652881	96
9	0.32654713	64.65147578	0.01546755	108
10	0.28836321	68.31713175	0.01463762	120
11	0.25464423	71.55415402	0.01397543	132
12	0.22486809	74.41266374	0.01343857	144
13	0.19857374	76.93692126	0.01299766	156
14	0.17535405	79.16601147	0.01263168	168
15	0.15484949	81.13444896	0.01232522	180
16	0.13674258	82.87271248	0.01206670	192
17	0.12075295	84.40771679	0.01184726	204
18	0.10663303	85.76322947	0.01166001	216
19	0.09416418	86.96023890	0.01149951	228
20	0.08315334	88.01727922	0.01136141	240
21	0.07343003	88.95071736	0.01124218	252
22	0.06484368	89.77500640	0.01113896	264
23	0.05726136	90.50290940	0.01104937	276
24	0.05056566	91.14569701	0.01097144	288
25	0.04465290	91.71332197	0.01090354	300
26	0.03943153	92.21457322	0.01084427	312
27	0.03482071	92.65721199	0.01079247	324
28	0.03074904	93.04809198	0.01074713	336
29	0.02715348	93.39326546	0.01070741	348
30	0.02397836	93.69807700	0.01067258	360
31	0.02117452	93.96724622	0.01064201	372
32	0.01869853	94.20494086	0.01061515	384
33	0.01651207	94.41484130	0.01059156	396
34	0.01458127	94.60019760	0.01057080	408
35	0.01287625	94.76387976	0.01055254	420
36	0.01137060	94.90842218	0.01053647	432
37	0.01004101	95.03606292	0.01052232	444
38	0.00886689	95.14877833	0.01050986	456
39	0.00783007	95.24831366	0.01049887	468
40	0.00691448	95.33621009	0.01048919	480
41	0.00610595	95.41382859	0.01048066	492
42	0.00539197	95.48237098	0.01047314	504
43	0.00476147	95.54289855	0.01046650	516
44	0.00420470	95.59634849	0.01046065	528
45	0.00371304	95.64354840	0.01045549	540
46	0.00327886	95.68522911	0.01045093	552
47	0.00289546	95.72203601	0.01044692	564
48	0.00255689	95.75453898	0.01044337	576
49	0.00225790	95.78324131	0.01044024	588
50	0.00199388	95.80858741	0.01043748	600

	Future Value of 1	Future Value of 1 per Period	Payment for Sinking Fund of 1	**12.50%** Monthly
Months				
1	1.01041667	1.00000000	1.00000000	
2	1.02094184	2.01041667	0.49740933	
3	1.03157665	3.03135851	0.32988510	
4	1.04232224	4.06293516	0.24612748	
5	1.05317976	5.10525740	0.19587651	
6	1.06415039	6.15843716	0.16237886	
7	1.07523529	7.22258755	0.13845453	
8	1.08643565	8.29782284	0.12051354	
9	1.09775269	9.38425849	0.10656143	
10	1.10918762	10.48201119	0.09540154	
11	1.12074165	11.59119880	0.08627235	Years
12	1.13241605	12.71194046	0.07866620	1
24	1.28236610	27.10714581	0.03689064	2
36	1.45217195	43.40850734	0.02303696	3
48	1.64446282	61.86843072	0.01616333	4
60	1.86221609	82.77274417	0.01208127	5
72	2.10880338	106.44512416	0.00939451	6
84	2.38804278	133.25210712	0.00750457	7
96	2.70425797	163.60876478	0.00611214	8
108	3.06234511	197.98513102	0.00505088	9
120	3.46784875	236.91347978	0.00422095	10
132	3.92704757	280.99656657	0.00355876	11
144	4.44705168	330.91696143	0.00302191	12
156	5.03591268	387.44761760	0.00258099	13
168	5.70274833	451.46383978	0.00221502	14
180	6.45788372	523.95683700	0.00190855	15
192	7.31301115	606.04907030	0.00165003	16
204	8.28137117	699.01163258	0.00143059	17
216	9.37795760	804.28392982	0.00124334	18
228	10.61974967	923.49596845	0.00108284	19
240	12.02597494	1058.49359393	0.00094474	20
252	13.61840699	1211.36707125	0.00082551	21
264	15.42170260	1384.48345004	0.00072229	22
276	17.46378349	1580.52321528	0.00063270	23
288	19.77626866	1802.52179117	0.00055478	24
300	22.39496397	2053.91654079	0.00048687	25
312	25.36041655	2338.59998925	0.00042761	26
324	28.71854265	2660.98009442	0.00037580	27
336	32.52133853	3026.04849867	0.00033046	28
348	36.82768560	3439.45781747	0.00029074	29
360	41.70426212	3907.60916393	0.00025591	30
372	47.22657563	4437.75126081	0.00022534	31
384	53.48013206	5038.09267820	0.00019849	32
396	60.56175971	5717.92893257	0.00017489	33
408	68.58110850	6487.78641596	0.00015414	34
420	77.66234775	7359.58538361	0.00013588	35
432	87.94608879	8346.82452382	0.00011981	36
444	99.59156216	9464.78996784	0.00010565	37
456	112.77908308	10730.79197599	0.00009319	38
468	127.71284338	12164.43296481	0.00008221	39
480	144.62407318	13787.91102534	0.00007253	40
492	163.77462117	15626.36363210	0.00006399	41
504	185.46100901	17708.25686457	0.00005647	42
516	210.01902258	20065.82616794	0.00004984	43
528	237.82891123	22735.57547761	0.00004398	44
540	269.32127537	25758.84243578	0.00003882	45
552	304.98373387	29182.43845182	0.00003427	46
564	345.36847413	33059.37351682	0.00003025	47
576	391.10080203	37449.67699534	0.00002670	48
588	442.88882399	42421.32710305	0.00002357	49
600	501.53441106	48051.30346218	0.00002081	50

13.00% Monthly	Present Value of 1	Present Value of 1 per Period	Payment to Pay Off a Loan of 1	Months
	0.98928277	0.98928277	1.01083333	1
	0.97868040	1.96796317	0.50813959	2
	0.96819166	2.93615483	0.34058150	3
	0.95781532	3.89397015	0.25680731	4
	0.94755020	4.84152034	0.20654669	5
	0.93739508	5.77891543	0.17304285	6
	0.92734880	6.70626423	0.14911432	7
	0.91741019	7.62367443	0.13117034	8
	0.90757810	8.53125252	0.11721608	9
	0.89785137	9.42910390	0.10605462	10
Years	0.88822889	10.31733279	0.09692427	11
1	0.87870954	11.19604233	0.08931728	12
2	0.77213046	21.03411156	0.04754182	24
3	0.67847840	29.67891685	0.03369395	36
4	0.59618544	37.27518975	0.02682750	48
5	0.52387004	43.95010720	0.02275307	60
6	0.46033294	49.81542090	0.02007411	72
7	0.40449895	54.96932798	0.01819196	84
8	0.35543708	59.49811532	0.01680726	96
9	0.31232596	63.47760396	0.01575359	108
10	0.27444380	66.97441860	0.01493107	120
11	0.24115638	70.04710298	0.01427611	132
12	0.21190642	72.74710007	0.01374625	144
13	0.18620419	75.11961327	0.01331210	156
14	0.16361940	77.20436326	0.01295264	168
15	0.14377393	79.03625297	0.01265242	180
16	0.12633552	80.64595193	0.01239988	192
17	0.11101223	82.06040977	0.01218614	204
18	0.09754750	83.30330737	0.01200433	216
19	0.08571592	84.39545335	0.01184898	228
20	0.07531940	85.35513244	0.01171576	240
21	0.06618387	86.19841162	0.01160114	252
22	0.05815640	86.93940907	0.01150226	264
23	0.05110259	87.59053061	0.01141676	276
24	0.04490433	88.16267731	0.01134267	288
25	0.03945786	88.66542808	0.01127835	300
26	0.03467200	89.10719998	0.01122244	312
27	0.03046662	89.49538916	0.01117376	324
28	0.02677131	89.83649470	0.01113131	336
29	0.02352420	90.13622739	0.01109432	348
30	0.02067094	90.39960537	0.01106200	360
31	0.01816375	90.63103811	0.01103375	372
32	0.01596066	90.83044026	0.01100904	384
33	0.01402479	91.01309653	0.01098743	396
34	0.01232371	91.17011865	0.01096851	408
35	0.01082897	91.30809548	0.01095193	420
36	0.00951552	91.42933704	0.01093741	432
37	0.00836137	91.53587315	0.01092468	444
38	0.00734722	91.62948745	0.01091352	456
39	0.00645607	91.71174723	0.01090373	468
40	0.00567301	91.78402968	0.01089514	480
41	0.00498493	91.84754496	0.01088761	492
42	0.00438031	91.90335644	0.01088100	504
43	0.00384902	91.95239853	0.01087519	516
44	0.00338217	91.99549227	0.01087010	528
45	0.00297194	92.03335916	0.01086563	540
46	0.00261147	92.06663315	0.01086170	552
47	0.00229473	92.09587133	0.01085825	564
48	0.00201640	92.12156319	0.01085522	576
49	0.00177183	92.14413888	0.01085256	588
50	0.00155692	92.16397635	0.01085023	600

	Future Value of 1	Future Value of 1 per Period	Payment for Sinking Fund of 1	**13.00%** Monthly
Months				
1	1.01083333	1.00000000	1.00000000	
2	1.02178403	2.01083333	0.49730626	
3	1.03285335	3.03261736	0.32974816	
4	1.04404260	4.06547072	0.24597398	
5	1.05535306	5.10951332	0.19571336	
6	1.06678605	6.16486638	0.16220952	
7	1.07834290	7.23165243	0.13828098	
8	1.09002495	8.30999533	0.12033701	
9	1.10183355	9.40002028	0.10638275	
10	1.11377008	10.50185383	0.09522128	
11	1.12583593	11.61562392	0.08609094	Years
12	1.13803248	12.74145984	0.07848394	1
24	1.29511793	27.24165500	0.03670849	2
36	1.47388627	43.74334809	0.02286062	3
48	1.67733045	62.52281082	0.01599416	4
60	1.90885654	83.89444940	0.01191974	5
72	2.17234074	108.21606828	0.00924077	6
84	2.47219432	135.89486058	0.00735863	7
96	2.81343744	167.39422526	0.00597392	8
108	3.20178319	203.24152543	0.00492025	9
120	3.64373327	244.03691739	0.00409774	10
132	4.14668682	290.46339854	0.00344277	11
144	4.71906429	343.29824210	0.00291292	12
156	5.37044844	403.42601024	0.00247877	13
168	6.11174477	471.85336342	0.00211930	14
180	6.95536407	549.72591397	0.00181909	15
192	7.91543023	638.34740592	0.00156655	16
204	9.00801671	739.20154234	0.00135281	17
216	10.25141561	853.97682548	0.00117099	18
228	11.66644395	984.59482578	0.00101565	19
240	13.27679216	1133.24235281	0.00088242	20
252	15.10942072	1302.40806688	0.00076781	21
264	17.19501156	1494.92414427	0.00066893	22
276	19.56848168	1714.01369357	0.00058343	23
288	22.26956777	1963.34471705	0.00050933	24
300	25.34349147	2247.09152045	0.00044502	25
312	28.84171649	2570.00459927	0.00038910	26
324	32.82281019	2937.49017171	0.00034043	27
336	37.35342414	3355.70068967	0.00029800	28
348	42.50940997	3831.63784326	0.00026098	29
360	48.37708932	4373.26978325	0.00022866	30
372	55.05469901	4989.66452404	0.00020041	31
384	62.65403574	5691.14176056	0.00017571	32
396	71.30232778	6489.44564083	0.00015410	33
408	81.14436502	7397.94138677	0.00013517	34
420	92.34492310	8431.83905506	0.00011860	35
432	105.09152200	9608.44818424	0.00010408	36
444	119.59756557	10947.46759141	0.00009135	37
456	136.10591434	12471.31517028	0.00008018	38
468	154.89295146	14205.50321206	0.00007040	39
480	176.27320994	16179.06553284	0.00006181	40
492	200.60463855	18425.04355837	0.00005427	41
504	228.29459463	20981.03950442	0.00004766	42
516	259.80666407	23889.84591390	0.00004186	43
528	295.66842265	27200.16209060	0.00003676	44
540	336.48026876	30967.40942411	0.00003229	45
552	382.92547527	35254.65925592	0.00002837	46
564	435.78162890	40133.68882130	0.00002492	47
576	495.93364858	45686.18294547	0.00002189	48
588	564.38860080	52005.10161274	0.00001923	49
600	642.29255997	59196.23630477	0.00001689	50

14.00% Monthly	Present Value of 1	Present Value of 1 per Period	Payment to Pay Off a Loan of 1	Months
	0.98846787	0.98846787	1.01166667	1
	0.97706874	1.96553661	0.50876692	2
	0.96580106	2.93133767	0.34114118	3
	0.95466452	3.88600100	0.25733395	4
	0.94365402	4.82965502	0.20705413	5
	0.93277169	5.76242671	0.17353800	6
	0.92201485	6.68444156	0.14960113	7
	0.91138206	7.59582362	0.13165129	8
	0.90087189	8.49669550	0.11769281	9
	0.89048292	9.38717842	0.10652828	10
Years	0.88021376	10.26739218	0.09739571	11
1	0.87006302	11.13745520	0.08978712	12
2	0.75700966	20.82774314	0.04801288	24
3	0.65864612	29.25890435	0.03417763	36
4	0.57306363	36.59454596	0.02732648	48
5	0.49860147	42.97701647	0.02326825	60
6	0.43381471	48.53016806	0.02060574	72
7	0.37744613	53.36175991	0.01874001	84
8	0.32840192	57.56554932	0.01737150	96
9	0.28573037	61.22311104	0.01633370	108
10	0.24860343	64.40542025	0.01552664	120
11	0.21630065	67.17422982	0.01488666	132
12	0.18819520	69.58326864	0.01437127	144
13	0.16374168	71.67928424	0.01395103	156
14	0.14246558	73.50294991	0.01360640	168
15	0.12395404	75.08965398	0.01331741	180
16	0.10784782	76.47018651	0.01307699	192
17	0.09383440	77.67133682	0.01287476	204
18	0.08164184	78.71641329	0.01270383	216
19	0.07103355	79.62569568	0.01255876	228
20	0.06180367	80.41682866	0.01243521	240
21	0.05377308	81.10516422	0.01232967	252
22	0.04678597	81.70405954	0.01223929	264
23	0.04070674	82.22513620	0.01216173	276
24	0.03541743	82.67850574	0.01209504	288
25	0.03081540	83.07296582	0.01203761	300
26	0.02681134	83.41617094	0.01198808	312
27	0.02332755	83.71478103	0.01194532	324
28	0.02029644	83.97459062	0.01190836	336
29	0.01765918	84.20064134	0.01187639	348
30	0.01536460	84.39731972	0.01184872	360
31	0.01336817	84.56844230	0.01182474	372
32	0.01163115	84.71732973	0.01180396	384
33	0.01011984	84.84687118	0.01178594	396
34	0.00880490	84.95958040	0.01177030	408
35	0.00766081	85.05764453	0.01175673	420
36	0.00666539	85.14296650	0.01174495	432
37	0.00579931	85.21720199	0.01173472	444
38	0.00504577	85.28179155	0.01172583	456
39	0.00439013	85.33798853	0.01171811	468
40	0.00381969	85.38688345	0.01171140	480
41	0.00332337	85.42942511	0.01170557	492
42	0.00289154	85.46643904	0.01170050	504
43	0.00251583	85.49864348	0.01169609	516
44	0.00218893	85.52666338	0.01169226	528
45	0.00190450	85.55104246	0.01168893	540
46	0.00165704	85.57225380	0.01168603	552
47	0.00144173	85.59070900	0.01168351	564
48	0.00125439	85.60676618	0.01168132	576
49	0.00109140	85.62073694	0.01167941	588
50	0.00094959	85.63289239	0.01167776	600

	Future Value of 1	Future Value of 1 per Period	Payment for Sinking Fund of 1	**14.00%** Monthly
Months				
1	1.01166667	1.00000000	1.00000000	
2	1.02346944	2.01166667	0.49710025	
3	1.03540992	3.03513611	0.32947452	
4	1.04748970	4.07054603	0.24566729	
5	1.05971042	5.11803574	0.19538746	
6	1.07207371	6.17774615	0.16187133	
7	1.08458123	7.24981986	0.13793446	
8	1.09723468	8.33440109	0.11998463	
9	1.11003575	9.43163577	0.10602615	
10	1.12298617	10.54167152	0.09486162	
11	1.13608767	11.66465769	0.08572905	Years
12	1.14934203	12.80074536	0.07812045	1
24	1.32098710	27.51318001	0.03634622	2
36	1.51826599	44.42279950	0.02251096	3
48	1.74500692	63.85773588	0.01565981	4
60	2.00560979	86.19512510	0.01160158	5
72	2.30513163	111.86842535	0.00893907	6
84	2.64938466	141.37582836	0.00707334	7
96	3.04504915	175.28992681	0.00570483	8
108	3.49980296	214.26882554	0.00466703	9
120	4.02247064	259.06891210	0.00385998	10
132	4.62319457	310.55953450	0.00321999	11
144	5.31363183	369.73987093	0.00270460	12
156	6.10718039	437.75831889	0.00228437	13
168	7.01923910	515.93477990	0.00193823	14
180	8.06750651	605.78627223	0.00165075	15
192	9.27232430	709.05636675	0.00141033	16
204	10.65707203	827.74903104	0.00120810	17
216	12.24862079	964.16749637	0.00103716	18
228	14.07785467	1120.95897214	0.00089209	19
240	16.18027006	1301.16600506	0.00076854	20
252	18.59666442	1508.28552195	0.00066300	21
264	21.37392802	1746.33668778	0.00057263	22
276	24.56595381	2019.93889777	0.00049506	23
288	28.23468320	2334.40141700	0.00042838	24
300	32.45130808	2695.82640696	0.00037094	25
312	37.29765228	3111.22733832	0.00032142	26
324	42.86775936	3588.66504877	0.00027866	27
336	49.26971753	4137.40435942	0.00024170	28
348	56.62775712	4768.09346747	0.00020973	29
360	65.08466128	5492.97096671	0.00018205	30
372	74.80453666	6326.10314261	0.00015808	31
384	85.97599796	7283.65696826	0.00013729	32
396	98.81582796	8384.21382531	0.00011927	33
408	113.57318423	9649.13007665	0.00010364	34
420	130.53443402	11102.95148775	0.00009007	35
432	150.02871128	12773.88953847	0.00007828	36
444	172.43430346	14694.36886838	0.00006805	37
456	198.18599225	16901.65647846	0.00005917	38
468	227.78349049	19438.58489928	0.00005144	39
480	261.80113918	22354.38335841	0.00004473	40
492	300.89905256	25705.63307619	0.00003890	41
504	345.83592765	29557.36522721	0.00003383	42
516	397.48376686	33984.32287362	0.00002943	43
528	456.84479918	39072.41135815	0.00002559	44
540	525.07092852	44920.36530176	0.00002226	45
552	603.48608646	51641.66455401	0.00001936	46
564	693.61192321	59366.73627550	0.00001684	47
576	797.19733531	68245.48588365	0.00001465	48
588	916.25240304	78450.20597511	0.00001275	49
600	1053.08739618	90178.91967251	0.00001109	50

15.00% Monthly	Present Value of 1	Present Value of 1 per Period	Payment to Pay Off a Loan of 1	
				Months
	0.98765432	0.98765432	1.01250000	1
	0.97546106	1.96311538	0.50939441	2
	0.96341833	2.92653371	0.34170117	3
	0.95152428	3.87805798	0.25786102	4
	0.93977706	4.81783504	0.20756211	5
	0.92817488	5.74600992	0.17403381	6
	0.91671593	6.66272585	0.15008872	7
	0.90539845	7.56812429	0.13213314	8
	0.89422069	8.46234498	0.11817055	9
	0.88318093	9.34552591	0.10700307	10
Years	0.87227746	10.21780338	0.09786839	11
1	0.86150860	11.07931197	0.09025831	12
2	0.74219707	20.62423451	0.04848665	24
3	0.63940916	28.84726737	0.03466533	36
4	0.55085649	35.93148091	0.02783075	48
5	0.47456760	42.03459179	0.02378993	60
6	0.40884407	47.29247431	0.02114501	72
7	0.35222268	51.82218532	0.01929675	84
8	0.30344287	55.72457031	0.01794541	96
9	0.26141864	59.08650855	0.01692434	108
10	0.22521441	61.98284725	0.01613350	120
11	0.19402415	64.47806795	0.01550915	132
12	0.16715347	66.62772204	0.01500877	144
13	0.14400416	68.47966753	0.01460287	156
14	0.12406082	70.07513450	0.01427040	168
15	0.10687946	71.44964301	0.01399587	180
16	0.09207758	72.63379392	0.01376770	192
17	0.07932562	73.65395011	0.01357700	204
18	0.06833971	74.53282344	0.01341691	216
19	0.05887525	75.28998037	0.01328198	228
20	0.05072153	75.94227758	0.01316790	240
21	0.04369703	76.50423724	0.01307117	252
22	0.03764537	76.98837032	0.01298897	264
23	0.03243181	77.40545513	0.01291899	276
24	0.02794028	77.76477728	0.01285929	288
25	0.02407079	78.07433640	0.01280831	300
26	0.02073720	78.34102425	0.01276470	312
27	0.01786527	78.57077382	0.01272738	324
28	0.01539109	78.76871306	0.01269540	336
29	0.01325955	78.93923571	0.01266797	348
30	0.01142322	79.08614244	0.01264444	360
31	0.00984120	79.21270385	0.01262424	372
32	0.00847828	79.32173760	0.01260688	384
33	0.00730411	79.41567111	0.01259197	396
34	0.00629255	79.49659563	0.01257916	408
35	0.00542109	79.56631281	0.01256813	420
36	0.00467032	79.62637476	0.01255865	432
37	0.00402352	79.67811864	0.01255050	444
38	0.00346629	79.72269644	0.01254348	456
39	0.00298624	79.76110060	0.01253744	468
40	0.00257267	79.79418611	0.01253224	480
41	0.00221638	79.82268956	0.01252777	492
42	0.00190943	79.84724553	0.01252391	504
43	0.00164499	79.86840071	0.01252060	516
44	0.00141717	79.88662608	0.01251774	528
45	0.00122091	79.90232740	0.01251528	540
46	0.00105182	79.91585421	0.01251316	552
47	0.00090615	79.92750768	0.01251134	564
48	0.00078066	79.93754724	0.01250977	576
49	0.00067254	79.94619641	0.01250841	588
50	0.00057940	79.95364775	0.01250725	600

	Future Value of 1	Future Value of 1 per Period	Payment for Sinking Fund of 1	**15.00%** Monthly
Months				
1	1.01250000	1.00000000	1.00000000	
2	1.02515625	2.01250000	0.49689441	
3	1.03797070	3.03765625	0.32920117	
4	1.05094534	4.07562695	0.24536102	
5	1.06408215	5.12657229	0.19506211	
6	1.07738318	6.19065444	0.16153381	
7	1.09085047	7.26803762	0.13758872	
8	1.10448610	8.35888809	0.11963314	
9	1.11829218	9.46337420	0.10567055	
10	1.13227083	10.58166637	0.09450307	
11	1.14642422	11.71393720	0.08536839	Years
12	1.16075452	12.86036142	0.07775831	1
24	1.34735105	27.78808403	0.03598665	2
36	1.56394382	45.11550550	0.02216533	3
48	1.81535485	65.22838824	0.01533075	4
60	2.10718135	88.57450776	0.01128993	5
72	2.44592027	115.67362145	0.00864501	6
84	2.83911300	147.12904010	0.00679675	7
96	3.29551324	183.64105940	0.00544541	8
108	3.82528188	226.02255076	0.00442434	9
120	4.44021323	275.21705832	0.00363350	10
132	5.15399757	332.31980521	0.00300915	11
144	5.98252596	398.60207665	0.00250877	12
156	6.94424403	475.53952266	0.00210287	13
168	8.06056263	564.84501070	0.00177040	14
180	9.35633449	668.50675940	0.00149587	15
192	10.86040753	788.83260252	0.00126770	16
204	12.60626711	928.50136852	0.00107700	17
216	14.63278150	1090.62251964	0.00091691	18
228	16.98506723	1278.80537822	0.00078198	19
240	19.71549352	1497.23948148	0.00066790	20
252	22.88484817	1750.78785365	0.00057117	21
264	26.56369090	2045.09527212	0.00048897	22
276	30.83392422	2386.71393771	0.00041899	23
288	35.79061684	2783.24934712	0.00035929	24
300	41.54412019	3243.52961504	0.00030831	25
312	48.22252519	3777.80201544	0.00026470	26
324	55.97451397	4397.96111791	0.00022738	27
336	64.97266997	5117.81359780	0.00019540	28
348	75.41732020	5953.38561593	0.00016797	29
360	87.54099514	6923.27961085	0.00014444	30
372	101.61360559	8049.08844718	0.00012424	31
384	117.94845175	9355.87614003	0.00010688	32
396	136.90919823	10872.73585821	0.00009197	33
408	158.91797036	12633.43762885	0.00007916	34
420	184.46475204	14677.18016348	0.00006813	35
432	214.11824430	17049.46354361	0.00005865	36
444	248.53877743	19803.10219441	0.00005050	37
456	288.49250873	22999.40069851	0.00004348	38
468	334.86898284	26709.51862214	0.00003744	39
480	388.70068468	31016.05477407	0.00003224	40
492	451.18607578	36014.88606237	0.00002777	41
504	523.71627579	41817.30206359	0.00002391	42
516	607.90603313	48552.48265072	0.00002060	43
528	705.62967431	56370.37394491	0.00001774	44
540	819.06283230	65445.02658470	0.00001528	45
552	950.73088289	75978.47063095	0.00001316	46
564	1103.56516745	88205.21339598	0.00001134	47
576	1280.96825372	102397.46029752	0.00000977	48
588	1486.88968756	118871.17500513	0.00000841	49
600	1725.91392220	137993.11377567	0.00000725	50

16.00% Monthly	Present Value of 1	Present Value of 1 per Period	Payment to Pay Off a Loan of 1	Months
	0.98684211	0.98684211	1.01333333	1
	0.97385734	1.96069945	0.51002208	2
	0.96104343	2.92174287	0.34226147	3
	0.94839812	3.87014099	0.25838852	4
	0.93591920	4.80606019	0.20807064	5
	0.92360447	5.72966466	0.17453028	6
	0.91145178	6.64111644	0.15057709	7
	0.89945899	7.54057544	0.13261587	8
	0.88762401	8.42819945	0.11864930	9
	0.87594474	9.30414419	0.10747899	10
Years	0.86441916	10.16856334	0.09834231	11
1	0.85304522	11.02160856	0.09073086	12
2	0.72768615	20.42353906	0.04896311	24
3	0.62074919	28.44381091	0.03515703	36
4	0.52952713	35.28546548	0.02834028	48
5	0.45171058	41.12170620	0.02431806	60
6	0.38532955	46.10028344	0.02169184	72
7	0.32870353	50.34723495	0.01986206	84
8	0.28039898	53.97007664	0.01852879	96
9	0.23919301	57.06052442	0.01752525	108
10	0.20404245	59.69681612	0.01675131	120
11	0.17405744	61.94569215	0.01614317	132
12	0.14847887	63.86408510	0.01565825	144
13	0.12665919	65.50056104	0.01526704	156
14	0.10804601	66.89654901	0.01494845	168
15	0.09216814	68.08738987	0.01468701	180
16	0.07862359	69.10323098	0.01447110	192
17	0.06706947	69.96978938	0.01429188	204
18	0.05721329	70.70900288	0.01414247	216
19	0.04880553	71.33958542	0.01401746	228
20	0.04163332	71.87750084	0.01391256	240
21	0.03551511	72.33636702	0.01382430	252
22	0.03029599	72.72780062	0.01374990	264
23	0.02584385	73.06171118	0.01368706	276
24	0.02204597	73.34655199	0.01363391	288
25	0.01880621	73.58953408	0.01358889	300
26	0.01604255	73.79680879	0.01355072	312
27	0.01368502	73.97362349	0.01351833	324
28	0.01167394	74.12445443	0.01349082	336
29	0.00995840	74.25312003	0.01346745	348
30	0.00849497	74.36287762	0.01344757	360
31	0.00724659	74.45650580	0.01343066	372
32	0.00618167	74.53637487	0.01341627	384
33	0.00527324	74.60450680	0.01340402	396
34	0.00449831	74.66262641	0.01339358	408
35	0.00383727	74.71220508	0.01338469	420
36	0.00327336	74.75449792	0.01337712	432
37	0.00279233	74.79057562	0.01337067	444
38	0.00238198	74.82135153	0.01336517	456
39	0.00203194	74.84760478	0.01336048	468
40	0.00173333	74.86999999	0.01335648	480
41	0.00147861	74.88910411	0.01335308	492
42	0.00126132	74.90540079	0.01335017	504
43	0.00107597	74.91930260	0.01334769	516
44	0.00091785	74.93116147	0.01334558	528
45	0.00078297	74.94127762	0.01334378	540
46	0.00066790	74.94990715	0.01334224	552
47	0.00056975	74.95726854	0.01334093	564
48	0.00048602	74.96354813	0.01333982	576
49	0.00041460	74.96890491	0.01333886	588
50	0.00035367	74.97347448	0.01333805	600

	Future Value of 1	Future Value of 1 per Period	Payment for Sinking Fund of 1	**16.00%** Monthly
Months				
1	1.01333333	1.00000000	1.00000000	
2	1.02684444	2.01333333	0.49668874	
3	1.04053570	3.04017778	0.32892813	
4	1.05440951	4.08071348	0.24505519	
5	1.06846831	5.13512299	0.19473730	
6	1.08271455	6.20359330	0.16119695	
7	1.09715074	7.28630585	0.13724376	
8	1.11177942	8.38345660	0.11928254	
9	1.12660315	9.49523602	0.10531597	
10	1.14162452	10.62183916	0.09414565	
11	1.15684618	11.76346369	0.08500898	Years
12	1.17227080	12.92030987	0.07739752	1
24	1.37421882	28.06641183	0.03562978	2
36	1.61095660	45.82174487	0.02182370	3
48	1.88847738	66.63580331	0.01500695	4
60	2.21380688	91.03551621	0.01098472	5
72	2.59518116	119.63858713	0.00835851	6
84	3.04225509	153.16913190	0.00652873	7
96	3.56634681	192.47601039	0.00519545	8
108	4.18072422	238.55431622	0.00419192	9
120	4.90094091	292.57056857	0.00341798	10
132	5.74522992	355.89224383	0.00280984	11
144	6.73496526	430.12239464	0.00232492	12
156	7.89520310	517.14023279	0.00193371	13
168	9.25531604	619.14870337	0.00161512	14
180	10.84973673	738.73025461	0.00135367	15
192	12.71882954	878.91221514	0.00113777	16
204	14.90991245	1043.24343391	0.00095855	17
216	17.47845497	1235.88412292	0.00080914	18
228	20.48948236	1461.71117720	0.00068413	19
240	24.01922185	1726.44163839	0.00057923	20
252	28.15703237	2036.77742745	0.00049097	21
264	33.00766681	2400.57501062	0.00041657	22
276	38.69392392	2827.04429385	0.00035373	23
288	45.35975708	3326.98178093	0.00030057	24
300	53.17391864	3913.04389800	0.00025556	25
312	62.33423205	4600.06740379	0.00021739	26
324	73.07259996	5405.44499736	0.00018500	27
336	85.66087509	6349.56563187	0.00015749	28
348	100.41774242	7456.33068174	0.00013411	29
360	117.71678707	8753.75903023	0.00011424	30
372	137.99595195	10274.69639601	0.00009733	31
384	161.76862475	12057.64685588	0.00008293	32
396	189.63663486	14147.74761474	0.00007068	33
408	222.30548933	16597.91169976	0.00006025	34
420	260.60223343	19470.16750758	0.00005136	35
432	305.49638822	22837.22911622	0.00004379	36
444	358.12449488	26784.33711596	0.00003734	37
456	419.81888749	31411.41656163	0.00003184	38
468	492.14142236	36835.60667701	0.00002715	39
480	576.92301805	43194.22635348	0.00002315	40
492	676.31000690	50648.25051744	0.00001974	41
504	792.81847166	59386.38537436	0.00001684	42
516	929.39794265	69629.84569838	0.00001436	43
528	1089.50606812	81637.95510935	0.00001225	44
540	1277.19614819	95714.71111413	0.00001045	45
552	1497.21974817	112216.48111275	0.00000891	46
564	1755.14698936	131561.02420171	0.00000760	47
576	2057.50756227	154238.06717057	0.00000648	48
588	2411.95603245	180821.70243381	0.00000553	49
600	2827.46562353	211984.92176449	0.00000472	50

	Present Value of 1	Present Value of 1 per Period	Payment to Pay Off a Loan of 1	
5.00% Quarterly				
				Quarters
	0.98765432	0.98765432	1.01250000	1
	0.97546106	1.96311538	0.50939441	2
Years	0.96341833	2.92653371	0.34170117	3
1	0.95152428	3.87805798	0.25786102	4
2	0.90539845	7.56812429	0.13213314	8
3	0.86150860	11.07931197	0.09025831	12
4	0.81974635	14.42029227	0.06934672	16
5	0.78000855	17.59931613	0.05682039	20
6	0.74219707	20.62423451	0.04848665	24
7	0.70621853	23.50251778	0.04254863	28
8	0.67198407	26.24127418	0.03810791	32
9	0.63940916	28.84726257	0.03466533	36
10	0.60841334	31.32693316	0.03192141	40
11	0.57892006	33.68639536	0.02968557	44
12	0.55085649	35.93148091	0.02783075	48
13	0.52415332	38.06773431	0.02626897	52
14	0.49874461	40.10043128	0.02493739	56
15	0.47456760	42.03459179	0.02378993	60
16	0.45156259	43.87499247	0.02279203	64
17	0.42967277	45.62617840	0.02191724	68
18	0.40884407	47.29247431	0.02114501	72
19	0.38902506	48.87799533	0.02045910	76
20	0.37016679	50.38665706	0.01984652	80
21	0.35222268	51.82218532	0.01929675	84
22	0.33514843	53.18812531	0.01880119	88
23	0.31890187	54.48785037	0.01835272	92
24	0.30344287	55.72457031	0.01794541	96
25	0.28873326	56.90133936	0.01757428	100
26	0.27473670	58.02106368	0.01723512	104
27	0.26141864	59.08650855	0.01692434	108
28	0.24874618	60.10030520	0.01663885	112
29	0.23668803	61.06495733	0.01637600	116
30	0.22521441	61.98284725	0.01613350	120
31	0.21429698	62.85624179	0.01590932	124
32	0.20390878	63.68729789	0.01570172	128
33	0.19402415	64.47806795	0.01550915	132
34	0.18461869	65.23050485	0.01533025	136
35	0.17566916	65.94646664	0.01516381	140
36	0.16715347	66.62772204	0.01500877	144
37	0.15905059	67.27595291	0.01486415	148
38	0.15134050	67.89276031	0.01472911	152
39	0.14400416	68.47966753	0.01460287	156
40	0.13702345	69.03812400	0.01448475	160
41	0.13038114	69.56950888	0.01437411	164
42	0.12406082	70.07513450	0.01427040	168
43	0.11804688	70.55624955	0.01417309	172
44	0.11232447	71.01404220	0.01408172	176
45	0.10687946	71.44964301	0.01399587	180
46	0.10169840	71.86412777	0.01391515	184
47	0.09676850	72.25852007	0.01383920	188
48	0.09207758	72.63379392	0.01376770	192
49	0.08761405	72.99087610	0.01370034	196
50	0.08336689	73.33064846	0.01363686	200

	Future Value of 1	Future Value of 1 per Period	Payment for Sinking Fund of 1	**5.00%** Quarterly
Quarters				
1	1.01250000	1.00000000	1.00000000	
2	1.02515625	2.01250000	0.49689441	
3	1.03797070	3.03765625	0.32920117	Years
4	1.05094534	4.07562695	0.24536102	1
8	1.10448610	8.35888809	0.11963314	2
12	1.16075452	12.86036142	0.07775831	3
16	1.21988955	17.59116382	0.05684672	4
20	1.28203723	22.56297854	0.04432039	5
24	1.34735105	27.78808403	0.03598665	6
28	1.41599230	33.27938429	0.03004863	7
32	1.48813051	39.05044069	0.02560791	8
36	1.56394382	45.11550550	0.02216533	9
40	1.64361946	51.48955708	0.01942141	10
44	1.72735421	58.18833687	0.01718557	11
48	1.81535485	65.22838824	0.01533075	12
52	1.90783872	72.62709741	0.01376897	13
56	2.00503420	80.40273631	0.01243739	14
60	2.10718135	88.57450776	0.01128993	15
64	2.21453241	97.16259285	0.01029203	16
68	2.32735251	106.18820083	0.00941724	17
72	2.44592027	115.67362145	0.00864501	18
76	2.57052850	125.64228002	0.00795910	19
80	2.70148494	136.11879526	0.00734652	20
84	2.83911300	147.12904010	0.00679675	21
88	2.98375257	158.70020557	0.00630119	22
92	3.13576085	170.86086796	0.00585272	23
96	3.29551324	183.64105940	0.00544541	24
100	3.46340427	197.07234200	0.00507428	25
104	3.63984857	211.18788581	0.00473512	26
108	3.82528188	226.02255076	0.00442434	27
112	4.02016216	241.61297271	0.00413885	28
116	4.22497067	257.99765396	0.00387600	29
120	4.44021323	275.21705832	0.00363350	30
124	4.66642139	293.31371103	0.00340932	31
128	4.90415380	312.33230381	0.00320172	32
132	5.15399757	332.31980521	0.00300915	33
136	5.41656971	353.32557660	0.00283025	34
140	5.69251868	375.40149410	0.00266381	35
144	5.98252596	398.60207665	0.00250877	36
148	6.28730776	422.98462069	0.00236415	37
152	6.60761677	448.60934165	0.00222911	38
156	6.94424403	475.53952266	0.00210287	39
160	7.29802089	503.84167081	0.00198475	40
164	7.66982102	533.58568143	0.00187411	41
168	8.06056263	564.84501070	0.00177040	42
172	8.47121071	597.69685703	0.00167309	43
176	8.90277940	632.22235173	0.00158172	44
180	9.35633449	668.50675940	0.00149587	45
184	9.83299611	706.63968844	0.00141515	46
188	10.33394140	746.71531240	0.00133920	47
192	10.86040753	788.83260252	0.00126770	48
196	11.41369465	833.09557218	0.00120034	49
200	11.99516917	879.61353374	0.00113686	50

5.50% Quarterly	Present Value of 1	Present Value of 1 per Period	Payment to Pay Off a Loan of 1	
				Quarters
	0.98643650	0.98643650	1.01375000	1
	0.97305696	1.95949346	0.51033597	2
Years	0.95985890	2.91935237	0.34254173	3
1	0.94683986	3.86619222	0.25865243	4
2	0.89650571	7.52685712	0.13285758	8
3	0.84884734	10.99292054	0.09096764	12
4	0.80372250	14.27472754	0.07005388	16
5	0.76099649	17.38207320	0.05753054	20
6	0.72054181	20.32423193	0.04920235	24
7	0.68223771	23.10998508	0.04327134	28
8	0.64596985	25.74764719	0.03883850	32
9	0.61163000	28.24509080	0.03540438	36
10	0.57911566	30.60976996	0.03266931	40
11	0.54832979	32.84874243	0.03044257	44
12	0.51918050	34.96869081	0.02859701	48
13	0.49158079	36.97594243	0.02704461	52
14	0.46544829	38.87648826	0.02572249	56
15	0.44070499	40.67600081	0.02458452	60
16	0.41727705	42.37985101	0.02359612	64
17	0.39509454	43.99312429	0.02273082	68
18	0.37409126	45.52063573	0.02196806	72
19	0.35420451	46.96694445	0.02129157	76
20	0.33537495	48.33636719	0.02068836	80
21	0.31754637	49.63299122	0.02014789	84
22	0.30066556	50.86068653	0.01966155	88
23	0.28468214	52.02311738	0.01922222	92
24	0.26954839	53.12375324	0.01882397	96
25	0.25521916	54.16587914	0.01846181	100
26	0.24165167	55.15260548	0.01813151	104
27	0.22880544	56.08687730	0.01782948	108
28	0.21664211	56.97148311	0.01755264	112
29	0.20512538	57.80906314	0.01729833	116
30	0.19422089	58.60211729	0.01706423	120
31	0.18389608	59.35301258	0.01684834	124
32	0.17412014	60.06399016	0.01664891	128
33	0.16486388	60.73717207	0.01646438	132
34	0.15609970	61.37456754	0.01629339	136
35	0.14780141	61.97807897	0.01613474	140
36	0.13994427	62.54950765	0.01598734	144
37	0.13250481	63.09055910	0.01585023	148
38	0.12546084	63.60284817	0.01572257	152
39	0.11879132	64.08790389	0.01560357	156
40	0.11247636	64.54717397	0.01549255	160
41	0.10649710	64.98202919	0.01538887	164
42	0.10083570	65.39376745	0.01529198	168
43	0.09547526	65.78361764	0.01520135	172
44	0.09039978	66.15274334	0.01511653	176
45	0.08559411	66.50224626	0.01503709	180
46	0.08104392	66.83316956	0.01496263	184
47	0.07673561	67.14650092	0.01489281	188
48	0.07265634	67.44317555	0.01482730	192
49	0.06879391	67.72407891	0.01476580	196
50	0.06513682	67.99004941	0.01470803	200

	Future Value of 1	Future Value of 1 per Period	Payment for Sinking Fund of 1	**5.50%** Quarterly
Quarters				
1	1.01375000	1.00000000	1.00000000	
2	1.02768906	2.01375000	0.49658597	
3	1.04181979	3.04143906	0.32879173	Years
4	1.05614481	4.08325885	0.24490243	1
8	1.11544186	8.39577149	0.11910758	2
12	1.17806813	12.95040933	0.07721764	3
16	1.24421054	17.76076644	0.05630388	4
20	1.31406650	22.84120013	0.04378054	5
24	1.38784451	28.20687380	0.03545235	6
28	1.46576478	33.87380220	0.02952134	7
32	1.54805986	39.85889921	0.02508850	8
36	1.63497539	46.18002835	0.02165438	9
40	1.72677077	52.85605608	0.01891931	10
44	1.82371999	59.90690811	0.01669257	11
48	1.92611240	67.35362888	0.01484701	12
52	2.03425361	75.21844437	0.01329461	13
56	2.14846639	83.52482843	0.01197249	14
60	2.26909163	92.29757283	0.01083452	15
64	2.39648934	101.56286130	0.00984612	16
68	2.53103978	111.34834761	0.00898082	17
72	2.67314453	121.68323819	0.00821806	18
76	2.82322771	132.59837923	0.00754157	19
80	2.98173730	144.12634878	0.00693836	20
84	3.14914637	156.30155398	0.00639789	21
88	3.32595459	169.16033375	0.00591155	22
92	3.51268967	182.74106726	0.00547222	23
96	3.70990897	197.08428847	0.00507397	24
100	3.91820110	212.23280708	0.00471181	25
104	4.13818775	228.23183639	0.00438151	26
108	4.37052551	245.12912814	0.00407948	27
112	4.61590783	262.97511512	0.00380264	28
116	4.87506710	281.82306162	0.00354833	29
120	5.14877681	301.72922249	0.00331423	30
124	5.43785390	322.75301096	0.00309834	31
128	5.74316117	344.95717603	0.00289891	32
132	6.06560986	368.40798970	0.00271459	33
136	6.40616237	393.17544483	0.00254339	34
140	6.76583513	419.33346401	0.00238474	35
144	7.14570165	446.96012018	0.00223734	36
148	7.54689571	476.13786968	0.00210023	37
152	7.97061473	506.95379837	0.00197257	38
156	8.41812337	539.49988150	0.00185357	39
160	8.89075730	573.87325825	0.00174255	40
164	9.38992717	610.17652167	0.00163887	41
168	9.91712284	648.51802490	0.00154198	42
172	10.47391781	689.01220451	0.00145135	43
176	11.06197393	731.77992210	0.00136653	44
180	11.68304634	776.94882504	0.00128709	45
184	12.33898875	824.65372742	0.00121263	46
188	13.03175892	875.03701244	0.00114281	47
192	13.76342454	928.24905738	0.00107730	48
196	14.53616938	984.44868243	0.00101580	49
200	15.35229984	1043.80362470	0.00095803	50

6.00% Quarterly	Present Value of 1	Present Value of 1 per Period	Payment to Pay Off a Loan of 1	
				Quarters
	0.98522167	0.98522167	1.01500000	1
	0.97066175	1.95588342	0.51127792	2
Years	0.95631699	2.91220042	0.34338296	3
1	0.94218423	3.85438465	0.25944479	4
2	0.88771112	7.48592508	0.13358402	8
3	0.83638742	10.90750521	0.09167999	12
4	0.78803104	14.13126405	0.07076508	16
5	0.74247042	17.16863879	0.05824574	20
6	0.69954392	20.03040537	0.04992410	24
7	0.65909925	22.72671671	0.04400108	28
8	0.62099292	25.26713874	0.03957710	32
9	0.58508974	27.66068431	0.03615240	36
10	0.55126232	29.91584520	0.03342710	40
11	0.51939067	32.04062223	0.03121038	44
12	0.48936170	34.04255365	0.02937500	48
13	0.46106887	35.92874185	0.02783287	52
14	0.43441182	37.70587863	0.02652106	56
15	0.40929597	39.38026889	0.02539343	60
16	0.38563221	40.95785298	0.02441534	64
17	0.36333658	42.44422783	0.02356033	68
18	0.34233000	43.84466697	0.02280779	72
19	0.32253793	45.16413826	0.02214146	76
20	0.30389015	46.40732349	0.02154832	80
21	0.28632050	47.57863301	0.02101784	84
22	0.26976666	48.68222237	0.02054138	88
23	0.25416990	49.72200686	0.02011182	92
24	0.23947487	50.70167541	0.01972321	96
25	0.22562944	51.62470367	0.01937057	100
26	0.21258450	52.49436634	0.01904966	104
27	0.20029377	53.31374879	0.01875669	108
28	0.18871363	54.08575801	0.01848916	112
29	0.17780301	54.81313293	0.01824380	116
30	0.16752319	55.49845411	0.01801852	120
31	0.15783771	56.14415291	0.01781129	124
32	0.14871220	56.75252015	0.01762036	128
33	0.14011429	57.32571416	0.01744418	132
34	0.13201347	57.86576852	0.01728137	136
35	0.12438101	58.37459922	0.01713074	140
36	0.11718983	58.85401148	0.01699120	144
37	0.11041441	59.30570615	0.01686178	148
38	0.10403071	59.73128575	0.01674165	152
39	0.09801610	60.13226014	0.01663001	156
40	0.09234922	60.51005188	0.01652618	160
41	0.08700998	60.86600130	0.01642953	164
42	0.08197943	61.20137124	0.01633950	168
43	0.07723973	61.51735150	0.01625558	172
44	0.07277405	61.81506312	0.01617729	176
45	0.06856657	62.09556231	0.01610421	180
46	0.06460234	62.35984423	0.01603596	184
47	0.06086730	62.60884648	0.01597218	188
48	0.05734821	62.84345248	0.01591256	192
49	0.05403258	63.06449455	0.01585678	196
50	0.05090865	63.27275690	0.01580459	200

	Future Value of 1	Future Value of 1 per Period	Payment for Sinking Fund of 1	**6.00%** Quarterly
Quarters				
1	1.01500000	1.00000000	1.00000000	
2	1.03022500	2.01500000	0.49627792	
3	1.04567838	3.04522500	0.32838296	Years
4	1.06136355	4.09090338	0.24444479	1
8	1.12649259	8.43283911	0.11858402	2
12	1.19561817	13.04121143	0.07667999	3
16	1.26898555	17.93236984	0.05576508	4
20	1.34685501	23.12366710	0.04324574	5
24	1.42950281	28.63352080	0.03492410	6
28	1.51722218	34.48147867	0.02900108	7
32	1.61032432	40.68828801	0.02457710	8
36	1.70913954	47.27596921	0.02115240	9
40	1.81401841	54.26789391	0.01842710	10
44	1.92533302	61.68886794	0.01621038	11
48	2.04347829	69.56521929	0.01437500	12
52	2.16887337	77.92489152	0.01283287	13
56	2.30196314	86.79754292	0.01152106	14
60	2.44321978	96.21465171	0.01039343	15
64	2.59314442	106.20962774	0.00941534	16
68	2.75226896	116.81793098	0.00856033	17
72	2.92115796	128.07719738	0.00780779	18
76	3.10041059	140.02737234	0.00714146	19
80	3.29066279	152.71085247	0.00654832	20
84	3.49258954	166.17263597	0.00601784	21
88	3.70690723	180.46048230	0.00554138	22
92	3.93437622	195.62508162	0.00511182	23
96	4.17580352	211.72023459	0.00472321	24
100	4.43204565	228.80304330	0.00437057	25
104	4.70401171	246.93411381	0.00404966	26
108	4.99266657	266.17777118	0.00375689	27
112	5.29903432	286.60228769	0.00348916	28
116	5.62420188	308.28012505	0.00324380	29
120	5.96932287	331.28819149	0.00301852	30
124	6.33562172	355.70811457	0.00281129	31
128	6.72439796	381.62653084	0.00262036	32
132	7.13703090	409.13539316	0.00244418	33
136	7.57498445	438.33229695	0.00228137	34
140	8.03981240	469.32082642	0.00213074	35
144	8.53316383	502.21092209	0.00199120	36
148	9.05678906	537.11927060	0.00186178	37
152	9.61254580	574.16971974	0.00174165	38
156	10.20240574	613.49371578	0.00163001	39
160	10.82846158	655.23077185	0.00152618	40
164	11.49293443	699.52896186	0.00142953	41
168	12.19818169	746.54544610	0.00133950	42
172	12.94670543	796.44702875	0.00125558	43
176	13.74116125	849.41074969	0.00117729	44
180	14.58436769	905.62451261	0.00110421	45
184	15.47931627	965.28775161	0.00103596	46
188	16.42918208	1028.61213880	0.00097218	47
192	17.43733503	1095.82233523	0.00091256	48
196	18.50735182	1167.15678795	0.00085678	49
200	19.64302864	1242.86857597	0.00080459	50

6.50% Quarterly	Present Value of 1	Present Value of 1 per Period	Payment to Pay Off a Loan of 1	
				Quarters
	0.98400984	0.98400984	1.01625000	1
	0.96827537	1.95228521	0.51222024	2
Years	0.95279249	2.90507769	0.34422487	3
1	0.93755718	3.84263488	0.26023810	4
2	0.87901347	7.44532481	0.13431247	8
3	0.82412539	10.82305263	0.09239537	12
4	0.77266468	13.98986562	0.07148031	16
5	0.72441732	16.95893388	0.05896597	20
6	0.67918267	19.74260515	0.05065188	24
7	0.63677259	22.35245615	0.04473184	28
8	0.59701071	24.79934071	0.04032365	32
9	0.55973168	27.09343490	0.03690903	36
10	0.52478046	29.24427938	0.03419472	40
11	0.49201169	31.26081908	0.03198893	44
12	0.46128909	33.15144036	0.03016460	48
13	0.43248490	34.92400592	0.02863360	52
14	0.40547933	36.58588750	0.02733294	56
15	0.38016006	38.14399650	0.02621645	60
16	0.35642179	39.60481280	0.02524946	64
17	0.33416581	40.97441161	0.02440548	68
18	0.31329956	42.25848881	0.02366368	72
19	0.29373625	43.46238461	0.02300840	76
20	0.27539453	44.59110577	0.02242600	80
21	0.25819812	45.64934640	0.02190612	84
22	0.24207550	46.64150750	0.02144013	88
23	0.22695963	47.57171528	0.02102089	92
24	0.21278763	48.44383825	0.02064246	96
25	0.19950057	49.26150341	0.02029983	100
26	0.18704319	50.02811126	0.01998876	104
27	0.17536369	50.74684995	0.01970566	108
28	0.16441349	51.42070858	0.01944742	112
29	0.15414704	52.05248957	0.01921138	116
30	0.14452167	52.64482038	0.01899522	120
31	0.13549733	53.20016439	0.01879693	124
32	0.12703649	53.72083115	0.01861475	128
33	0.11910398	54.20898601	0.01844713	132
34	0.11166679	54.66665911	0.01829269	136
35	0.10469400	55.09575381	0.01815022	140
36	0.09815661	55.49805462	0.01801865	144
37	0.09202744	55.87523465	0.01789702	148
38	0.08628098	56.22886249	0.01778446	152
39	0.08089336	56.56040881	0.01768021	156
40	0.07584215	56.87125244	0.01758358	160
41	0.07110635	57.16268612	0.01749393	164
42	0.06666627	57.43592187	0.01741071	168
43	0.06250344	57.69209600	0.01733340	172
44	0.05860055	57.93227390	0.01726154	176
45	0.05494137	58.15745441	0.01719470	180
46	0.05151067	58.36857402	0.01713251	184
47	0.04829420	58.56651072	0.01707460	188
48	0.04527857	58.75208770	0.01702067	192
49	0.04245125	58.92607674	0.01697042	196
50	0.03980048	59.08920140	0.01692357	200

	Future Value of 1	Future Value of 1 per Period	Payment for Sinking Fund of 1	**6.50%** Quarterly
Quarters				
1	1.01625000	1.00000000	1.00000000	
2	1.03276406	2.01625000	0.49597024	
3	1.04954648	3.04901406	0.32797487	Years
4	1.06660161	4.09856054	0.24398810	1
8	1.13763899	8.47009181	0.11806247	2
12	1.21340758	13.13277409	0.07614537	3
16	1.29422248	18.10599851	0.05523031	4
20	1.38041977	23.41044768	0.04271597	5
24	1.47235795	29.06818170	0.03440188	6
28	1.57041936	35.10272991	0.02848781	7
32	1.67501182	41.53918874	0.02407365	8
36	1.78657030	48.40432608	0.02065931	9
40	1.90555875	55.72669261	0.01794472	10
44	2.03247203	63.53674053	0.01573893	11
48	2.16783794	71.86695020	0.01391460	12
52	2.31221944	80.75196525	0.01238360	13
56	2.46621697	90.22873659	0.01108294	14
60	2.63047099	100.33667614	0.00996645	15
64	2.80566459	111.11782074	0.00899946	16
68	2.99252636	122.61700690	0.00815548	17
72	3.19183343	134.88205737	0.00741388	18
76	3.40441467	147.96397993	0.00675840	19
80	3.63115417	161.91717958	0.00617600	20
84	3.87299488	176.79968477	0.00565612	21
88	4.13094257	192.67338875	0.00519013	22
92	4.40606999	209.60430695	0.00477089	23
96	4.69952134	227.66285155	0.00439246	24
100	5.01251702	246.92412426	0.00404983	25
104	5.34635872	267.46822873	0.00373876	26
108	5.70243481	289.38060360	0.00345566	27
112	6.08222614	312.75237790	0.00319742	28
116	6.48731219	337.68074996	0.00296138	29
120	6.91937762	364.26939171	0.00274522	30
124	7.38021930	392.62887977	0.00254693	31
128	7.87175377	422.87715536	0.00236475	32
132	8.39602524	455.14001477	0.00219713	33
136	8.95521403	489.55163252	0.00204269	34
140	9.55164569	526.25511937	0.00190022	35
144	10.18780066	565.40311750	0.00176865	36
148	10.86632457	607.15843526	0.00164702	37
152	11.59003927	651.69472440	0.00153446	38
156	12.36195453	699.19720203	0.00143021	39
160	13.18528059	749.86342109	0.00133358	40
164	14.06344149	803.90409185	0.00124393	41
168	15.00008932	861.54395822	0.00116071	42
172	15.99911940	923.02273242	0.00108340	43
176	17.06468649	988.59609189	0.00101154	44
180	18.20122207	1058.53674260	0.00094470	45
184	19.41345274	1133.13555316	0.00088251	46
188	20.70641992	1212.70276452	0.00082460	47
192	22.08550080	1297.56928017	0.00077067	48
196	23.55643069	1388.08804228	0.00072042	49
200	25.12532687	1484.63549959	0.00067357	50

7.00% Quarterly	Present Value of 1	Present Value of 1 per Period	Payment to Pay Off a Loan of 1	
				Quarters
	0.98280098	0.98280098	1.01750000	1
	0.96589777	1.94869875	0.51316295	2
Years	0.94928528	2.89798403	0.34506746	3
1	0.93295851	3.83094254	0.26103237	4
2	0.87041157	7.40505297	0.13504292	8
3	0.81205788	10.73954969	0.09311377	12
4	0.75761631	13.85049677	0.07219958	16
5	0.70682458	16.75288130	0.05969122	20
6	0.65943800	19.46068565	0.05138565	24
7	0.61522829	21.98695474	0.04548151	28
8	0.57398247	24.34385897	0.04107812	32
9	0.53550183	26.54275283	0.03767507	36
10	0.49960098	28.59422955	0.03497209	40
11	0.46610699	30.50817221	0.03277810	44
12	0.43485948	32.29380129	0.03096569	48
13	0.40570492	33.95971913	0.02944665	52
14	0.37850585	35.51395135	0.02815795	56
15	0.35313025	36.96398552	0.02705336	60
16	0.32945587	38.31680723	0.02609821	64
17	0.30736866	39.57893375	0.02526597	68
18	0.28676221	40.75644542	0.02453600	72
19	0.26753724	41.85501495	0.02389200	76
20	0.24960114	42.87993474	0.02332093	80
21	0.23286751	43.83614237	0.02281223	84
22	0.21725572	44.72824441	0.02235724	88
23	0.20269057	45.56053860	0.02194882	92
24	0.18910190	46.33703455	0.02158101	96
25	0.17642422	47.06147304	0.02124880	100
26	0.16459648	47.73744410	0.02094796	104
27	0.15356168	48.36790375	0.02067487	108
28	0.14326668	48.95618974	0.02042643	112
29	0.13366187	49.50503616	0.02019997	116
30	0.12470098	50.01708709	0.01999317	120
31	0.11634084	50.49480936	0.01980402	124
32	0.10854117	50.94050442	0.01963074	128
33	0.10126441	51.35631942	0.01947180	132
34	0.09447549	51.74425755	0.01932582	136
35	0.08814171	52.10618774	0.01919158	140
36	0.08223256	52.44385358	0.01906801	144
37	0.07671957	52.75888180	0.01895415	148
38	0.07157617	53.05279006	0.01884915	152
39	0.06677760	53.32699427	0.01875223	156
40	0.06230073	53.58281542	0.01866270	160
41	0.05812400	53.82148594	0.01857994	164
42	0.05422728	54.04415563	0.01850339	168
43	0.05059180	54.25189721	0.01843254	172
44	0.04720005	54.44571148	0.01836692	176
45	0.04403569	54.62653216	0.01830612	180
46	0.04108347	54.79523035	0.01824976	184
47	0.03832917	54.95261875	0.01819749	188
48	0.03575953	55.09945561	0.01814900	192
49	0.03336215	55.23644830	0.01810399	196
50	0.03112551	55.36425680	0.01806219	200

	Future Value of 1	Future Value of 1 per Period	Payment for Sinking Fund of 1	**7.00%** Quarterly
Quarters				
1	1.01750000	1.00000000	1.00000000	
2	1.03530625	2.01750000	0.49566295	
3	1.05342411	3.05280625	0.32756746	Years
4	1.07185903	4.10623036	0.24353237	1
8	1.14888178	8.50753045	0.11754292	2
12	1.23143931	13.22510371	0.07561377	3
16	1.31992935	18.28167721	0.05469958	4
20	1.41477820	23.70161119	0.04219122	5
24	1.51644279	29.51101637	0.03388565	6
28	1.62541290	35.73787977	0.02798151	7
32	1.74221349	42.41219955	0.02357812	8
36	1.86740727	49.56612949	0.02017507	9
40	2.00159734	57.23413390	0.01747209	10
44	2.14543019	65.45315367	0.01527810	11
48	2.29959872	74.26278425	0.01346569	12
52	2.46484566	83.70546635	0.01194665	13
56	2.64196708	93.82669043	0.01065795	14
60	2.83181628	104.67521588	0.00955336	15
64	3.03530785	116.30330585	0.00859821	16
68	3.25342213	128.76697910	0.00776597	17
72	3.48720990	142.12627984	0.00703600	18
76	3.73779742	156.44556699	0.00639200	19
80	4.00639192	171.79382424	0.00582093	20
84	4.29428737	188.24499239	0.00531223	21
88	4.60287070	205.87832555	0.00485724	22
92	4.93362853	224.77877295	0.00444882	23
96	5.28815429	245.03738819	0.00408101	24
100	5.66815594	266.75176789	0.00374880	25
104	6.07546413	290.02652188	0.00344796	26
108	6.51204110	314.97377716	0.00317487	27
112	6.97999007	341.71371802	0.00292643	28
116	7.48156539	370.37516514	0.00269997	29
120	8.01918343	401.09619608	0.00249317	30
124	8.59543418	434.02481054	0.00230402	31
128	9.21309376	469.31964334	0.00213074	32
132	9.87513775	507.15072863	0.00197180	33
136	10.58475558	547.70031907	0.00182582	34
140	11.34536587	591.16376380	0.00169158	35
144	12.16063287	637.75044955	0.00156801	36
148	13.03448416	687.68480942	0.00145415	37
152	13.97112957	741.20740402	0.00134915	38
156	14.97508141	798.57608042	0.00125223	39
160	16.05117625	860.06721433	0.00116270	40
164	17.20459823	925.97704155	0.00107994	41
168	18.44090399	996.62308511	0.00100339	42
172	19.76604949	1072.34568493	0.00093254	43
176	21.18641865	1153.50963741	0.00086692	44
180	22.70885418	1240.50595290	0.00080612	45
184	24.34069044	1333.75373934	0.00074976	46
188	26.08978887	1433.70222139	0.00069749	47
192	27.96457583	1540.83290453	0.00064900	48
196	29.97408316	1655.66189479	0.00060399	49
200	32.12799174	1778.74238505	0.00056219	50

7.50% Quarterly	Present Value of 1	Present Value of 1 per Period	Payment to Pay Off a Loan of 1	
				Quarters
	0.98159509	0.98159509	1.01875000	1
	0.96352892	1.94512402	0.51410604	2
Years	0.94579526	2.89091928	0.34591073	3
1	0.92838799	3.81930727	0.26182759	4
2	0.86190426	7.36510626	0.13577537	8
3	0.80018156	10.65698346	0.09383518	12
4	0.74287895	13.71312271	0.07292285	16
5	0.68967989	16.55040568	0.06042148	20
6	0.64029053	19.18450511	0.05212540	24
7	0.59443804	21.62997138	0.04623215	28
8	0.55186913	23.90031290	0.04184046	32
9	0.51234867	26.00807069	0.03844960	36
10	0.47565836	27.96488770	0.03575913	40
11	0.44159550	29.78157312	0.03357781	44
12	0.40997196	31.46816204	0.03177015	48
13	0.38061305	33.03397093	0.03027187	52
14	0.35335658	34.48764910	0.02899589	56
15	0.32805200	35.83722645	0.02790395	60
16	0.30455954	37.09015786	0.02696133	64
17	0.28274942	38.25336432	0.02614149	68
18	0.26250116	39.33327123	0.02542377	72
19	0.24370293	40.33584384	0.02479185	76
20	0.22625087	41.26662020	0.02423266	80
21	0.21004859	42.13074180	0.02373564	84
22	0.19500659	42.93298191	0.02329212	88
23	0.18104178	43.67777199	0.02289494	92
24	0.16807701	44.36922616	0.02253814	96
25	0.15604068	45.01116391	0.02221671	100
26	0.14486629	45.60713120	0.02192640	104
27	0.13449212	46.16042007	0.02166358	108
28	0.12486087	46.67408682	0.02142516	112
29	0.11591933	47.15096885	0.02120847	116
30	0.10761812	47.59370041	0.02101118	120
31	0.09991137	48.00472707	0.02083128	124
32	0.09275651	48.38631928	0.02066700	128
33	0.08611403	48.74058491	0.02051678	132
34	0.07994723	49.06948086	0.02037922	136
35	0.07422205	49.37482391	0.02025324	140
36	0.06890684	49.65830073	0.02013762	144
37	0.06397230	49.92147721	0.02003146	148
38	0.05939112	50.16580709	0.01993390	152
39	0.05513800	50.39264001	0.01984417	156
40	0.05118946	50.60322898	0.01976158	160
41	0.04752368	50.79873724	0.01968553	164
42	0.04412041	50.98024476	0.01961544	168
43	0.04096086	51.14875417	0.01955082	172
44	0.03802757	51.30519628	0.01949120	176
45	0.03530434	51.45043525	0.01943618	180
46	0.03277612	51.58527337	0.01938538	184
47	0.03042896	51.71045546	0.01933845	188
48	0.02824988	51.82667301	0.01929508	192
49	0.02622685	51.93456798	0.01925500	196
50	0.02434869	52.03473638	0.01921793	200

96

	Future Value of 1	Future Value of 1 per Period	Payment for Sinking Fund of 1	**7.50%** Quarterly
Quarters				
1	1.01875000	1.00000000	1.00000000	
2	1.03785156	2.01875000	0.49535604	
3	1.05731128	3.05660156	0.32716073	Years
4	1.07713587	4.11391284	0.24307759	1
8	1.16022167	8.54515591	0.11702537	2
12	1.24971638	13.31820675	0.07508518	3
16	1.34611433	18.45934100	0.05417285	4
20	1.44994803	23.99722804	0.04167148	5
24	1.56179102	29.96218784	0.03337540	6
28	1.68226112	36.38725998	0.02748215	7
32	1.81202379	43.30793563	0.02309046	8
36	1.95179582	50.76244358	0.01969960	9
40	2.10234928	58.79196146	0.01700913	10
44	2.26451581	67.44084315	0.01482781	11
48	2.43919120	76.75686381	0.01302815	12
52	2.62734032	86.79148380	0.01152187	13
56	2.83000249	97.60013289	0.01024589	14
60	3.04829718	109.24251648	0.00915395	15
64	3.28343023	121.78294541	0.00821133	16
68	3.53670046	135.29069118	0.00739149	17
72	3.80950691	149.84036862	0.00667377	18
76	4.10335653	165.51234803	0.00604185	19
80	4.41987248	182.39319913	0.00548266	20
84	4.76080317	200.57616930	0.00498564	21
88	5.12803185	220.16169862	0.00454212	22
92	5.52358703	241.25797469	0.00414494	23
96	5.94965369	263.98153029	0.00378814	24
100	6.40858538	288.45788702	0.00346671	25
104	6.90291716	314.82224872	0.00317640	26
108	7.43537966	343.22024829	0.00291358	27
112	8.00891410	373.80875214	0.00267516	28
116	8.62668863	406.75672671	0.00245847	29
120	9.29211572	442.24617183	0.00226118	30
124	10.00887111	480.47312603	0.00208128	31
128	10.78091405	521.64874943	0.00191700	32
132	11.61250919	566.00049019	0.00176678	33
136	12.50825014	613.77334088	0.00162927	34
140	13.47308485	665.23119177	0.00150324	35
144	14.51234291	720.65828853	0.00138762	36
148	15.63176504	780.36080239	0.00128146	37
152	16.83753478	844.66852135	0.00118390	38
156	18.13631260	913.93667189	0.00109417	39
160	19.53527277	988.54788119	0.00101158	40
164	21.04214295	1068.91429071	0.00093553	41
168	22.66524687	1155.47983282	0.00086544	42
172	24.41355031	1248.72268296	0.00080082	43
176	26.29671065	1349.15790108	0.00074120	44
180	28.32513019	1457.34027670	0.00068618	45
184	30.51001363	1573.86739352	0.00063538	46
188	32.86342994	1699.38293039	0.00058845	47
192	35.39837907	1834.58021687	0.00054508	48
196	38.12886368	1980.20606309	0.00050500	49
200	41.06996659	2137.06488504	0.00046793	50

8.00% Quarterly

Years	Present Value of 1	Present Value of 1 per Period	Payment to Pay Off a Loan of 1	Quarters
	0.98039216	0.98039216	1.02000000	1
	0.96116878	1.94156094	0.51504950	2
Years	0.94232233	2.88388327	0.34675467	3
1	0.92384543	3.80772870	0.26262375	4
2	0.85349037	7.32548144	0.13650980	8
3	0.78849318	10.57534122	0.09455960	12
4	0.72844581	13.57770931	0.07365013	16
5	0.67297133	16.35143334	0.06115672	20
6	0.62172149	18.91392560	0.05287110	24
7	0.57437455	21.28127236	0.04698967	28
8	0.53063330	23.46833482	0.04261061	32
9	0.49022315	25.48884248	0.03923285	36
10	0.45289042	27.35547924	0.03655575	40
11	0.41840074	29.07996307	0.03438794	44
12	0.38653761	30.67011957	0.03260104	48
13	0.35710100	32.14494992	0.03110909	52
14	0.32990613	33.50469365	0.02984656	56
15	0.30478227	34.76088668	0.02876797	60
16	0.28157170	35.92141486	0.02783855	64
17	0.26012873	36.99356351	0.02703173	68
18	0.24031874	37.98406314	0.02632683	72
19	0.22201737	38.89913170	0.02570725	76
20	0.20510973	39.74451359	0.02516071	80
21	0.18948968	40.52551579	0.02467581	84
22	0.17505918	41.24704110	0.02424416	88
23	0.16172762	41.91361895	0.02385859	92
24	0.14941132	42.52943386	0.02351313	96
25	0.13803297	43.09835164	0.02320274	100
26	0.12752113	43.62394373	0.02292319	104
27	0.11780981	44.10950958	0.02267085	108
28	0.10883805	44.55809737	0.02244261	112
29	0.10054954	44.97252314	0.02223580	116
30	0.09289223	45.35538850	0.02204810	120
31	0.08581806	45.70909691	0.02187748	124
32	0.07928262	46.03586881	0.02172209	128
33	0.07324489	46.33775553	0.02158067	132
34	0.06766696	46.61665220	0.02145156	136
35	0.06251381	46.87430961	0.02133365	140
36	0.05775310	47.11234523	0.02122586	144
37	0.05335493	47.33225335	0.02112724	148
38	0.04929171	47.53541446	0.02103695	152
39	0.04553792	47.72310392	0.02095421	156
40	0.04207000	47.89649997	0.02087835	160
41	0.03886618	48.05669112	0.02080876	164
42	0.03590634	48.20468298	0.02074487	168
43	0.03317191	48.34140458	0.02068620	172
44	0.03064572	48.46771421	0.02063229	176
45	0.02831190	48.58440478	0.02058274	180
46	0.02615582	48.69220883	0.02053717	184
47	0.02416394	48.79180311	0.02049525	188
48	0.02232374	48.88381283	0.02045667	192
49	0.02062369	48.96881559	0.02042116	196
50	0.01905310	49.04734500	0.02038846	200

	Future Value of 1	Future Value of 1 per Period	Payment for Sinking Fund of 1	**8.00%** Quarterly
Quarters				
1	1.02000000	1.00000000	1.00000000	
2	1.04040000	2.02000000	0.49504950	
3	1.06120800	3.06040000	0.32675467	Years
4	1.08243216	4.12160800	0.24262375	1
8	1.17165938	8.58296905	0.11650980	2
12	1.26824179	13.41208973	0.07455960	3
16	1.37278571	18.63928525	0.05365013	4
20	1.48594740	24.29736980	0.04115672	5
24	1.60843725	30.42186247	0.03287110	6
28	1.74102421	37.05121031	0.02698967	7
32	1.88454059	44.22702961	0.02261061	8
36	2.03988734	51.99436719	0.01923285	9
40	2.20803966	60.40198318	0.01655575	10
44	2.39005314	69.50265712	0.01438794	11
48	2.58707039	79.35351927	0.01260184	12
52	2.80032819	90.01640927	0.01110909	13
56	3.03116529	101.55826432	0.00984656	14
60	3.28103079	114.05153942	0.00876797	15
64	3.55149324	127.57466216	0.00783855	16
68	3.84425050	142.21252513	0.00703173	17
72	4.16114038	158.05701875	0.00632683	18
76	4.50415216	175.20760821	0.00570751	19
80	4.87543916	193.77195780	0.00516071	20
84	5.27733214	213.86660683	0.00467581	21
88	5.71235402	235.61770119	0.00424416	22
92	6.18323570	259.16178523	0.00385859	23
96	6.69293318	284.64665898	0.00351313	24
100	7.24464612	312.23230591	0.00320274	25
104	7.84183795	342.09189731	0.00292319	26
108	8.48825759	374.41287932	0.00267085	27
112	9.18796299	409.39814970	0.00244261	28
116	9.94534663	447.26733148	0.00223580	29
120	10.76516303	488.25815171	0.00204810	30
124	11.65255868	532.62793379	0.00187748	31
128	12.61310426	580.65521285	0.00172219	32
132	13.65282969	632.64148426	0.00158067	33
136	14.77826193	688.91309632	0.00145156	34
140	15.99646598	749.82329890	0.00133365	35
144	17.31508922	815.75446104	0.00122586	36
148	18.74240943	887.12047130	0.00112724	37
152	20.28738672	964.36933593	0.00103695	38
156	21.95971983	1047.98599133	0.00095421	39
160	23.76990696	1138.49534824	0.00087835	40
164	25.72931174	1236.46558695	0.00080876	41
168	27.85023448	1342.51172404	0.00074487	42
172	30.14598047	1457.29947328	0.00068620	43
176	32.63098849	1581.54942463	0.00063229	44
180	35.32083136	1716.04156785	0.00058274	45
184	38.23240378	1861.62018894	0.00053717	46
188	41.38398340	2019.19917021	0.00049525	47
192	44.79535455	2189.76772728	0.00045667	48
196	48.48793238	2374.39661894	0.00042116	49
200	52.48489738	2574.24486894	0.00038846	50

8.50% Quarterly	Present Value of 1	Present Value of 1 per Period	Payment to Pay Off a Loan of 1	
				Quarters
	0.97919217	0.97919217	1.02125000	1
	0.95881730	1.93800947	0.51599335	2
Years	0.93886639	2.87687585	0.34759929	3
1	0.91933061	3.79620647	0.26342087	4
2	0.84516878	7.28617528	0.13724622	8
3	0.77698953	10.49461045	0.09528701	12
4	0.71431026	13.44423312	0.07438139	16
5	0.65668729	16.15589234	0.06189692	20
6	0.60371273	18.64881287	0.05362272	24
7	0.55501159	20.94063103	0.04775405	28
8	0.51023915	23.04756962	0.04338852	32
9	0.46907847	24.98454276	0.04002475	36
10	0.43123819	26.76526147	0.03736186	40
11	0.39645047	28.40233069	0.03520838	44
12	0.36446906	29.90733854	0.03343661	48
13	0.33506756	31.29093832	0.03195813	52
14	0.30803787	32.56292396	0.03070977	56
15	0.28318864	33.73229930	0.02964518	60
16	0.26034399	34.80734185	0.02872957	64
17	0.23934220	35.79566137	0.02793635	68
18	0.22003461	36.70425376	0.02724480	72
19	0.20228455	37.53955056	0.02663857	76
20	0.18596638	38.30746448	0.02610457	80
21	0.17096459	39.01343125	0.02563220	84
22	0.15717298	39.66244812	0.02521277	88
23	0.14449393	40.25910919	0.02483910	92
24	0.13283769	40.80763798	0.02450522	96
25	0.12212176	41.31191729	0.02420609	100
26	0.11227027	41.77551670	0.02393747	104
27	0.10321350	42.20171782	0.02369572	108
28	0.09488733	42.59353756	0.02347774	112
29	0.08723282	42.95374945	0.02328085	116
30	0.08019581	43.28490326	0.02310274	120
31	0.07372646	43.58934310	0.02294139	124
32	0.06777899	43.86922396	0.02279502	128
33	0.06231130	44.12652700	0.02266211	132
34	0.05728469	44.36307357	0.02254127	136
35	0.05266357	44.58053806	0.02243101	140
36	0.04841523	44.78045983	0.02233117	144
37	0.04450960	44.96425404	0.02223989	148
38	0.04091904	45.13322168	0.02215663	152
39	0.03761813	45.28855880	0.02208063	156
40	0.03458349	45.43136497	0.02201123	160
41	0.03179367	45.56265105	0.02194780	164
42	0.02922889	45.68334637	0.02188981	168
43	0.02687101	45.79430527	0.02183678	172
44	0.02470334	45.89631318	0.02178824	176
45	0.02271054	45.99009218	0.02174381	180
46	0.02087850	46.07630608	0.02170313	184
47	0.01919424	46.15556516	0.02166586	188
48	0.01764585	46.22843046	0.02163171	192
49	0.01622237	46.29541776	0.02160041	196
50	0.01491372	46.35700124	0.02157171	200

	Future Value of 1	Future Value of 1 per Period	Payment for Sinking Fund of 1	**8.50%** Quarterly
Quarters				
1	1.02125000	1.00000000	1.00000000	
2	1.04295156	2.02125000	0.49474335	
3	1.06511428	3.06420156	0.32634929	Years
4	1.08774796	4.12931585	0.24217087	1
8	1.18319563	8.62097074	0.11599622	2
12	1.28701863	13.50675920	0.07403701	3
16	1.39995189	18.82126563	0.05313139	4
20	1.52279482	24.60210917	0.04064692	5
24	1.65641696	30.89020995	0.03237272	6
28	1.80176417	37.73007876	0.02650405	7
32	1.95986531	45.17013211	0.02213852	8
36	2.13183949	53.26303498	0.01877475	9
40	2.31890406	62.06607358	0.01611186	10
44	2.52238317	71.64156087	0.01395838	11
48	2.74371715	82.05727766	0.01218661	12
52	2.98447274	93.38695237	0.01070813	13
56	3.24635414	105.71078293	0.00945977	14
60	3.53121510	119.11600451	0.00839518	15
64	3.84107202	133.69750696	0.00747957	16
68	4.17811826	149.55850653	0.00668635	17
72	4.54473963	166.81127649	0.00599480	18
76	4.94353126	185.57794183	0.00538857	19
80	5.37731606	205.99134382	0.00485457	20
84	5.84916458	228.19598021	0.00438220	21
88	6.36241685	252.34902820	0.00396277	22
92	6.92070596	278.62145691	0.00358910	23
96	7.52798380	307.19923769	0.00325522	24
100	8.18854904	338.28466049	0.00295609	25
104	8.90707752	372.07916591	0.00268747	26
108	9.68865542	408.87790212	0.00244572	27
112	10.53881519	448.88542047	0.00222774	28
116	11.46357474	492.40351701	0.00203085	29
120	12.46948005	539.74023782	0.00185274	30
124	13.56365151	591.23065939	0.00169139	31
128	14.75383429	647.23926051	0.00154502	32
132	16.04845317	708.16250221	0.00141211	33
136	17.45667223	774.43163419	0.00129127	34
140	18.98845963	846.51574743	0.00118131	35
144	20.65465826	924.92509468	0.00108117	36
148	22.46706242	1010.21470233	0.00098989	37
152	24.43850136	1102.98829920	0.00090663	38
156	26.58293004	1203.90259011	0.00083063	39
160	28.91552797	1313.67190434	0.00076123	40
164	31.45280661	1433.07325217	0.00069780	41
168	34.21272628	1562.95182489	0.00063981	42
172	37.21482327	1704.22697764	0.00058678	43
176	40.48034816	1857.89873708	0.00053824	44
180	44.03241620	2025.05488019	0.00049381	45
184	47.89617098	2206.87863414	0.00045313	46
188	52.09896235	2404.65705190	0.00041586	47
192	56.67054011	2619.79012269	0.00038171	48
196	61.64326449	2853.80068194	0.00035041	49
200	67.05233530	3108.34519078	0.00032171	50

9.00% Quarterly	Present Value of 1	Present Value of 1 per Period	Payment to Pay Off a Loan of 1	
				Quarters
	0.97799511	0.97799511	1.02250000	1
	0.95647444	1.93446955	0.51693758	2
Years	0.93542732	2.86989687	0.34844458	3
1	0.91484335	3.78474021	0.26421893	4
2	0.83693835	7.24718461	0.13798462	8
3	0.76566748	10.41477882	0.09601740	12
4	0.70046580	13.31263131	0.07511663	16
5	0.64081647	15.96371237	0.06264207	20
6	0.58624668	18.38903624	0.05438023	24
7	0.53632388	20.60782764	0.04852525	28
8	0.49065233	22.63767419	0.04417415	32
9	0.44887002	24.49466579	0.04082522	36
10	0.41064575	26.19352221	0.03817738	40
11	0.37567653	27.74770969	0.03603901	44
12	0.34368518	29.16954777	0.03428233	48
13	0.31441810	30.47030687	0.03281884	52
14	0.28764330	31.66029768	0.03158530	56
15	0.26314856	32.74895285	0.03053533	60
16	0.24073971	33.74490179	0.02963411	64
17	0.22023912	34.65603905	0.02885500	68
18	0.20148429	35.48958691	0.02817728	72
19	0.18432657	36.25215262	0.02758457	76
20	0.16862993	36.94978079	0.02706376	80
21	0.15426997	37.58800127	0.02660423	84
22	0.14113286	38.17187304	0.02619730	88
23	0.12911445	38.70602423	0.02583577	92
24	0.11811950	39.19468890	0.02551366	96
25	0.10806084	39.64174052	0.02522594	100
26	0.09885874	40.05072272	0.02496804	104
27	0.09044026	40.42487737	0.02473724	108
28	0.08273867	40.76717025	0.02452954	112
29	0.07569292	41.08031462	0.02434226	116
30	0.06924717	41.36679266	0.02417398	120
31	0.06335031	41.62887519	0.02402179	124
32	0.05795561	41.86863965	0.02388422	128
33	0.05302030	42.08796657	0.02375975	132
34	0.04850527	42.28865464	0.02364700	136
35	0.04437472	42.47223449	0.02354499	140
36	0.04059592	42.64018129	0.02345206	144
37	0.03713891	42.79382631	0.02336786	148
38	0.03397628	42.93438742	0.02329135	152
39	0.03108298	43.06297883	0.02322180	156
40	0.02843605	43.18061982	0.02315854	160
41	0.02601453	43.28824290	0.02310096	164
42	0.02379922	43.38670115	0.02304854	168
43	0.02177256	43.47677503	0.02300079	172
44	0.01991848	43.55917852	0.02295727	176
45	0.01822229	43.63456481	0.02291761	180
46	0.01667054	43.70353145	0.02288145	184
47	0.01525093	43.76662512	0.02284846	188
48	0.01395222	43.82434595	0.02281837	192
49	0.01276409	43.87715146	0.02279091	196
50	0.01167714	43.92546023	0.02276584	200

	Future Value of 1	Future Value of 1 per Period	Payment for Sinking Fund of 1	**9.00%** Quarterly
Quarters				
1	1.02250000	1.00000000	1.00000000	
2	1.04550625	2.02250000	0.49443758	
3	1.06903014	3.06800625	0.32594458	Years
4	1.09308332	4.13703639	0.24171893	1
8	1.19483114	8.65916186	0.11548462	2
12	1.30604999	13.60222177	0.07351740	3
16	1.42762146	19.00539811	0.05261663	4
20	1.56050920	24.91152003	0.04014207	5
24	1.70576658	31.36740338	0.03188023	6
28	1.86454499	38.42421178	0.02602525	7
32	2.03810303	46.13791226	0.02167415	8
36	2.22781642	54.56961864	0.01832522	9
40	2.43518897	63.78617624	0.01567738	10
44	2.66186444	73.86064161	0.01353901	11
48	2.90963961	84.87287165	0.01178233	12
52	3.18047852	96.91015661	0.01031884	13
56	3.47652802	110.06791200	0.00908530	14
60	3.80013479	124.45043493	0.00803533	15
64	4.15386394	140.17173083	0.00713411	16
68	4.54051939	157.35641713	0.00635500	17
72	4.96316600	176.14071106	0.00567728	18
76	5.42415396	196.67350941	0.00508457	19
80	5.93014530	219.11756877	0.00456376	20
84	6.48214290	243.65079567	0.00410423	21
88	7.08552228	270.46765674	0.00369730	22
92	7.74506621	299.78072025	0.00333577	23
96	8.46600267	331.82234099	0.00301366	24
100	9.25404630	366.84650213	0.00272594	25
104	10.11544364	405.13082842	0.00246834	26
108	11.05702270	446.97878687	0.00223724	27
112	12.08624707	492.72220917	0.00202954	28
116	13.21127506	542.72333614	0.00184256	29
120	14.44102439	597.37886184	0.00167398	30
124	15.78524287	657.12190526	0.00152179	31
128	17.25458566	722.42602944	0.00138422	32
132	18.86069976	793.80887824	0.00125975	33
136	20.61631629	871.83627950	0.00114700	34
140	22.53535143	957.12673022	0.00104479	35
144	24.63301673	1050.35629917	0.00095206	36
148	26.92593968	1152.26398579	0.00086786	37
152	29.43229551	1263.65757810	0.00079135	38
156	32.17195125	1385.42005568	0.00072180	39
160	35.16662325	1518.51658877	0.00065854	40
164	38.44004925	1664.00218887	0.00060096	41
168	42.01817661	1823.03007148	0.00054854	42
172	45.92936794	1996.86079717	0.00050079	43
176	50.20462593	2186.87226373	0.00045727	44
180	54.87783913	2394.57062819	0.00041761	45
184	59.98605053	2621.60224573	0.00038145	46
188	65.56975119	2869.76671970	0.00034846	47
192	71.67320125	3141.03116651	0.00031837	48
196	78.34478069	3437.54580830	0.00029091	49
200	85.63737288	3761.66101701	0.00026584	50

9.50% Quarterly	Present Value of 1	Present Value of 1 per Period	Payment to Pay Off a Loan of 1	
				Quarters
	0.97680098	0.97680098	1.02375000	1
	0.95414015	1.93094113	0.51788218	2
Years	0.93200503	2.86294615	0.34929054	3
1	0.91038342	3.77332958	0.26501793	4
2	0.82879798	7.20850627	0.13872500	8
3	0.75452394	10.33583419	0.09675078	12
4	0.68690609	13.18290168	0.07585583	16
5	0.62534791	15.77482473	0.06339215	20
6	0.56930637	18.13446850	0.05514361	24
7	0.51828708	20.28264908	0.04930322	28
8	0.47183997	22.23831706	0.04496743	32
9	0.42955529	24.01872477	0.04163418	36
10	0.39106001	25.63957844	0.03900220	40
11	0.35601455	27.11517675	0.03687972	44
12	0.32410975	28.45853699	0.03513884	48
13	0.29506414	29.68150988	0.03369101	52
14	0.26862150	30.79488413	0.03247293	56
15	0.24454856	31.80848159	0.03143816	60
16	0.22263296	32.73124391	0.03055185	64
17	0.20268135	33.57131143	0.02978734	68
18	0.18451774	34.33609498	0.02912387	72
19	0.16798190	35.03234124	0.02854505	76
20	0.15292793	35.66619230	0.02803776	80
21	0.13922306	36.24323979	0.02759135	84
22	0.12674636	36.76857426	0.02719714	88
23	0.11538779	37.24683005	0.02684792	92
24	0.10504713	37.68222620	0.02653771	96
25	0.09563316	38.07860363	0.02626147	100
26	0.08706285	38.43945908	0.02601493	104
27	0.07926057	38.76797589	0.02579449	108
28	0.07215751	39.06705216	0.02559702	112
29	0.06569100	39.33932623	0.02541986	116
30	0.05980400	39.58720003	0.02526069	120
31	0.05444457	39.81286023	0.02511751	124
32	0.04956543	40.01829753	0.02498857	128
33	0.04512355	40.20532425	0.02487233	132
34	0.04107973	40.37559027	0.02476744	136
35	0.03739831	40.53059764	0.02467272	140
36	0.03404680	40.67171377	0.02458711	144
37	0.03099564	40.80018356	0.02450969	148
38	0.02821792	40.91714033	0.02443964	152
39	0.02568912	41.02361583	0.02437620	156
40	0.02338695	41.12054936	0.02431874	160
41	0.02129109	41.20879604	0.02426666	164
42	0.01938306	41.28913436	0.02421945	168
43	0.01764602	41.36227303	0.02417662	172
44	0.01606464	41.42885726	0.02413776	176
45	0.01462498	41.48947444	0.02410250	180
46	0.01331434	41.54465932	0.02407048	184
47	0.01212116	41.59489871	0.02404141	188
48	0.01103490	41.64063583	0.02401500	192
49	0.01004599	41.68227414	0.02399101	196
50	0.00914570	41.72018097	0.02396922	200

	Future Value of 1	Future Value of 1 per Period	Payment for Sinking Fund of 1	**9.50%** Quarterly
Quarters				
1	1.02375000	1.00000000	1.00000000	
2	1.04806406	2.02375000	0.49413218	
3	1.07295558	3.07181406	0.32554054	Years
4	1.09843828	4.14476965	0.24126793	1
8	1.20656665	8.69754328	0.11497500	2
12	1.32533900	13.69848412	0.07300078	3
16	1.45580309	19.19170897	0.05210583	4
20	1.59910984	25.22567743	0.03964215	5
24	1.75652346	31.85361935	0.03139361	6
28	1.92943261	39.13400446	0.02555322	7
32	2.11936263	47.13105817	0.02121743	8
36	2.32798904	55.91532807	0.01788418	9
40	2.55715228	65.56430639	0.01525220	10
44	2.80887395	76.16311352	0.01312972	11
48	3.08537466	87.80524900	0.01138884	12
52	3.38909364	100.59341625	0.00994101	13
56	3.72271018	114.64042868	0.00872293	14
60	4.08916737	130.07020485	0.00768816	15
64	4.49169796	147.01886162	0.00680185	16
68	4.93385298	165.63591500	0.00603734	17
72	5.41953298	186.08559908	0.00537387	18
76	5.95302248	208.54831486	0.00479505	19
80	6.53902777	233.22222173	0.00428776	20
84	7.18271841	260.32498554	0.00384135	21
88	7.88977285	290.09569877	0.00344714	22
92	8.66642851	322.79698978	0.00309792	23
96	9.51953682	358.71733960	0.00278771	24
100	10.45662364	398.17362684	0.00251147	25
104	11.48595567	441.51392309	0.00226493	26
108	12.61661338	489.12056353	0.00204449	27
112	13.85857109	541.41351972	0.00184702	28
116	15.22278498	598.85410454	0.00166986	29
120	16.72128974	661.94904167	0.00151069	30
124	18.36730473	731.25493583	0.00136751	31
128	20.17535059	807.38318295	0.00123857	32
132	22.16137739	891.00536370	0.00112233	33
136	24.34290524	982.85916080	0.00101744	34
140	26.73917894	1083.75490277	0.00092272	35
144	29.37133770	1194.58264001	0.00083711	36
148	32.26260164	1316.32006899	0.00075969	37
152	35.43847662	1450.04112098	0.00068964	38
156	38.92697928	1596.92544320	0.00062620	39
160	42.75888413	1758.26880534	0.00056874	40
164	46.96799510	1935.49453038	0.00051666	41
168	51.59144371	2130.16605082	0.00046945	42
172	56.67001664	2344.00070071	0.00042662	43
176	62.24851556	2578.88486555	0.00038776	44
180	68.37615231	2836.89062337	0.00035250	45
184	75.10698307	3120.29402399	0.00032048	46
188	82.50038523	3431.59516766	0.00029141	47
192	90.62158118	3773.54026019	0.00026500	48
196	99.54221368	4149.14538918	0.00024101	49
200	109.34097789	4561.72538499	0.00021922	50

10.00% Quarterly	Present Value of 1	Present Value of 1 per Period	Payment to Pay Off a Loan of 1	
				Quarters
	0.97560976	0.97560976	1.02500000	1
	0.95181440	1.92742415	0.51882716	2
Years	0.92859941	2.85602356	0.35013717	3
1	0.90595064	3.76197421	0.26581788	4
2	0.82074657	7.17013717	0.13946735	8
3	0.74355589	10.25776460	0.09748713	12
4	0.67362493	13.05500266	0.07659899	16
5	0.61027094	15.58916229	0.06414713	20
6	0.55287535	17.88498583	0.05591282	24
7	0.50087778	19.96488866	0.05008793	28
8	0.45377055	21.84917796	0.04576831	32
9	0.41109372	23.55625107	0.04245158	36
10	0.37243062	25.10277505	0.03983623	40
11	0.33740376	26.50384945	0.03773037	44
12	0.30567116	27.77315371	0.03600599	48
13	0.27692298	28.92308072	0.03457446	52
14	0.25087855	29.96485784	0.03337243	56
15	0.22728359	30.90865649	0.03235340	60
16	0.20590771	31.76369148	0.03148249	64
17	0.18654223	32.53831099	0.03073300	68
18	0.16899805	33.24007803	0.03008417	72
19	0.15310389	33.87584433	0.02951956	76
20	0.13870457	34.45181722	0.02902605	80
21	0.12565949	34.97362023	0.02859298	84
22	0.11384130	35.44634801	0.02821165	88
23	0.10313460	35.87461604	0.02787486	92
24	0.09343486	36.26260574	0.02757662	96
25	0.08464737	36.61410526	0.02731188	100
26	0.07668634	36.93254648	0.02707039	104
27	0.06947404	37.22103851	0.02686653	108
28	0.06294005	37.48239804	0.02667919	112
29	0.05702058	37.71917688	0.02651171	116
30	0.05165783	37.93368683	0.02636179	120
31	0.04679944	38.12802225	0.02622743	124
32	0.04239799	38.30408055	0.02610688	128
33	0.03841048	38.46358068	0.02599862	132
34	0.03479800	38.60807993	0.02590131	136
35	0.03152527	38.73898911	0.02581379	140
36	0.02856034	38.85758637	0.02573500	144
37	0.02587426	38.96502964	0.02566404	148
38	0.02344080	39.06236793	0.02560009	152
39	0.02123621	39.15055162	0.02554242	156
40	0.01923896	39.23044170	0.02549041	160
41	0.01742955	39.30281816	0.02544347	164
42	0.01579031	39.36838766	0.02540109	168
43	0.01430524	39.42779039	0.02536282	172
44	0.01295984	39.48160634	0.02532825	176
45	0.01174098	39.53036093	0.02529701	180
46	0.01063675	39.57453018	0.02526878	184
47	0.00963637	39.61454534	0.02524325	188
48	0.00873007	39.65079710	0.02522017	192
49	0.00790901	39.68363941	0.02519930	196
50	0.00716518	39.71339292	0.02518042	200

	Future Value of 1	Future Value of 1 per Period	Payment for Sinking Fund of 1	**10.00%** Quarterly
Quarters				
1	1.02500000	1.00000000	1.00000000	
2	1.05062500	2.02500000	0.49382716	
3	1.07689062	3.07562500	0.32513717	Years
4	1.10381289	4.15251562	0.24081788	1
8	1.21840290	8.73611590	0.11446735	2
12	1.34488882	13.79555297	0.07248713	3
16	1.48450562	19.38022483	0.05159899	4
20	1.63861644	25.54465761	0.03914713	5
24	1.80872595	32.34903798	0.03091282	6
28	1.99649502	39.85980005	0.02508793	7
32	2.20375694	48.15027751	0.02076831	8
36	2.43253532	57.30141263	0.01745158	9
40	2.68506384	67.40255354	0.01483623	10
44	2.96380808	78.55232308	0.01273037	11
48	3.27148956	90.85958243	0.01100599	12
52	3.61111235	104.44449395	0.00957446	13
56	3.98599236	119.43969440	0.00837243	14
60	4.39978975	135.99158995	0.00735340	15
64	4.85654464	154.26178563	0.00648249	16
68	5.36071658	174.42866314	0.00573300	17
72	5.91722806	196.68912249	0.00508417	18
76	6.53151261	221.26050447	0.00451956	19
80	7.20956782	248.38271265	0.00402605	20
84	7.95801389	278.32055566	0.00359298	21
88	8.78415832	311.36633268	0.00321165	22
92	9.69606718	347.84268735	0.00287486	23
96	10.70264395	388.10575783	0.00257662	24
100	11.81371635	432.54865404	0.00231188	25
104	13.04013239	481.60529578	0.00207639	26
108	14.39386623	535.75464930	0.00186653	27
112	15.88813509	595.52540373	0.00167919	28
116	17.53752832	661.50113296	0.00151171	29
120	19.35814983	734.32599335	0.00136179	30
124	21.36777533	814.71101301	0.00122743	31
128	23.58602585	903.44103392	0.00110688	32
132	26.03455937	1001.38237478	0.00099862	33
136	28.73728223	1109.49128935	0.00090131	34
140	31.72058257	1228.82330285	0.00081379	35
144	35.01358794	1360.54351761	0.00073500	36
148	38.64844972	1505.93798862	0.00066404	37
152	42.66065700	1666.42627995	0.00060009	38
156	47.08938312	1843.57532470	0.00054242	39
160	51.97786810	2039.11472387	0.00049041	40
164	57.37384083	2254.95363330	0.00044347	41
168	63.32998510	2493.19940382	0.00040109	42
172	69.90445391	2756.17815646	0.00036282	43
176	77.16143734	3046.45749359	0.00032825	44
180	85.17178919	3366.87156779	0.00029701	45
184	94.01371883	3720.54875323	0.00026878	46
188	103.77355474	4110.94218964	0.00024325	47
192	114.54658743	4541.86349716	0.00022017	48
196	126.43799978	5017.51999125	0.00019930	49
200	139.56389402	5542.55576093	0.00018042	50

10.50% Quarterly	Present Value of 1	Present Value of 1 per Period	Payment to Pay Off a Loan of 1	
				Quarters
	0.97442144	0.97442144	1.02625000	1
	0.94949714	1.92391857	0.51977252	2
Years	0.92521037	2.84912894	0.35098447	3
1	0.90154481	3.75067375	0.26661876	4
2	0.81278305	7.13207423	0.14021166	8
3	0.73276035	10.18055828	0.09822644	12
4	0.66061629	12.92890328	0.07734608	16
5	0.59557519	15.40665946	0.06490700	20
6	0.53693772	17.64046769	0.05668784	24
7	0.48407342	19.65434591	0.05087933	28
8	0.43641388	21.46994738	0.04657673	32
9	0.39344667	23.10679347	0.04327732	36
10	0.35470981	24.58248358	0.04067937	40
11	0.31978679	25.91288434	0.03859084	44
12	0.28830212	27.11230024	0.03688363	48
13	0.25991728	28.19362743	0.03546901	52
14	0.23432708	29.16849235	0.03428357	56
15	0.21125636	30.04737676	0.03328078	60
16	0.19045708	30.83973045	0.03242570	64
17	0.17170559	31.55407280	0.03169163	68
18	0.15480028	32.19808445	0.03105775	72
19	0.13955939	32.77868981	0.03050763	76
20	0.12581905	33.30213156	0.03002811	80
21	0.11343151	33.77403776	0.02960854	84
22	0.10226359	34.19948234	0.02924021	88
23	0.09219521	34.58303970	0.02891591	92
24	0.08311811	34.92883384	0.02862964	96
25	0.07493470	35.24058276	0.02837638	100
26	0.06755699	35.52163838	0.02815185	104
27	0.06090566	35.77502262	0.02795246	108
28	0.05490918	36.00345987	0.02777511	112
29	0.04950309	36.20940628	0.02761713	116
30	0.04462925	36.39507621	0.02747624	120
31	0.04023527	36.56246596	0.02735045	124
32	0.03627390	36.71337533	0.02723803	128
33	0.03270254	36.84942688	0.02713746	132
34	0.02948281	36.97208346	0.02704743	136
35	0.02658007	37.08266386	0.02696678	140
36	0.02396313	37.18235704	0.02689448	144
37	0.02160383	37.27223492	0.02682962	148
38	0.01947682	37.35326385	0.02677142	152
39	0.01755923	37.42631506	0.02671917	156
40	0.01583043	37.49217400	0.02667223	160
41	0.01427184	37.55154879	0.02663006	164
42	0.01286671	37.60507782	0.02659215	168
43	0.01159991	37.65333664	0.02655807	172
44	0.01045784	37.69684413	0.02652742	176
45	0.00942821	37.73606808	0.02649985	180
46	0.00849996	37.77143023	0.02647504	184
47	0.00766309	37.80331080	0.02645271	188
48	0.00690862	37.83205255	0.02643261	192
49	0.00622843	37.85796453	0.02641452	196
50	0.00561521	37.88132535	0.02639823	200

	Future Value of 1	Future Value of 1 per Period	Payment for Sinking Fund of 1	**10.50%** Quarterly
Quarters				
1	1.02625000	1.00000000	1.00000000	
2	1.05318906	2.02625000	0.49352252	
3	1.08083528	3.07943906	0.32473447	Years
4	1.10920720	4.16027434	0.24036876	1
8	1.23034062	8.77488059	0.11396166	2
12	1.36470267	13.89343508	0.07197644	3
16	1.51373803	19.57097258	0.05109608	4
20	1.67904912	25.86853807	0.03865700	5
24	1.86241338	32.85384305	0.03043784	6
28	2.06580233	40.60199364	0.02462933	7
32	2.29140282	49.19629807	0.02032673	8
36	2.54164051	58.72916244	0.01702732	9
40	2.81920596	69.30308425	0.01442937	10
44	3.12708355	81.03175446	0.01234084	11
48	3.46858360	94.04127993	0.01063363	12
52	3.84737791	108.47153926	0.00921901	13
56	4.26753928	124.47768683	0.00803357	14
60	4.73358530	142.23182098	0.00703078	15
64	5.25052690	161.92483443	0.00617570	16
68	5.82392225	183.76846677	0.00544163	17
72	6.45993650	207.99758107	0.00480775	18
76	7.16540809	234.87268912	0.00425763	19
80	7.94792225	264.68275252	0.00377811	20
84	8.81589260	297.74828951	0.00335854	21
88	9.77865156	334.42482126	0.00299021	22
92	10.84655073	375.10669439	0.00266591	23
96	12.03107218	420.23132104	0.00237964	24
100	13.34495190	470.28388188	0.00212638	25
104	14.80231675	525.80254280	0.00190185	26
108	16.41883633	587.38424132	0.00170246	27
112	18.21189150	655.69110478	0.00152511	28
116	20.20076120	731.45756963	0.00136713	29
120	22.40682980	815.49827807	0.00122624	30
124	24.85381697	908.71683707	0.00110045	31
128	27.56803277	1012.11513403	0.00098803	32
132	30.57866047	1126.80611330	0.00088746	33
136	33.91807041	1254.02112730	0.00079743	34
140	37.62216795	1395.13020766	0.00071678	35
144	41.73077962	1551.64874752	0.00064448	36
148	46.28808128	1725.26023908	0.00057962	37
152	51.34307309	1917.83135576	0.00052142	38
156	56.95010641	2131.43262516	0.00046917	39
160	63.16946815	2368.36069140	0.00042223	40
164	70.06802898	2631.16300868	0.00038006	41
168	77.71996233	2922.66523155	0.00034215	42
172	86.20754190	3246.00159636	0.00030807	43
176	95.62202629	3604.64862068	0.00027742	44
180	106.06464017	4002.46248280	0.00024985	45
184	117.64766269	4443.72048348	0.00022504	46
188	130.49563468	4933.16703548	0.00020271	47
192	144.74669774	5476.06467565	0.00018261	48
196	160.55407950	6078.25064774	0.00016452	49
200	178.08774119	6746.19966454	0.00014823	50

11.00% Quarterly	Present Value of 1	Present Value of 1 per Period	Payment to Pay Off a Loan of 1	
				Quarters
	0.97323601	0.97323601	1.02750000	1
	0.94718833	1.92042434	0.52071825	2
Years	0.92183779	2.84226213	0.35183243	3
1	0.89716573	3.73942787	0.26742059	4
2	0.80490635	7.09431441	0.14095795	8
3	0.72213440	10.10420366	0.09896871	12
4	0.64787424	12.80457315	0.07809710	16
5	0.58125057	15.22725213	0.06567173	20
6	0.52147809	17.40079670	0.05746863	24
7	0.46785227	19.35082640	0.05167738	28
8	0.41974103	21.10032623	0.04739263	32
9	0.37657727	22.66991753	0.04411132	36
10	0.33785222	24.07810106	0.04153151	40
11	0.30310944	25.34147507	0.03946100	44
12	0.27193940	26.47493094	0.03777158	48
13	0.24397471	27.49182871	0.03637444	52
14	0.21888575	28.40415454	0.03520612	56
15	0.19637679	29.22266201	0.03422002	60
16	0.17618253	29.95699887	0.03338118	64
17	0.15806493	30.61582074	0.03266285	68
18	0.14181044	31.20689314	0.03204420	72
19	0.12722747	31.73718304	0.03150308	76
20	0.11414412	32.21294098	0.03104342	80
21	0.10240620	32.63977469	0.03063747	84
22	0.09187533	33.02271527	0.03028219	88
23	0.08242740	33.36627644	0.02997038	92
24	0.07395104	33.67450775	0.02969605	96
25	0.06634634	33.95104232	0.02945418	100
26	0.05952366	34.19913966	0.02924050	104
27	0.05340259	34.42172409	0.02905142	108
28	0.04791097	34.62141921	0.02888385	112
29	0.04298408	34.80057884	0.02873515	116
30	0.03856385	34.96131471	0.02860304	120
31	0.03459816	35.10552143	0.02848555	124
32	0.03104028	35.23489875	0.02838095	128
33	0.02784828	35.35097166	0.02828777	132
34	0.02498452	35.45510829	0.02820468	136
35	0.02241526	35.54853611	0.02813055	140
36	0.02011020	35.63235634	0.02806438	144
37	0.01804218	35.70755699	0.02800524	148
38	0.01618683	35.77502443	0.02795246	152
39	0.01452227	35.83555391	0.02790525	156
40	0.01302888	35.88985888	0.02786302	160
41	0.01168907	35.93857944	0.02782525	164
42	0.01048703	35.98228986	0.02779145	168
43	0.00940860	36.02150534	0.02776119	172
44	0.00844108	36.05668814	0.02773411	176
45	0.00757304	36.08825293	0.02770985	180
46	0.00679428	36.11657179	0.02768812	184
47	0.00609559	36.14197849	0.02766866	188
48	0.00546876	36.16477251	0.02765122	192
49	0.00490638	36.18522253	0.02763559	196
50	0.00440184	36.20356959	0.02762159	200

	Future Value of 1	Future Value of 1 per Period	Payment for Sinking Fund of 1	**11.00%** Quarterly
Quarters				
1	1.02750000	1.00000000	1.00000000	
2	1.05575625	2.02750000	0.49321825	
3	1.08478955	3.08325625	0.32433243	Years
4	1.11462126	4.16804580	0.23992059	1
8	1.24238055	8.81383825	0.11345795	2
12	1.38478378	13.99213729	0.07146871	3
16	1.54350944	19.76397948	0.05059710	4
20	1.72042843	26.19739750	0.03817173	5
24	1.91762610	33.36822199	0.02996863	6
28	2.13742682	41.36097542	0.02417738	7
32	2.38242138	50.26986831	0.01989263	8
36	2.65549752	60.19990972	0.01661132	9
40	2.95987399	71.26814499	0.01403151	10
44	3.29913847	83.60503532	0.01196100	11
48	3.67728988	97.35599556	0.01027158	12
52	4.09878547	112.68310818	0.00887444	13
56	4.56859343	129.76703375	0.00770612	14
60	5.09225136	148.80914038	0.00672002	15
64	5.67593162	170.03387726	0.00588118	16
68	6.32651406	193.69142022	0.00516285	17
72	7.05166706	220.06062054	0.00454420	18
76	7.85993802	249.45229131	0.00400878	19
80	8.76085402	282.21287345	0.00354342	20
84	9.76503414	318.72851423	0.00313747	21
88	10.88431465	359.42962374	0.00278219	22
92	12.13188851	404.79594568	0.00247038	23
96	13.52246085	455.36221257	0.00219605	24
100	15.07242234	511.72444867	0.00195418	25
104	16.80004237	574.54699524	0.00174050	26
108	18.72568438	644.57034123	0.00155142	27
112	20.87204591	722.61985131	0.00138385	28
116	23.26442610	809.61549455	0.00123515	29
120	25.93102392	906.58268797	0.00110304	30
124	28.90327054	1014.66438322	0.00098555	31
128	32.21619981	1135.13453851	0.00088095	32
132	35.90886120	1269.41313471	0.00078777	33
136	40.02478010	1419.08291273	0.00070468	34
140	44.61247080	1585.90802920	0.00063055	35
144	49.72600839	1771.85485061	0.00056438	36
148	55.42566610	1979.11513089	0.00050528	37
152	61.77862575	2210.13184551	0.00045246	38
156	68.85976964	2467.62798691	0.00040525	39
160	76.75256316	2754.63866033	0.00036302	40
164	85.55003861	3074.54685861	0.00032525	41
168	95.35589178	3431.12333747	0.00029145	42
172	106.28570419	3828.57106141	0.00026119	43
176	118.46830546	4271.57474402	0.00023411	44
180	132.04729183	4765.35606666	0.00020985	45
184	147.18271873	5315.73522637	0.00018812	46
188	164.05298731	5929.19953853	0.00016866	47
192	182.85694733	6612.97990275	0.00015122	48
196	203.81624092	7375.13603348	0.00013559	49
200	227.17791514	8224.65145978	0.00012159	50

11.50% Quarterly	Present Value of 1	Present Value of 1 per Period	Payment to Pay Off a Loan of 1	
				Quarters
	0.97205346	0.97205346	1.02875000	1
	0.94488793	1.91694140	0.52166436	2
Years	0.91848159	2.83542299	0.35268107	3
1	0.89281321	3.72823620	0.26822335	4
2	0.79711543	7.05685472	0.14170619	8
3	0.71167518	10.02868931	0.09971393	12
4	0.63539300	12.68198248	0.07885203	16
5	0.56728727	15.05087768	0.06644131	20
6	0.50648157	17.16585860	0.05825517	24
7	0.45219343	19.05414150	0.05248203	28
8	0.40372427	20.74002542	0.04821595	32
9	0.36045036	22.24520486	0.04495351	36
10	0.32181484	23.58904894	0.04239255	40
11	0.28732054	24.78885068	0.04034072	44
12	0.25652358	25.86004953	0.03866969	48
13	0.22902764	26.81643001	0.03729057	52
14	0.20447890	27.67029914	0.03613983	56
15	0.18256146	28.43264477	0.03517084	60
16	0.16299329	29.11327703	0.03434859	64
17	0.14552256	29.72095449	0.03364629	68
18	0.12992446	30.26349696	0.03304311	72
19	0.11599828	30.74788605	0.03252256	76
20	0.10356479	31.18035502	0.03207148	80
21	0.09246402	31.56646903	0.03167918	84
22	0.08255309	31.91119672	0.03133696	88
23	0.07370449	32.21897415	0.03103761	92
24	0.06580435	32.49376191	0.03077514	96
25	0.05875099	32.73909605	0.03054452	100
26	0.05245366	32.95813361	0.03034152	104
27	0.04683132	33.15369324	0.03016255	108
28	0.04181162	33.32829146	0.03000454	112
29	0.03732997	33.48417506	0.02986485	116
30	0.03332869	33.62334999	0.02974124	120
31	0.02975629	33.74760721	0.02963173	124
32	0.02656681	33.85854570	0.02953464	128
33	0.02371920	33.95759305	0.02944849	132
34	0.02117681	34.04602383	0.02937201	136
35	0.01890694	34.12497600	0.02930405	140
36	0.01688037	34.19546553	0.02924364	144
37	0.01507101	34.25839952	0.02918992	148
38	0.01345560	34.31458782	0.02914212	152
39	0.01201334	34.36475348	0.02909958	156
40	0.01072567	34.40954204	0.02906171	160
41	0.00957602	34.44952986	0.02902797	164
42	0.00854959	34.48523151	0.02899792	168
43	0.00763319	34.51710641	0.02897114	172
44	0.00681501	34.54556475	0.02894728	176
45	0.00608453	34.57097273	0.02892600	180
46	0.00543235	34.59365731	0.02890703	184
47	0.00485008	34.61391040	0.02889012	188
48	0.00433021	34.63199263	0.02887504	192
49	0.00386607	34.64813668	0.02886158	196
50	0.00345168	34.66255031	0.02884958	200

	Future Value of 1	Future Value of 1 per Period	Payment for Sinking Fund of 1	**11.50%** Quarterly
Quarters				
1	1.02875000	1.00000000	1.00000000	
2	1.05832656	2.02875000	0.49291436	
3	1.08875345	3.08707656	0.32393107	Years
4	1.12005511	4.17583001	0.23947335	1
8	1.25452346	8.85298977	0.11295619	2
12	1.40513541	14.09166647	0.07096393	3
16	1.57382910	19.95927309	0.05010203	4
20	1.76277533	26.53131589	0.03769131	5
24	1.97440552	33.89236603	0.02950517	6
28	2.21144300	42.13714787	0.02373203	7
32	2.47693804	51.37175793	0.01946595	8
36	2.77430712	61.71503014	0.01620351	9
40	3.10736787	73.00006507	0.01364255	10
44	3.48043335	86.27594267	0.01159072	11
48	3.89827717	100.80964072	0.00991969	12
52	4.36628528	117.08818353	0.00854057	13
56	4.89048015	135.32104864	0.00738983	14
60	5.47760729	155.74286242	0.00642084	15
64	6.13522206	178.61641937	0.00559859	16
68	6.87178683	204.23606377	0.00489629	17
72	7.69677998	232.93147748	0.00429311	18
76	8.62081777	265.07192232	0.00377256	19
80	9.65579102	301.07099189	0.00332148	20
84	10.81501810	341.39193382	0.00292918	21
88	12.11341632	386.55361099	0.00258696	22
92	13.56769388	437.13717841	0.00228761	23
96	15.19656490	493.79356173	0.00202514	24
100	17.02099021	557.25183355	0.00179452	25
104	19.06444712	628.32859535	0.00159152	26
108	21.35323147	707.93848581	0.00141255	27
112	23.91679608	797.10595066	0.00125454	28
116	26.78812973	896.97842556	0.00111485	29
120	30.00418167	1008.84110172	0.00099124	30
124	33.60633709	1134.13346409	0.00088173	31
128	37.64094969	1274.46781517	0.00078464	32
132	42.15993815	1431.65002262	0.00069849	33
136	47.22145428	1607.70275772	0.00062201	34
140	52.89063131	1804.89152381	0.00055405	35
144	59.24042202	2025.75380947	0.00049364	36
148	66.35253758	2273.13174178	0.00043992	37
152	74.31849897	2550.20865967	0.00039212	38
156	83.24081475	2860.55007822	0.00034958	39
160	93.23430016	3208.14957081	0.00031171	40
164	104.42755459	3597.48015973	0.00027797	41
168	116.96461645	4033.55187645	0.00024792	42
172	131.00681668	4521.97623235	0.00022114	43
176	146.73485485	5069.03842944	0.00019728	44
180	164.35112441	5681.77824035	0.00017600	45
184	184.08231721	6368.08059845	0.00015703	46
188	206.18234058	7136.77706362	0.00014012	47
192	230.93558475	7997.75946970	0.00012504	48
196	258.66058245	8962.10721574	0.00011158	49
200	289.71410788	10042.22983930	0.00009958	50

12.00% Quarterly	Present Value of 1	Present Value of 1 per Period	Payment to Pay Off a Loan of 1	
				Quarters
	0.97087379	0.97087379	1.03000000	1
	0.94259591	1.91346970	0.52261084	2
Years	0.91514166	2.82861135	0.35353036	3
1	0.88848705	3.71709840	0.26902705	4
2	0.78940923	7.01969219	0.14245639	8
3	0.70137988	9.95400399	0.10046209	12
4	0.62316694	12.56110203	0.07961086	16
5	0.55367575	14.87747486	0.06721571	20
6	0.49193374	16.93554212	0.05904742	24
7	0.43707675	18.76410823	0.05329323	28
8	0.38833703	20.38876553	0.04904662	32
9	0.34503243	21.83225250	0.04580379	36
10	0.30655684	23.11477197	0.04326238	40
11	0.27237178	24.25427392	0.04122985	44
12	0.24199890	25.26670664	0.03957777	48
13	0.21501280	26.16623999	0.03821718	52
14	0.19103609	26.96546373	0.03708447	56
15	0.16973309	27.67556367	0.03613296	60
16	0.15080565	28.30647826	0.03532760	64
17	0.13398887	28.86703771	0.03464159	68
18	0.11904737	29.36508752	0.03405404	72
19	0.10577205	29.80759833	0.03354849	76
20	0.09397710	30.20076345	0.03311175	80
21	0.08349743	30.55008556	0.03273313	84
22	0.07418639	30.86045374	0.03240320	88
23	0.06591364	31.13621184	0.03211694	92
24	0.05856342	31.38121934	0.03186619	96
25	0.05203284	31.59890534	0.03164667	100
26	0.04623050	31.79231652	0.03145414	104
27	0.04107520	31.96415986	0.03128504	108
28	0.03649479	32.11684043	0.03113631	112
29	0.03242515	32.25249515	0.03100535	116
30	0.02880932	32.37302261	0.03088992	120
31	0.02559671	32.48010969	0.03078807	124
32	0.02274234	32.57525518	0.03069815	128
33	0.02020628	32.65979071	0.03061869	132
34	0.01795302	32.73489944	0.03054844	136
35	0.01595102	32.80163257	0.03048629	140
36	0.01417228	32.86092409	0.03043128	144
37	0.01259188	32.91360384	0.03038257	148
38	0.01118773	32.96040911	0.03033943	152
39	0.00994015	33.00199499	0.03030120	156
40	0.00883169	33.03894351	0.03026731	160
41	0.00784685	33.07177179	0.03023727	164
42	0.00697182	33.10093929	0.03021062	168
43	0.00619437	33.12685423	0.03018699	172
44	0.00550362	33.14987933	0.03016602	176
45	0.00488990	33.17033683	0.03014742	180
46	0.00434461	33.18851305	0.03013091	184
47	0.00386013	33.20466239	0.03011625	188
48	0.00342967	33.21901086	0.03010324	192
49	0.00304722	33.23175930	0.03009170	196
50	0.00270742	33.24308612	0.03008144	200

	Future Value of 1	Future Value of 1 per Period	Payment for Sinking Fund of 1	**12.00%** Quarterly
Quarters				
1	1.03000000	1.00000000	1.00000000	
2	1.06090000	2.03000000	0.49261084	
3	1.09272700	3.09090000	0.32353036	Years
4	1.12550881	4.18362700	0.23902705	1
8	1.26677008	8.89233605	0.11245639	2
12	1.42576089	14.19202956	0.07046209	3
16	1.60470644	20.15688130	0.04961085	4
20	1.80611123	26.87037449	0.03721571	5
24	2.03279411	34.42647022	0.02904742	6
28	2.28792768	42.93092252	0.02329323	7
32	2.57508276	52.50275852	0.01904662	8
36	2.89827833	63.27594427	0.01580379	9
40	3.26203779	75.40125973	0.01326238	10
44	3.67145227	89.04840911	0.01122985	11
48	4.13225188	104.40839598	0.00957777	12
52	4.65088590	121.69619651	0.00821718	13
56	5.23461305	141.15376831	0.00708447	14
60	5.89160310	163.05343680	0.00613296	15
64	6.63105120	187.70170662	0.00532760	16
68	7.46330654	215.44355145	0.00464159	17
72	8.40001727	246.66724222	0.00405404	18
76	9.45429344	281.80978126	0.00354849	19
80	10.64089056	321.36301855	0.00311175	20
84	11.97641607	365.88053558	0.00273313	21
88	13.47956180	415.98539321	0.00240393	22
92	15.17136556	472.37885189	0.00211694	23
96	17.07550559	535.85018645	0.00186619	24
100	19.21863198	607.28773270	0.00164667	25
104	21.63073961	687.69132035	0.00145414	26
108	24.34558800	778.18626662	0.00128504	27
112	27.40117378	880.03912590	0.00113631	28
116	30.84026249	994.67541634	0.00100535	29
120	34.71098714	1123.69957119	0.00088992	30
124	39.06752182	1268.91739416	0.00078807	31
128	43.97084000	1432.36133329	0.00069815	32
132	49.48956780	1616.31892673	0.00061869	33
136	55.70094456	1823.36481880	0.00054844	34
140	62.69190383	2056.39679440	0.00048629	35
144	70.56029008	2318.67630299	0.00043128	36
148	79.41622812	2613.87427066	0.00038257	37
152	89.38366441	2946.12214686	0.00033943	38
156	100.60210176	3320.07005862	0.00030120	39
160	113.22855183	3740.95172780	0.00026731	40
164	127.43973263	4214.65775442	0.00023727	41
168	143.43454182	4747.81806074	0.00021062	42
172	161.43684048	5347.89468263	0.00018699	43
176	181.69858622	6023.28620726	0.00016602	44
180	204.50335955	6783.44531842	0.00014742	45
184	230.17033285	7639.01109503	0.00013091	46
188	259.05873742	8601.95791415	0.00011625	47
192	291.57289128	9685.76304262	0.00010324	48
196	328.16785789	10905.59526305	0.00009170	49
200	369.35581522	12278.52717385	0.00008144	50

12.50% Quarterly	Present Value of 1	Present Value of 1 per Period	Payment to Pay Off a Loan of 1	Quarters
	0.96969697	0.96969697	1.03125000	1
	0.94031221	1.91000918	0.52355769	2
Years	0.91181790	2.82182709	0.35438033	3
1	0.88418706	3.70601414	0.26983167	4
2	0.78178675	6.98282389	0.14320854	8
3	0.69124573	9.88013665	0.10121317	12
4	0.61119053	12.44190310	0.08037356	16
5	0.54040675	14.70698385	0.06799491	20
6	0.47782066	16.70973892	0.05984534	24
7	0.42248284	18.48054904	0.05411095	28
8	0.37355386	20.04627643	0.04988458	32
9	0.33029149	21.43067233	0.04666209	36
10	0.29203946	22.65473726	0.04414088	40
11	0.25821751	23.73703963	0.04212825	44
12	0.22831258	24.69899730	0.04049567	48
13	0.20187103	25.54012704	0.03915407	52
14	0.17849175	26.28826393	0.03803979	56
15	0.15782010	26.94975689	0.03710609	60
16	0.13954249	27.53464040	0.03631789	64
17	0.12338166	28.05178683	0.03564835	68
18	0.10909247	28.50904102	0.03507609	72
19	0.09645815	28.91333925	0.03458611	76
20	0.08528705	29.27081451	0.03416372	80
21	0.07540970	29.58688951	0.03379875	84
22	0.06667628	29.86635894	0.03348249	88
23	0.05895431	30.11346218	0.03320774	92
24	0.05212664	30.33194768	0.03296854	96
25	0.04608970	30.52512973	0.03275989	100
26	0.04075191	30.69593879	0.03257760	104
27	0.03603231	30.84696596	0.03241810	108
28	0.03185931	30.98050222	0.03227837	112
29	0.02816959	31.09857326	0.03215582	116
30	0.02490718	31.20927014	0.03204823	120
31	0.02202261	31.29527651	0.03195370	124
32	0.01947211	31.37689261	0.03187059	128
33	0.01721698	31.44905651	0.03179746	132
34	0.01522303	31.51286290	0.03173307	136
35	0.01346001	31.56927968	0.03167636	140
36	0.01190117	31.61916267	0.03162639	144
37	0.01052286	31.66326856	0.03158234	148
38	0.00930417	31.70226642	0.03154349	152
39	0.00822663	31.73674782	0.03150921	156
40	0.00727388	31.76723583	0.03147897	160
41	0.00643147	31.79419293	0.03145228	164
42	0.00568662	31.81802806	0.03142872	168
43	0.00502804	31.83910276	0.03140792	172
44	0.00444573	31.85773674	0.03138955	176
45	0.00393085	31.87421267	0.03137332	180
46	0.00347561	31.88878047	0.03135899	184
47	0.00307309	31.90166113	0.03134633	188
48	0.00271719	31.91305005	0.03133514	192
49	0.00240250	31.92311998	0.03132526	196
50	0.00212426	31.93202368	0.03131652	200

Quarters	Future Value of 1	Future Value of 1 per Period	Payment for Sinking Fund of 1	**12.50%** Quarterly
1	1.03125000	1.00000000	1.00000000	
2	1.06347656	2.03125000	0.49230769	
3	1.09671021	3.09472656	0.32313033	Years
4	1.13098240	4.19143677	0.23858167	1
8	1.27912119	8.93187798	0.11195854	2
12	1.44666355	14.29323355	0.06996317	3
16	1.63615101	20.35683234	0.04912356	4
20	1.85045800	27.21465584	0.03674491	5
24	2.09283542	34.97073352	0.02859534	6
28	2.36696003	43.74272086	0.02286095	7
32	2.67699013	53.66368414	0.01863458	8
36	3.02762872	64.88411899	0.01541209	9
40	3.42419479	77.57423332	0.01289088	10
44	3.87270404	91.92652927	0.01087825	11
48	4.37996011	108.15872337	0.00924567	12
52	4.95365779	126.51704920	0.00790407	13
56	5.60249977	147.27999259	0.00678979	14
60	6.33632863	170.76251611	0.00585609	15
64	7.16627615	197.32083689	0.00506789	16
68	8.10493220	227.35783024	0.00439835	17
72	9.16653566	261.32914104	0.00382659	18
76	10.36719049	299.75009563	0.00333611	19
80	11.72510997	343.20351902	0.00291372	20
84	13.26089300	392.34857605	0.00254875	21
88	14.99783658	447.93077055	0.00223249	22
92	16.96228919	510.79325422	0.00195774	23
96	19.18405053	581.88961681	0.00171854	24
100	21.69682349	662.29835154	0.00150989	25
104	24.53872548	753.23921523	0.00132760	26
108	27.75286661	856.09173142	0.00116810	27
112	31.38800365	972.41611693	0.00102837	28
116	35.49927967	1103.97694950	0.00090582	29
120	40.14906049	1252.76993554	0.00079823	30
124	45.40788075	1421.05218384	0.00070370	31
128	51.35551390	1611.37644474	0.00062059	32
132	58.08218231	1826.62983391	0.00054746	33
136	65.68992589	2070.07762838	0.00048307	34
140	74.29414997	2345.41279900	0.00042636	35
144	84.02537596	2656.81203080	0.00037639	36
148	95.03122128	3008.99908102	0.00033234	37
152	107.47863862	3407.31643596	0.00029349	38
156	121.55644855	3857.80635362	0.00025921	39
160	137.47820379	4367.30252141	0.00022897	40
164	155.48542874	4943.53371954	0.00020228	41
168	175.85128320	5595.24106236	0.00017872	42
172	198.88470614	6332.31059639	0.00015792	43
176	224.93510207	7165.92326620	0.00013955	44
180	254.39764135	8108.72452333	0.00012332	45
184	287.71925472	9175.01615088	0.00010899	46
188	325.40541293	10380.97321384	0.00009633	47
192	368.02779456	11744.88942597	0.00008514	48
196	416.23295799	13287.45465559	0.00007526	49
200	470.75214936	15032.06877957	0.00006652	50

13.00% Quarterly	Present Value of 1	Present Value of 1 per Period	Payment to Pay Off a Loan of 1	
				Quarters
	0.96852300	0.96852300	1.03250000	1
	0.93803681	1.90655981	0.52450492	2
Years	0.90851022	2.81507003	0.35523095	3
1	0.87991305	3.69498308	0.27063723	4
2	0.77424698	6.94624692	0.14396263	8
3	0.68127002	9.80707639	0.10196719	12
4	0.59945838	12.32435758	0.08114013	16
5	0.52747125	14.53934615	0.06877888	20
6	0.46412884	16.48834349	0.06064891	24
7	0.40839302	18.20329169	0.05493512	28
8	0.35935035	19.71229699	0.05072976	32
9	0.31619706	21.04009045	0.04752831	36
10	0.27822592	22.20843324	0.04502794	40
11	0.24481462	23.23647330	0.04303579	44
12	0.21541558	24.14105917	0.04142320	48
13	0.18954698	24.93701809	0.04010103	52
14	0.16678486	25.63738896	0.03900553	56
15	0.14675617	26.25365619	0.03808993	60
16	0.12913267	26.79591777	0.03731912	64
17	0.11362552	27.27306081	0.03666622	68
18	0.09998058	27.69290520	0.03611033	72
19	0.08797422	28.06233175	0.03563496	76
20	0.07740966	28.38739500	0.03522690	80
21	0.06811377	28.67342239	0.03487550	84
22	0.05993420	28.92510163	0.03457205	88
23	0.05273688	29.14655747	0.03430937	92
24	0.04640387	29.34141936	0.03408151	96
25	0.04083137	29.51288088	0.03388351	100
26	0.03592806	29.66375211	0.03371118	104
27	0.03161357	29.79650567	0.03356098	108
28	0.02781719	29.91331726	0.03342993	112
29	0.02447671	30.01610130	0.03331545	116
30	0.02153737	30.10654232	0.03321537	120
31	0.01895102	30.18612256	0.03312781	124
32	0.01667525	30.25614624	0.03305114	128
33	0.01467277	30.31776100	0.03298397	132
34	0.01291076	30.37197663	0.03292509	136
35	0.01136035	30.41968167	0.03287345	140
36	0.00999612	30.46165795	0.03282815	144
37	0.00879571	30.49859343	0.03278840	148
38	0.00773946	30.53109345	0.03275349	152
39	0.00681005	30.55969063	0.03272284	156
40	0.00599226	30.58485367	0.03269592	160
41	0.00527266	30.60699495	0.03267227	164
42	0.00463949	30.62647736	0.03265149	168
43	0.00408234	30.64362018	0.03263322	172
44	0.00359211	30.65870437	0.03261716	176
45	0.00316074	30.67197715	0.03260305	180
46	0.00278118	30.68365604	0.03259064	184
47	0.00244720	30.69393245	0.03257973	188
48	0.00215332	30.70297479	0.03257013	192
49	0.00189473	30.71093127	0.03256170	196
50	0.00166720	30.71793228	0.03255427	200

	Future Value of 1	Future Value of 1 per Period	Payment for Sinking Fund of 1	**13.00%** Quarterly
Quarters				
1	1.03250000	1.00000000	1.00000000	
2	1.06605625	2.03250000	0.49200492	
3	1.10070308	3.09855625	0.32273095	Years
4	1.13647593	4.19925933	0.23813723	1
8	1.29157754	8.97161647	0.11146263	2
12	1.46784678	14.39528548	0.06946719	3
16	1.66817253	20.55915476	0.04864013	4
20	1.89583792	27.56424382	0.03627888	5
24	2.15457416	35.52535890	0.02814891	6
28	2.44862167	44.57297456	0.02243512	7
32	2.78279959	54.85537196	0.01822976	8
36	3.16258475	66.54106909	0.01502831	9
40	3.59420143	79.82158259	0.01252794	10
44	4.08472341	94.91456649	0.01053579	11
48	4.64218983	112.06737937	0.00892320	12
52	5.27573700	131.56113832	0.00760103	13
56	5.99574810	153.71532611	0.00650553	14
60	6.81402339	178.89302724	0.00558993	15
64	7.74397355	207.50687850	0.00481912	16
68	8.80083953	240.02583168	0.00416622	17
72	10.00194227	276.98283916	0.00361033	18
76	11.36696663	318.98358855	0.00313496	19
80	12.91828395	366.71642920	0.00272690	20
84	14.68131874	420.96365357	0.00237550	21
88	16.68496534	482.61431825	0.00207205	22
92	18.96206147	552.67881460	0.00180937	23
96	21.54992641	632.30542813	0.00158151	24
100	24.49097262	722.79915765	0.00138351	25
104	27.83340084	825.64310289	0.00121118	26
108	31.63199006	942.52277102	0.00106098	27
112	35.94899526	1075.35370034	0.00092993	28
116	40.85516776	1226.31285402	0.00081545	29
120	46.43091470	1397.87429832	0.00077537	30
124	52.76761687	1592.84974997	0.00062781	31
128	59.96912636	1814.43465735	0.00055114	32
132	68.15346855	2066.26057064	0.00048397	33
136	77.45477642	2352.45465917	0.00042509	34
140	88.02548893	2677.70735157	0.00037345	35
144	100.03884923	3047.34920706	0.00032815	36
148	113.69174403	3467.43827786	0.00028840	37
152	129.20793032	3944.85939451	0.00025349	38
156	146.84170254	4487.43700118	0.00022284	39
160	166.88206019	5104.06339033	0.00019592	40
164	189.65744424	5804.84443826	0.00017227	41
168	215.54111998	6601.26523015	0.00015149	42
172	244.95729439	7506.37828882	0.00013322	43
176	278.38806850	8535.01749226	0.00011716	44
180	316.38133854	9704.04118574	0.00010305	45
184	359.55977537	11032.60847284	0.00009064	46
188	408.63102944	12542.49321357	0.00007973	47
192	464.39932846	14258.44087571	0.00007013	48
196	527.77865785	16208.57408772	0.00006170	49
200	599.80774005	18424.85353988	0.00005427	50

14.00%
Quarterly

	Present Value of 1	Present Value of 1 per Period	Payment to Pay Off a Loan of 1	
				Quarters
	0.96618357	0.96618357	1.03500000	1
	0.93351070	1.89969428	0.52640049	2
Years	0.90194271	2.80163698	0.35693418	3
1	0.87144223	3.67307921	0.27225114	4
2	0.75941156	6.87395554	0.14547665	8
3	0.66178330	9.66333433	0.10348395	12
4	0.57670591	12.09411681	0.08268483	16
5	0.50256588	14.21240330	0.07036108	20
6	0.43795713	16.05836760	0.06227283	24
7	0.38165434	17.66701885	0.05660265	28
8	0.33258971	19.06886547	0.05244150	32
9	0.28983272	20.29049381	0.04928416	36
10	0.25257247	21.35507234	0.04682728	40
11	0.22010231	22.28279102	0.04487768	44
12	0.19180645	23.09124425	0.04330646	48
13	0.16714824	23.79576454	0.04202429	52
14	0.14566004	24.40971327	0.04096730	56
15	0.12693431	24.94473412	0.04008862	60
16	0.11061591	25.41097388	0.03935308	64
17	0.09639538	25.81727489	0.03873375	68
18	0.08400300	26.17134275	0.03820973	72
19	0.07320376	26.47989244	0.03776450	76
20	0.06379285	26.74877567	0.03738489	80
21	0.05559178	26.98309186	0.03706025	84
22	0.04844503	27.18728489	0.03678190	88
23	0.04221704	27.36522732	0.03654273	92
24	0.03678971	27.52029387	0.03633682	96
25	0.03206011	27.65542540	0.03615927	100
26	0.02793853	27.77318473	0.03600595	104
27	0.02434682	27.87580518	0.03587340	108
28	0.02121685	27.96523297	0.03575869	112
29	0.01848926	28.04316413	0.03565931	116
30	0.01611232	28.11107663	0.03557317	120
31	0.01404095	28.17025845	0.03549843	124
32	0.01223588	28.22183199	0.03543356	128
33	0.01066286	28.26677534	0.03537722	132
34	0.00929207	28.30594088	0.03532827	136
35	0.00809750	28.34007139	0.03528573	140
36	0.00705650	28.36981415	0.03524873	144
37	0.00614934	28.39573325	0.03521656	148
38	0.00535879	28.41832025	0.03518857	152
39	0.00466988	28.43800352	0.03516421	156
40	0.00406953	28.45515634	0.03514302	160
41	0.00354636	28.47010404	0.03512456	164
42	0.00309045	28.48313010	0.03510850	168
43	0.00269315	28.49448155	0.03509451	172
44	0.00234692	28.50437369	0.03508234	176
45	0.00204521	28.51299412	0.03507173	180
46	0.00178228	28.52050632	0.03506249	184
47	0.00155315	28.52705277	0.03505444	188
48	0.00135348	28.53275763	0.03504744	192
49	0.00117948	28.53772908	0.03504133	196
50	0.00102785	28.54206141	0.03503601	200

	Future Value of 1	Future Value of 1 per Period	Payment for Sinking Fund of 1	**14.00%** Quarterly
Quarters				
1	1.03500000	1.00000000	1.00000000	
2	1.07122500	2.03500000	0.49140049	
3	1.10871788	3.10622500	0.32193418	Years
4	1.14752300	4.21494288	0.23725114	1
8	1.31680904	9.05168677	0.11047665	2
12	1.51106866	14.60196164	0.06848395	3
16	1.73398604	20.97102971	0.04768483	4
20	1.98978886	28.27968181	0.03536108	5
24	2.28332849	36.66652821	0.02727283	6
28	2.62017196	46.29062734	0.02160265	7
32	3.00670759	57.33450247	0.01744150	8
36	3.45026611	70.00760318	0.01428416	9
40	3.95925972	84.55027775	0.01182728	10
44	4.54334160	101.23833130	0.00987768	11
48	5.21358898	120.38825659	0.00830646	12
52	5.98271327	142.36323631	0.00702429	13
56	6.86530108	167.58003099	0.00596730	14
60	7.87809090	196.51688288	0.00508862	15
64	9.04029051	229.72258599	0.00435308	16
68	10.37394129	267.82689406	0.00373375	17
72	11.90433624	311.55246400	0.00320973	18
76	13.66049964	361.72856121	0.00276450	19
80	15.67573754	419.30678685	0.00238489	20
84	17.98826938	485.37912510	0.00206025	21
88	20.64195285	561.19865295	0.00178190	22
92	23.68711568	648.20330506	0.00154273	23
96	27.18151006	748.04314451	0.00133682	24
100	31.19140798	862.61165666	0.00115927	25
104	35.79285808	994.08165950	0.00100595	26
108	41.07312791	1144.94651165	0.00087340	27
112	47.13235898	1318.06739948	0.00075869	28
116	54.08546601	1516.72760015	0.00065931	29
120	62.06431624	1744.69474973	0.00057317	30
124	71.22023040	2006.29229726	0.00049843	31
128	81.72685250	2306.48149996	0.00043356	32
132	93.78344301	2650.95551459	0.00037722	33
136	107.61865793	3046.24736951	0.00032827	34
140	123.49488527	3499.85386498	0.00028573	35
144	141.71322131	4020.37712176	0.00024873	36
148	162.61918095	4617.69088422	0.00021656	37
152	186.60925048	5303.12144230	0.00018857	38
156	214.13840706	6089.66877302	0.00016421	39
160	245.72874741	6992.24992610	0.00014302	40
164	281.97938957	8027.98255920	0.00012456	41
168	323.57783524	9216.50957817	0.00010850	42
172	371.31300843	10580.37166930	0.00009451	43
176	426.09021760	12145.43478856	0.00008234	44
180	488.94832504	13941.38071534	0.00007173	45
184	561.07944910	16002.26997420	0.00006249	46
188	643.85157302	18367.18780048	0.00005444	47
192	738.83448903	21080.98540072	0.00004744	48
196	847.82956981	24195.13056605	0.00004133	49
200	972.90393197	27768.68377054	0.00003601	50

15.00% Quarterly	Present Value of 1	Present Value of 1 per Period	Payment to Pay Off a Loan of 1	
				Quarters
	0.96385542	0.96385542	1.03750000	1
	0.92901727	1.89287270	0.52829755	2
Years	0.89543834	2.78831103	0.35864005	3
1	0.86307310	3.65138413	0.27386875	4
2	0.74489517	6.80279553	0.14699839	8
3	0.64289898	9.52269392	0.10501230	12
4	0.55486881	11.87016504	0.08424483	16
5	0.47889234	13.89620421	0.07196210	20
6	0.41331910	15.64482411	0.06391890	24
7	0.35672459	17.15401089	0.05829540	28
8	0.30787940	18.45654941	0.05418131	32
9	0.26572242	19.58073533	0.05107060	36
10	0.22933788	20.55098999	0.04865946	40
11	0.19793535	21.38839067	0.04675434	44
12	0.17083268	22.11112866	0.04522609	48
13	0.14744109	22.73490438	0.04398523	52
14	0.12725243	23.27326842	0.04296775	56
15	0.10982815	23.73791594	0.04212670	60
16	0.09478972	24.13894071	0.04142684	64
17	0.08181046	24.48505440	0.04084124	68
18	0.07060841	24.78377582	0.04034898	72
19	0.06094022	25.04159423	0.03993356	76
20	0.05259586	25.26411037	0.03958184	80
21	0.04539407	25.45615806	0.03928323	84
22	0.03917840	25.62190926	0.03902910	88
23	0.03381383	25.76496466	0.03881240	92
24	0.02918380	25.88843192	0.03862729	96
25	0.02518776	25.99499320	0.03846895	100
26	0.02173887	26.08696337	0.03833332	104
27	0.01876224	26.16634035	0.03821704	108
28	0.01619318	26.23484848	0.03811724	112
29	0.01397590	26.29397601	0.03803152	116
30	0.01206222	26.34500739	0.03795786	120
31	0.01041058	26.38905120	0.03789450	124
32	0.00898509	26.42706422	0.03784400	128
33	0.00775479	26.45987224	0.03779308	132
34	0.00669295	26.48818796	0.03775268	136
35	0.00577651	26.51262650	0.03771788	140
36	0.00498555	26.53371874	0.03768789	144
37	0.00430289	26.55192289	0.03766206	148
38	0.00371371	26.56763440	0.03763978	152
39	0.00320520	26.58119458	0.03762058	156
40	0.00276632	26.59289801	0.03760402	160
41	0.00238754	26.60299892	0.03758975	164
42	0.00206062	26.61171675	0.03757743	168
43	0.00177847	26.61924087	0.03756681	172
44	0.00153495	26.62573474	0.03755765	176
45	0.00132477	26.63133942	0.03754974	180
46	0.00114337	26.63617667	0.03754293	184
47	0.00098682	26.64035157	0.03753704	188
48	0.00085169	26.64395482	0.03753197	192
49	0.00073507	26.64706468	0.03752759	196
50	0.00063442	26.64974872	0.03752381	200

	Future Value of 1	Future Value of 1 per Period	Payment for Sinking Fund of 1	**15.00%** Quarterly
Quarters				
1	1.03750000	1.00000000	1.00000000	
2	1.07640625	2.03750000	0.49079755	
3	1.11677148	3.11390625	0.32114005	Years
4	1.15865042	4.23067773	0.23636875	1
8	1.34247078	9.13255425	0.10949839	2
12	1.55545433	14.81211550	0.06751230	3
16	1.80222781	21.39274151	0.04674483	4
20	2.08815200	29.01738656	0.03446210	5
24	2.41943818	37.85168472	0.02641890	6
28	2.80328305	48.08754794	0.02079540	7
32	3.24802507	59.94733512	0.01668131	8
36	3.76332559	73.68868245	0.01357060	9
40	4.36037876	89.61010024	0.01115946	10
44	5.05215466	108.05745757	0.00925434	11
48	5.85368109	129.43149579	0.00772609	12
52	6.78237003	154.19653405	0.00648523	13
56	7.85839585	182.89055591	0.00546775	14
60	9.10513361	216.13689625	0.00462670	15
64	10.54966684	254.65778228	0.00392684	16
68	12.22337586	299.29002287	0.00334124	17
72	14.16261951	351.00318695	0.00284898	18
76	16.40952497	410.92066597	0.00243356	19
80	19.01290292	480.34407791	0.00208184	20
84	22.02930786	560.78154296	0.00178323	21
88	25.52426670	653.98044524	0.00152910	22
92	29.57370220	761.96539204	0.00131240	23
96	34.26558233	887.08219546	0.00112729	24
100	39.70183119	1032.04883168	0.00096895	25
104	46.00054318	1200.01448490	0.00083332	26
108	53.29854845	1394.62795872	0.00071704	27
112	61.75438528	1620.11694093	0.00061724	28
116	71.55174414	1881.37984375	0.00053152	29
120	82.90345805	2184.09221454	0.00045786	30
124	96.05612607	2534.83002860	0.00039450	31
128	111.29547034	2941.21254242	0.00034000	32
132	128.95254290	3412.06781073	0.00029308	33
136	149.41091735	3957.62446278	0.00025268	34
140	173.11502140	4589.73390410	0.00021788	35
144	200.57979140	5322.12777064	0.00018789	36
148	232.40185855	6170.71622808	0.00016206	37
152	269.27250987	7153.93359649	0.00013978	38
156	311.99270532	8293.13880847	0.00012058	39
160	361.49047751	9613.07940014	0.00010402	40
164	418.84109179	11142.42911451	0.00008975	41
168	485.29040484	12914.41079581	0.00007743	42
172	562.28192899	14967.51810628	0.00006681	43
176	651.48819039	17346.35174368	0.00005765	44
180	754.84706219	20102.58832497	0.00004974	45
184	874.60386189	23296.10298382	0.00004293	46
188	1013.36012758	26996.27006873	0.00003704	47
192	1174.13013240	31283.47019737	0.00003197	48
196	1360.40636522	36250.83640578	0.00002759	49
200	1576.23539968	42006.27732481	0.00002381	50

16.00% Quarterly	Present Value of 1	Present Value of 1 per Period	Payment to Pay Off a Loan of 1	
				Quarters
	0.96153846	0.96153846	1.04000000	1
	0.92455621	1.88609467	0.53019608	2
Years	0.88899636	2.77509103	0.36034854	3
1	0.85480419	3.62989522	0.27549005	4
2	0.73069021	6.73274487	0.14852783	8
3	0.62459705	9.38507376	0.10655217	12
4	0.53390818	11.65229561	0.08582000	16
5	0.45638695	13.59032634	0.07358175	20
6	0.39012147	15.24696314	0.06558683	24
7	0.33347747	16.66306322	0.06001298	28
8	0.28505794	17.87355150	0.05594859	32
9	0.24366872	18.90828195	0.05288688	36
10	0.20828904	19.79277388	0.05052349	40
11	0.17804635	20.54884129	0.04866454	44
12	0.15219476	21.19513088	0.04718065	48
13	0.13009672	21.74758193	0.04598212	52
14	0.11120722	22.21981940	0.04500487	56
15	0.09506040	22.62348997	0.04420185	60
16	0.08125803	22.96854927	0.04353780	64
17	0.06945970	23.26350740	0.04298578	68
18	0.05937445	23.51563885	0.04252489	72
19	0.05075353	23.73116187	0.04213869	76
20	0.04338433	23.91539185	0.04181408	80
21	0.03708510	24.07287241	0.04154054	84
22	0.03170050	24.20748745	0.04130953	88
23	0.02709772	24.32255695	0.04111410	92
24	0.02316325	24.42091884	0.04094850	96
25	0.01980004	24.50499900	0.04080800	100
26	0.01692516	24.57687107	0.04068866	104
27	0.01446770	24.63830762	0.04058720	108
28	0.01236705	24.69082383	0.04050088	112
29	0.01057140	24.73571492	0.04042737	116
30	0.00903648	24.77408800	0.04036476	120
31	0.00772442	24.80688948	0.04031138	124
32	0.00660287	24.83492832	0.04026587	128
33	0.00564416	24.85889603	0.04022705	132
34	0.00482465	24.87933874	0.04019392	136
35	0.00412413	24.89689671	0.04016565	140
36	0.00352532	24.91186688	0.04014151	144
37	0.00301346	24.92466344	0.04012090	148
38	0.00257592	24.93560199	0.04010330	152
39	0.00220191	24.94495231	0.04008827	156
40	0.00188220	24.95294501	0.04007543	160
41	0.00160891	24.95977719	0.04006446	164
42	0.00137530	24.96561738	0.04005509	168
43	0.00117562	24.97060959	0.04004708	172
44	0.00100492	24.97487695	0.04004024	176
45	0.00085901	24.97852472	0.04003439	180
46	0.00073429	24.98164284	0.04002939	184
47	0.00062767	24.98430822	0.04002512	188
48	0.00053654	24.98658660	0.04002090	192
49	0.00045863	24.98853417	0.04001835	196
50	0.00039204	24.99019896	0.04001569	200

	Future Value of 1	Future Value of 1 per Period	Payment for Sinking Fund of 1	**16.00%** Quarterly
Quarters				
1	1.04000000	1.00000000	1.00000000	
2	1.08160000	2.04000000	0.49019608	
3	1.12486400	3.12160000	0.32034854	Years
4	1.16985856	4.24646400	0.23549005	1
8	1.36856905	9.21422626	0.10852783	2
12	1.60103222	15.02580546	0.06655217	3
16	1.87298125	21.82453114	0.04582000	4
20	2.19112314	29.77807858	0.03358175	5
24	2.56330416	39.08260412	0.02558683	6
28	2.99870332	49.96758298	0.02001298	7
32	3.50805875	62.70146867	0.01594859	8
36	4.10393255	77.59831383	0.01288688	9
40	4.80102063	95.02551570	0.01052349	10
44	5.61651508	115.41287696	0.00866454	11
48	6.57052824	139.26320604	0.00718065	12
52	7.68658871	167.16471768	0.00598212	13
56	8.99222160	199.80553991	0.00500487	14
60	10.51962741	237.99068520	0.00420185	15
64	12.30647617	282.66190428	0.00353780	16
68	14.39683649	334.92091231	0.00298578	17
72	16.84226241	396.05656019	0.00252489	18
76	19.70306485	467.57662118	0.00213869	19
80	23.04979907	551.24497675	0.00181408	20
84	26.96500475	649.12511870	0.00154054	21
88	31.54524163	763.63104063	0.00130953	22
92	36.90347094	897.58677356	0.00111410	23
96	43.17184138	1054.29603439	0.00094850	24
100	50.50494818	1237.62370461	0.00080800	25
104	59.08364596	1452.09114889	0.00068866	26
108	69.11950898	1702.98772443	0.00058720	27
112	80.86004924	1996.50123100	0.00050088	28
116	94.59482077	2339.87051914	0.00042737	29
120	110.66256080	2741.56402011	0.00036476	30
124	129.45954403	3211.48860071	0.00031138	31
128	151.44935576	3761.23389388	0.00026587	32
132	177.17432524	4404.35813092	0.00022705	33
136	207.26890099	5156.72252476	0.00019392	34
140	242.47529805	6036.88245114	0.00016565	35
144	283.66180301	7066.54507518	0.00014151	36
148	331.84418839	8271.10470982	0.00012090	37
152	388.21076438	9680.26910944	0.00010330	38
156	454.15168579	11328.79214479	0.00008827	39
160	531.29323716	13257.33092904	0.00007543	40
164	621.53794136	15513.44853409	0.00006446	41
168	727.11148107	18152.78702672	0.00005509	42
172	850.61759020	21240.43975507	0.00004708	43
176	995.10226919	24852.55672963	0.00004024	44
180	1164.12890768	29078.22269204	0.00003439	45
184	1361.86616759	34021.65418987	0.00002939	46
188	1593.19079374	39804.76984338	0.00002512	47
192	1863.80788776	46570.19719411	0.00002147	48
196	2180.39161170	54484.79029242	0.00001835	49
200	2550.74979110	63743.74477739	0.00001569	50

5.00% Semi-Annually	Present Value of 1	Present Value of 1 per Period	Payment to Pay Off a Loan of 1	
Years	0.97560976	0.97560976	1.02500000	Half Years
				1
1	0.95181440	1.92742415	0.51882716	2
2	0.90595064	3.76197421	0.26581788	4
3	0.86229687	5.50812536	0.18154997	6
4	0.82074657	7.17013717	0.13946735	8
5	0.78119840	8.75206393	0.11425876	10
6	0.74355589	10.25776460	0.09748713	12
7	0.70772720	11.69091217	0.08553652	14
8	0.67362493	13.05500266	0.07659899	16
9	0.64116591	14.35336363	0.06967008	18
10	0.61027094	15.58916229	0.06414713	20
11	0.58086467	16.76541324	0.05964661	22
12	0.55287535	17.88498583	0.05591282	24
13	0.52623472	18.95061114	0.05276875	26
14	0.50007770	19.96400000	0.05008793	28
15	0.47674269	20.93029259	0.04777764	30
16	0.45377055	21.84917796	0.04576831	32
17	0.43190534	22.72378628	0.04400675	34
18	0.41109372	23.55625037	0.04245158	36
19	0.39128492	24.34860304	0.04107012	38
20	0.37243062	25.10277505	0.03983623	40
21	0.35448483	25.82060683	0.03872876	42
22	0.33740376	26.50384945	0.03773037	44
23	0.32114576	27.15416962	0.03682676	46
24	0.30567116	27.77315371	0.03600599	48
25	0.29094221	28.36231168	0.03525806	50
26	0.27692298	28.92308072	0.03457446	52
27	0.26357928	29.45682876	0.03394749	54
28	0.25087855	29.96485784	0.03337243	56
29	0.23878982	30.44840722	0.03284244	58
30	0.22728359	30.90865649	0.03235340	60
31	0.21633179	31.34672836	0.03190126	62
32	0.20590771	31.76369148	0.03148249	64
33	0.19598593	32.16056298	0.03109398	66
34	0.18654223	32.53831099	0.03073300	68
35	0.17755358	32.89785698	0.03039712	70
36	0.16899805	33.24007803	0.03008417	72
37	0.16085478	33.56580895	0.02979222	74
38	0.15310389	33.87584433	0.02951956	76
39	0.14572649	34.17094047	0.02926463	78
40	0.13870457	34.45181722	0.02902605	80
41	0.13202101	34.71915976	0.02880254	82
42	0.12565949	34.97362023	0.02859298	84
43	0.11960452	35.21581938	0.02839633	86
44	0.11384130	35.44634801	0.02821165	88
45	0.10835579	35.66576848	0.02803809	90
46	0.10313460	35.87461604	0.02787486	92
47	0.09816500	36.07340016	0.02772126	94
48	0.09343486	36.26260574	0.02757662	96
49	0.08893264	36.44269434	0.02744034	98
50	0.08464737	36.61410526	0.02731188	100

	Future Value of 1	Future Value of 1 per Period	Payment for Sinking Fund of 1	**5.00%** Semi-Annually
Half Years				
1	1.02500000	1.00000000	1.00000000	Years
2	1.05062500	2.02500000	0.49382716	1
4	1.10381289	4.15251562	0.24081788	2
6	1.15969342	6.38773673	0.15654997	3
8	1.21840290	8.73611590	0.11446735	4
10	1.28008454	11.20338177	0.08925876	5
12	1.34488882	13.79555297	0.07248713	6
14	1.41297382	16.51895284	0.06053652	7
16	1.48450562	19.38022483	0.05159899	8
18	1.55965872	22.38634871	0.04467008	9
20	1.63861644	25.54465761	0.03914713	10
22	1.72157140	28.86285590	0.03464661	11
24	1.80872595	32.34903798	0.03091282	12
26	1.90029270	36.01170803	0.02776875	13
28	1.99649502	39.85980075	0.02508793	14
30	2.09756758	43.90270316	0.02277764	15
32	2.20375694	48.15027751	0.02076831	16
34	2.31532213	52.61288531	0.01900675	17
36	2.43253532	57.30141263	0.01745158	18
38	2.55568242	62.22729664	0.01607012	19
40	2.68506384	67.40255354	0.01483623	20
42	2.82099520	72.83980781	0.01372876	21
44	2.96380808	78.55232308	0.01273037	22
46	3.11385086	84.55403443	0.01182676	23
48	3.27148956	90.85958243	0.01100599	24
50	3.43710872	97.48434879	0.01025806	25
52	3.61111235	104.44449395	0.00957446	26
54	3.79392491	111.75699645	0.00894799	27
56	3.98599236	119.43969440	0.00837243	28
58	4.18778322	127.51132893	0.00784244	29
60	4.39978975	135.99158995	0.00735340	30
62	4.62252910	144.90116419	0.00690126	31
64	4.85564464	154.26178563	0.00648249	32
66	5.10240721	164.09628853	0.00609398	33
68	5.36071658	174.42866314	0.00573300	34
70	5.63210286	185.28411421	0.00539712	35
72	5.91722806	196.68912429	0.00508417	36
74	6.21678773	208.67150931	0.00479222	37
76	6.53151261	221.26050447	0.00451956	38
78	6.86217044	234.48681751	0.00426463	39
80	7.20956782	248.38271265	0.00402605	40
82	7.57455219	262.98208748	0.00380254	41
84	7.95801389	278.32055566	0.00359298	42
86	8.36088834	294.43553379	0.00339633	43
88	8.78415832	311.36633268	0.00321165	44
90	9.22885633	329.15425328	0.00303809	45
92	9.69606718	347.84268735	0.00287486	46
94	10.18693058	367.47722339	0.00272126	47
96	10.70264395	388.10575783	0.00257662	48
98	11.24446530	409.77861182	0.00244034	49
100	11.81371635	432.54865404	0.00231188	50

5.50% Semi-Annually	Present Value of 1	Present Value of 1 per Period	Payment to Pay Off a Loan of 1	
				Half Years
Years	0.97323601	0.97323601	1.02750000	1
1	0.94718833	1.92042434	0.52071825	2
2	0.89716573	3.73942787	0.26742059	4
3	0.84978491	5.46236678	0.18307083	6
4	0.80490635	7.09431441	0.14095795	8
5	0.76239791	8.64007616	0.11573972	10
6	0.72213440	10.10420366	0.09896871	12
7	0.68399728	11.49100814	0.08702457	14
8	0.64787424	12.80457315	0.07809710	16
9	0.61365892	14.04876661	0.07118063	18
10	0.58125057	15.22725213	0.06567173	20
11	0.55055375	16.34349987	0.06118640	22
12	0.52147809	17.40079670	0.05746863	24
13	0.49393796	18.40225592	0.05434116	26
14	0.46785227	19.35082640	0.05167738	28
15	0.44314421	20.24930130	0.04938442	30
16	0.41974103	21.10032623	0.04739263	32
17	0.39757380	21.90640712	0.04564875	34
18	0.37657727	22.66991753	0.04411132	36
19	0.35668959	23.39310568	0.04274764	38
20	0.33785222	24.07810106	0.04153151	40
21	0.32000968	24.72692069	0.04044175	42
22	0.30310944	25.34147507	0.03946100	44
23	0.28710172	25.92357381	0.03857043	46
24	0.27193940	26.47493094	0.03777158	48
25	0.25757783	26.99716998	0.03704092	50
26	0.24397471	27.49182871	0.03637444	52
27	0.23109000	27.96036368	0.03576491	54
28	0.21888575	28.40415454	0.03520612	56
29	0.20732603	28.82450806	0.03469270	58
30	0.19637679	29.22266201	0.03422002	60
31	0.18600581	29.59978879	0.03378402	62
32	0.17618253	29.95699887	0.03338118	64
33	0.16687804	30.29534409	0.03300837	66
34	0.15806493	30.61582074	0.03266285	68
35	0.14971726	30.91937247	0.03234218	70
36	0.14181044	31.20689314	0.03204420	72
37	0.13432119	31.47922936	0.03176698	74
38	0.12722747	31.73718304	0.03150878	76
39	0.12050837	31.98151377	0.03126806	78
40	0.11414412	32.21294098	0.03104342	80
41	0.10811598	32.43214613	0.03083361	82
42	0.10240620	32.63977469	0.03063747	84
43	0.09699795	32.83643804	0.03045397	86
44	0.09187533	33.02271527	0.03028219	88
45	0.08702324	33.19915489	0.03012125	90
46	0.08242740	33.36627644	0.02997038	92
47	0.07807427	33.52457202	0.02982887	94
48	0.07395104	33.67450775	0.02969605	96
49	0.07004556	33.81652512	0.02957134	98
50	0.06634634	33.95104232	0.02945418	100

	Future Value of 1	Future Value of 1 per Period	Payment for Sinking Fund of 1	**5.50%** Semi-Annually
Half Years				
1	1.02750000	1.00000000	1.00000000	Years
2	1.05575625	2.02750000	0.49321825	1
4	1.11462126	4.16804580	0.23992059	2
6	1.17676836	6.42794040	0.15557083	3
8	1.24238055	8.81383825	0.11345795	4
10	1.31165103	11.33276482	0.08823972	5
12	1.38478378	13.99213729	0.07146871	6
14	1.46199413	16.79978639	0.05952457	7
16	1.54350944	19.76397948	0.05059710	8
18	1.62956973	22.89344487	0.04368063	9
20	1.72042843	26.19739750	0.03817173	10
22	1.81635307	29.68556615	0.03368640	11
24	1.91762610	33.36822199	0.02996863	12
26	2.02454575	37.25620892	0.02684116	13
28	2.13742682	41.36097542	0.02417738	14
30	2.25660173	45.69460831	0.02188442	15
32	2.38242138	50.26986831	0.01989263	16
34	2.51525626	55.10022765	0.01814875	17
36	2.65549752	60.19990972	0.01661132	18
38	2.80355810	65.58393094	0.01524764	19
40	2.95987399	71.26814499	0.01403151	20
42	3.12490546	77.26928950	0.01294175	21
44	3.29913847	83.60503532	0.01196100	22
46	3.48308606	90.29403857	0.01107493	23
48	3.67728988	97.35599556	0.01027158	24
50	3.88232177	104.81170079	0.00954092	25
52	4.09878547	112.68310818	0.00887444	26
54	4.32731838	120.99339573	0.00826491	27
56	4.56859343	129.76703375	0.00770612	28
58	4.82332107	139.02985692	0.00719270	29
60	5.09225136	148.80914038	0.00672002	30
62	5.37617620	159.13368002	0.00628402	31
64	5.67593162	170.03387726	0.00588118	32
66	5.99240029	181.54182863	0.00550837	33
68	6.32651406	193.69142022	0.00516285	34
70	6.67925676	206.51842746	0.00484218	35
72	7.05166706	220.06062054	0.00454420	36
74	7.44484158	234.35787551	0.00426698	37
76	7.85993802	249.45229181	0.00400878	38
78	8.29817869	265.38831615	0.00376806	39
80	8.76085402	282.21287345	0.00354342	40
82	9.24932639	299.97550498	0.00333361	41
84	9.76503414	318.72851423	0.00313747	42
86	10.30949583	338.52712095	0.00295397	43
88	10.88431465	359.42962374	0.00278219	44
90	11.49118322	381.49757170	0.00262125	45
92	12.13188851	404.79594568	0.00247038	46
94	12.80831711	429.39334962	0.00232887	47
96	13.52246085	455.36221257	0.00219605	48
98	14.27642255	482.77900194	0.00207134	49
100	15.07242234	511.72444867	0.00195418	50

6.00% Semi-Annually	Present Value of 1	Present Value of 1 per Period	Payment to Pay Off a Loan of 1	
				Half Years
Years	0.97087379	0.97087379	1.03000000	1
1	0.94259591	1.91346970	0.52261084	2
2	0.88848705	3.71709840	0.26902705	4
3	0.83748426	5.41719144	0.18459750	6
4	0.78940923	7.01969219	0.14245639	8
5	0.74409391	8.53020284	0.11723051	10
6	0.70137988	9.95400399	0.10046209	12
7	0.66111781	11.29607314	0.08852634	14
8	0.62316694	12.56110203	0.07961085	16
9	0.58739461	13.75351308	0.07270870	18
10	0.55367575	14.87747486	0.06721571	20
11	0.52189250	15.93691664	0.06274739	22
12	0.49193374	16.93554212	0.05904742	24
13	0.46369473	17.87684242	0.05593829	26
14	0.43707675	18.76110822	0.05329323	28
15	0.41198676	19.60044135	0.05101926	30
16	0.38833703	20.38876553	0.04904662	32
17	0.36604490	21.13183668	0.04732196	34
18	0.34503243	21.83225250	0.04580379	36
19	0.32522615	22.49246159	0.04445934	38
20	0.30655684	23.11477197	0.04326238	40
21	0.28895922	23.70135920	0.04219167	42
22	0.27237178	24.25427392	0.04122945	44
23	0.25673653	24.77544907	0.04036254	46
24	0.24199880	25.26670664	0.03957777	48
25	0.22810708	25.72976401	0.03886645	50
26	0.21501280	26.16623999	0.03821718	52
27	0.20267019	26.57766047	0.03762558	54
28	0.19103609	26.96546373	0.03708447	56
29	0.18006984	27.33100549	0.03658848	58
30	0.16973309	27.67556367	0.03613296	60
31	0.15998972	28.00034279	0.03571385	62
32	0.15080565	28.30647826	0.03532760	64
33	0.14214879	28.59504031	0.03497110	66
34	0.13398887	28.86703771	0.03464159	68
35	0.12629736	29.12342135	0.03433663	70
36	0.11904737	29.36508752	0.03405404	72
37	0.11221357	29.59288107	0.03379191	74
38	0.10577205	29.80759833	0.03354849	76
39	0.09970030	30.00998994	0.03332224	78
40	0.09397710	30.20076345	0.03311175	80
41	0.08858243	30.38058577	0.03291576	82
42	0.08349743	30.55008556	0.03273313	84
43	0.07870434	30.70985537	0.03256284	86
44	0.07418639	30.86045374	0.03240393	88
45	0.06992779	31.00240714	0.03225556	90
46	0.06591364	31.13621184	0.03211694	92
47	0.06212993	31.26233560	0.03198737	94
48	0.05856342	31.38121934	0.03186619	96
49	0.05520164	31.49327867	0.03175281	98
50	0.05203284	31.59890534	0.03164667	100

Half Years	Future Value of 1	Future Value of 1 per Period	Payment for Sinking Fund of 1	**6.00%** Semi-Annually
1	1.03000000	1.00000000	1.00000000	Years
2	1.06090000	2.03000000	0.49261084	1
4	1.12550881	4.18362700	0.23902705	2
6	1.19405230	6.46840988	0.15459750	3
8	1.26677008	8.89233605	0.11245639	4
10	1.34391638	11.46387931	0.08723051	5
12	1.42576089	14.19202956	0.07046209	6
14	1.51258972	17.08632416	0.05852634	7
16	1.60470644	20.15688130	0.04961085	8
18	1.70243306	23.41443537	0.04270870	9
20	1.80611123	26.87037449	0.03721571	10
22	1.91610341	30.53678030	0.03274739	11
24	2.03279411	34.42647022	0.02904742	12
26	2.15659127	38.55304225	0.02593829	13
28	2.28792768	42.93092252	0.02329323	14
30	2.42726247	47.57541571	0.02101926	15
32	2.57508276	52.50275852	0.01904662	16
34	2.73190530	57.73017652	0.01732196	17
36	2.89827833	63.27594427	0.01580379	18
38	3.07478348	69.15944927	0.01445934	19
40	3.26203779	75.40125973	0.01326238	20
42	3.46069589	82.02319645	0.01219167	21
44	3.67145227	89.04840911	0.01122985	22
46	3.89504372	96.50145723	0.01036254	23
48	4.13225188	104.40839598	0.00957777	24
50	4.38390602	112.79686729	0.00886549	25
52	4.65088590	121.69619651	0.00821718	26
54	4.93412485	131.13749488	0.00762558	27
56	5.23461305	141.15376831	0.00708447	28
58	5.55340098	151.78003280	0.00658848	29
60	5.89160310	163.05343680	0.00613296	30
62	6.25040173	175.01339110	0.00571385	31
64	6.63105120	187.70170662	0.00532760	32
66	7.03488222	201.16274055	0.00497110	33
68	7.46330654	215.44355145	0.00464159	34
70	7.91782191	230.59406374	0.00433663	35
72	8.40001727	246.66724222	0.00405404	36
74	8.91157832	263.71927727	0.00379191	37
76	9.45429344	281.80978126	0.00354849	38
78	10.03005991	301.00199693	0.00332224	39
80	10.64089056	321.36301855	0.00311175	40
82	11.28892079	342.96402638	0.00291576	41
84	11.97641607	365.88053558	0.00273313	42
86	12.70577981	390.19266020	0.00256284	43
88	13.47956180	415.98539321	0.00240393	44
90	14.30046711	443.34890365	0.00225556	45
92	15.17136556	472.37885189	0.00211694	46
94	16.09530172	503.17672397	0.00198737	47
96	17.07550559	535.85018645	0.00186619	48
98	18.11540388	570.51346281	0.00175281	49
100	19.21863198	607.28773270	0.00164667	50

6.50% Semi-Annually	Present Value of 1	Present Value of 1 per Period	Payment to Pay Off a Loan of 1	
				Half Years
Years	0.96852300	0.96852300	1.03250000	1
1	0.93803681	1.90655981	0.52450492	2
2	0.87991305	3.69498308	0.27063723	4
3	0.82539083	5.37258994	0.18612997	6
4	0.77424698	6.94624692	0.14396263	8
5	0.72627216	8.42239508	0.11873107	10
6	0.68127002	9.80707639	0.10196719	12
7	0.63905635	11.10595842	0.09004176	14
8	0.59945838	12.32435758	0.08114013	16
9	0.56231402	13.46726083	0.07425415	18
10	0.52747125	14.53934615	0.06877888	20
11	0.49478745	15.54500163	0.06432936	22
12	0.46412884	16.48834349	0.06064891	24
13	0.43536993	17.37323288	0.05755981	26
14	0.40039302	18.20329169	0.05492512	28
15	0.38308768	18.98191741	0.05268172	30
16	0.35935035	19.71229699	0.05072976	32
17	0.33708385	20.39741992	0.04902581	34
18	0.31619706	21.04009045	0.04752831	36
19	0.29660448	21.64293905	0.04620445	38
20	0.27822592	22.20843324	0.04502794	40
21	0.26098615	22.73888759	0.04397753	42
22	0.24481462	23.23647330	0.04303579	44
23	0.22964512	23.70322701	0.04218835	46
24	0.21541558	24.14105917	0.04142320	48
25	0.20206774	24.55176185	0.04073027	50
26	0.18954698	24.93701609	0.04010103	52
27	0.17780204	25.29839873	0.03952819	54
28	0.16678486	25.63738896	0.03900553	56
29	0.15645034	25.95537427	0.03852767	58
30	0.14675617	26.25365619	0.03808993	60
31	0.13766269	26.53345561	0.03768827	62
32	0.12913267	26.79591777	0.03731912	64
33	0.12113120	27.04211693	0.03697935	66
34	0.11362552	27.27306081	0.03666622	68
35	0.10658492	27.48969467	0.03637727	70
36	0.09998058	27.69290520	0.03611033	72
37	0.09378546	27.88352416	0.03586347	74
38	0.08797422	28.06233175	0.03563496	76
39	0.08252305	28.23005986	0.03542323	78
40	0.07740966	28.38739500	0.03522690	80
41	0.07261311	28.53498115	0.03504471	82
42	0.06811377	28.67342239	0.03487550	84
43	0.06389323	28.80328537	0.03471826	86
44	0.05993420	28.92510163	0.03457205	88
45	0.05622048	29.03936976	0.03443601	90
46	0.05273688	29.14655747	0.03430937	92
47	0.04946914	29.24710349	0.03419142	94
48	0.04640387	29.34141936	0.03408151	96
49	0.04352854	29.42989112	0.03397906	98
50	0.04083137	29.51288088	0.03388351	100

	Future Value of 1	Future Value of 1 per Period	Payment for Sinking Fund of 1	**6.50%** Semi-Annually
Half Years				
1	1.03250000	1.00000000	1.00000000	Years
2	1.06605625	2.03250000	0.49200492	1
4	1.13647593	4.19925933	0.23813723	2
6	1.21154727	6.50914665	0.15362997	3
8	1.29157754	8.97161647	0.11146263	4
10	1.37689430	11.59674781	0.08623107	5
12	1.46784678	14.39528548	0.06946719	6
14	1.56480723	17.37868406	0.05754176	7
16	1.66817253	20.55915476	0.04864013	8
18	1.77836575	23.94971543	0.04175415	9
20	1.89583792	27.56424382	0.03627888	10
22	2.02106987	31.41753440	0.03182936	11
24	2.15457416	35.52535890	0.02814891	12
26	2.29689725	39.90743089	0.02505981	13
28	2.44862167	44.57297456	0.02243512	14
30	2.61036844	49.54979811	0.02018172	15
32	2.78279959	54.85537196	0.01822976	16
34	2.96662089	60.51141213	0.01652581	17
36	3.16258475	66.54106909	0.01502831	18
38	3.37149323	72.96902259	0.01370445	19
40	3.59420143	79.82158259	0.01252794	20
42	3.83162090	87.12679700	0.01147753	21
44	4.08472341	94.91456649	0.01053579	22
46	4.35454492	103.21676682	0.00968835	23
48	4.64218983	112.06737937	0.00892320	24
50	4.94883548	121.50263020	0.00823027	25
52	5.27573700	131.56113832	0.00760103	26
54	5.62423240	142.28407376	0.00702819	27
56	5.99574810	153.71532611	0.00650553	28
58	6.39180473	165.90168412	0.00602767	29
60	6.81402339	178.89302724	0.00558993	30
62	7.26413222	192.74252977	0.00518827	31
64	7.74397355	207.50687850	0.00481912	32
66	8.25551140	223.24650475	0.00447935	33
68	8.80083953	240.02583168	0.00416622	34
70	9.38218999	257.91353802	0.00387727	35
72	10.00194227	276.98283916	0.00361033	36
74	10.66263307	297.31178683	0.00336347	37
76	11.36696663	318.98358855	0.00313496	38
78	12.11782582	342.08694822	0.00292323	39
80	12.91828395	366.71642920	0.00272690	40
82	13.77161734	392.97284132	0.00254471	41
84	14.68131874	420.96365357	0.00237550	42
86	15.65111160	450.80343392	0.00221826	43
88	16.68496534	482.61431825	0.00207205	44
90	17.78711158	516.52651031	0.00193601	45
92	18.96206147	552.67881460	0.00180937	46
94	20.21462415	591.21920455	0.00169142	47
96	21.54992641	632.30542813	0.00158151	48
98	22.97343374	676.10565357	0.00147906	49
100	24.49097262	722.79915765	0.00138351	50

7.00% Semi- Annually	Present Value of 1	Present Value of 1 per Period	Payment to Pay Off a Loan of 1	
Years	0.96618357	0.96618357	1.03500000	Half Years 1
1	0.93351070	1.89969428	0.52640049	2
2	0.87144223	3.67307921	0.27225114	4
3	0.81350064	5.32855302	0.18766821	6
4	0.75941156	6.87395554	0.14547665	8
5	0.70891881	8.31660532	0.12024137	10
6	0.66178330	9.66333433	0.10348395	12
7	0.61778179	10.92052028	0.09157073	14
8	0.57670591	12.09411681	0.08268483	16
9	0.53836114	13.18968173	0.07581684	18
10	0.50256588	14.21240330	0.07036108	20
11	0.46915063	15.16712484	0.06593207	22
12	0.43795713	16.05836760	0.06227283	24
13	0.40883767	16.89035226	0.05920540	26
14	0.38165434	17.66701885	0.05660265	28
15	0.35627841	18.39204541	0.05437133	30
16	0.33258971	19.06886547	0.05244150	32
17	0.31047605	19.70068423	0.05075966	34
18	0.28983272	20.29049381	0.04928416	36
19	0.27056194	20.84108736	0.04798214	38
20	0.25257247	21.35507234	0.04682728	40
21	0.23577910	21.83488281	0.04579828	42
22	0.22010231	22.28279102	0.04487768	44
23	0.20546787	22.70091813	0.04405108	46
24	0.19180645	23.09124425	0.04330646	48
25	0.17905337	23.45561787	0.04263371	50
26	0.16714824	23.79576454	0.04202429	52
27	0.15603467	24.11329510	0.04147090	54
28	0.14566004	24.40971327	0.04096730	56
29	0.13597520	24.68642281	0.04050810	58
30	0.12693431	24.94473412	0.04008862	60
31	0.11849453	25.18587049	0.03970480	62
32	0.11061591	25.41097388	0.03935308	64
33	0.10326114	25.62111030	0.03903031	66
34	0.09639548	25.81727489	0.03873375	68
35	0.08998612	26.00039664	0.03846095	70
36	0.08400300	26.17134275	0.03820973	72
37	0.07841770	26.33092278	0.03797816	74
38	0.07320376	26.47989244	0.03776450	76
39	0.06833650	26.61895721	0.03756721	78
40	0.06379285	26.74877567	0.03738489	80
41	0.05955131	26.86996258	0.03721628	82
42	0.05559178	26.98309186	0.03706025	84
43	0.05189553	27.08869926	0.03691576	86
44	0.04844503	27.18728489	0.03678190	88
45	0.04522395	27.27931564	0.03665781	90
46	0.04221704	27.36522732	0.03654273	92
47	0.03941006	27.44542680	0.03643594	94
48	0.03678971	27.52029387	0.03633682	96
49	0.03434359	27.59018308	0.03624478	98
50	0.03206011	27.65542540	0.03615927	100

	Future Value of 1	Future Value of 1 per Period	Payment for Sinking Fund of 1	**7.00%** Semi-Annually
Half Years				
1	1.03500000	1.00000000	1.00000000	Years
2	1.07122500	2.03500000	0.49140049	1
4	1.14752300	4.21494288	0.23725114	2
6	1.22925533	6.55015218	0.15266821	3
8	1.31680904	9.05168677	0.11047665	4
10	1.41059876	11.73139316	0.08524137	5
12	1.51106866	14.60196164	0.06848395	6
14	1.61869452	17.67698636	0.05657073	7
16	1.73398604	20.97102971	0.04768483	8
18	1.85748920	24.49969130	0.04081684	9
20	1.98978886	28.27968181	0.03536108	10
22	2.13151158	32.32890215	0.03093207	11
24	2.28332849	36.66652821	0.02727283	12
26	2.44595856	41.31310268	0.02420540	13
28	2.62017196	46.29062734	0.02160265	14
30	2.80679370	51.62267728	0.01937133	15
32	3.00670759	57.33450247	0.01744150	16
34	3.22086033	63.45315240	0.01575966	17
36	3.45026611	70.00760318	0.01428416	18
38	3.69601132	77.02889472	0.01298214	19
40	3.95925972	84.55027775	0.01182728	20
42	4.24125799	92.60737128	0.01079828	21
44	4.54334160	101.23833130	0.00987768	22
46	4.86694110	110.48403145	0.00905108	23
48	5.21358898	120.38825659	0.00830646	24
50	5.58492686	130.99791016	0.00763371	25
52	5.98271327	142.36323631	0.00702429	26
54	6.40883202	154.53805782	0.00647090	27
56	6.86530108	167.58003099	0.00596730	28
58	7.35428215	181.55091869	0.00550810	29
60	7.87809090	196.51688288	0.00508862	30
62	8.43920793	212.54879786	0.00470480	31
64	9.04029051	229.72258599	0.00435308	32
66	9.68418520	248.11957718	0.00403031	33
68	10.37394129	267.82689406	0.00373375	34
70	11.11282526	288.93786459	0.00346095	35
72	11.90433624	311.55246400	0.00320973	36
74	12.75222259	335.77778824	0.00297816	37
76	13.66049964	361.72856121	0.00276450	38
78	14.63346873	389.52767798	0.00256721	39
80	15.67573754	419.30678685	0.00238489	40
82	16.79224195	451.20691274	0.00221628	41
84	17.98826938	485.37912510	0.00206025	42
86	19.26948387	521.98525329	0.00191576	43
88	20.64195285	561.19865295	0.00178190	44
90	22.11217595	603.20502701	0.00165781	45
92	23.68711568	648.20330506	0.00154273	46
94	25.37423049	696.40658546	0.00143594	47
96	27.18151006	748.04314451	0.00133682	48
98	29.11751311	803.35751748	0.00124478	49
100	31.19140798	862.61165666	0.00115927	50

7.50% Semi-Annually	Present Value of 1	Present Value of 1 per Period	Payment to Pay Off a Loan of 1	
				Half Years
Years	0.96385542	0.96385542	1.03750000	1
1	0.92901727	1.89287270	0.52829755	2
2	0.86307310	3.65138413	0.27386875	4
3	0.80180981	5.28507162	0.18921219	6
4	0.74489517	6.80279553	0.14699839	8
5	0.69202048	8.21278725	0.12176134	10
6	0.64289898	9.52269392	0.10501230	12
7	0.59726426	10.73961984	0.09311317	14
8	0.55486881	11.87016504	0.08424483	16
9	0.51548271	12.92046106	0.07739662	18
10	0.47889234	13.89620421	0.07196210	20
11	0.44489926	14.80268645	0.06755531	22
12	0.41331910	15.64482411	0.06391890	24
13	0.38398058	16.42718454	0.06087470	26
14	0.35672459	17.15401089	0.05829540	28
15	0.33140331	17.82924513	0.05608762	30
16	0.30787940	18.45654941	0.05418131	32
17	0.28602528	19.03932591	0.05252287	34
18	0.26572242	19.58073535	0.05107000	36
19	0.24686072	20.08371407	0.04979159	38
20	0.22933788	20.55098999	0.04865946	40
21	0.21305885	20.98509739	0.04765286	42
22	0.19793535	21.38839067	0.04675434	44
23	0.18388536	21.76305709	0.04594943	46
24	0.17083268	22.11112866	0.04522609	48
25	0.15870651	22.43449317	0.04457422	50
26	0.14744109	22.73490438	0.04398523	52
27	0.13697532	23.01399159	0.04345183	54
28	0.12725243	23.27326842	0.04296775	56
29	0.11821971	23.51414108	0.04252760	58
30	0.10982815	23.73791594	0.04212670	60
31	0.10203225	23.94580665	0.04176097	62
32	0.09478972	24.13894071	0.04142684	64
33	0.08806129	24.31836559	0.04112118	66
34	0.08181046	24.48505440	0.04084124	68
35	0.07600333	24.63991119	0.04058456	70
36	0.07060841	24.78377582	0.04034898	72
37	0.06559643	24.91742854	0.04013255	74
38	0.06094022	25.04159423	0.03993356	76
39	0.05661451	25.15694631	0.03975045	78
40	0.05259586	25.26411037	0.03958184	80
41	0.04886246	25.36366764	0.03942647	82
42	0.04539407	25.45615806	0.03928323	84
43	0.04217188	25.54208326	0.03915107	86
44	0.03917840	25.62190926	0.03902910	88
45	0.03639741	25.69606899	0.03891646	90
46	0.03381383	25.76496466	0.03881240	92
47	0.03141363	25.82896993	0.03871622	94
48	0.02918380	25.88843192	0.03862729	96
49	0.02711226	25.94367315	0.03854504	98
50	0.02518776	25.99499320	0.03846895	100

	Future Value of 1	Future Value of 1 per Period	Payment for Sinking Fund of 1	
Half Years				Years
1	1.03750000	1.00000000	1.00000000	
2	1.07640625	2.03750000	0.49079755	1
4	1.15865042	4.23067773	0.23636875	2
6	1.24717855	6.59142796	0.15171219	3
8	1.34247078	9.13255425	0.10949839	4
10	1.44504394	11.86783847	0.08426134	5
12	1.55545433	14.81211550	0.06751230	6
14	1.67430076	17.98135370	0.05561317	7
16	1.80222781	21.39274151	0.04674483	8
18	1.93992927	25.06478067	0.03989662	9
20	2.08815200	29.01738656	0.03446210	10
22	2.24769986	33.27199626	0.03005531	11
24	2.41943818	37.85168472	0.02641890	12
26	2.60429838	42.78129001	0.02337470	13
28	2.80328305	48.08754794	0.02079540	14
30	3.01747139	53.79923715	0.01858762	15
32	3.24802507	59.94733512	0.01668131	16
34	3.49619448	66.56518619	0.01502287	17
36	3.76332559	73.68868245	0.01357060	18
38	4.05086719	81.35645834	0.01229159	19
40	4.36037876	89.61010024	0.01115946	20
42	4.69353895	98.49437196	0.01015286	21
44	5.05215466	108.05745757	0.00925434	22
46	5.43817085	118.35122269	0.00844943	23
48	5.85368109	129.43149579	0.00772609	24
50	6.30093891	141.35837102	0.00707422	25
52	6.78237003	154.19653405	0.00648523	26
54	7.30058549	168.01561298	0.00595183	27
56	7.85839585	182.89055591	0.00546775	28
58	8.45882640	198.90203745	0.00502760	29
60	9.10513361	216.13689625	0.00462670	30
62	9.80082272	234.68860598	0.00426097	31
64	10.54966684	254.65778228	0.00392684	32
66	11.35572732	276.15272846	0.00362118	33
68	12.22337586	299.29002287	0.00334124	34
70	13.15731817	324.19515118	0.00308456	35
72	14.16261951	351.00318695	0.00284898	36
74	15.24473216	379.85952420	0.00263255	37
76	16.40952497	410.92066597	0.00243356	38
78	17.66331524	444.35507310	0.00225045	39
80	19.01290292	480.34407791	0.00208184	40
82	20.46560754	519.08286761	0.00192647	41
84	22.02930786	560.78154296	0.00178323	42
86	23.71248466	605.66625773	0.00165107	43
88	25.52426670	653.98044524	0.00152910	44
90	27.47448020	705.98613863	0.00141646	45
92	29.57370220	761.96539204	0.00131240	46
94	31.83331789	822.22181027	0.00121622	47
96	34.26558233	887.08219546	0.00112729	48
98	36.88368698	956.89831946	0.00104504	49
100	39.70183119	1032.04883168	0.00096895	50

8.00% Semi-Annually	Present Value of 1	Present Value of 1 per Period	Payment to Pay Off a Loan of 1	
	0.96153846	0.96153846	1.04000000	Half Years
Years				1
1	0.92455621	1.88609467	0.53019608	2
2	0.85480419	3.62989522	0.27549005	4
3	0.79031453	5.24213686	0.19076190	6
4	0.73069021	6.73274487	0.14852783	8
5	0.67556417	8.11089578	0.12329094	10
6	0.62459705	9.38507376	0.10655217	12
7	0.57747508	10.56312293	0.09466897	14
8	0.53390818	11.65229561	0.08582000	16
9	0.49362812	12.65929697	0.07899933	18
10	0.45638695	13.59032634	0.07358175	20
11	0.42195539	14.45111533	0.06919881	22
12	0.39012147	15.26696314	0.06558683	24
13	0.36068923	15.98276918	0.06256738	26
14	0.33347747	16.66306322	0.06001298	28
15	0.30831867	17.29203330	0.05783010	30
16	0.28505794	17.87355150	0.05594859	32
17	0.26355209	18.41119776	0.05431477	34
18	0.24366872	18.90828195	0.05288688	36
19	0.22528543	19.36786423	0.05163192	38
20	0.20828904	19.79277388	0.05052349	40
21	0.19257493	20.18562674	0.04954020	42
22	0.17804635	20.54884129	0.04866414	44
23	0.16461386	20.88465356	0.04788205	46
24	0.15219476	21.19513088	0.04718065	48
25	0.14071262	21.48218462	0.04655020	50
26	0.13009672	21.74758193	0.04598212	52
27	0.12028173	21.99295667	0.04546910	54
28	0.11120722	22.21981940	0.04500487	56
29	0.10281733	22.42956676	0.04458401	58
30	0.09506040	22.62348997	0.04420185	60
31	0.08788868	22.80278289	0.04385430	62
32	0.08125803	22.96854927	0.04353780	64
33	0.07512762	23.12180961	0.04324921	66
34	0.06945970	23.26350740	0.04298578	68
35	0.06421940	23.39451498	0.04274506	70
36	0.05937445	23.51563885	0.04252489	72
37	0.05489501	23.62762468	0.04232334	74
38	0.05075353	23.73116187	0.04213869	76
39	0.04692449	23.82688782	0.04196939	78
40	0.04338433	23.91539185	0.04181408	80
41	0.04011125	23.99721879	0.04167150	82
42	0.03708510	24.07287241	0.04154054	84
43	0.03428726	24.14281842	0.04142018	86
44	0.03170050	24.20748745	0.04130953	88
45	0.02930890	24.26727759	0.04120775	90
46	0.02709772	24.32255695	0.04111410	92
47	0.02505337	24.37366582	0.04102789	94
48	0.02316325	24.42091884	0.04094850	96
49	0.02141572	24.46460692	0.04087538	98
50	0.01980004	24.50499900	0.04080800	100

	Future Value of 1	Future Value of 1 per Period	Payment for Sinking Fund of 1	**8.00%** Semi-Annually
Half Years				
1	1.04000000	1.00000000	1.00000000	Years
2	1.08160000	2.04000000	0.49019608	1
4	1.16985856	4.24646400	0.23549005	2
6	1.26531902	6.63297546	0.15076190	3
8	1.36856905	9.21422626	0.10852783	4
10	1.48024428	12.00610712	0.08329094	5
12	1.60103222	15.02580546	0.06655217	6
14	1.73167645	18.29191119	0.05466897	7
16	1.87298125	21.82453114	0.04582000	8
18	2.02581652	25.64541288	0.03899333	9
20	2.19112314	29.77807858	0.03358175	10
22	2.36991879	34.24796979	0.02919881	11
24	2.56330416	39.08260412	0.02558683	12
26	2.77246978	44.31174462	0.02256738	13
28	2.99870332	49.96758298	0.02001298	14
30	3.24339751	56.08493775	0.01783010	15
32	3.50805875	62.70146867	0.01594859	16
34	3.79431634	69.85790851	0.01431477	17
36	4.10393255	77.59831385	0.01288688	18
38	4.43881345	85.97033626	0.01163192	19
40	4.80102063	95.02551570	0.01052349	20
42	5.19278391	104.81959778	0.00954020	21
44	5.61651508	115.41287696	0.00866454	22
46	6.07482271	126.87056772	0.00788205	23
48	6.57052824	139.26320604	0.00718065	24
50	7.10668335	152.66708366	0.00655020	25
52	7.68658871	167.16471768	0.00598212	26
54	8.31381435	182.84535865	0.00546910	27
56	8.99222160	199.80553991	0.00500487	28
58	9.72598688	218.14967197	0.00458401	29
60	10.51962741	237.99068520	0.00420185	30
62	11.37802900	259.45072511	0.00385430	31
64	12.30647617	282.66190428	0.00353780	32
66	13.31068463	307.76711567	0.00324921	33
68	14.39683649	334.92091231	0.00298578	34
70	15.57161835	364.29045876	0.00274506	35
72	16.84226241	396.05656019	0.00252489	36
74	18.21659102	430.41477550	0.00232334	37
76	19.70306485	467.57662118	0.00213869	38
78	21.31083494	507.77087347	0.00196939	39
80	23.04979907	551.24497675	0.00181408	40
82	24.93066267	598.26656685	0.00167150	41
84	26.96500475	649.12511870	0.00154054	42
86	29.16534914	704.13372869	0.00142018	43
88	31.54524163	763.63104063	0.00130953	44
90	34.11933334	827.98333354	0.00120775	45
92	36.90347094	897.58677356	0.00111410	46
94	39.91479417	972.86985428	0.00102789	47
96	43.17184138	1054.29603439	0.00094850	48
98	46.69466363	1142.36659080	0.00087538	49
100	50.50494818	1237.62370461	0.00080800	50

8.50% Semi-Annually	Present Value of 1	Present Value of 1 per Period	Payment to Pay Off a Loan of 1	
Years	0.95923261	0.95923261	1.04250000	Half Years
				1
1	0.92012721	1.87935982	0.53209608	2
2	0.84663408	3.60860993	0.27711502	4
3	0.77901105	5.19974000	0.19231731	6
4	0.71678926	6.66378206	0.15006493	8
5	0.65953730	8.01088700	0.12483012	10
6	0.60685822	9.25039491	0.10810349	12
7	0.55838676	10.39089986	0.09623806	14
8	0.51378685	11.44030949	0.08741022	16
9	0.47274926	12.40589985	0.08060681	18
10	0.43498945	13.29436581	0.07521983	20
11	0.40024563	14.11186751	0.07086234	22
12	0.36827689	14.86407307	0.06727631	24
13	0.33886159	15.55619787	0.06428306	26
14	0.31179577	16.19304072	0.06175492	28
15	0.28689177	16.77901717	0.05959825	30
16	0.26397692	17.31819003	0.05774275	32
17	0.24289235	17.81429766	0.05613469	34
18	0.22349186	18.27077978	0.05473220	36
19	0.20564094	18.69080140	0.05350225	38
20	0.18921582	19.07727472	0.05241839	40
21	0.17410263	19.43287934	0.05145918	42
22	0.16019657	19.76760082	0.05060708	44
23	0.14740122	20.06114781	0.04984760	46
24	0.13562787	20.33816774	0.04916864	48
25	0.12479489	20.59306131	0.04856005	50
26	0.11482718	20.82759582	0.04801322	52
27	0.10565561	21.04339740	0.04752084	54
28	0.09721660	21.24196231	0.04707663	56
29	0.08945164	21.42466729	0.04667517	58
30	0.08230689	21.59277911	0.04631178	60
31	0.07573281	21.74746337	0.04598237	62
32	0.06968382	21.88979256	0.04568339	64
33	0.06411798	22.02075352	0.04541171	66
34	0.05899669	22.14125427	0.04516456	68
35	0.05428446	22.25213029	0.04493952	70
36	0.04994861	22.35415032	0.04473442	72
37	0.04595908	22.44802174	0.04454736	74
38	0.04228820	22.53439538	0.04437661	76
39	0.03891052	22.61387012	0.04422065	78
40	0.03580263	22.68699698	0.04407811	80
41	0.03294297	22.75428300	0.04394777	82
42	0.03031173	22.81619470	0.04382852	84
43	0.02789064	22.87316134	0.04371936	86
44	0.02566294	22.92557790	0.04361940	88
45	0.02361317	22.97380779	0.04352783	90
46	0.02172712	23.01818543	0.04344391	92
47	0.01999171	23.05901851	0.04336698	94
48	0.01839492	23.09659013	0.04329643	96
49	0.01692567	23.13116080	0.04323173	98
50	0.01557377	23.16297022	0.04317236	100

	Future Value of 1	Future Value of 1 per Period	Payment for Sinking Fund of 1	**8.50%** Semi-Annually
Half Years				
1	1.04250000	1.00000000	1.00000000	Years
2	1.08680625	2.04250000	0.48959608	1
4	1.18114783	4.26230177	0.23461502	2
6	1.28367884	6.67479620	0.14981731	3
8	1.39511018	9.29671023	0.10756493	4
10	1.51621447	12.14622278	0.08233012	5
12	1.64783136	15.24309083	0.06560349	6
14	1.79087342	18.60878638	0.05373806	7
16	1.94633243	22.26664534	0.04491022	8
18	2.11528625	26.24202933	0.03810681	9
20	2.29890631	30.56250149	0.03271983	10
22	2.49846575	35.25801763	0.02836234	11
24	2.71534819	40.36113392	0.02477631	12
26	2.95105739	45.90723260	0.02178306	13
28	3.20722761	51.93476732	0.01925492	14
30	3.48563501	58.48552971	0.01709825	15
32	3.78820992	65.60493922	0.01524275	16
34	4.11705021	73.34235798	0.01363469	17
36	4.47443590	81.75143304	0.01223220	18
38	4.86284491	90.89046838	0.01100225	19
40	5.28497024	100.82282910	0.00991839	20
42	5.74373868	111.61738080	0.00895918	21
44	6.24233110	123.34896707	0.00810708	22
46	6.78420445	136.09892834	0.00734760	23
48	7.37311580	149.95566594	0.00666864	24
50	8.01314834	165.01525496	0.00606005	25
52	8.70873969	181.38211044	0.00551322	26
54	9.46471273	199.16971127	0.00502084	27
56	10.28630895	218.50138701	0.00457663	28
58	11.17922485	239.51117304	0.00417517	29
60	12.14965144	262.34473980	0.00381178	30
62	13.20431712	287.16040287	0.00348237	31
64	14.35053438	314.13022060	0.00318339	32
66	15.59625045	343.44118706	0.00291171	33
68	16.95010247	375.29652866	0.00266456	34
70	18.42147730	409.91711289	0.00243952	35
72	20.02057666	447.54298027	0.00223442	36
74	21.75848784	488.43500810	0.00204736	37
76	23.64726058	532.87671952	0.00187661	38
78	25.69999059	581.17624926	0.00172065	39
80	27.93091040	633.66848004	0.00157811	40
82	30.35548799	690.71736454	0.00144777	41
84	32.99053407	752.71844876	0.00132852	42
86	35.85431862	820.10161461	0.00121936	43
88	38.96669757	893.33406039	0.00111940	44
90	42.34925046	972.92354017	0.00102783	45
92	46.02543008	1059.42188423	0.00094391	46
94	50.02072507	1153.42882517	0.00086698	47
96	54.36283664	1255.59615612	0.00079643	48
98	59.08187062	1366.63224995	0.00073173	49
100	64.21054625	1487.30697069	0.00067236	50

9.00% Semi-Annually	Present Value of 1	Present Value of 1 per Period	Payment to Pay Off a Loan of 1	
Years				Half Years
	0.95693780	0.95693780	1.04500000	1
1	0.91572995	1.87266775	0.53399756	2
2	0.83856134	3.58752570	0.27874365	4
3	0.76789574	5.15787248	0.19387839	6
4	0.70318513	6.59588607	0.15160965	8
5	0.64392768	7.91271818	0.12637882	10
6	0.58966386	9.11858078	0.10966619	12
7	0.53997286	10.22282528	0.09782032	14
8	0.49446932	11.23401505	0.08901537	16
9	0.45280037	12.15999180	0.08223690	18
10	0.41464286	13.00793645	0.07687614	20
11	0.37970089	13.78442476	0.07254565	22
12	0.34770347	14.49547837	0.06898703	24
13	0.31840248	15.14661145	0.06602137	26
14	0.29157069	15.74287351	0.06352081	28
15	0.26700002	16.28888854	0.06139154	30
16	0.24449991	16.78889086	0.05956320	32
17	0.22389589	17.24675796	0.05798191	34
18	0.20502817	17.66604058	0.05660578	36
19	0.18775044	18.04999023	0.05540169	38
20	0.17192870	18.40158442	0.05434315	40
21	0.15744026	18.72354975	0.05340868	42
22	0.14417276	19.01838305	0.05258071	44
23	0.13202332	19.28837074	0.05184471	46
24	0.12089771	19.53560654	0.05118858	48
25	0.11070965	19.76200778	0.05060215	50
26	0.10138014	19.96933017	0.05007679	52
27	0.09283683	20.15918149	0.04960519	54
28	0.08501347	20.33303404	0.04918105	56
29	0.07784938	20.49223602	0.04879897	58
30	0.07128901	20.63802204	0.04845426	60
31	0.06528148	20.77152266	0.04814284	62
32	0.05978021	20.89377319	0.04786115	64
33	0.05474253	21.00572165	0.04760608	66
34	0.05012937	21.10823621	0.04737487	68
35	0.04590497	21.20211187	0.04716511	70
36	0.04203655	21.28807662	0.04697465	72
37	0.03849413	21.36679711	0.04680159	74
38	0.03525023	21.43888383	0.04664422	76
39	0.03227969	21.50489579	0.04650104	78
40	0.02955948	21.56534493	0.04637069	80
41	0.02706850	21.62070001	0.04625197	82
42	0.02478744	21.67139032	0.04614379	84
43	0.02269860	21.71780895	0.04604516	86
44	0.02078579	21.76031588	0.04595522	88
45	0.01903417	21.79924075	0.04587316	90
46	0.01743016	21.83488542	0.04579827	92
47	0.01596132	21.86752631	0.04572991	94
48	0.01461626	21.89741655	0.04566749	96
49	0.01338454	21.92478794	0.04561048	98
50	0.01225663	21.94985274	0.04555839	100

	Future Value of 1	Future Value of 1 per Period	Payment for Sinking Fund of 1	**9.00%** Semi-Annually
Half Years				
1	1.04500000	1.00000000	1.00000000	Years
2	1.09202500	2.04500000	0.48899756	1
4	1.19251860	4.27819113	0.23374365	2
6	1.30226012	6.71689166	0.14887839	3
8	1.42210061	9.38001362	0.10660965	4
10	1.55296942	12.28820937	0.08137882	5
12	1.69588143	15.46403184	0.06466619	6
14	1.85194492	18.93210937	0.05282032	7
16	2.02237015	22.71933673	0.04401537	8
18	2.20847877	26.85508370	0.03723690	9
20	2.41171402	31.37142277	0.03187614	10
22	2.63365201	36.30337795	0.02754565	11
24	2.87601383	41.68919631	0.02398703	12
26	3.14067901	47.57064460	0.02102137	13
28	3.42969999	53.99333317	0.01852081	14
30	3.74531813	61.00706966	0.01639154	15
32	4.08998104	68.66624524	0.01456320	16
34	4.46636154	77.03025646	0.01298191	17
36	4.87737846	86.16396581	0.01160578	18
38	5.32621921	96.13820476	0.01040169	19
40	5.81636454	107.03032306	0.00934315	20
42	6.35161548	118.92478854	0.00840868	21
44	6.93612290	131.91384220	0.00758071	22
46	7.57441961	146.09821353	0.00684471	23
48	8.27145557	161.58790163	0.00618858	24
50	9.03263627	178.50302828	0.00560215	25
52	9.86386463	196.97476946	0.00507679	26
54	10.77158677	217.14637262	0.00460519	27
56	11.76284204	239.17426756	0.00418105	28
58	12.84531758	263.22927953	0.00379897	29
60	14.02740793	289.49795398	0.00345426	30
62	15.31828014	318.18400319	0.00314284	31
64	16.72794487	349.50988608	0.00286115	32
66	18.26733400	383.71853335	0.00260608	33
68	19.94838541	421.07523138	0.00237487	34
70	21.78413558	461.86967955	0.00216511	35
72	23.78882066	506.41823466	0.00197465	36
74	25.97798688	555.06637505	0.00180159	37
76	28.36861112	608.19135822	0.00164422	38
78	30.97923256	666.20516796	0.00150104	39
80	33.83009643	729.55769854	0.00137069	40
82	36.94331106	798.74024575	0.00125197	41
84	40.34301926	874.28931686	0.00114379	42
86	44.05558561	956.79079125	0.00104516	43
88	48.10980087	1046.88446381	0.00095522	44
90	52.53710530	1145.26900659	0.00087316	45
92	57.37183241	1252.70738692	0.00079827	46
94	62.65147529	1370.03278420	0.00072991	47
96	68.41697730	1498.15505117	0.00066749	48
98	74.71304964	1638.06776976	0.00061048	49
100	81.58851803	1790.85595627	0.00055839	50

9.50% Semi-Annually	Present Value of 1	Present Value of 1 per Period	Payment to Pay Off a Loan of 1	
Years	0.95465394	0.95465394	1.04750000	Half Years
				1
1	0.91136414	1.86601808	0.53590049	2
2	0.83058460	3.56664004	0.28037592	4
3	0.75696502	5.11652592	0.19544512	6
4	0.68987077	6.52903633	0.15316196	8
5	0.62872349	7.81634767	0.12793699	10
6	0.57299604	8.98955706	0.11124019	12
7	0.52220804	10.05877803	0.09941565	14
8	0.47592169	11.03322768	0.09063531	16
9	0.43373796	11.92130615	0.08388343	18
10	0.39529322	12.73066902	0.07855047	20
11	0.36025607	13.46829332	0.07424846	22
12	0.32832446	14.14053765	0.07071867	24
13	0.29922314	14.75319703	0.06778192	26
14	0.27270124	15.31155282	0.06531016	28
15	0.24853013	15.82041827	0.06320945	30
16	0.22650145	16.28417999	0.06140929	32
17	0.20642530	16.70683579	0.05985574	34
18	0.18812862	17.09202913	0.05850680	36
19	0.17145367	17.44308053	0.05732932	38
20	0.15625673	17.76301619	0.05629675	40
21	0.14240678	18.05459407	0.05538756	42
22	0.12978443	18.32032770	0.05458418	44
23	0.11828088	18.56250780	0.05387203	46
24	0.10779695	18.78322206	0.05323900	48
25	0.09824228	18.98437312	0.05267490	50
26	0.08953449	19.16769499	0.05217111	52
27	0.08159852	19.33476796	0.05172030	54
28	0.07436597	19.48703228	0.05131618	56
29	0.06777448	19.62580052	0.05095334	58
30	0.06176723	19.75226891	0.05062710	60
31	0.05629244	19.86752767	0.05033339	62
32	0.05130291	19.97257038	0.05006867	64
33	0.04675563	20.06830253	0.04982982	66
34	0.04261140	20.15554938	0.04961413	68
35	0.03883451	20.23506303	0.04941917	70
36	0.03539238	20.30752892	0.04924282	72
37	0.03225534	20.37357174	0.04908320	74
38	0.02939636	20.43376079	0.04893862	76
39	0.02679079	20.48861493	0.04880759	78
40	0.02441617	20.53860703	0.04868879	80
41	0.02225202	20.58416804	0.04858103	82
42	0.02027969	20.62569071	0.04848322	84
43	0.01848218	20.66353298	0.04839443	86
44	0.01684400	20.69802107	0.04831380	88
45	0.01535102	20.72945227	0.04824054	90
46	0.01399037	20.75809755	0.04817397	92
47	0.01275032	20.78420383	0.04811346	94
48	0.01162018	20.80799615	0.04805845	96
49	0.01059022	20.82967962	0.04800842	98
50	0.00965154	20.84944116	0.04796292	100

	Future Value of 1	Future Value of 1 per Period	Payment for Sinking Fund of 1	**9.50%** Semi-Annually
Half Years				
1	1.04750000	1.00000000	1.00000000	Years
2	1.09725625	2.04750000	0.48840049	1
4	1.20397128	4.29413217	0.23287592	2
6	1.32106501	6.75926336	0.14794512	3
8	1.44954684	9.46414397	0.10566196	4
10	1.59052433	12.43209112	0.08043699	5
12	1.74521276	15.68868969	0.06374019	6
14	1.91494561	19.26201281	0.05191565	7
16	2.10118604	23.18286395	0.04313531	8
18	2.30553951	27.48504236	0.03638343	9
20	2.52976764	32.20563451	0.03105047	10
22	2.77580335	37.38533375	0.02674846	11
24	3.04576758	43.06879111	0.02321867	12
26	3.34198751	49.30500023	0.02028192	13
28	3.66701668	56.14771966	0.01781016	14
30	4.02365698	63.65593632	0.01570945	15
32	4.41498276	71.89437398	0.01390929	16
34	4.84436743	80.93405119	0.01235574	17
36	5.31551244	90.85289350	0.01100680	18
38	5.83247925	101.73640522	0.00982932	19
40	6.39972431	113.67840648	0.00879675	20
42	7.02213750	126.78184201	0.00788756	21
44	7.70508426	141.15966853	0.00708418	22
46	8.45445186	156.93582854	0.00637203	23
48	9.27670014	174.24631871	0.00573900	24
50	10.17891721	193.24036225	0.00517490	25
52	11.16888052	214.08169523	0.00467111	26
54	12.25512396	236.94997810	0.00422030	27
56	13.44701136	262.04234441	0.00381618	28
58	14.75481726	289.57510017	0.00345334	29
60	16.18981545	319.78558850	0.00312710	30
62	17.76437619	352.93423564	0.00283339	31
64	19.49207281	389.30679590	0.00256867	32
66	21.38779871	429.21681497	0.00232982	33
68	23.46789581	473.00833283	0.00211413	34
70	25.75029535	521.05884950	0.00191917	35
72	28.25467251	573.78257923	0.00174282	36
74	31.00261601	631.63402120	0.00158320	37
76	34.01781418	695.11187747	0.00143862	38
78	37.32625922	764.76335201	0.00130759	39
80	40.95647122	841.18886776	0.00118879	40
82	44.93974402	925.04724258	0.00108103	41
84	49.31041500	1017.06136847	0.00098322	42
86	54.10616105	1118.02444319	0.00089443	43
88	59.36832338	1228.80680794	0.00081380	44
90	65.14226388	1350.36345005	0.00074054	45
92	71.47775618	1483.74223534	0.00067397	46
94	78.42941470	1630.09294112	0.00061346	47
96	86.05716547	1790.67716772	0.00055845	48
98	94.42676267	1966.87921402	0.00050842	49
100	103.61035550	2160.21801057	0.00046292	50

10.00% Semi-Annually	Present Value of 1	Present Value of 1 per Period	Payment to Pay Off a Loan of 1	
				Half Years
Years	0.95238095	0.95238095	1.05000000	1
1	0.90702948	1.85941043	0.53780488	2
2	0.82270247	3.54595050	0.28201183	4
3	0.74621540	5.07569207	0.19701747	6
4	0.67683936	6.46321276	0.15472181	8
5	0.61391325	7.72173493	0.12950457	10
6	0.55683742	8.86325164	0.11282541	12
7	0.50506795	9.89864094	0.10102397	14
8	0.45811152	10.83776956	0.09226991	16
9	0.41552065	11.68958690	0.08554622	18
10	0.37688948	12.46221034	0.08024259	20
11	0.34184987	13.16300258	0.07597051	22
12	0.31006791	13.79864179	0.07247090	24
13	0.28124073	14.37518550	0.06956432	26
14	0.25509364	14.89812726	0.06712253	28
15	0.23137745	15.37245103	0.06505144	30
16	0.20986617	15.80267667	0.06328042	32
17	0.19035480	16.19290401	0.06175545	34
18	0.17265741	16.54585551	0.06043446	36
19	0.15660536	16.86789271	0.05928423	38
20	0.14204568	17.15908635	0.05827816	40
21	0.12883962	17.42320758	0.05739471	42
22	0.11686133	17.66277331	0.05661625	44
23	0.10599668	17.88006650	0.05592820	46
24	0.09614211	18.07715782	0.05531843	48
25	0.08720373	18.25592546	0.05477674	50
26	0.07909635	18.41807298	0.05429450	52
27	0.07174272	18.56514556	0.05386438	54
28	0.06507276	18.69854473	0.05348010	56
29	0.05902291	18.81954170	0.05313626	58
30	0.05353552	18.92928953	0.05282818	60
31	0.04855830	19.02883404	0.05255183	62
32	0.04404381	19.11912384	0.05230365	64
33	0.03994903	19.20101936	0.05208057	66
34	0.03623495	19.27530101	0.05187986	68
35	0.03286617	19.34267665	0.05169915	70
36	0.02981058	19.40378834	0.05153633	72
37	0.02703908	19.45921845	0.05138953	74
38	0.02452524	19.50949519	0.05125709	76
39	0.02224512	19.55509768	0.05113756	78
40	0.02017698	19.59646048	0.05102962	80
41	0.01830111	19.63397776	0.05093211	82
42	0.01659965	19.66800704	0.05084399	84
43	0.01505637	19.69887264	0.05076433	86
44	0.01365657	19.72686857	0.05069228	88
45	0.01238691	19.75226174	0.05062711	90
46	0.01123530	19.77529410	0.05056815	92
47	0.01019074	19.79618512	0.05051478	94
48	0.00924331	19.81513390	0.05046648	96
49	0.00838395	19.83232100	0.05042274	98
50	0.00760449	19.84791020	0.05038314	100

	Future Value of 1	Future Value of 1 per Period	Payment for Sinking Fund of 1	**10.00%** Semi-Annually
Half Years				
1	1.05000000	1.00000000	1.00000000	Years
2	1.10250000	2.05000000	0.48780488	1
4	1.21550625	4.31012500	0.23201183	2
6	1.34009564	6.80191281	0.14701747	3
8	1.47745544	9.54910888	0.10472181	4
10	1.62889463	12.57789254	0.07950457	5
12	1.79585633	15.91712652	0.06282541	6
14	1.97993160	19.59863199	0.05102397	7
16	2.18287459	23.65749177	0.04226991	8
18	2.40661923	28.13238467	0.03554622	9
20	2.65329771	33.06595410	0.03024259	10
22	2.92526072	38.50521440	0.02597051	11
24	3.22509994	44.50199887	0.02247090	12
26	3.55567269	51.11345376	0.01956432	13
28	3.92012914	58.40258277	0.01712253	14
30	4.32194238	66.43884750	0.01505144	15
32	4.76494147	75.29882937	0.01328042	16
34	5.25334797	85.06695938	0.01175545	17
36	5.79181614	95.83632272	0.01043446	18
38	6.38547729	107.70954580	0.00928423	19
40	7.03998871	120.79977424	0.00827816	20
42	7.76158756	135.23175110	0.00739471	21
44	8.55715028	151.14300559	0.00661625	22
46	9.43425818	168.68516366	0.00592820	23
48	10.40126965	188.02539294	0.00531843	24
50	11.46739979	209.34799572	0.00477674	25
52	12.64280826	232.85616528	0.00429450	26
54	13.93869611	258.77392222	0.00386438	27
56	15.36741246	287.34824924	0.00348010	28
58	16.94257224	318.85144479	0.00313626	29
60	18.67918589	353.58371788	0.00282818	30
62	20.59380245	391.87604897	0.00255183	31
64	22.70466720	434.09334398	0.00230365	32
66	25.03189559	480.63791174	0.00208057	33
68	27.59766488	531.95329770	0.00187986	34
70	30.42642554	588.52851071	0.00169915	35
72	33.54513415	650.90268306	0.00153633	36
74	36.98351040	719.67020807	0.00138953	37
76	40.77432022	795.48640440	0.00125709	38
78	44.95368804	879.07376085	0.00113756	39
80	49.56144107	971.22882134	0.00102962	40
82	54.64148878	1072.82977552	0.00093211	41
84	60.24224138	1184.84482752	0.00084399	42
86	66.41707112	1308.34142234	0.00076433	43
88	73.22482091	1444.49641812	0.00069228	44
90	80.73036505	1594.60730098	0.00062711	45
92	89.00522747	1760.10454933	0.00056815	46
94	98.12826328	1942.56526564	0.00051478	47
96	108.18641027	2143.72820537	0.00046648	48
98	119.27551732	2365.51034642	0.00042274	49
100	131.50125785	2610.02515693	0.00038314	50

10.50% Semi-Annually	Present Value of 1	Present Value of 1 per Period	Payment to Pay Off a Loan of 1	
Years	0.95011876	0.95011876	1.05250000	Half Years 1
1	0.90272567	1.85284443	0.53971072	2
2	0.81491363	3.52545466	0.28365136	4
3	0.73564345	5.03536284	0.19859542	6
4	0.66408423	6.39839571	0.15628918	8
5	0.59948588	7.62884047	0.13108152	10
6	0.54117129	8.73959454	0.11442178	12
7	0.48852921	9.74230074	0.10264516	14
8	0.44100786	10.64746937	0.09391903	16
9	0.39810911	11.46458833	0.08722511	18
10	0.35938331	12.20222258	0.08195228	20
11	0.32442454	12.86810395	0.07771153	22
12	0.29286636	13.46921216	0.07424339	24
13	0.26437798	14.01184797	0.07136817	26
14	0.23868079	14.50169921	0.06895744	28
15	0.21544522	14.94390055	0.06691693	30
16	0.19448793	15.34308703	0.06517593	32
17	0.17556925	15.70344291	0.06368030	34
18	0.15849087	16.02874541	0.06238791	36
19	0.14307377	16.32240433	0.06126548	38
20	0.12915637	16.58749778	0.06028637	40
21	0.11659277	16.82680443	0.05942899	42
22	0.10525128	17.04283269	0.05867569	44
23	0.09501304	17.23784695	0.05801189	46
24	0.08577071	17.41389132	0.05742542	48
25	0.07742742	17.57281109	0.05690609	50
26	0.06989572	17.71627205	0.05644528	52
27	0.06309666	17.84577794	0.05603566	54
28	0.05695897	17.96268624	0.05567096	56
29	0.05141833	18.06822235	0.05534579	58
30	0.04641664	18.16349251	0.05505549	60
31	0.04190150	18.24949533	0.05479604	62
32	0.03782556	18.32713228	0.05456391	64
33	0.03414610	18.39721715	0.05435605	66
34	0.03082456	18.46048456	0.05416976	68
35	0.02782612	18.51759768	0.05400269	70
36	0.02511935	18.56915515	0.05385275	72
37	0.02267589	18.61569741	0.05371811	74
38	0.02047010	18.65771230	0.05359714	76
39	0.01847889	18.69564022	0.05348841	78
40	0.01668137	18.72987872	0.05339063	80
41	0.01505870	18.76078670	0.05330267	82
42	0.01359387	18.78868813	0.05322351	84
43	0.01227154	18.81387546	0.05315226	86
44	0.01107783	18.83661271	0.05308810	88
45	0.01000024	18.85713821	0.05303032	90
46	0.00902748	18.87566711	0.05297826	92
47	0.00814934	18.89239362	0.05293136	94
48	0.00735661	18.90749307	0.05288908	96
49	0.00664100	18.92112373	0.05285098	98
50	0.00599500	18.93342848	0.05281664	100

	Future Value of 1	Future Value of 1 per Period	Payment for Sinking Fund of 1	**10.50%** Semi-Annually
Half Years				
1	1.05250000	1.00000000	1.00000000	Years
2	1.10775625	2.05250000	0.48721072	1
4	1.22712391	4.32616970	0.23115136	2
6	1.35935418	6.84484153	0.14609542	3
8	1.50583309	9.63491598	0.10378918	4
10	1.66809602	12.72563840	0.07858152	5
12	1.84784709	16.14940547	0.06192178	6
14	2.04696050	19.94210484	0.05014516	7
16	2.26753329	24.14349128	0.04141903	8
18	2.51187418	28.79760336	0.03472511	9
20	2.78254432	33.95322511	0.02945228	10
22	3.08238086	39.66439732	0.02521153	11
24	3.41452666	45.99098403	0.02174339	12
26	3.78246325	52.99930001	0.01886817	13
28	4.19004731	60.76280583	0.01645744	14
30	4.64155109	69.36287792	0.01441693	15
32	5.14170723	78.88966154	0.01267593	16
34	5.69575832	89.44301563	0.01118030	17
36	6.30951188	101.13355958	0.00988791	18
38	6.98940122	114.08382271	0.00876548	19
40	7.74255288	128.42957871	0.00778637	20
42	8.57686135	144.32116850	0.00692899	21
44	9.50107176	161.92517642	0.00617569	22
46	10.52487163	181.42612621	0.00551189	23
48	11.65899232	203.02842522	0.00492542	24
50	12.91532162	226.95850696	0.00440609	25
52	14.30702824	253.46720458	0.00394528	26
54	15.84869995	282.83238004	0.00353566	27
56	17.55649643	315.36183669	0.00317096	28
58	19.44831864	351.39654561	0.00284579	29
60	21.54399653	391.31421963	0.00255549	30
62	23.86549681	435.53327251	0.00229604	31
64	26.43715325	484.51720470	0.00206391	32
66	29.28592174	538.77946174	0.00185605	33
68	32.44166285	598.88881611	0.00166976	34
70	35.93745478	665.47532911	0.00150269	35
72	39.80994014	739.23695504	0.00135275	36
74	44.09971000	820.94685717	0.00121811	37
76	48.85172938	911.46151195	0.00109714	38
78	54.11580854	1011.72968650	0.00098841	39
80	59.94712514	1122.80238353	0.00089063	40
82	66.40680254	1245.84385787	0.00080267	41
84	73.56255055	1382.14382008	0.00072351	42
86	81.48937514	1533.13095509	0.00065226	43
88	90.27036462	1700.38789757	0.00058810	44
90	99.99756060	1885.66782096	0.00053032	45
92	110.77292274	2090.91281410	0.00047826	46
94	122.70939750	2318.27423802	0.00043136	47
96	135.93210201	2570.13527638	0.00038908	48
98	150.57963558	2849.13591576	0.00035098	49
100	166.80553243	3158.20061778	0.00031664	50

11.00% Semi-Annually	Present Value of 1	Present Value of 1 per Period	Payment to Pay Off a Loan of 1	
				Half Years
Years	0.94786730	0.94786730	1.05500000	1
1	0.89845242	1.84631971	0.54161800	2
2	0.80721674	3.50515012	0.28529449	4
3	0.72524583	4.99553031	0.20017895	6
4	0.65159887	6.33456599	0.15786401	8
5	0.58543058	7.53762583	0.13266777	10
6	0.52598152	8.61851785	0.11602923	12
7	0.47256937	9.58964790	0.10427912	14
8	0.42458109	10.46216203	0.09558254	16
9	0.38146590	11.24607447	0.08891992	18
10	0.34272896	11.95038248	0.08367933	20
11	0.30792567	12.58316973	0.07947123	22
12	0.27665656	13.15169895	0.07603580	24
13	0.24856275	13.66249541	0.07319307	26
14	0.22332181	14.12142172	0.07081440	28
15	0.20064402	14.53374517	0.06880539	30
16	0.18026910	14.90419817	0.06709519	32
17	0.16196321	15.23703257	0.06562958	34
18	0.14551624	15.53606843	0.06436635	36
19	0.13073941	15.80473793	0.06327217	38
20	0.11746314	16.04612469	0.06232034	40
21	0.10553504	16.26299920	0.06148927	42
22	0.09481822	16.45785063	0.06076128	44
23	0.08518965	16.63291537	0.06012175	46
24	0.07653885	16.79020271	0.05955854	48
25	0.06876652	16.93151790	0.05906145	50
26	0.06178344	17.05848287	0.05862186	52
27	0.05550948	17.17255486	0.05823245	54
28	0.04987263	17.27504311	0.05788698	56
29	0.04480818	17.36712393	0.05758006	58
30	0.04025802	17.44985416	0.05730707	60
31	0.03616992	17.52418334	0.05706400	62
32	0.03249695	17.59096457	0.05684737	64
33	0.02919696	17.65096433	0.05665413	66
34	0.02623208	17.70487125	0.05648160	68
35	0.02356828	17.75330406	0.05632754	70
36	0.02117498	17.79681864	0.05618982	72
37	0.01902471	17.83591441	0.05606665	74
38	0.01709279	17.87104010	0.05595645	76
39	0.01535706	17.90259887	0.05585781	78
40	0.01379759	17.93095291	0.05576948	80
41	0.01239648	17.95642767	0.05569036	82
42	0.01113765	17.97931554	0.05561947	84
43	0.01000664	17.99987919	0.05555593	86
44	0.00899049	18.01835466	0.05549896	88
45	0.00807753	18.03495398	0.05544788	90
46	0.00725728	18.04986769	0.05540207	92
47	0.00652032	18.06326694	0.05536097	94
48	0.00585820	18.07530553	0.05532410	96
49	0.00526331	18.08612164	0.05529101	98
50	0.00472883	18.09583939	0.05526132	100

	Future Value of 1	Future Value of 1 per Period	Payment for Sinking Fund of 1	**11.00%** Semi-Annually
Half Years 1	1.05500000	1.00000000	1.00000000	Years
2	1.11302500	2.05500000	0.48661800	1
4	1.23882465	4.34226637	0.23029449	2
6	1.37884281	6.88805103	0.14517895	3
8	1.53468651	9.72157300	0.10286401	4
10	1.70814446	12.87535379	0.07766777	5
12	1.90120749	16.38559065	0.06102923	6
14	2.11609146	20.29257203	0.04927912	7
16	2.35526270	24.64113996	0.04058254	8
18	2.62146627	29.48120483	0.03391992	9
20	2.91775749	34.86831801	0.02867933	10
22	3.24753703	40.86430965	0.02447123	11
24	3.61458990	47.53799825	0.02103580	12
26	4.02312893	54.96598051	0.01819307	13
28	4.47784307	63.23351045	0.01581440	14
30	4.98395129	72.43547797	0.01380539	15
32	5.54726238	82.67749787	0.01209519	16
34	6.17424171	94.07712207	0.01062958	17
36	6.87208538	106.76518879	0.00936635	18
38	7.64880283	120.88732425	0.00827217	19
40	8.51330877	136.60561407	0.00732034	20
42	9.47552550	154.10046360	0.00648927	21
44	10.54649677	173.57266850	0.00576128	22
46	11.73851456	195.24571936	0.00512175	23
48	13.06526017	219.36836679	0.00455854	24
50	14.54196120	246.21747645	0.00406145	25
52	16.18556637	276.10120672	0.00362186	26
54	18.01494001	309.36254561	0.00323245	27
56	20.05107860	346.38324733	0.00288698	28
58	22.31735176	387.58821386	0.00258006	29
60	24.83977045	433.45037173	0.00230707	30
62	27.64728550	484.49609999	0.00206400	31
64	30.77211994	541.31127170	0.00184737	32
66	34.25013880	604.54797818	0.00165413	33
68	38.12126074	674.93201341	0.00148163	34
70	42.42991623	753.27120423	0.00132754	35
72	47.22555751	840.46468209	0.00118982	36
74	52.56322615	937.51320278	0.00106665	37
76	58.50418479	1045.53063252	0.00095645	38
78	65.11662027	1165.75673226	0.00085781	39
80	72.47642628	1299.57138693	0.00076948	40
82	80.66807436	1448.51044294	0.00069036	41
84	89.78558347	1614.28333575	0.00061947	42
86	99.93359904	1798.79270977	0.00055593	43
88	111.22859407	2004.15625579	0.00049896	44
90	123.80020591	2232.73101660	0.00044788	45
92	137.79272419	2487.14043976	0.00040207	46
94	153.36674684	2770.30448796	0.00036097	47
96	170.70102340	3085.47315271	0.00032410	48
98	189.99450657	3436.26375580	0.00029101	49
100	211.46863567	3826.70246680	0.00026132	50

11.50% Semi-Annually	Present Value of 1	Present Value of 1 per Period	Payment to Pay Off a Loan of 1	
	0.94562648	0.94562648	1.05750000	Half Years
Years				1
1	0.89420944	1.83983591	0.54352673	2
2	0.79961051	3.48503454	0.28694120	4
3	0.71501927	4.95618668	0.20176803	6
4	0.63937697	6.27170481	0.15944628	8
5	0.57173692	7.44805352	0.13426327	10
6	0.51125255	8.49995565	0.11764767	12
7	0.45716685	9.44057645	0.10592574	14
8	0.40880291	10.28168845	0.09726029	16
9	0.36555542	11.03381873	0.09063045	18
10	0.32688311	11.70638072	0.08542350	20
11	0.29230196	12.30779201	0.08124934	22
12	0.26137917	12.84557965	0.07784779	24
13	0.23372772	13.32647443	0.07503860	26
14	0.20900150	13.75649509	0.07269293	28
15	0.18689114	14.14102361	0.07071624	30
16	0.16711982	14.48487265	0.06903754	32
17	0.14944012	14.79234570	0.06760253	34
18	0.13363077	15.06729100	0.06636893	36
19	0.11949389	15.31314969	0.06530335	38
20	0.10685257	15.53299884	0.06437907	40
21	0.09554857	15.72959003	0.06357445	42
22	0.08544044	15.90534373	0.06287179	44
23	0.07640164	16.06258011	0.06225650	46
24	0.06831907	16.20314660	0.06171641	48
25	0.06109156	16.32884248	0.06124133	50
26	0.05462865	16.44124092	0.06082266	52
27	0.04884945	16.54114867	0.06045310	54
28	0.04368164	16.63162364	0.06012642	56
29	0.03906054	16.71199069	0.05983728	58
30	0.03492830	16.78385567	0.05958107	60
31	0.03123321	16.84811801	0.05935381	62
32	0.02792904	16.90558200	0.05915206	64
33	0.02497441	16.95696684	0.05897281	66
34	0.02233235	17.00291565	0.05881344	68
35	0.01996980	17.04400351	0.05867166	70
36	0.01785718	17.08074466	0.05854546	72
37	0.01596806	17.11359895	0.05843306	74
38	0.01427879	17.14297756	0.05833292	76
39	0.01276823	17.16924819	0.05824367	78
40	0.01141747	17.19273964	0.05816409	80
41	0.01020961	17.21374591	0.05809311	82
42	0.00912953	17.23252992	0.05802978	84
43	0.00816371	17.24932675	0.05797328	86
44	0.00730007	17.26434664	0.05792284	88
45	0.00652779	17.27777704	0.05787781	90
46	0.00583721	17.28978763	0.05783761	92
47	0.00521969	17.30052714	0.05780171	94
48	0.00466750	17.31013051	0.05776964	96
49	0.00417372	17.31871794	0.05774099	98
50	0.00373218	17.32639690	0.05771540	100

Half Years	Future Value of 1	Future Value of 1 per Period	Payment for Sinking Fund of 1	**11.50%** Semi-Annually
1	1.05750000	1.00000000	1.00000000	Years
2	1.11830625	2.05750000	0.48602673	1
4	1.25060887	4.35841511	0.22944120	2
6	1.39856371	6.93154286	0.14426803	3
8	1.56402254	9.80908770	0.10194628	4
10	1.74905618	13.02706408	0.07676327	5
12	1.95598046	16.62574718	0.06014767	6
14	2.18738518	20.65017698	0.04842574	7
16	2.44616651	25.15072349	0.03976029	8
18	2.73556330	30.18370959	0.03313045	9
20	3.05919754	35.81213108	0.02792350	10
22	3.42111973	42.10643001	0.02374934	11
24	3.82585957	49.14538385	0.02034779	12
26	4.27848267	57.01708991	0.01753860	13
28	4.78465391	65.82006801	0.01519293	14
30	5.35070837	75.66449343	0.01321624	15
32	5.98373061	86.67357590	0.01153754	16
34	6.69164334	98.98510164	0.01010253	17
36	7.48330657	112.75315782	0.00886893	18
38	8.36862851	128.15006110	0.00780335	19
40	9.35868957	145.36851427	0.00687907	20
42	10.46588104	164.62401806	0.00607445	21
44	11.70406018	186.15756830	0.00537179	22
46	13.08872365	210.23867211	0.00475650	23
48	14.63720146	237.16872101	0.00421641	24
50	16.36887387	267.28476301	0.00374133	25
52	18.30541396	300.96372101	0.00332266	26
54	20.47105884	338.62711023	0.00295310	27
56	22.89291304	380.74631379	0.00262642	28
58	25.60128774	427.84848237	0.00233728	29
60	28.63008008	480.52313189	0.00208107	30
62	32.01719750	539.42952166	0.00185381	31
64	35.80503207	605.30490551	0.00165206	32
66	40.04099114	678.97375898	0.00147281	33
68	44.77809065	761.35809826	0.00131344	34
70	50.07561864	853.48901997	0.00117166	35
72	55.99987729	956.51960512	0.00104546	36
74	62.62501278	1071.73935265	0.00093306	37
76	70.03394320	1200.59031644	0.00083292	38
78	78.31939639	1344.68515456	0.00074367	39
80	87.58507048	1505.82731263	0.00066409	40
82	97.94693172	1686.03359513	0.00059311	41
84	109.53466591	1887.55940715	0.00052978	42
86	122.49330148	2112.92698226	0.00047328	43
88	136.98502463	2364.95695006	0.00042284	44
90	153.19120920	2646.80363823	0.00037781	45
92	171.31468669	2961.99455115	0.00033761	46
94	191.58228484	3314.47451902	0.00030171	47
96	214.24766653	3708.65507009	0.00026964	48
98	239.59450453	4149.46964397	0.00024099	49
100	267.94003188	4642.43533704	0.00021540	50

153

12.00% Semi-Annually	Present Value of 1	Present Value of 1 per Period	Payment to Pay Off a Loan of 1	
Years	0.94339623	0.94339623	1.06000000	Half Years 1
1	0.88999644	1.83339267	0.54543689	2
2	0.79209366	3.46510561	0.28859149	4
3	0.70496054	4.91732433	0.20336263	6
4	0.62741237	6.20979381	0.16103594	8
5	0.55839478	7.36008705	0.13586796	10
6	0.49696936	8.38384394	0.11927703	12
7	0.44230096	9.29498393	0.10758491	14
8	0.39364628	10.10589527	0.09895214	16
9	0.35034379	10.82760348	0.09235654	18
10	0.31180473	11.46992122	0.08718456	20
11	0.27750510	12.04158172	0.08304557	22
12	0.24697855	12.55035753	0.07967900	24
13	0.21981003	13.00316619	0.07690435	26
14	0.19563014	13.40616428	0.07459255	28
15	0.17411013	13.76483115	0.07264891	30
16	0.15495740	14.08404339	0.07100234	32
17	0.13791153	14.36814114	0.06959843	34
18	0.12274077	14.62098713	0.06839483	36
19	0.10923885	14.84601916	0.06735812	38
20	0.09722219	15.04629687	0.06646154	40
21	0.08652740	15.22454332	0.06568342	42
22	0.07700908	15.38318202	0.06500606	44
23	0.06853781	15.52436990	0.06441485	46
24	0.06099840	15.65002661	0.06389765	48
25	0.05428836	15.76186064	0.06344429	50
26	0.04831645	15.86139252	0.06304617	52
27	0.04300147	15.94997554	0.06269602	54
28	0.03827115	16.02881412	0.06238765	56
29	0.03406119	16.09898017	0.06211574	58
30	0.03031434	16.16142771	0.06187572	60
31	0.02697965	16.21700579	0.06166366	62
32	0.02401179	16.26647009	0.06147615	64
33	0.02137041	16.31049314	0.06131022	66
34	0.01901959	16.34967349	0.06116330	68
35	0.01692737	16.38454387	0.06103313	70
36	0.01506530	16.41557838	0.06091774	72
37	0.01340806	16.44319899	0.06081542	74
38	0.01193313	16.46778123	0.06072463	76
39	0.01062044	16.48965933	0.06064407	78
40	0.00945215	16.50913077	0.06057254	80
41	0.00841238	16.52646028	0.06050903	82
42	0.00748699	16.54188348	0.06045261	84
43	0.00666340	16.55561008	0.06040249	86
44	0.00593040	16.56782670	0.06035795	88
45	0.00527803	16.57869944	0.06031836	90
46	0.00469743	16.58837615	0.06028318	92
47	0.00418070	16.59698839	0.06025189	94
48	0.00372081	16.60465325	0.06022408	96
49	0.00331150	16.61147494	0.06019935	98
50	0.00294723	16.61754623	0.06017736	100

	Future Value of 1	Future Value of 1 per Period	Payment for Sinking Fund of 1	**12.00%** Semi-Annually
Half Years				
1	1.06000000	1.00000000	1.00000000	Years
2	1.12360000	2.06000000	0.48543689	1
4	1.26247696	4.37461600	0.22859149	2
6	1.41851911	6.97531854	0.14336263	3
8	1.59384807	9.89746791	0.10103594	4
10	1.79084770	13.18079494	0.07586796	5
12	2.01219647	16.86994120	0.05927703	6
14	2.26090396	21.01506593	0.04758491	7
16	2.54035168	25.67252808	0.03895214	8
18	2.85433915	30.90565255	0.03235654	9
20	3.20713547	36.78559120	0.02718456	10
22	3.60353742	43.39229028	0.02304557	11
24	4.04893464	50.81557735	0.01967900	12
26	4.54938296	59.15638272	0.01690435	13
28	5.11168670	68.52811162	0.01459255	14
30	5.74349117	79.05818622	0.01264891	15
32	6.45338668	90.88977803	0.01100234	16
34	7.25102528	104.18375460	0.00959843	17
36	8.14725200	119.12086666	0.00839483	18
38	9.15425235	135.90420578	0.00735812	19
40	10.28571794	154.76196562	0.00646154	20
42	11.55703267	175.95054457	0.00568342	21
44	12.98548191	199.75803188	0.00500606	22
46	14.59048748	226.50812462	0.00441485	23
48	16.39387173	256.56452882	0.00389765	24
50	18.42015427	290.33590458	0.00344429	25
52	20.69688534	328.28142239	0.00304617	26
54	23.25502037	370.91700620	0.00269602	27
56	26.12934089	418.82234816	0.00238765	28
58	29.35892742	472.64879040	0.00211574	29
60	32.98769085	533.12818089	0.00187572	30
62	37.06496944	601.08282405	0.00166366	31
64	41.64619967	677.43666110	0.00147615	32
66	46.79366994	763.22783241	0.00131022	33
68	52.57736755	859.62279250	0.00116330	34
70	59.07593018	967.93216965	0.00103313	35
72	66.37771515	1089.62858582	0.00091774	36
74	74.58200074	1226.36667903	0.00081542	37
76	83.80033603	1380.00560055	0.00072463	38
78	94.15805757	1552.63429278	0.00064407	39
80	105.79599348	1746.59989137	0.00057254	40
82	118.87237828	1964.53963794	0.00050903	41
84	133.56500423	2209.41673719	0.00045261	42
86	150.07363875	2484.56064591	0.00040249	43
88	168.62274050	2793.71234174	0.00035795	44
90	189.46451123	3141.07518718	0.00031836	45
92	212.88232482	3531.37208032	0.00028318	46
94	239.19458017	3969.90966944	0.00025189	47
96	268.75903028	4462.65050459	0.00022408	48
98	301.97764642	5016.29410696	0.00019935	49
100	339.30208351	5638.36805857	0.00017736	50

12.50% Semi-Annually	Present Value of 1	Present Value of 1 per Period	Payment to Pay Off a Loan of 1	
Years	0.94117647	0.94117647	1.06250000	Half Years
				1
1	0.88581315	1.82698962	0.54734848	2
2	0.78466493	3.44536105	0.29024534	4
3	0.69506652	4.87893574	0.20496273	6
4	0.61569906	6.14881505	0.16263296	8
5	0.54539432	7.27369084	0.13748179	10
6	0.48311746	8.27012060	0.12091722	12
7	0.42795180	9.15277119	0.10925653	14
8	0.37908533	9.93463469	0.10065795	16
9	0.33579877	10.62721966	0.09409799	18
10	0.29745497	11.24072053	0.08896227	20
11	0.26348952	11.78416766	0.08485962	22
12	0.23340248	12.26556028	0.08152909	24
13	0.20675099	12.69198419	0.07878989	26
14	0.18314274	13.06971610	0.07651276	28
15	0.16223025	13.40431599	0.07460284	30
16	0.14370569	13.70070898	0.07298892	32
17	0.12729639	13.96325778	0.07161653	34
18	0.11276081	14.19582696	0.07044324	36
19	0.09988501	14.40183980	0.06943557	38
20	0.08847946	14.58432868	0.06856675	40
21	0.07837627	14.74597973	0.06781509	42
22	0.06942673	14.88917236	0.06716290	44
23	0.06149911	15.01601427	0.06659557	46
24	0.05447672	15.12837250	0.06610096	48
25	0.04825619	15.22790090	0.06566893	50
26	0.04274597	15.31606446	0.06529092	52
27	0.03786494	15.39416091	0.06495970	54
28	0.03354126	15.46333977	0.06466908	56
29	0.02971129	15.52461931	0.06441382	58
30	0.02631865	15.57890153	0.06418938	60
31	0.02331341	15.62698544	0.06399187	62
32	0.02065133	15.66957880	0.06381792	64
33	0.01829322	15.70730856	0.06366463	66
34	0.01620437	15.74073007	0.06352945	68
35	0.01435404	15.77033529	0.06341019	70
36	0.01271500	15.79655998	0.06330492	72
37	0.01126312	15.81979015	0.06321196	74
38	0.00997702	15.84036775	0.06312985	76
39	0.00883777	15.85859565	0.06305729	78
40	0.00782861	15.87474217	0.06299315	80
41	0.00693469	15.88904497	0.06293644	82
42	0.00614284	15.90171457	0.06288630	84
43	0.00544141	15.91293748	0.06284195	86
44	0.00482007	15.92287887	0.06280271	88
45	0.00426968	15.93168509	0.06276800	90
46	0.00378214	15.93948575	0.06273728	92
47	0.00335027	15.94639569	0.06271010	94
48	0.00296771	15.95251659	0.06268603	96
49	0.00262884	15.95793857	0.06266474	98
50	0.00232866	15.96274144	0.06264588	100

	Future Value of 1	Future Value of 1 per Period	Payment for Sinking Fund of 1	**12.50%** Semi-Annually
Half Years				
1	1.06250000	1.00000000	1.00000000	Years
2	1.12890625	2.06250000	0.48484848	1
4	1.27442932	4.39086914	0.22774534	2
6	1.43871123	7.01937962	0.14246273	3
8	1.62417009	9.98672152	0.10013296	4
10	1.83353577	13.33657234	0.07498179	5
12	2.06988999	17.11823987	0.05841722	6
14	2.33671175	21.38738798	0.04675653	7
16	2.63792850	26.20685596	0.03815795	8
18	2.97797397	31.64758348	0.03159799	9
20	3.36185342	37.78965479	0.02646227	10
22	3.79521734	44.72347748	0.02235962	11
24	4.28444458	52.55111325	0.01902909	12
26	4.83673626	61.38778019	0.01628989	13
28	5.46022180	71.36354873	0.01401276	14
30	6.16407851	82.62525619	0.01210284	15
32	6.95866676	95.33866812	0.01048892	16
34	7.85568239	109.69091830	0.00911653	17
36	8.86832895	125.89326324	0.00794324	18
38	10.01151198	144.18419170	0.00693557	19
40	11.30205845	164.83293517	0.00606675	20
42	12.75896442	188.14343071	0.00531509	21
44	14.40367468	214.45879483	0.00466290	22
46	16.26039837	244.16637385	0.00409557	23
48	18.35646534	277.70344548	0.00360096	24
50	20.72272845	315.56365525	0.00316893	25
52	23.39401767	358.30428268	0.00279092	26
54	26.40965276	406.55444412	0.00245970	27
56	29.81402206	461.02435294	0.00216908	28
58	33.65723584	522.51577343	0.00191382	29
60	37.99586390	591.93382235	0.00168938	30
62	42.89376823	670.30029164	0.00149187	31
64	48.42304304	758.76868861	0.00131792	32
66	54.66507593	858.64121487	0.00116463	33
68	61.71174587	971.38793398	0.00102945	34
70	69.66677562	1098.66840984	0.00091019	35
72	78.64725841	1242.35613455	0.00080492	36
74	88.78538156	1404.56610502	0.00071196	37
76	100.23037216	1587.68595449	0.00062985	38
78	113.15069357	1794.41109707	0.00055729	39
80	127.73652516	2027.78440255	0.00049315	40
82	144.20256161	2291.24098569	0.00043644	41
84	162.79117306	2588.65876900	0.00038630	42
86	183.77597272	2924.41556344	0.00034195	43
88	207.46584420	3303.45350717	0.00030271	44
90	234.20948818	3731.35181082	0.00026800	45
92	264.40055501	4214.40888019	0.00023728	46
94	298.84343906	4759.73502490	0.00021010	47
96	336.95981987	5375.35711795	0.00018603	48
98	380.39604665	6070.33674644	0.00016474	49
100	429.43147454	6854.90359266	0.00014588	50

	Present Value of 1	Present Value of 1 per Period	Payment to Pay Off a Loan of 1	
Years	0.93896714	0.93896714	1.06500000	Half Years
				1
1	0.88165928	1.82062642	0.54926150	2
2	0.77732309	3.42579860	0.29190274	4
3	0.68533412	4.84101356	0.20656831	6
4	0.60423119	6.08875096	0.16423730	8
5	0.53272604	7.18883022	0.13910469	10
6	0.46968285	8.15872532	0.12256817	12
7	0.41410025	9.01384233	0.11094048	14
8	0.36509533	9.76776418	0.10237757	16
9	0.32188969	10.43246638	0.09585641	18
10	0.28379703	11.01850725	0.09075640	20
11	0.25021228	11.53519562	0.08669120	22
12	0.22060198	11.99073871	0.08339770	24
13	0.19449579	12.39237251	0.08069480	26
14	0.17147902	12.74147668	0.07845305	28
15	0.15118607	13.05867591	0.07657744	30
16	0.13329460	13.33392925	0.07499665	32
17	0.11752042	13.57660892	0.07365610	34
18	0.10361297	13.79056970	0.07251332	36
19	0.09135134	13.97921021	0.07153480	38
20	0.08054075	14.14552687	0.07069373	40
21	0.07100950	14.29216149	0.06996842	42
22	0.06260619	14.42144327	0.06934119	44
23	0.05519733	14.53542575	0.06879743	46
24	0.04866524	14.63591946	0.06832505	48
25	0.04290616	14.72452067	0.06791393	50
26	0.03782861	14.80263675	0.06755553	52
27	0.03335195	14.87150852	0.06724267	54
28	0.02940505	14.93222996	0.06696923	56
29	0.02592524	14.98576557	0.06672999	58
30	0.02285723	15.03296574	0.06652047	60
31	0.02015229	15.07458022	0.06633684	62
32	0.01776745	15.11127000	0.06617577	64
33	0.01566484	15.14361789	0.06603442	66
34	0.01381105	15.17213771	0.06591029	68
35	0.01217664	15.19728247	0.06580124	70
36	0.01073565	15.21945158	0.06570539	72
37	0.00946518	15.23899718	0.06562112	74
38	0.00834507	15.25622974	0.06554699	76
39	0.00735751	15.27142299	0.06548178	78
40	0.00648681	15.28481826	0.06542440	80
41	0.00571916	15.29662832	0.06537388	82
42	0.00504235	15.30704078	0.06532941	84
43	0.00444563	15.31622101	0.06529026	86
44	0.00391953	15.32431485	0.06525577	88
45	0.00345569	15.33145086	0.06522540	90
46	0.00304674	15.33774239	0.06519864	92
47	0.00268619	15.34328937	0.06517507	94
48	0.00236831	15.34817992	0.06515431	96
49	0.00208804	15.35249172	0.06513601	98
50	0.00184094	15.35629326	0.06511988	100

	Future Value of 1	Future Value of 1 per Period	Payment for Sinking Fund of 1	**13.00%** Semi-Annually
Half Years				
1	1.06500000	1.00000000	1.00000000	Years
2	1.13422500	2.06500000	0.48426150	1
4	1.28646635	4.40717463	0.22690274	2
6	1.45914230	7.06372764	0.14156831	3
8	1.65499567	10.07685648	0.09923730	4
10	1.87713747	13.49442254	0.07410469	5
12	2.12909624	17.37071141	0.05756817	6
14	2.41487418	21.76729515	0.04594048	7
16	2.73901067	26.75401034	0.03737757	8
18	3.10665438	32.41006738	0.03085461	9
20	3.52364506	38.82530867	0.02576640	10
22	3.99660632	46.10163573	0.02169120	11
24	4.53305081	54.35462778	0.01839770	12
26	5.14149955	63.71537769	0.01569480	13
28	5.83161733	74.33257427	0.01345305	14
30	6.61436616	86.37486405	0.01157744	15
32	7.50217946	100.03353017	0.00999665	16
34	8.50915950	115.52553076	0.00865610	17
36	9.65130143	133.09694513	0.00751332	18
38	10.94674737	153.02688259	0.00653480	19
40	12.41607453	175.63191590	0.00569373	20
42	14.08262214	201.27110981	0.00496842	21
44	15.97286209	230.35172453	0.00434119	22
46	18.11681951	263.33568475	0.00379743	23
48	20.54854961	300.74691704	0.00332505	24
50	23.30667868	343.17967198	0.00291393	25
52	26.43501762	391.30796345	0.00255553	26
54	29.98325786	445.89627485	0.00224267	27
56	34.00776065	507.81170234	0.00196923	28
58	38.57245233	578.03772808	0.00172999	29
60	43.74983974	657.68984214	0.00152047	30
62	49.62216198	748.03326120	0.00133684	31
64	56.28269667	850.50302568	0.00117577	32
66	63.83724163	966.72679430	0.00103442	33
68	72.40579539	1098.55069827	0.00091029	34
70	82.12446327	1248.06866574	0.00080124	35
72	93.14761936	1417.65568240	0.00070539	36
74	105.65035856	1610.00551637	0.00062112	37
76	119.83127794	1828.17350681	0.00054699	38
78	135.91563122	2075.62509576	0.00048178	39
80	154.15890683	2356.29087423	0.00042440	40
82	174.85088609	2674.62901683	0.00037388	41
84	198.32024628	3035.69609661	0.00032941	42
86	224.93978134	3445.22740518	0.00029026	43
88	255.13232349	3909.72805364	0.00025577	44
90	289.37745961	4436.57630164	0.00022540	45
92	328.21914912	5034.14075573	0.00019864	46
94	372.27436441	5711.91329867	0.00017507	47
96	422.24289098	6480.65986118	0.00015431	48
98	478.91844302	7352.59143105	0.00013601	49
100	543.20127103	8341.55801588	0.00011988	50

14.00% Semi-Annually	Present Value of 1	Present Value of 1 per Period	Payment to Pay Off a Loan of 1	
				Half Years
Years	0.93457944	0.93457944	1.07000000	1
1	0.87343873	1.80801817	0.55309179	2
2	0.76289521	3.38721126	0.29522812	4
3	0.66634222	4.76653966	0.20979580	6
4	0.58200910	5.97129851	0.16746776	8
5	0.50834929	7.02358154	0.14237750	10
6	0.44401196	7.94268630	0.12590199	12
7	0.38781724	8.74546799	0.11434494	14
8	0.33873460	9.44664860	0.10585765	16
9	0.29586392	10.05908691	0.09941260	18
10	0.25841900	10.59401425	0.09439293	20
11	0.22571317	11.06124050	0.09040577	22
12	0.19714662	11.46933400	0.08718902	24
13	0.17219549	11.82577867	0.08456103	26
14	0.13040221	12.13711125	0.08239193	28
15	0.13136712	12.40904118	0.08058640	30
16	0.11474113	12.64655532	0.07907292	32
17	0.10021934	12.85400936	0.07779674	34
18	0.08753546	13.03520776	0.07671531	36
19	0.07645686	13.19347345	0.07579505	38
20	0.06678038	13.33170884	0.07500914	40
21	0.05832857	13.45244898	0.07433591	42
22	0.05094643	13.55790810	0.07375769	44
23	0.04449859	13.65002018	0.07325996	46
24	0.03886679	13.73047443	0.07283070	48
25	0.03394776	13.80074629	0.07245985	50
26	0.02965129	13.86212446	0.07213901	52
27	0.02589858	13.91573453	0.07186110	54
28	0.02262083	13.96255964	0.07162011	56
29	0.01975791	14.00345850	0.07141093	58
30	0.01725732	14.03918115	0.07122923	60
31	0.01507321	14.07038270	0.07107127	62
32	0.01316553	14.09763534	0.07093388	64
33	0.01149928	14.12143885	0.07081431	66
34	0.01004392	14.14222976	0.07071021	68
35	0.00877275	14.16038934	0.07061953	70
36	0.00766246	14.17625063	0.07054051	72
37	0.00669269	14.19010449	0.07047164	74
38	0.00584565	14.20220498	0.07041160	76
39	0.00510582	14.21277403	0.07035924	78
40	0.00445962	14.22200544	0.07031357	80
41	0.00389520	14.23006851	0.07027373	82
42	0.00340222	14.23711111	0.07023897	84
43	0.00297163	14.24326239	0.07020863	86
44	0.00259554	14.24863516	0.07018216	88
45	0.00226704	14.25332794	0.07015905	90
46	0.00198012	14.25742680	0.07013888	92
47	0.00172952	14.26100690	0.07012128	94
48	0.00151063	14.26413390	0.07010590	96
49	0.00131944	14.26686514	0.07009248	98
50	0.00115245	14.26925071	0.07008076	100

	Future Value of 1	Future Value of 1 per Period	Payment for Sinking Fund of 1	**14.00%** Semi-Annually
Half Years				
1	1.07000000	1.00000000	1.00000000	Years
2	1.14490000	2.07000000	0.48309179	1
4	1.31079601	4.43994300	0.22522812	2
6	1.50073035	7.15329074	0.13979580	3
8	1.71818618	10.25980257	0.09746776	4
10	1.96715136	13.81644796	0.07237750	5
12	2.25219159	17.88845127	0.05590199	6
14	2.57853415	22.55048786	0.04434494	7
16	2.95216375	27.88805355	0.03585765	8
18	3.37993228	33.99903251	0.02941260	9
20	3.86968446	40.99549232	0.02439293	10
22	4.43040174	49.00573916	0.02040577	11
24	5.07236695	58.17667076	0.01718902	12
26	5.80735292	68.67647036	0.01456103	13
28	6.64883836	80.69769091	0.01239193	14
30	7.61225504	94.46078632	0.01058640	15
32	8.71527080	110.21815426	0.00907292	16
34	9.97811354	128.25876481	0.00779674	17
36	11.42394219	148.91345984	0.00671531	18
38	13.07927141	172.56102017	0.00579505	19
40	14.97445784	199.63511199	0.00500914	20
42	17.14425678	230.63223972	0.00433591	21
44	19.62845959	266.12085125	0.00375769	22
46	22.47262338	306.75176260	0.00325996	23
48	25.72890651	353.27009300	0.00283070	24
50	29.45702506	406.52892947	0.00245985	25
52	33.72534799	467.50497135	0.00213901	26
54	38.61215092	537.31644170	0.00186110	27
56	44.20705159	617.24357984	0.00162011	28
58	50.61265336	708.75219089	0.00141093	29
60	57.94642683	813.52038335	0.00122923	30
62	66.34286408	933.46948690	0.00107127	31
64	75.95594509	1070.79921555	0.00093388	32
66	86.96196153	1228.02802188	0.00081431	33
68	99.56274976	1408.03928225	0.00071021	34
70	113.98939220	1614.13417425	0.00061953	35
72	130.50645513	1850.09221610	0.00054051	36
74	149.41684047	2120.24057821	0.00047164	37
76	171.06734066	2429.53343800	0.00041160	38
78	195.85499832	2783.64283316	0.00035924	39
80	224.23438758	3189.06267969	0.00031357	40
82	256.72595034	3653.22786198	0.00027373	41
84	293.92554054	4184.65057918	0.00023897	42
86	336.51535137	4793.07644810	0.00020863	43
88	385.27642578	5489.66322543	0.00018216	44
90	441.10297988	6287.18542679	0.00015905	45
92	505.01880166	7200.26859513	0.00013888	46
94	578.19602602	8245.65751457	0.00012128	47
96	661.97663019	9442.52328843	0.00010590	48
98	757.89704390	10812.81491292	0.00009248	49
100	867.71632557	12381.66179381	0.00008076	50

15.00% Semi-Annually	Present Value of 1	Present Value of 1 per Period	Payment to Pay Off a Loan of 1	
Years	0.93023256	0.93023256	1.07500000	Half Years 1
1	0.86533261	1.79556517	0.55692771	2
2	0.74880053	3.34932627	0.29856751	4
3	0.64796152	4.69384642	0.21304489	6
4	0.56070223	5.85730355	0.17072702	8
5	0.48519393	6.86408096	0.14568593	10
6	0.41985413	7.73527827	0.12927783	12
7	0.36331347	8.48915373	0.11779737	14
8	0.31438699	9.14150674	0.10939116	16
9	0.27204932	9.70600908	0.10302896	18
10	0.23541315	10.19449136	0.09809219	20
11	0.20371067	10.61719101	0.09418687	22
12	0.17627749	10.98296680	0.09105008	24
13	0.15253866	11.29948452	0.08849961	26
14	0.13199668	11.57337763	0.08640520	28
15	0.11422103	11.81038627	0.08467124	30
16	0.09883918	12.01547757	0.08322599	32
17	0.08552877	12.19294976	0.08201461	34
18	0.07401083	12.34652224	0.08099447	36
19	0.06404399	12.47941351	0.08013197	38
20	0.05541935	12.59440866	0.07940031	40
21	0.04795617	12.69391772	0.07877789	42
22	0.04149804	12.78002615	0.07824710	44
23	0.03590961	12.85453858	0.07779354	46
24	0.03107375	12.91901662	0.07740527	48
25	0.02688913	12.97481157	0.07707241	50
26	0.02326804	13.02309276	0.07678668	52
27	0.02013460	13.06487205	0.07654112	54
28	0.01742312	13.10102503	0.07632991	56
29	0.01507680	13.13230938	0.07614807	58
30	0.01304644	13.15938075	0.07599142	60
31	0.01128951	13.18280649	0.07585638	62
32	0.00976918	13.20307755	0.07573992	64
33	0.00845359	13.22061875	0.07563942	66
34	0.00731517	13.23579773	0.07555268	68
35	0.00633006	13.24893260	0.07547778	70
36	0.00547760	13.26029862	0.07541308	72
37	0.00473995	13.27013402	0.07535719	74
38	0.00410163	13.27864490	0.07530889	76
39	0.00354928	13.28600965	0.07526714	78
40	0.00307130	13.29238261	0.07523106	80
41	0.00265770	13.29789734	0.07519986	82
42	0.00229979	13.30266941	0.07517288	84
43	0.00199009	13.30679884	0.07514955	86
44	0.00172209	13.31037217	0.07512938	88
45	0.00149018	13.31346429	0.07511193	90
46	0.00128950	13.31614000	0.07509684	92
47	0.00111585	13.31845538	0.07508378	94
48	0.00096558	13.32045896	0.07507249	96
49	0.00083555	13.32219272	0.07506272	98
50	0.00072303	13.32369299	0.07505427	100

	Future Value of 1	Future Value of 1 per Period	Payment for Sinking Fund of 1	**15.00%** Semi-Annually
Half Years				
1	1.07500000	1.00000000	1.00000000	Years
2	1.15562500	2.07500000	0.48192771	1
4	1.33546914	4.47292188	0.22356751	2
6	1.54330153	7.24402034	0.13804489	3
8	1.78347783	10.44637101	0.09572702	4
10	2.06103156	14.14708750	0.07068593	5
12	2.38177960	18.42372799	0.05427783	6
14	2.75244405	23.36592066	0.04279737	7
16	3.18079315	29.07724206	0.03439116	8
18	3.67580409	35.67738785	0.02802896	9
20	4.24785110	43.30468134	0.02309219	10
22	4.90892293	52.11897237	0.01918687	11
24	5.67287406	62.30498744	0.01605008	12
26	6.55571508	74.07620112	0.01349961	13
28	7.57594824	87.67930991	0.01140520	14
30	8.75495519	103.39940252	0.00967124	15
32	10.11744509	121.56593454	0.00822599	16
34	11.69197248	142.55963310	0.00701461	17
36	13.51153570	166.82047600	0.00599447	18
38	15.61426844	194.85691258	0.00513197	19
40	18.04423897	227.25651960	0.00440031	20
42	20.85237366	264.69831546	0.00377789	21
44	24.09752431	307.96699080	0.00324710	22
46	27.84770153	357.96935375	0.00279354	23
48	32.18150008	415.75333442	0.00240527	24
50	37.18974603	482.52994709	0.00207241	25
52	42.97740026	559.69867011	0.00178668	26
54	49.66575817	648.87677565	0.00154112	27
56	57.39499179	751.93322386	0.00132991	28
58	66.32708739	871.02783182	0.00114807	29
60	76.64924036	1008.65653814	0.00099142	30
62	88.57777839	1167.70371189	0.00085638	31
64	102.36269515	1351.50260206	0.00073992	32
66	118.29288959	1563.90519450	0.00063942	33
68	136.70222053	1809.36294040	0.00055268	34
70	157.97650360	2093.02004800	0.00047778	35
72	182.56159697	2420.82112996	0.00041308	36
74	210.97274550	2799.63660668	0.00035719	37
76	243.80537902	3237.40505360	0.00030889	38
78	281.74759113	3743.30121506	0.00026714	39
80	325.59456000	4327.92746666	0.00023106	40
82	376.26521340	5003.53617866	0.00019986	41
84	434.82148723	5784.28649646	0.00017288	42
86	502.49058119	6686.54108247	0.00014955	43
88	580.69067788	7729.20903843	0.00012938	44
90	671.06066463	8934.14219504	0.00011193	45
92	775.49448056	10326.59307414	0.00009684	46
94	896.18080910	11935.74412130	0.00008378	47
96	1035.64894751	13795.31930018	0.00007249	48
98	1196.82181497	15944.29086627	0.00006272	49
100	1383.07720993	18427.69613233	0.00005427	50

16.00% Semi-Annually	Present Value of 1	Present Value of 1 per Period	Payment to Pay Off a Loan of 1	
				Half Years
Years	0.92592593	0.92592593	1.08000000	1
1	0.85733882	1.78326475	0.56076923	2
2	0.73502985	3.31212684	0.30192080	4
3	0.63016963	4.62287966	0.21631539	6
4	0.54026888	5.74663894	0.17401476	8
5	0.46319349	6.71008140	0.14902949	10
6	0.39711376	7.53607802	0.13269502	12
7	0.34046104	8.24423698	0.12129685	14
8	0.29189047	8.85136916	0.11297687	16
9	0.25024903	9.37188714	0.10670210	18
10	0.21454821	9.81814741	0.10185221	20
11	0.18394051	10.20074366	0.09803207	22
12	0.15769934	10.52875828	0.09497796	24
13	0.13520176	10.80997795	0.09250713	26
14	0.11591372	11.05107049	0.09040091	28
15	0.09937733	11.25778334	0.08882743	30
16	0.08520005	11.43499944	0.08745081	32
17	0.07304531	11.58693367	0.08630411	34
18	0.06262458	11.71719279	0.08534467	36
19	0.05369048	11.82886899	0.08453894	38
20	0.04603093	11.92461333	0.08386016	40
21	0.03946411	12.00669867	0.08328684	42
22	0.03383411	12.07707362	0.08280152	44
23	0.02900730	12.13740880	0.08238991	46
24	0.02486908	12.18913649	0.08204027	48
25	0.02132123	12.23348464	0.08174286	50
26	0.01827952	12.27150604	0.08148959	52
27	0.01567174	12.30410326	0.08127370	54
28	0.01343599	12.33205012	0.08108952	56
29	0.01151920	12.35601005	0.08093227	58
30	0.00987585	12.37655182	0.08079795	60
31	0.00846695	12.39416308	0.08068314	62
32	0.00725905	12.40926190	0.08058497	64
33	0.00622346	12.42220671	0.08050099	66
34	0.00533562	12.43330479	0.08042914	68
35	0.00457443	12.44281961	0.08036764	70
36	0.00392184	12.45097703	0.08031498	72
37	0.00336234	12.45797070	0.08026989	74
38	0.00288267	12.46396665	0.08023128	76
39	0.00247142	12.46910721	0.08019820	78
40	0.00211885	12.47351441	0.08016987	80
41	0.00181657	12.47729288	0.08014559	82
42	0.00155742	12.48053230	0.08012479	84
43	0.00133523	12.48330959	0.08010696	86
44	0.00114475	12.48569066	0.08009168	88
45	0.00098144	12.48773205	0.08007859	90
46	0.00084142	12.48948221	0.08006737	92
47	0.00072138	12.49098269	0.08005775	94
48	0.00061847	12.49226911	0.08004951	96
49	0.00053024	12.49337201	0.08004244	98
50	0.00045459	12.49431757	0.08003638	100

	Future Value of 1	Future Value of 1 per Period	Payment for Sinking Fund of 1	**16.00%** Semi-Annually
Half Years				
1	1.08000000	1.00000000	1.00000000	Years
2	1.16640000	2.08000000	0.48076923	1
4	1.36048896	4.50611200	0.22192080	2
6	1.58687432	7.33592904	0.13631539	3
8	1.85093021	10.63662763	0.09401476	4
10	2.15892500	14.48656247	0.06902949	5
12	2.51817012	18.97721646	0.05269502	6
14	2.93719362	24.21492030	0.04129685	7
16	3.42594264	30.32428304	0.03297687	8
18	3.99601950	37.45024374	0.02670210	9
20	4.66095714	45.76196430	0.02185221	10
22	5.43654041	55.45675516	0.01803207	11
24	6.34118074	66.76475922	0.01497796	12
26	7.39635321	79.95441435	0.01250713	13
28	8.62710639	95.33882983	0.01048891	14
30	10.06265689	113.28211111	0.00882743	15
32	11.73708300	134.21353744	0.00745081	16
34	13.69013361	158.62667007	0.00630411	17
36	15.96817184	187.10214797	0.00534467	18
38	18.62527563	220.31594540	0.00453894	19
40	21.72452150	259.05651871	0.00386016	20
42	25.33948187	304.24352342	0.00328684	21
44	29.55597166	356.94964572	0.00280152	22
46	34.47408534	418.42606677	0.00238991	23
48	40.21057314	490.13216428	0.00204027	24
50	46.90161251	573.77015642	0.00174286	25
52	54.70604084	671.32551044	0.00148959	26
54	63.80912603	785.11407538	0.00127370	27
56	74.42696460	917.83705752	0.00108952	28
58	86.81161151	1072.64514390	0.00093227	29
60	101.25706367	1253.21329984	0.00079795	30
62	118.10623906	1463.82798827	0.00068314	31
64	137.75911724	1709.48896552	0.00058497	32
66	160.68223435	1996.02792938	0.00050099	33
68	187.41975815	2330.24697683	0.00042914	34
70	218.60640590	2720.08007377	0.00036764	35
72	254.98251184	3174.78139805	0.00031498	36
74	297.41160181	3705.14502268	0.00026989	37
76	346.90089236	4323.76115445	0.00023128	38
78	404.62520084	5045.31501056	0.00019820	39
80	471.95483426	5886.93542831	0.00016987	40
82	550.48811869	6868.60148358	0.00014559	41
84	642.08934164	8013.61677045	0.00012479	42
86	748.93300808	9349.16260105	0.00010696	43
88	873.55546063	10906.94325787	0.00009168	44
90	1018.91508928	12723.93861598	0.00007859	45
92	1188.46256013	14843.28200168	0.00006737	46
94	1386.22273014	17315.28412676	0.00005775	47
96	1616.89019244	20198.62740545	0.00004951	48
98	1885.94072046	23561.75900572	0.00004244	49
100	2199.76125634	27484.51570427	0.00003638	50

Years	Present Value of 1	Present Value of 1 per Period	Payment to Pay Off a Loan of 1	Years
1	0.95238095	0.95238095	1.05000000	1
2	0.90702948	1.85941043	0.53780488	2
3	0.86383760	2.72324803	0.36720856	3
4	0.82270247	3.54595050	0.28201183	4
5	0.78352617	4.32947667	0.23097480	5
6	0.74621540	5.07569207	0.19701747	6
7	0.71068133	5.78637340	0.17281982	7
8	0.67683936	6.46321276	0.15472181	8
9	0.64460892	7.10782168	0.14069008	9
10	0.61391325	7.72173493	0.12950457	10
11	0.58467929	8.30641422	0.12038889	11
12	0.55683742	8.86325164	0.11282541	12
13	0.53032135	9.39357299	0.10645577	13
14	0.50506795	9.89864094	0.10102397	14
15	0.48101710	10.37965804	0.09634229	15
16	0.45811152	10.83776956	0.09226991	16
17	0.43629669	11.27406625	0.08869914	17
18	0.41552065	11.68958690	0.08554622	18
19	0.39573396	12.08532086	0.08274501	19
20	0.37688948	12.46221034	0.08024259	20
21	0.35894236	12.82115271	0.07799611	21
22	0.34184987	13.16300258	0.07597051	22
23	0.32557131	13.48857388	0.07413682	23
24	0.31006791	13.79864179	0.07247090	24
25	0.29530277	14.09394457	0.07095246	25
26	0.28124073	14.37518530	0.06956432	26
27	0.26784832	14.64303362	0.06829186	27
28	0.25509364	14.89812726	0.06712253	28
29	0.24294632	15.14107358	0.06604551	29
30	0.23137745	15.37245103	0.06505144	30
31	0.22035947	15.59281050	0.06413212	31
32	0.20986617	15.80267667	0.06328042	32
33	0.19987254	16.00254921	0.06249004	33
34	0.19035480	16.19290401	0.06175545	34
35	0.18129029	16.37419429	0.06107171	35
36	0.17265741	16.54685171	0.06043446	36
37	0.16443563	16.71128734	0.05983979	37
38	0.15660536	16.86789271	0.05928423	38
39	0.14914797	17.01704067	0.05876462	39
40	0.14204568	17.15908635	0.05827816	40
41	0.13528160	17.29436796	0.05782229	41
42	0.12883962	17.42320758	0.05739471	42
43	0.12270440	17.54591198	0.05699333	43
44	0.11686133	17.66277331	0.05661625	44
45	0.11129651	17.77406982	0.05626173	45
46	0.10599668	17.88006650	0.05592820	46
47	0.10094921	17.98101571	0.05561421	47
48	0.09614211	18.07715782	0.05531843	48
49	0.09156391	18.16872173	0.05503965	49
50	0.08720373	18.25592546	0.05477674	50

Years	Future Value of 1	Future Value of 1 per Period	Payment for Sinking Fund of 1	**5.00%** Yearly Years
1	1.05000000	1.00000000	1.00000000	1
2	1.10250000	2.05000000	0.48780488	2
3	1.15762500	3.15250000	0.31720856	3
4	1.21550625	4.31012500	0.23201183	4
5	1.27628156	5.52563125	0.18097480	5
6	1.34009564	6.80191281	0.14701747	6
7	1.40710042	8.14200845	0.12281982	7
8	1.47745544	9.54910888	0.10472181	8
9	1.55132822	11.02656432	0.09069008	9
10	1.62889463	12.57789254	0.07950457	10
11	1.71033936	14.20678716	0.07038889	11
12	1.79585633	15.91726652	0.06282541	12
13	1.88564914	17.71298285	0.05645577	13
14	1.97993160	19.59863199	0.05102397	14
15	2.07892818	21.57856359	0.04634229	15
16	2.18287459	23.65749177	0.04226991	16
17	2.29201832	25.84036636	0.03869914	17
18	2.40661923	28.13238467	0.03554622	18
19	2.52695020	30.53900391	0.03274501	19
20	2.65329771	33.06595410	0.03024259	20
21	2.78596259	35.71925181	0.02799611	21
22	2.92526072	38.50521440	0.02597051	22
23	3.07152376	41.43047512	0.02413682	23
24	3.22509994	44.50199887	0.02247090	24
25	3.38635494	47.72709882	0.02095246	25
26	3.55567269	51.11345376	0.01956432	26
27	3.73345632	54.66912645	0.01829186	27
28	3.92012914	58.40258277	0.01712253	28
29	4.11613560	62.32271191	0.01604551	29
30	4.32194238	66.43884750	0.01505144	30
31	4.53803949	70.76078988	0.01413212	31
32	4.76494147	75.29882937	0.01328042	32
33	5.00318854	80.06377084	0.01249004	33
34	5.25334797	85.06695938	0.01175545	34
35	5.51601537	90.32030735	0.01107171	35
36	5.79181614	95.83632272	0.01043446	36
37	6.08140694	101.62813886	0.00983979	37
38	6.38547729	107.70954580	0.00928423	38
39	6.70475115	114.09502309	0.00876462	39
40	7.03998871	120.79977424	0.00827816	40
41	7.39198815	127.83976295	0.00782229	41
42	7.76158756	135.23175110	0.00739471	42
43	8.14966693	142.99333866	0.00699333	43
44	8.55715028	151.14300559	0.00661625	44
45	8.98500779	159.70015588	0.00626173	45
46	9.43425818	168.68516366	0.00592820	46
47	9.90597109	178.11942185	0.00561421	47
48	10.40126965	188.02539294	0.00531843	48
49	10.92133313	198.42666259	0.00503965	49
50	11.46739979	209.34799572	0.00477674	50

5.50%
Yearly

Years	Present Value of 1	Present Value of 1 per Period	Payment to Pay Off a Loan of 1	Years
1	0.94786730	0.94786730	1.05500000	1
2	0.89845242	1.84631971	0.54161800	2
3	0.85161366	2.69793338	0.37065407	3
4	0.80721674	3.50515012	0.28529449	4
5	0.76513435	4.27028448	0.23417644	5
6	0.72524583	4.99553031	0.20017895	6
7	0.68743681	5.68296712	0.17596442	7
8	0.65159887	6.33456599	0.15786401	8
9	0.61762926	6.95219525	0.14383946	9
10	0.58543058	7.53762583	0.13266777	10
11	0.55491050	8.09253633	0.12357065	11
12	0.52598152	8.61851785	0.11602923	12
13	0.49856068	9.11707853	0.10968426	13
14	0.47256937	9.58964790	0.10427912	14
15	0.44793305	10.03758094	0.09962560	15
16	0.42458109	10.46216203	0.09558251	16
17	0.40244653	10.86460856	0.09204197	17
18	0.38146590	11.24607447	0.08891992	18
19	0.36157906	11.60765352	0.08615006	19
20	0.34272896	11.95038248	0.08367933	20
21	0.32486158	12.27524406	0.08146478	21
22	0.30792567	12.58316973	0.07947123	22
23	0.29187267	12.87504239	0.07766965	23
24	0.27665656	13.15169895	0.07603580	24
25	0.26223370	13.41393266	0.07454935	25
26	0.24856275	13.66249541	0.07319307	26
27	0.23560450	13.89809991	0.07195228	27
28	0.22332181	14.12142172	0.07081440	28
29	0.21167944	14.33310116	0.06976857	29
30	0.20064402	14.53374517	0.06880539	30
31	0.19018390	14.72392907	0.06791665	31
32	0.18026910	14.90419817	0.06709519	32
33	0.17087119	15.07506936	0.06633469	33
34	0.16196321	15.23703257	0.06562958	34
35	0.15351963	15.39055220	0.06497493	35
36	0.14551624	15.53606843	0.06436635	36
37	0.13793008	15.67399851	0.06379993	37
38	0.13073941	15.80473793	0.06327217	38
39	0.12392362	15.92866154	0.06277991	39
40	0.11746314	16.04612469	0.06232034	40
41	0.11133947	16.15746416	0.06189090	41
42	0.10553504	16.26299920	0.06148927	42
43	0.10003322	16.36303242	0.06111337	43
44	0.09481822	16.45785063	0.06076128	44
45	0.08987509	16.54772572	0.06043127	45
46	0.08518965	16.63291537	0.06012175	46
47	0.08074849	16.71366386	0.05983129	47
48	0.07653885	16.79020271	0.05955854	48
49	0.07254867	16.86275139	0.05930230	49
50	0.06876652	16.93151790	0.05906145	50

	Future Value of 1	Future Value of 1 per Period	Payment for Sinking Fund of 1	**5.50%** Yearly
Years				Years
1	1.05500000	1.00000000	1.00000000	1
2	1.11302500	2.05500000	0.48661800	2
3	1.17424137	3.16802500	0.31565407	3
4	1.23882465	4.34226637	0.23029449	4
5	1.30696001	5.58109103	0.17917644	5
6	1.37884281	6.88805103	0.14517895	6
7	1.45467916	8.26689384	0.12096442	7
8	1.53468651	9.72157300	0.10286401	8
9	1.61909427	11.25625951	0.08883946	9
10	1.70814446	12.87535379	0.07766777	10
11	1.80209240	14.58349825	0.06857065	11
12	1.90120749	16.38559065	0.06102923	12
13	2.00577390	18.28679814	0.05468426	13
14	2.11609146	20.29257203	0.04927912	14
15	2.23247649	22.40866350	0.04462560	15
16	2.35526270	24.64113999	0.04058254	16
17	2.48480215	26.99640269	0.03704197	17
18	2.62146627	29.48120483	0.03391992	18
19	2.76564691	32.10267110	0.03115006	19
20	2.91775749	34.86831801	0.02867933	20
21	3.07823415	37.78607550	0.02646478	21
22	3.24753003	40.86430965	0.02447123	22
23	3.42615157	44.11184669	0.02266965	23
24	3.61458990	47.53799825	0.02103580	24
25	3.81339235	51.15258816	0.01954935	25
26	4.02312893	54.96598051	0.01819307	26
27	4.24440102	58.98910943	0.01695228	27
28	4.47784307	63.23351045	0.01581440	28
29	4.72412444	67.71135353	0.01476857	29
30	4.98395129	72.43547797	0.01380539	30
31	5.25806861	77.41942926	0.01291665	31
32	5.54726238	82.67749787	0.01209519	32
33	5.85236181	88.22476025	0.01133469	33
34	6.17424171	94.07712207	0.01062958	34
35	6.51382501	100.25136378	0.00997493	35
36	6.87208538	106.76518879	0.00936635	36
37	7.25005008	113.63727417	0.00879993	37
38	7.64880283	120.88732425	0.00827217	38
39	8.06948699	128.53612708	0.00777991	39
40	8.51330877	136.60561407	0.00732034	40
41	8.98154076	145.11892285	0.00689090	41
42	9.47552550	154.10046360	0.00648927	42
43	9.99667940	163.57598910	0.00611337	43
44	10.54649677	173.57266850	0.00576128	44
45	11.12655409	184.11916527	0.00543127	45
46	11.73851456	195.24571936	0.00512175	46
47	12.38413287	206.98423392	0.00483129	47
48	13.06526017	219.36836679	0.00455854	48
49	13.78384948	232.43362696	0.00430230	49
50	14.54196120	246.21747645	0.00406145	50

6.00% Yearly	Present Value of 1	Present Value of 1 per Period	Payment to Pay Off a Loan of 1	
Years				Years
1	0.94339623	0.94339623	1.06000000	1
2	0.88999644	1.83339267	0.54543689	2
3	0.83961928	2.67301195	0.37410981	3
4	0.79209366	3.46510561	0.28859149	4
5	0.74725817	4.21236379	0.23739640	5
6	0.70496054	4.91732433	0.20336263	6
7	0.66505711	5.58238144	0.17913502	7
8	0.62741237	6.20979381	0.16103594	8
9	0.59189846	6.80169227	0.14702224	9
10	0.55839478	7.36008705	0.13586796	10
11	0.52678753	7.88687458	0.12679294	11
12	0.49696936	8.38384394	0.11927703	12
13	0.46883902	8.85268296	0.11296001	13
14	0.44230096	9.29498393	0.10758491	14
15	0.41726506	9.71224899	0.10296276	15
16	0.39364628	10.10589527	0.09895214	16
17	0.37136442	10.47725969	0.09544480	17
18	0.35034379	10.82760348	0.09235654	18
19	0.33051301	11.15811649	0.08962086	19
20	0.31180473	11.46992122	0.08718456	20
21	0.29415540	11.76407662	0.08500455	21
22	0.27750510	12.04158172	0.08304557	22
23	0.26179726	12.30337898	0.08127848	23
24	0.24697855	12.55035753	0.07967900	24
25	0.23299863	12.78335616	0.07822672	25
26	0.21981003	13.00316619	0.07690435	26
27	0.20736795	13.21053414	0.07569717	27
28	0.19563014	13.40616428	0.07459255	28
29	0.18455674	13.59072102	0.07357961	29
30	0.17411013	13.76483115	0.07264891	30
31	0.16425484	13.92908599	0.07179222	31
32	0.15495740	14.08404339	0.07100234	32
33	0.14618622	14.23022961	0.07027293	33
34	0.13791153	14.36814114	0.06959843	34
35	0.13010522	14.49824636	0.06897386	35
36	0.12274077	14.62098713	0.06839483	36
37	0.11579318	14.73678031	0.06785743	37
38	0.10923885	14.84601916	0.06735812	38
39	0.10305552	14.94907468	0.06689377	39
40	0.09722219	15.04629687	0.06646154	40
41	0.09171905	15.13801592	0.06605886	41
42	0.08652740	15.22454332	0.06568342	42
43	0.08162962	15.30617294	0.06533312	43
44	0.07700908	15.38318202	0.06500606	44
45	0.07265007	15.45583209	0.06470050	45
46	0.06853781	15.52436990	0.06441485	46
47	0.06465831	15.58902821	0.06414768	47
48	0.06099840	15.65002661	0.06389765	48
49	0.05754566	15.70757227	0.06366356	49
50	0.05428836	15.76186064	0.06344429	50

Years	Future Value of 1	Future Value of 1 per Period	Payment for Sinking Fund of 1	**6.00%** Yearly Years
1	1.06000000	1.00000000	1.00000000	1
2	1.12360000	2.06000000	0.48543689	2
3	1.19101600	3.18360000	0.31410981	3
4	1.26247696	4.37461600	0.22859149	4
5	1.33822558	5.63709296	0.17739640	5
6	1.41851911	6.97531854	0.14336263	6
7	1.50363026	8.39383765	0.11913502	7
8	1.59384807	9.89746791	0.10103594	8
9	1.68947896	11.49131598	0.08702224	9
10	1.79084770	13.18079494	0.07586796	10
11	1.89829856	14.97164264	0.06679294	11
12	2.01219647	16.86994120	0.05927703	12
13	2.13292826	18.88213767	0.05296011	13
14	2.26090396	21.01506593	0.04758491	14
15	2.39655819	23.27596988	0.04296276	15
16	2.54035168	25.67252808	0.03895214	16
17	2.69277279	28.21287976	0.03544480	17
18	2.85433915	30.90565255	0.03235654	18
19	3.02559950	33.75999170	0.02962086	19
20	3.20713547	36.78559120	0.02718456	20
21	3.39956360	39.99272668	0.02500455	21
22	3.60353742	43.39229028	0.02304557	22
23	3.81974966	46.99582769	0.02127848	23
24	4.04893464	50.81557735	0.01967900	24
25	4.29187072	54.86451200	0.01822672	25
26	4.54938296	59.15638272	0.01690435	26
27	4.82234594	63.70576568	0.01569717	27
28	5.11168670	68.52811162	0.01459255	28
29	5.41838790	73.63979832	0.01357961	29
30	5.74349117	79.05818622	0.01264891	30
31	6.08810064	84.80167739	0.01179222	31
32	6.45338668	90.88977803	0.01100234	32
33	6.84058988	97.34316471	0.01027293	33
34	7.25102528	104.18375460	0.00959843	34
35	7.68608679	111.43477987	0.00897386	35
36	8.14725200	119.12086666	0.00839483	36
37	8.63608712	127.26811866	0.00785743	37
38	9.15425235	135.90420578	0.00735812	38
39	9.70350749	145.05845813	0.00689377	39
40	10.28571794	154.76196562	0.00646154	40
41	10.90286101	165.04768356	0.00605886	41
42	11.55703267	175.95054457	0.00568342	42
43	12.25045463	187.50757724	0.00533312	43
44	12.98548191	199.75803188	0.00500606	44
45	13.76461083	212.74351379	0.00470050	45
46	14.59048748	226.50812462	0.00441485	46
47	15.46591673	241.09861210	0.00414768	47
48	16.39387173	256.56452882	0.00389765	48
49	17.37750403	272.95840055	0.00366356	49
50	18.42015427	290.33590458	0.00344429	50

6.50%	Present Value of 1	Present Value of 1 per Period	Payment to Pay Off a Loan of 1	
Yearly				
Years				Years
1	0.93896714	0.93896714	1.06500000	1
2	0.88165928	1.82062642	0.54926150	2
3	0.82784909	2.64847551	0.37757570	3
4	0.77732309	3.42579860	0.29190274	4
5	0.72988084	4.15567944	0.24063454	5
6	0.68533412	4.84101356	0.20656831	6
7	0.64350621	5.48451977	0.18233137	7
8	0.60423119	6.08875096	0.16423730	8
9	0.56735323	6.65610419	0.15023803	9
10	0.53272604	7.18883022	0.13910469	10
11	0.50021224	7.68904246	0.13005521	11
12	0.46968285	8.15872532	0.12256817	12
13	0.44101676	8.59974208	0.11628256	13
14	0.41410025	9.01384233	0.11094048	14
15	0.38882652	9.40266885	0.10635278	15
16	0.36509533	9.76776418	0.10237757	16
17	0.34281251	10.11057670	0.09890633	17
18	0.32188969	10.43246638	0.09585461	18
19	0.30224384	10.73471022	0.09315575	19
20	0.28379703	11.01850725	0.09075640	20
21	0.26647608	11.28498333	0.08861333	21
22	0.25021228	11.53519562	0.08669120	22
23	0.23494111	11.77013673	0.08496078	23
24	0.22060198	11.99073871	0.08339770	24
25	0.20713801	12.19787673	0.08198148	25
26	0.19449579	12.39237251	0.08069480	26
27	0.18262515	12.57499766	0.07952288	27
28	0.17147902	12.74647668	0.07845305	28
29	0.16101316	12.90748984	0.07747440	29
30	0.15118607	13.05867591	0.07657744	30
31	0.14195875	13.20063465	0.07575393	31
32	0.13329460	13.33392925	0.07499665	32
33	0.12515925	13.45908850	0.07429924	33
34	0.11752042	13.57660892	0.07365610	34
35	0.11034781	13.68695673	0.07306226	35
36	0.10361297	13.79056970	0.07251302	36
37	0.09728917	13.88785887	0.07200534	37
38	0.09135134	13.97921021	0.07153480	38
39	0.08577590	14.06498611	0.07109854	39
40	0.08054075	14.14552687	0.07069373	40
41	0.07562512	14.22115199	0.07031779	41
42	0.07100950	14.29216149	0.06996842	42
43	0.06667559	14.35883708	0.06964352	43
44	0.06260619	14.42144327	0.06934119	44
45	0.05878515	14.48022842	0.06905968	45
46	0.05519733	14.53542575	0.06879743	46
47	0.05182848	14.58725422	0.06855300	47
48	0.04866524	14.63591946	0.06832505	48
49	0.04569506	14.68161451	0.06811240	49
50	0.04290616	14.72452067	0.06791393	50

Years	Future Value of 1	Future Value of 1 per Period	Payment for Sinking Fund of 1	**6.50%** Yearly Years
1	1.06500000	1.00000000	1.00000000	1
2	1.13422500	2.06500000	0.48426150	2
3	1.20794963	3.19922500	0.31257570	3
4	1.28646635	4.40717463	0.22690274	4
5	1.37008666	5.69364098	0.17563454	5
6	1.45914230	7.06372764	0.14156831	6
7	1.55398655	8.52286994	0.11733137	7
8	1.65499567	10.07685648	0.09923730	8
9	1.76257039	11.73185215	0.08523803	9
10	1.87713747	13.49442254	0.07410469	10
11	1.99915140	15.37156001	0.06505521	11
12	2.12909624	17.37071141	0.05756817	12
13	2.26748750	19.49980765	0.05128256	13
14	2.41487418	21.76729515	0.04594048	14
15	2.57184101	24.18216933	0.04135278	15
16	2.73901067	26.75401034	0.03737757	16
17	2.91704637	29.49302101	0.03390633	17
18	3.10665438	32.41006738	0.03085461	18
19	3.30858691	35.51672176	0.02815575	19
20	3.52364506	38.82530867	0.02575640	20
21	3.75268199	42.34895373	0.02361333	21
22	3.99660632	46.10163573	0.02169120	22
23	4.25638573	50.09824205	0.01996078	23
24	4.53305081	54.35462778	0.01839770	24
25	4.82769911	58.88767859	0.01698148	25
26	5.14149955	63.71537769	0.01569480	26
27	5.47569702	68.85687725	0.01452288	27
28	5.83161733	74.33257427	0.01345305	28
29	6.21067245	80.16419159	0.01247440	29
30	6.61436616	86.37486405	0.01157744	30
31	7.04429996	92.98923021	0.01075393	31
32	7.50217946	100.03353017	0.00999665	32
33	7.98982113	107.53570963	0.00929924	33
34	8.50915950	115.52553076	0.00865610	34
35	9.06225487	124.03469026	0.00806226	35
36	9.65130143	133.09694513	0.00751332	36
37	10.27863603	142.74824656	0.00700534	37
38	10.94674737	153.02688259	0.00653480	38
39	11.65828595	163.97362996	0.00609854	39
40	12.41607453	175.63191590	0.00569373	40
41	13.22311938	188.04799044	0.00531779	41
42	14.08262214	201.27110981	0.00496842	42
43	14.99799258	215.35373195	0.00464352	43
44	15.97286209	230.35172453	0.00434119	44
45	17.01109813	246.32458662	0.00405968	45
46	18.11681951	263.33568475	0.00379743	46
47	19.29441278	281.45250426	0.00355300	47
48	20.54854961	300.74691704	0.00332505	48
49	21.88420533	321.29546665	0.00311240	49
50	23.30667868	343.17967198	0.00291393	50

7.00% Yearly	Present Value of 1	Present Value of 1 per Period	Payment to Pay Off a Loan of 1	
Years				Years
1	0.93457944	0.93457944	1.07000000	1
2	0.87343873	1.80801817	0.55309179	2
3	0.81629788	2.62431604	0.38105167	3
4	0.76289521	3.38721126	0.29522812	4
5	0.71298618	4.10019744	0.24389069	5
6	0.66634222	4.76653966	0.20979580	6
7	0.62274974	5.38928940	0.18555322	7
8	0.58200910	5.97129851	0.16746776	8
9	0.54393374	6.51523225	0.15348647	9
10	0.50834929	7.02358154	0.14237750	10
11	0.47509280	7.49867434	0.13335690	11
12	0.44401196	7.94268630	0.12590109	12
13	0.41496445	8.35765074	0.11965085	13
14	0.38781724	8.74546799	0.11434494	14
15	0.36244602	9.10791401	0.10979462	15
16	0.33873460	9.44664860	0.10585765	16
17	0.31657439	9.76322299	0.10242519	17
18	0.29586392	10.05908691	0.09941260	18
19	0.27650833	10.33559524	0.09675301	19
20	0.25841900	10.59401425	0.09439293	20
21	0.24151309	10.83552733	0.09228900	21
22	0.22571317	11.06124050	0.09040577	22
23	0.21094688	11.27218738	0.08871393	23
24	0.19714662	11.46933400	0.08718902	24
25	0.18424918	11.65358318	0.08581052	25
26	0.17219549	11.82577867	0.08456103	26
27	0.16093037	11.98670904	0.08342573	27
28	0.15040221	12.13711125	0.08239193	28
29	0.14056282	12.27767407	0.08144865	29
30	0.13136712	12.40904118	0.08058640	30
31	0.12277301	12.53181419	0.07979691	31
32	0.11474113	12.64655532	0.07907292	32
33	0.10723470	12.75379002	0.07840807	33
34	0.10021934	12.85400936	0.07779674	34
35	0.09366294	12.94767230	0.07723396	35
36	0.08753546	13.03520776	0.07671531	36
37	0.08180884	13.11701660	0.07623685	37
38	0.07645686	13.19347345	0.07579505	38
39	0.07145501	13.26492846	0.07538676	39
40	0.06678038	13.33170884	0.07500914	40
41	0.06241157	13.39412041	0.07465962	41
42	0.05832857	13.45244898	0.07433591	42
43	0.05451268	13.50696167	0.07403590	43
44	0.05094643	13.55790810	0.07375769	44
45	0.04761349	13.60552159	0.07349957	45
46	0.04449859	13.65002018	0.07325996	46
47	0.04158747	13.69160764	0.07303744	47
48	0.03886679	13.73047443	0.07283070	48
49	0.03632410	13.76679853	0.07263853	49
50	0.03394776	13.80074629	0.07245985	50

Years	Future Value of 1	Future Value of 1 per Period	Payment for Sinking Fund of 1	**7.00%** Yearly Years
1	1.07000000	1.00000000	1.00000000	1
2	1.14490000	2.07000000	0.48309179	2
3	1.22504300	3.21490000	0.31105167	3
4	1.31079601	4.43994300	0.22522812	4
5	1.40255173	5.75073901	0.17389069	5
6	1.50073035	7.15329074	0.13979580	6
7	1.60578148	8.65402109	0.11555322	7
8	1.71818618	10.25980257	0.09746776	8
9	1.83845921	11.97798875	0.08348647	9
10	1.96715136	13.81644796	0.07237750	10
11	2.10485195	15.78359932	0.06335690	11
12	2.25219159	17.88845127	0.05590199	12
13	2.40984500	20.14064286	0.04965085	13
14	2.57853415	22.55048786	0.04434494	14
15	2.75903154	25.12902201	0.03979462	15
16	2.95216375	27.88805355	0.03585765	16
17	3.15881521	30.84021730	0.03242519	17
18	3.37993228	33.99903251	0.02941260	18
19	3.61652754	37.37896479	0.02675301	19
20	3.86968446	40.99549232	0.02439225	20
21	4.14056237	44.86517678	0.02228900	21
22	4.43040174	49.00573916	0.02040577	22
23	4.74052986	53.43614090	0.01871393	23
24	5.07236695	58.17667076	0.01718902	24
25	5.42743264	63.24903772	0.01581052	25
26	5.80735292	68.67647036	0.01456103	26
27	6.21386763	74.48382328	0.01342573	27
28	6.64883836	80.69769091	0.01239193	28
29	7.11425705	87.34652927	0.01144865	29
30	7.61225504	94.46078632	0.01058640	30
31	8.14511290	102.07304137	0.00979691	31
32	8.71527080	110.21815426	0.00907292	32
33	9.32533975	118.93342506	0.00840807	33
34	9.97811354	128.25876481	0.00779674	34
35	10.67658148	138.23687835	0.00723396	35
36	11.42394219	148.91345984	0.00671531	36
37	12.22361814	160.33740202	0.00623685	37
38	13.07927141	172.56102017	0.00579505	38
39	13.99482041	185.64029158	0.00538676	39
40	14.97445784	199.63511199	0.00500914	40
41	16.02266989	214.60956983	0.00465962	41
42	17.14426678	230.63223972	0.00433591	42
43	18.34435475	247.77649650	0.00403590	43
44	19.62845959	266.12085125	0.00375769	44
45	21.00245176	285.74931084	0.00349957	45
46	22.47262338	306.75176260	0.00325996	46
47	24.04570702	329.22438598	0.00303744	47
48	25.72890651	353.27009300	0.00283070	48
49	27.52992997	378.99899951	0.00263853	49
50	29.45702506	406.52892947	0.00245985	50

7.50% Yearly	Present Value of 1	Present Value of 1 per Period	Payment to Pay Off a Loan of 1	
Years				Years
1	0.93023256	0.93023256	1.07500000	1
2	0.86533261	1.79556517	0.55692771	2
3	0.80496057	2.60052574	0.38453763	3
4	0.74880053	3.34932627	0.29856751	4
5	0.69655863	4.04588490	0.24716472	5
6	0.64796152	4.69384642	0.21304489	6
7	0.60275490	5.29660132	0.18880032	7
8	0.56070223	5.85730355	0.17072702	8
9	0.52158347	6.37888703	0.15676716	9
10	0.48519393	6.86408096	0.14568593	10
11	0.45134319	7.31542415	0.13669747	11
12	0.41985413	7.73527827	0.12927783	12
13	0.39056198	8.12584026	0.12306420	13
14	0.36331347	8.48915373	0.11779737	14
15	0.33796602	8.82711975	0.11328724	15
16	0.31438699	9.14150674	0.10939116	16
17	0.29245302	9.43395976	0.10600003	17
18	0.27204932	9.70600908	0.10302896	18
19	0.25306913	9.95907821	0.10041090	19
20	0.23541315	10.19449136	0.09809219	20
21	0.21898897	10.41348033	0.09602937	21
22	0.20371067	10.61719101	0.09418687	22
23	0.18949830	10.80668931	0.09253528	23
24	0.17627749	10.98296680	0.09105008	24
25	0.16397906	11.14694586	0.08971067	25
26	0.15253866	11.29948452	0.08849961	26
27	0.14189643	11.44138095	0.08740204	27
28	0.13199668	11.57337763	0.08640520	28
29	0.12278761	11.69616524	0.08549811	29
30	0.11422103	11.81038627	0.08467124	30
31	0.10625212	11.91663839	0.08391628	31
32	0.09883918	12.01547757	0.08322599	32
33	0.09194343	12.10742099	0.08259397	33
34	0.08552877	12.19294976	0.08201461	34
35	0.07956164	12.27251141	0.08148293	35
36	0.07401083	12.34652224	0.08099447	36
37	0.06884729	12.41536952	0.08054533	37
38	0.06404399	12.47941351	0.08013197	38
39	0.05957580	12.53898931	0.07975124	39
40	0.05541935	12.59440866	0.07940031	40
41	0.05155288	12.64596155	0.07907663	41
42	0.04795617	12.69391772	0.07877789	42
43	0.04461039	12.73852811	0.07850201	43
44	0.04149804	12.78002615	0.07824710	44
45	0.03860283	12.81862898	0.07801146	45
46	0.03590961	12.85453858	0.07779354	46
47	0.03340428	12.88794287	0.07759190	47
48	0.03107375	12.91901662	0.07740527	48
49	0.02890582	12.94792244	0.07723247	49
50	0.02688913	12.97481157	0.07707241	50

	Future Value of 1	Future Value of 1 per Period	Payment for Sinking Fund of 1	**7.50%**
Years				Yearly Years
1	1.07500000	1.00000000	1.00000000	1
2	1.15562500	2.07500000	0.48192771	2
3	1.24229688	3.23062500	0.30953763	3
4	1.33546914	4.47292188	0.22356751	4
5	1.43562933	5.80839102	0.17216472	5
6	1.54330153	7.24402034	0.13804489	6
7	1.65904914	8.78732187	0.11380032	7
8	1.78347783	10.44637101	0.09572702	8
9	1.91723866	12.22984883	0.08176716	9
10	2.06103156	14.14708750	0.07068593	10
11	2.21560893	16.20811906	0.06169747	11
12	2.38177960	18.42372799	0.05427983	12
13	2.56041307	20.80550759	0.04806420	13
14	2.75244405	23.36592066	0.04279737	14
15	2.95887735	26.11836470	0.03828724	15
16	3.18079315	29.07724206	0.03439116	16
17	3.41935264	32.25803521	0.03100003	17
18	3.67580409	35.67738785	0.02802896	18
19	3.95148940	39.35319194	0.02541090	19
20	4.24785110	43.30468134	0.02309219	20
21	4.56643993	47.55253244	0.02102937	21
22	4.90892293	52.11897237	0.01918687	22
23	5.27709215	57.02789530	0.01753528	23
24	5.67287406	62.30498744	0.01605008	24
25	6.09833961	67.97786150	0.01471067	25
26	6.55571508	74.07620112	0.01349961	26
27	7.04739371	80.63191620	0.01240204	27
28	7.57594824	87.67930991	0.01140520	28
29	8.14414436	95.25525816	0.01049811	29
30	8.75495519	103.39940252	0.00967124	30
31	9.41157683	112.15435771	0.00891628	31
32	10.11744509	121.56593454	0.00822599	32
33	10.87625347	131.68337963	0.00759397	33
34	11.69197248	142.55963310	0.00701461	34
35	12.56887042	154.25160558	0.00648291	35
36	13.51153570	166.82047600	0.00599447	36
37	14.52490088	180.33201170	0.00554533	37
38	15.61426844	194.85691258	0.00513197	38
39	16.78533858	210.47118102	0.00475124	39
40	18.04423897	227.25651960	0.00440031	40
41	19.39755689	245.30075857	0.00407663	41
42	20.85237366	264.69831546	0.00377789	42
43	22.41630168	285.55068912	0.00350201	43
44	24.09752431	307.96699080	0.00324710	44
45	25.90483863	332.06451511	0.00301146	45
46	27.84770153	357.96935375	0.00279354	46
47	29.93627915	385.81705528	0.00259190	47
48	32.18150008	415.75333442	0.00240527	48
49	34.59511259	447.93483451	0.00223247	49
50	37.18974603	482.52994709	0.00207241	50

8.00% Yearly	Present Value of 1	Present Value of 1 per Period	Payment to Pay Off a Loan of 1	
Years				Years
1	0.92592593	0.92592593	1.08000000	1
2	0.85733882	1.78326475	0.56076923	2
3	0.79383224	2.57709699	0.38803351	3
4	0.73502985	3.31212684	0.30192080	4
5	0.68058320	3.99271004	0.25045645	5
6	0.63016963	4.62287966	0.21631539	6
7	0.58349040	5.20637006	0.19207240	7
8	0.54026888	5.74663894	0.17401476	8
9	0.50024897	6.24688791	0.16007971	9
10	0.46319349	6.71008140	0.14902949	10
11	0.42888286	7.13896426	0.14007634	11
12	0.39711376	7.53607802	0.13269502	12
13	0.36769792	7.90377594	0.12652181	13
14	0.34046104	8.24423698	0.12129685	14
15	0.31524170	8.55947869	0.11682954	15
16	0.29189047	8.85136916	0.11297687	16
17	0.27026895	9.12163811	0.10962943	17
18	0.25024903	9.37188714	0.10670210	18
19	0.23171206	9.60359920	0.10412763	19
20	0.21454821	9.81814941	0.10185221	20
21	0.19865575	10.01680316	0.09983225	21
22	0.18394051	10.20074366	0.09803207	22
23	0.17031528	10.37105895	0.09642217	23
24	0.15769934	10.52875828	0.09497796	24
25	0.14601790	10.67477619	0.09367878	25
26	0.13520176	10.80997795	0.09250713	26
27	0.12518682	10.93516477	0.09144810	27
28	0.11591372	11.05107849	0.09048891	28
29	0.10732752	11.15840601	0.08961854	29
30	0.09937733	11.25778334	0.08882743	30
31	0.09201605	11.34979939	0.08810728	31
32	0.08520005	11.43499944	0.08745081	32
33	0.07888893	11.51388837	0.08685163	33
34	0.07304531	11.58693367	0.08630411	34
35	0.06763454	11.65456822	0.08580204	35
36	0.06262458	11.71719279	0.08534467	36
37	0.05798572	11.77517851	0.08492440	37
38	0.05369048	11.82886899	0.08453894	38
39	0.04971341	11.87858240	0.08418513	39
40	0.04603093	11.92461333	0.08386016	40
41	0.04262123	11.96723457	0.08356149	41
42	0.03946411	12.00669867	0.08328684	42
43	0.03654084	12.04323951	0.08303414	43
44	0.03383411	12.07707362	0.08280152	44
45	0.03132788	12.10840150	0.08258728	45
46	0.02900730	12.13740880	0.08238991	46
47	0.02685861	12.16426741	0.08220799	47
48	0.02486908	12.18913649	0.08204027	48
49	0.02302693	12.21216341	0.08188557	49
50	0.02132123	12.23348464	0.08174286	50

Years	Future Value of 1	Future Value of 1 per Period	Payment for Sinking Fund of 1	**8.00%** Yearly Years
1	1.08000000	1.00000000	1.00000000	1
2	1.16640000	2.08000000	0.48076923	2
3	1.25971200	3.24640000	0.30803351	3
4	1.36048896	4.50611200	0.22192080	4
5	1.46932808	5.86660096	0.17045645	5
6	1.58687432	7.33592904	0.13631539	6
7	1.71382427	8.92280336	0.11207240	7
8	1.85093021	10.63662763	0.09401476	8
9	1.99900463	12.48755784	0.08007971	9
10	2.15892500	14.48656247	0.06902949	10
11	2.33163900	16.64548746	0.06007634	11
12	2.51817012	18.97712646	0.05269502	12
13	2.71962373	21.49529658	0.04652181	13
14	2.93719362	24.21492030	0.04129685	14
15	3.17216911	27.15211393	0.03682954	15
16	3.42594264	30.32428304	0.03297687	16
17	3.70001805	33.75022569	0.02962943	17
18	3.99601950	37.45024374	0.02670210	18
19	4.31570106	41.44626324	0.02412763	19
20	4.66095714	45.76196430	0.02185221	20
21	5.03383372	50.42292144	0.01983225	21
22	5.43654041	55.45675516	0.01803207	22
23	5.87146365	60.89329557	0.01642217	23
24	6.34118074	66.76475922	0.01497796	24
25	6.84847520	73.10593995	0.01367878	25
26	7.39635321	79.95441515	0.01250713	26
27	7.98806147	87.35076836	0.01144810	27
28	8.62710639	95.33882983	0.01048891	28
29	9.31727490	103.96593622	0.00961854	29
30	10.06265689	113.28321111	0.00882743	30
31	10.86766944	123.34586800	0.00810728	31
32	11.73708300	134.21353744	0.00745081	32
33	12.67604964	145.95062044	0.00685163	33
34	13.69013361	158.62667007	0.00630411	34
35	14.78534429	172.31680368	0.00580326	35
36	15.96817184	187.10214797	0.00534467	36
37	17.24562558	203.07031981	0.00492440	37
38	18.62527563	220.31594540	0.00453894	38
39	20.11529768	238.94122103	0.00418513	39
40	21.72452150	259.05651871	0.00386016	40
41	23.46248322	280.78104021	0.00356149	41
42	25.33948187	304.24352342	0.00328684	42
43	27.36664042	329.58300530	0.00303414	43
44	29.55597166	356.94964572	0.00280152	44
45	31.92044939	386.50561738	0.00258728	45
46	34.47408534	418.42606677	0.00238991	46
47	37.23201217	452.90015211	0.00220799	47
48	40.21057314	490.13216428	0.00204027	48
49	43.42741899	530.34273742	0.00188557	49
50	46.90161251	573.77015642	0.00174286	50

8.50% Yearly	Present Value of 1	Present Value of 1 per Period	Payment to Pay Off a Loan of 1	
Years				Years
1	0.92165899	0.92165899	1.08500000	1
2	0.84945529	1.77111427	0.56461631	2
3	0.78290810	2.55402237	0.39153925	3
4	0.72157428	3.27559666	0.30528789	4
5	0.66504542	3.94064208	0.25376575	5
6	0.61294509	4.55358717	0.21960708	6
7	0.56492635	5.11851352	0.19536922	7
8	0.52066945	5.63918297	0.17733065	8
9	0.47987968	6.11906264	0.16342372	9
10	0.44228542	6.56134806	0.15240771	10
11	0.40763633	6.96898439	0.14349293	11
12	0.37570168	7.34468607	0.13615286	12
13	0.34626883	7.69095490	0.13002287	13
14	0.31914178	8.01009668	0.12484244	14
15	0.29413989	8.30423658	0.12042046	15
16	0.27109667	8.57533325	0.11661354	16
17	0.24985869	8.82519194	0.11331198	17
18	0.23028450	9.05547644	0.11043041	18
19	0.21224378	9.26772022	0.10790140	19
20	0.19561639	9.46333661	0.10567097	20
21	0.18029160	9.64362821	0.10369541	21
22	0.16616738	9.80979559	0.10193892	22
23	0.15314965	9.96294524	0.10037193	23
24	0.14115176	10.10409700	0.09896975	24
25	0.13009378	10.23419078	0.09771168	25
26	0.11990210	10.35409288	0.09658017	26
27	0.11050885	10.46460174	0.09556025	27
28	0.10185148	10.56645321	0.09463914	28
29	0.09387233	10.66032554	0.09380577	29
30	0.08651828	10.74684382	0.09305058	30
31	0.07974035	10.82658416	0.09236524	31
32	0.07349341	10.90007757	0.09174247	32
33	0.06773586	10.96781343	0.09117588	33
34	0.06242936	11.03024279	0.09065984	34
35	0.05753858	11.08778137	0.09018937	35
36	0.05303095	11.14081233	0.08976006	36
37	0.04887645	11.18968878	0.08936799	37
38	0.04504742	11.23473620	0.08900966	38
39	0.04151836	11.27625457	0.08868193	39
40	0.03826577	11.31452034	0.08838201	40
41	0.03526799	11.34978833	0.08810737	41
42	0.03250506	11.38229339	0.08785576	42
43	0.02995858	11.41225197	0.08762512	43
44	0.02761160	11.43986357	0.08741363	44
45	0.02544848	11.46531205	0.08721961	45
46	0.02345482	11.48876686	0.08704154	46
47	0.02161734	11.51038420	0.08687807	47
48	0.01992382	11.53030802	0.08672795	48
49	0.01836297	11.54867099	0.08659005	49
50	0.01692439	11.56559538	0.08646334	50

Years	Future Value of 1	Future Value of 1 per Period	Payment for Sinking Fund of 1	**8.50%** Yearly Years
1	1.08500000	1.00000000	1.00000000	1
2	1.17722500	2.08500000	0.47961631	2
3	1.27728913	3.26222500	0.30653925	3
4	1.38585870	4.53951413	0.22028789	4
5	1.50365669	5.92537283	0.16876575	5
6	1.63146751	7.42902952	0.13460708	6
7	1.77014225	9.06049702	0.11036922	7
8	1.92060434	10.83063927	0.09233065	8
9	2.08385571	12.75124361	0.07842372	9
10	2.26098344	14.83509932	0.06740771	10
11	2.45316703	17.09608276	0.05849293	11
12	2.66168623	19.54924979	0.05115286	12
13	2.88792956	22.21093603	0.04502287	13
14	3.13340357	25.09886559	0.03984244	14
15	3.39974288	28.23226916	0.03542046	15
16	3.68872102	31.63201204	0.03161354	16
17	4.00226231	35.32073306	0.02831198	17
18	4.34245461	39.32299538	0.02543041	18
19	4.71156325	43.66544998	0.02290140	19
20	5.11204612	48.37701323	0.02067097	20
21	5.54657005	53.48905936	0.01869541	21
22	6.01802850	59.03562940	0.01693892	22
23	6.52956092	65.05365790	0.01537193	23
24	7.08457360	71.58321882	0.01396975	24
25	7.68676236	78.66779242	0.01271168	25
26	8.34013716	86.35455478	0.01158017	26
27	9.04904881	94.69469193	0.01056025	27
28	9.81821796	103.74374075	0.00963914	28
29	10.65276649	113.56195871	0.00880577	29
30	11.55825164	124.21472520	0.00805058	30
31	12.54070303	135.77297684	0.00736524	31
32	13.60666279	148.31367987	0.00674247	32
33	14.76322913	161.92034266	0.00617588	33
34	16.01810360	176.68357179	0.00565984	34
35	17.37964241	192.70167539	0.00518937	35
36	18.85691201	210.08131780	0.00476006	36
37	20.45974953	228.93822981	0.00436799	37
38	22.19882824	249.39797935	0.00400966	38
39	24.08572865	271.59680759	0.00368193	39
40	26.13301558	295.68253624	0.00338201	40
41	28.35432190	321.81555182	0.00310737	41
42	30.76443927	350.16987372	0.00285576	42
43	33.37941660	380.93431299	0.00262512	43
44	36.21666702	414.31372959	0.00241363	44
45	39.29508371	450.53039661	0.00221961	45
46	42.63516583	489.82548032	0.00204154	46
47	46.25915492	532.46064615	0.00187807	47
48	50.19118309	578.71980107	0.00172795	48
49	54.45743365	628.91098416	0.00159005	49
50	59.08631551	683.36841782	0.00146334	50

9.00% Yearly	Present Value of 1	Present Value of 1 per Period	Payment to Pay Off a Loan of 1	
Years				Years
1	0.91743119	0.91743119	1.09000000	1
2	0.84167999	1.75911119	0.56846890	2
3	0.77218348	2.53129467	0.39505476	3
4	0.70842521	3.23971988	0.30866866	4
5	0.64993139	3.88965126	0.25709246	5
6	0.59626733	4.48591859	0.22291978	6
7	0.54703424	5.03295284	0.19869052	7
8	0.50186628	5.53481911	0.18067438	8
9	0.46042778	5.99524689	0.16679880	9
10	0.42241081	6.41765770	0.15582009	10
11	0.38753285	6.80519055	0.14694666	11
12	0.35553473	7.16072528	0.13965066	12
13	0.32617865	7.48690392	0.13356656	13
14	0.29924647	7.78615039	0.12843317	14
15	0.27453804	8.06068843	0.12405888	15
16	0.25186976	8.31255819	0.12029991	16
17	0.23107318	8.54363137	0.11704625	17
18	0.21199374	8.75562511	0.11421229	18
19	0.19448967	8.95011478	0.11173041	19
20	0.17843089	9.12854567	0.10954648	20
21	0.16369806	9.29224373	0.10761663	21
22	0.15018171	9.44242544	0.10590499	22
23	0.13778139	9.58020683	0.10438188	23
24	0.12640494	9.70661177	0.10302256	24
25	0.11596784	9.82257960	0.10180625	25
26	0.10639251	9.92897211	0.10071536	26
27	0.09760781	10.02657992	0.09973491	27
28	0.08954845	10.11612837	0.09885205	28
29	0.08215454	10.19828291	0.09805572	29
30	0.07537114	10.27365404	0.09733635	30
31	0.06914783	10.34280187	0.09668560	31
32	0.06343838	10.40624025	0.09609619	32
33	0.05820035	10.46444060	0.09556173	33
34	0.05339481	10.51783541	0.09507660	34
35	0.04898607	10.56682148	0.09463584	35
36	0.04494135	10.61176282	0.09423505	36
37	0.04123059	10.65299342	0.09387033	37
38	0.03782623	10.69081965	0.09353820	38
39	0.03470296	10.72552261	0.09323555	39
40	0.03183758	10.75736020	0.09295961	40
41	0.02920879	10.78656899	0.09270789	41
42	0.02679706	10.81336604	0.09247814	42
43	0.02458446	10.83795050	0.09226837	43
44	0.02255455	10.86050504	0.09207675	44
45	0.02069224	10.88119729	0.09190165	45
46	0.01898371	10.90018100	0.09174160	46
47	0.01741625	10.91759725	0.09159525	47
48	0.01597821	10.93357546	0.09146139	48
49	0.01465891	10.94823436	0.09133893	49
50	0.01344854	10.96168290	0.09122687	50

Years	Future Value of 1	Future Value of 1 per Period	Payment for Sinking Fund of 1	**9.00%** Yearly Years
1	1.09000000	1.00000000	1.00000000	1
2	1.18810000	2.09000000	0.47846890	2
3	1.29502900	3.27810000	0.30505476	3
4	1.41158161	4.57312900	0.21866866	4
5	1.53862395	5.98471061	0.16709246	5
6	1.67710011	7.52333456	0.13291978	6
7	1.82803912	9.20043468	0.10869052	7
8	1.99256264	11.02847380	0.09067438	8
9	2.17189328	13.02103644	0.07679880	9
10	2.36736367	15.19292972	0.06582009	10
11	2.58042641	17.56029339	0.05694666	11
12	2.81266478	20.14071980	0.04965066	12
13	3.06580461	22.95338458	0.04356656	13
14	3.34172703	26.01918919	0.03843317	14
15	3.64248246	29.36091622	0.03405888	15
16	3.97030588	33.00339868	0.03029991	16
17	4.32763341	36.97370456	0.02704625	17
18	4.71712042	41.30133797	0.02421229	18
19	5.14166125	46.01845839	0.02173041	19
20	5.60441077	51.16011964	0.01954648	20
21	6.10880774	56.76453041	0.01761663	21
22	6.65860043	62.87333815	0.01590499	22
23	7.25787447	69.53193858	0.01438188	23
24	7.91108317	76.78981305	0.01302256	24
25	8.62308066	84.70089623	0.01180625	25
26	9.39915792	93.32397689	0.01071536	26
27	10.24508213	102.72313481	0.00973491	27
28	11.16713952	112.96821694	0.00885205	28
29	12.17218208	124.13535646	0.00805572	29
30	13.26767847	136.30753855	0.00733635	30
31	14.46176953	149.57521702	0.00668560	31
32	15.76332879	164.03698655	0.00609619	32
33	17.18202838	179.80031534	0.00556173	33
34	18.72841093	196.98234372	0.00507660	34
35	20.41396792	215.71075465	0.00463584	35
36	22.25122503	236.12472257	0.00423505	36
37	24.25383528	258.37594760	0.00387033	37
38	26.43668046	282.62978288	0.00353820	38
39	28.81598170	309.06646334	0.00323555	39
40	31.40942005	337.88244504	0.00295961	40
41	34.23626786	369.29186510	0.00270789	41
42	37.31753197	403.52813296	0.00247814	42
43	40.67610984	440.84566492	0.00226837	43
44	44.33695973	481.52177477	0.00207675	44
45	48.32728610	525.85873450	0.00190165	45
46	52.67674185	574.18602060	0.00174160	46
47	57.41764862	626.86276245	0.00159525	47
48	62.58523700	684.28041107	0.00146139	48
49	68.21790833	746.86564807	0.00133893	49
50	74.35752008	815.08355640	0.00122687	50

Years	Present Value of 1	Present Value of 1 per Period	Payment to Pay Off a Loan of 1	Years
1	0.91324201	0.91324201	1.09500000	1
2	0.83401097	1.74725298	0.57232697	2
3	0.76165385	2.50890683	0.39857997	3
4	0.69557429	3.20448112	0.31206300	4
5	0.63522767	3.83970879	0.26043642	5
6	0.58011659	4.41982538	0.22625328	6
7	0.52978684	4.94961222	0.20203603	7
8	0.48382360	5.43343581	0.18404561	8
9	0.44184803	5.87528385	0.17020454	9
10	0.40351419	6.27879803	0.15926615	10
11	0.36850611	6.64730414	0.15043693	11
12	0.33653526	6.98383940	0.14318771	12
13	0.30733813	7.29117753	0.13715206	13
14	0.28067410	7.57185163	0.13206809	14
15	0.25632337	7.82817500	0.12774370	15
16	0.23408327	8.06226028	0.12403470	16
17	0.21377651	8.27603678	0.12083078	17
18	0.19522969	8.47126647	0.11804610	18
19	0.17829195	8.64955842	0.11561284	19
20	0.16282370	8.81238212	0.11347670	20
21	0.14869744	8.96107956	0.11159370	21
22	0.13579675	9.09687631	0.10992784	22
23	0.12401530	9.22089161	0.10844938	23
24	0.11325598	9.33414759	0.10713351	24
25	0.10343012	9.43757770	0.10595939	25
26	0.09445673	9.53203443	0.10490940	26
27	0.08626185	9.61829629	0.10396852	27
28	0.07877795	9.69707423	0.10312389	28
29	0.07194333	9.76901756	0.10236444	29
30	0.06570167	9.83471924	0.10168058	30
31	0.06000153	9.89472076	0.10106399	31
32	0.05479592	9.94951668	0.10050739	32
33	0.05004193	9.99955861	0.10000441	33
34	0.04570039	10.04525901	0.09954945	34
35	0.04173552	10.08699453	0.09913756	35
36	0.03811463	10.12510916	0.09876423	36
37	0.03480788	10.15991704	0.09842600	37
38	0.03178802	10.19170506	0.09811901	38
39	0.02903015	10.22073521	0.09784032	39
40	0.02651156	10.24724677	0.09758719	40
41	0.02421147	10.27145824	0.09735716	41
42	0.02211093	10.29356917	0.09714803	42
43	0.02019263	10.31376180	0.09695783	43
44	0.01844076	10.33220255	0.09678478	44
45	0.01684087	10.34904343	0.09662729	45
46	0.01537979	10.36442322	0.09648390	46
47	0.01404547	10.37846870	0.09635333	47
48	0.01282692	10.39129561	0.09623439	48
49	0.01171408	10.40300969	0.09612603	49
50	0.01069779	10.41370748	0.09602728	50

	Future Value of 1	Future Value of 1 per Period	Payment for Sinking Fund of 1	**9.50%**
Years				Yearly
				Years
1	1.09500000	1.00000000	1.00000000	1
2	1.19902500	2.09500000	0.47732697	2
3	1.31293238	3.29402500	0.30357997	3
4	1.43766095	4.60695738	0.21706300	4
5	1.57423874	6.04461833	0.16543642	5
6	1.72379142	7.61885707	0.13125328	6
7	1.88755161	9.34264849	0.10703603	7
8	2.06686901	11.23020009	0.08904561	8
9	2.26322156	13.29706910	0.07520454	9
10	2.47822761	15.56029067	0.06426615	10
11	2.71365924	18.03851828	0.05543693	11
12	2.97145686	20.75217752	0.04818771	12
13	3.25374527	23.72363438	0.04215206	13
14	3.56285107	26.97737965	0.03706809	14
15	3.90132192	30.54023072	0.03274370	15
16	4.27194750	34.44155263	0.02903470	16
17	4.67778251	38.71350013	0.02583078	17
18	5.12217185	43.39128265	0.02304610	18
19	5.60877818	48.51345450	0.02061284	19
20	6.14161210	54.12223267	0.01847670	20
21	6.72506525	60.26384478	0.01659370	21
22	7.36394645	66.98891003	0.01492784	22
23	8.06352137	74.35285649	0.01344938	23
24	8.82955590	82.41637785	0.01213351	24
25	9.66836371	91.24593375	0.01095939	25
26	10.58685826	100.91429745	0.00990940	26
27	11.59260979	111.50115571	0.00896852	27
28	12.69390772	123.09376551	0.00812389	28
29	13.89982896	135.78767323	0.00736444	29
30	15.22031271	149.68750218	0.00668058	30
31	16.66624241	164.90781489	0.00606399	31
32	18.24953544	181.57405731	0.00550739	32
33	19.98324131	199.82359275	0.00500441	33
34	21.88164924	219.80683406	0.00454945	34
35	23.96040591	241.68848330	0.00413756	35
36	26.23664448	265.64888921	0.00376437	36
37	28.72912570	291.88553369	0.00342600	37
38	31.45839264	320.61465939	0.00311901	38
39	34.44693994	352.07305203	0.00284032	39
40	37.71939924	386.51999197	0.00258719	40
41	41.30274216	424.23939121	0.00235716	41
42	45.22650267	465.54213337	0.00214803	42
43	49.52302042	510.76863604	0.00195783	43
44	54.22770736	560.29165647	0.00178478	44
45	59.37933956	614.51936383	0.00162729	45
46	65.02037682	673.89870340	0.00148390	46
47	71.19731262	738.91908022	0.00135333	47
48	77.96105732	810.11639284	0.00123439	48
49	85.36735777	888.07745016	0.00112603	49
50	93.47725675	973.44480793	0.00102728	50

10.00% Yearly	Present Value of 1	Present Value of 1 per Period	Payment to Pay Off a Loan of 1	
Years				Years
1	0.90909091	0.90909091	1.10000000	1
2	0.82644628	1.73553719	0.57619048	2
3	0.75131480	2.48685199	0.40211480	3
4	0.68301346	3.16986545	0.31547080	4
5	0.62092132	3.79078677	0.26379748	5
6	0.56447393	4.35526070	0.22960738	6
7	0.51315812	4.86841882	0.20540550	7
8	0.46650738	5.33492620	0.18744402	8
9	0.42409762	5.75902382	0.17364054	9
10	0.38554329	6.14456711	0.16274539	10
11	0.35049390	6.49506101	0.15396314	11
12	0.31863082	6.81369182	0.14676332	12
13	0.28966438	7.10335620	0.14077852	13
14	0.26333125	7.36668746	0.13574622	14
15	0.23939205	7.60607951	0.13147378	15
16	0.21762914	7.82370864	0.12781662	16
17	0.19784467	8.02155331	0.12466413	17
18	0.17985879	8.20141210	0.12193022	18
19	0.16350799	8.36492009	0.11954687	19
20	0.14864363	8.51356372	0.11745962	20
21	0.13513057	8.64869429	0.11562439	21
22	0.12284597	8.77154026	0.11400506	22
23	0.11167816	8.88321842	0.11257181	23
24	0.10152560	8.98474402	0.11129978	24
25	0.09229600	9.07704002	0.11016807	25
26	0.08390545	9.16094547	0.10915944	26
27	0.07627768	9.23722316	0.10825764	27
28	0.06934335	9.30656651	0.10745101	28
29	0.06303941	9.36960591	0.10672807	29
30	0.05730855	9.42691447	0.10607925	30
31	0.05209868	9.47901315	0.10549621	31
32	0.04736244	9.52637559	0.10497172	32
33	0.04305676	9.56943236	0.10449941	33
34	0.03914251	9.60857487	0.10407371	34
35	0.03558410	9.64415897	0.10368971	35
36	0.03234918	9.67650816	0.10334306	36
37	0.02940835	9.70591651	0.10302994	37
38	0.02673486	9.73265137	0.10274692	38
39	0.02430442	9.75695579	0.10249098	39
40	0.02209493	9.77905072	0.10225941	40
41	0.02008630	9.79913702	0.10204980	41
42	0.01826027	9.81739729	0.10185999	42
43	0.01660025	9.83399753	0.10168805	43
44	0.01509113	9.84908867	0.10153224	44
45	0.01371921	9.86280788	0.10139100	45
46	0.01247201	9.87527989	0.10126295	46
47	0.01133819	9.88661808	0.10114682	47
48	0.01030745	9.89692553	0.10104148	48
49	0.00937041	9.90629594	0.10094590	49
50	0.00851855	9.91481449	0.10085917	50

Years	Future Value of 1	Future Value of 1 per Period	Payment for Sinking Fund of 1	**10.00%** Yearly Years
1	1.10000000	1.00000000	1.00000000	1
2	1.21000000	2.10000000	0.47619048	2
3	1.33100000	3.31000000	0.30211480	3
4	1.46410000	4.64100000	0.21547080	4
5	1.61051000	6.10510000	0.16379748	5
6	1.77156100	7.71561000	0.12960738	6
7	1.94871710	9.48717100	0.10540550	7
8	2.14358881	11.43588810	0.08744402	8
9	2.35794769	13.57947691	0.07364054	9
10	2.59374246	15.93742460	0.06274539	10
11	2.85311671	18.53116706	0.05396314	11
12	3.13842838	21.38428377	0.04676332	12
13	3.45227121	24.52271214	0.04077852	13
14	3.79749834	27.97498336	0.03574622	14
15	4.17724817	31.77248169	0.03147378	15
16	4.59497299	35.94972986	0.02781662	16
17	5.05447028	40.54470285	0.02466413	17
18	5.55991731	45.59917313	0.02193022	18
19	6.11590904	51.15909045	0.01954687	19
20	6.72749995	57.27499949	0.01745962	20
21	7.40024994	64.00249944	0.01562439	21
22	8.14027494	71.40274939	0.01400506	22
23	8.95430243	79.54302433	0.01257181	23
24	9.84973268	88.49732676	0.01129978	24
25	10.83470594	98.34705943	0.01016807	25
26	11.91817654	109.18176538	0.00915904	26
27	13.10999419	121.09994191	0.00825764	27
28	14.42099361	134.20993611	0.00745101	28
29	15.86309297	148.63092972	0.00672807	29
30	17.44940227	164.49402269	0.00607925	30
31	19.19434250	181.94342496	0.00549621	31
32	21.11377675	201.13776745	0.00497172	32
33	23.22515442	222.25154420	0.00449941	33
34	25.54766986	245.47669862	0.00407371	34
35	28.10243685	271.02436848	0.00368901	35
36	30.91268053	299.12680533	0.00334306	36
37	34.00394859	330.03948586	0.00302994	37
38	37.40434344	364.04343445	0.00274692	38
39	41.14477779	401.44777789	0.00249098	39
40	45.25925557	442.59255568	0.00225941	40
41	49.78518112	487.85181125	0.00204980	41
42	54.76369924	537.63699237	0.00185999	42
43	60.24006916	592.40069161	0.00168805	43
44	66.26407608	652.64076077	0.00153224	44
45	72.89048369	718.90483685	0.00139100	45
46	80.17953205	791.79532054	0.00126295	46
47	88.19748526	871.97485259	0.00114682	47
48	97.01723378	960.17233785	0.00104148	48
49	106.71895716	1057.18957163	0.00094590	49
50	117.39085288	1163.90852880	0.00085917	50

10.50%
Yearly

Years	Present Value of 1	Present Value of 1 per Period	Payment to Pay Off a Loan of 1	Years
1	0.90497738	0.90497738	1.10500000	1
2	0.81898405	1.72396143	0.58005938	2
3	0.74116204	2.46512346	0.40565920	3
4	0.67073487	3.13585834	0.31889196	4
5	0.60699989	3.74285822	0.26717550	5
6	0.54932116	4.29217939	0.23298187	6
7	0.49712323	4.78930261	0.20879867	7
8	0.44988527	5.23918789	0.19086928	8
9	0.40713599	5.64632388	0.17710638	9
10	0.36844886	6.01477274	0.16625732	10
11	0.33343788	6.34821062	0.15752670	11
12	0.30175374	6.64996437	0.15037675	12
13	0.27308031	6.92304468	0.14444512	13
14	0.24713150	7.17017618	0.13946659	14
15	0.22364842	7.39382459	0.13524800	15
16	0.20239676	7.59622135	0.13164440	16
17	0.18318449	7.77938584	0.12854485	17
18	0.16575972	7.94514556	0.12586302	18
19	0.15000879	8.09515435	0.12353069	19
20	0.13575456	8.23090891	0.12149327	20
21	0.12285481	8.35376372	0.11970652	21
22	0.11118082	8.46494455	0.11813426	22
23	0.10061613	8.56556067	0.11674509	23
24	0.09105532	8.65661599	0.11551858	24
25	0.08240301	8.73901900	0.11442932	25
26	0.07457286	8.81359186	0.11346112	26
27	0.06748675	8.88107860	0.11259894	27
28	0.06107398	8.94215258	0.11182990	28
29	0.05527057	8.99742315	0.11114293	29
30	0.05001861	9.04744176	0.11052848	30
31	0.04526571	9.09270748	0.10997824	31
32	0.04096445	9.13367193	0.10948499	32
33	0.03707190	9.17074383	0.10904241	33
34	0.03354923	9.20429305	0.10864495	34
35	0.03036129	9.23465435	0.10828776	35
36	0.02747628	9.26213063	0.10796652	36
37	0.02486542	9.28699605	0.10767744	37
38	0.02250264	9.30949868	0.10741717	38
39	0.02036438	9.32986306	0.10718271	39
40	0.01842930	9.34829237	0.10697141	40
41	0.01667810	9.36497047	0.10678090	41
42	0.01509330	9.38006377	0.10660908	42
43	0.01365910	9.39372287	0.10645407	43
44	0.01236118	9.40608404	0.10631417	44
45	0.01118658	9.41727063	0.10618788	45
46	0.01012361	9.42739423	0.10607385	46
47	0.00916163	9.43655587	0.10597087	47
48	0.00829107	9.44484694	0.10587784	48
49	0.00750323	9.45235017	0.10579380	49
50	0.00679026	9.45914043	0.10571785	50

	Future Value of 1	Future Value of 1 per Period	Payment for Sinking Fund of 1	**10.50%** Yearly
Years				Years
1	1.10500000	1.00000000	1.00000000	1
2	1.22102500	2.10500000	0.47505938	2
3	1.34923263	3.32602500	0.30065920	3
4	1.49090205	4.67525763	0.21389196	4
5	1.64744677	6.16615968	0.16217550	5
6	1.82042868	7.81360644	0.12798187	6
7	2.01157369	9.63403512	0.10379867	7
8	2.22278892	11.64560881	0.08586928	8
9	2.45618176	13.86839773	0.07210638	9
10	2.71408085	16.32457949	0.06125732	10
11	2.99905934	19.03866034	0.05252470	11
12	3.31396057	22.03771967	0.04537675	12
13	3.66192643	25.35168024	0.03944512	13
14	4.04642870	29.01360666	0.03446659	14
15	4.47130371	33.06003536	0.03024800	15
16	4.94079060	37.53133908	0.02664440	16
17	5.45957362	42.47212968	0.02354485	17
18	6.03282885	47.93170330	0.02086302	18
19	6.66627588	53.96453214	0.01853069	19
20	7.36623484	60.63080802	0.01649327	20
21	8.13968950	67.99704286	0.01470652	21
22	8.99435690	76.13673236	0.01313426	22
23	9.93876437	85.13108926	0.01174659	23
24	10.98233463	95.06985363	0.01051858	24
25	12.13547977	106.05218826	0.00942932	25
26	13.40970514	118.18766803	0.00846112	26
27	14.81772418	131.59737317	0.00759894	27
28	16.37358522	146.41509736	0.00682990	28
29	18.09281167	162.78868258	0.00614293	29
30	19.99255690	180.88149425	0.00552848	30
31	22.09177537	200.87405114	0.00497824	31
32	24.41141178	222.96582651	0.00448499	32
33	26.97461002	247.37723830	0.00404241	33
34	29.80694407	274.35184832	0.00364495	34
35	32.93667320	304.15879239	0.00328776	35
36	36.39502389	337.09546560	0.00296662	36
37	40.21650140	373.49048948	0.00267744	37
38	44.43923404	413.70699088	0.00241717	38
39	49.10535362	458.14622492	0.00218271	39
40	54.26141575	507.25157854	0.00197141	40
41	59.95886440	561.51299428	0.00178090	41
42	66.25454516	621.47185868	0.00160908	42
43	73.21127240	687.72640385	0.00145407	43
44	80.89845601	760.93767625	0.00131417	44
45	89.39279389	841.83613225	0.00118788	45
46	98.77903724	931.22892614	0.00107385	46
47	109.15083616	1030.00796339	0.00097087	47
48	120.61167395	1139.15879954	0.00087784	48
49	133.27589972	1259.77047349	0.00079380	49
50	147.26986919	1393.04637321	0.00071785	50

11.00% Yearly	Present Value of 1	Present Value of 1 per Period	Payment to Pay Off a Loan of 1	
Years				Years
1	0.90090090	0.90090090	1.11000000	1
2	0.81162243	1.71252333	0.58393365	2
3	0.73119138	2.44371472	0.40921307	3
4	0.65873097	3.10244569	0.32232635	4
5	0.59345133	3.69589702	0.27057031	5
6	0.53464084	4.23053785	0.23637656	6
7	0.48165841	4.71219626	0.21221527	7
8	0.43392650	5.14612276	0.19432105	8
9	0.39092477	5.53704753	0.18060166	9
10	0.35218448	5.88923201	0.16980143	10
11	0.31728331	6.20651533	0.16112101	11
12	0.28584082	6.49235615	0.15402729	12
13	0.25751426	6.74987040	0.14815099	13
14	0.23199482	6.98186523	0.14322820	14
15	0.20900435	7.19086958	0.13906524	15
16	0.18829220	7.37916178	0.13551675	16
17	0.16963262	7.54879440	0.13247148	17
18	0.15282218	7.70161657	0.12984287	18
19	0.13767764	7.83929421	0.12756250	19
20	0.12403391	7.96332812	0.12557564	20
21	0.11174226	8.07507038	0.12383793	21
22	0.10066870	8.17573908	0.12231310	22
23	0.09069252	8.26643160	0.12097118	23
24	0.08170498	8.34813658	0.11978721	24
25	0.07360809	8.42174466	0.11874024	25
26	0.06631359	8.48805826	0.11781258	26
27	0.05974197	8.54780023	0.11698916	27
28	0.05382160	8.60162183	0.11625715	28
29	0.04848793	8.65010976	0.11560547	29
30	0.04368282	8.69379257	0.11502460	30
31	0.03935389	8.73314646	0.11450627	31
32	0.03545395	8.76860042	0.11404329	32
33	0.03194050	8.80054092	0.11362938	33
34	0.02877522	8.82931614	0.11325905	34
35	0.02592363	8.85523977	0.11292749	35
36	0.02335462	8.87859438	0.11263044	36
37	0.02104020	8.89963458	0.11236416	37
38	0.01895513	8.91858971	0.11212535	38
39	0.01707670	8.93566641	0.11191107	39
40	0.01538441	8.95105082	0.11171873	40
41	0.01385983	8.96491065	0.11154601	41
42	0.01248633	8.97739698	0.11139086	42
43	0.01124895	8.98864593	0.11125146	43
44	0.01013419	8.99878011	0.11112617	44
45	0.00912990	9.00791001	0.11101354	45
46	0.00822513	9.01613515	0.11091227	46
47	0.00741003	9.02354518	0.11082119	47
48	0.00667570	9.03022088	0.11073926	48
49	0.00601415	9.03623503	0.11066556	49
50	0.00541815	9.04165318	0.11059924	50

Years	Future Value of 1	Future Value of 1 per Period	Payment for Sinking Fund of 1	**11.00%** Yearly Years
1	1.11000000	1.00000000	1.00000000	1
2	1.23210000	2.11000000	0.47393365	2
3	1.36763100	3.34210000	0.29921307	3
4	1.51807041	4.70973100	0.21232635	4
5	1.68505816	6.22780141	0.16057031	5
6	1.87041455	7.91285957	0.12637656	6
7	2.07616015	9.78327412	0.10221527	7
8	2.30453777	11.85943427	0.08432105	8
9	2.55803692	14.16397204	0.07060166	9
10	2.83942099	16.72200896	0.05980143	10
11	3.15175729	19.56142995	0.05112101	11
12	3.49845060	22.71318724	0.04402729	12
13	3.88328016	26.21163784	0.03815099	13
14	4.31044098	30.09491800	0.03322820	14
15	4.78458949	34.40535898	0.02906524	15
16	5.31089433	39.18994847	0.02551675	16
17	5.89509271	44.50084281	0.02247148	17
18	6.54355291	50.39593551	0.01984287	18
19	7.26334373	56.93948842	0.01756250	19
20	8.06231154	64.20283215	0.01557564	20
21	8.94916581	72.26514368	0.01383793	21
22	9.93357404	81.21430949	0.01231310	22
23	11.02626719	91.14788353	0.01097118	23
24	12.23915658	102.17415072	0.00978721	24
25	13.58546380	114.41330730	0.00874024	25
26	15.07986482	127.99877110	0.00781258	26
27	16.73864995	143.07863592	0.00698916	27
28	18.57990145	159.81728587	0.00625715	28
29	20.62369061	178.39718732	0.00560547	29
30	22.89229657	199.02087793	0.00502460	30
31	25.41044919	221.91317450	0.00450627	31
32	28.20559861	247.32362369	0.00404329	32
33	31.30821445	275.52922230	0.00362938	33
34	34.75211804	306.83743675	0.00325905	34
35	38.57485103	341.58955480	0.00292749	35
36	42.81808464	380.16440582	0.00263044	36
37	47.52807395	422.98249046	0.00236416	37
38	52.75616209	470.51056441	0.00212535	38
39	58.55933991	523.26672650	0.00191107	39
40	65.00086731	581.82606641	0.00171873	40
41	72.15096271	646.82693372	0.00154601	41
42	80.08756861	718.97789643	0.00139086	42
43	88.89720115	799.06546504	0.00125146	43
44	98.67589328	887.96266619	0.00112617	44
45	109.53024154	986.63855947	0.00101354	45
46	121.57856811	1096.16880101	0.00091227	46
47	134.95221060	1217.74736912	0.00082119	47
48	149.79695377	1352.69957973	0.00073926	48
49	166.27461868	1502.49653350	0.00066556	49
50	184.56482674	1668.77115218	0.00059924	50

11.50% Yearly	Present Value of 1	Present Value of 1 per Period	Payment to Pay Off a Loan of 1	
Years				Years
1	0.89686099	0.89686099	1.11500000	1
2	0.80435963	1.70122062	0.58781324	2
3	0.72139877	2.42261939	0.41277636	3
4	0.64699441	3.06961380	0.32577388	4
5	0.58026405	3.64987785	0.27398177	5
6	0.52041619	4.17029403	0.23979125	6
7	0.46674097	4.63703501	0.21565505	7
8	0.41860177	5.05563678	0.19779902	8
9	0.37542760	5.43106437	0.18412597	9
10	0.33670636	5.76777074	0.17337721	10
11	0.30197880	6.06974954	0.16475144	11
12	0.27083301	6.34058255	0.15771423	12
13	0.24289956	6.58348211	0.15189530	13
14	0.21784714	6.80132924	0.14703008	14
15	0.19537860	6.99670784	0.14292436	15
16	0.17522744	7.17193528	0.13943230	16
17	0.15715466	7.32908994	0.13644259	17
18	0.14094588	7.47003582	0.13386817	18
19	0.12640886	7.59644468	0.13164053	19
20	0.11337118	7.70981586	0.12970478	20
21	0.10167818	7.81149404	0.12801648	21
22	0.09119120	7.90268524	0.12653927	22
23	0.08178583	7.98447107	0.12524311	23
24	0.07335052	8.05782159	0.12410302	24
25	0.06578522	8.12360680	0.12309803	25
26	0.05900020	8.18260700	0.12221044	26
27	0.05291497	8.23552197	0.12142521	27
28	0.04745738	8.28297935	0.12072951	28
29	0.04256267	8.32554202	0.12011230	29
30	0.03817280	8.36371481	0.11956410	30
31	0.03423569	8.39795050	0.11907667	31
32	0.03070466	8.42865516	0.11864289	32
33	0.02753781	8.45619297	0.11825653	33
34	0.02469759	8.48089056	0.11791215	34
35	0.02215030	8.50304086	0.11760499	35
36	0.01986574	8.52290660	0.11733086	36
37	0.01781681	8.54072341	0.11708610	37
38	0.01597920	8.55670261	0.11686745	38
39	0.01433112	8.57103373	0.11667204	39
40	0.01285302	8.58388675	0.11649734	40
41	0.01152738	8.59541413	0.11634111	41
42	0.01033845	8.60575258	0.11620134	42
43	0.00927216	8.61502474	0.11607628	43
44	0.00831583	8.62334057	0.11596434	44
45	0.00745815	8.63079872	0.11586413	45
46	0.00668892	8.63748764	0.11577441	46
47	0.00599903	8.64348667	0.11569405	47
48	0.00538030	8.64886697	0.11562208	48
49	0.00482538	8.65369235	0.11555761	49
50	0.00432769	8.65802004	0.11549985	50

Years	Future Value of 1	Future Value of 1 per Period	Payment for Sinking Fund of 1	**11.50%** Yearly Years
1	1.11500000	1.00000000	1.00000000	1
2	1.24322500	2.11500000	0.47281324	2
3	1.38619587	3.35822500	0.29777636	3
4	1.54560840	4.74442087	0.21077388	4
5	1.72335337	6.29002928	0.15898177	5
6	1.92153900	8.01338264	0.12479125	6
7	2.14251599	9.93492165	0.10065505	7
8	2.38890533	12.07743764	0.08279902	8
9	2.66362944	14.46634296	0.06912597	9
10	2.96994683	17.12997240	0.05837721	10
11	3.31149071	20.09991923	0.04975144	11
12	3.69231214	23.41140994	0.04271422	12
13	4.11692804	27.10372209	0.03689530	13
14	4.59037476	31.22065013	0.03203008	14
15	5.11826786	35.81102489	0.02792436	15
16	5.70686867	40.92929275	0.02443238	16
17	6.36315856	46.63616142	0.02144259	17
18	7.09492180	52.99931998	0.01886817	18
19	7.91083780	60.09424178	0.01664053	19
20	8.82058415	68.00507958	0.01470478	20
21	9.83495133	76.82566374	0.01301648	21
22	10.96597073	86.66061507	0.01153927	22
23	12.22705737	97.62658580	0.01024311	23
24	13.63316896	109.85364317	0.00910302	24
25	15.20098340	123.48681213	0.00809803	25
26	16.94909649	138.68779553	0.00721044	26
27	18.89824258	155.63689201	0.00642521	27
28	21.07154048	174.53513459	0.00572951	28
29	23.49476763	195.60667507	0.00511230	29
30	26.19666591	219.10144270	0.00456410	30
31	29.20928249	245.29810861	0.00407667	31
32	32.56834998	274.50739111	0.00364289	32
33	36.31371022	307.07574108	0.00325653	33
34	40.48978690	343.38945131	0.00291215	34
35	45.14611239	383.87923821	0.00260499	35
36	50.33791532	429.02535060	0.00233086	36
37	56.12677558	479.36326592	0.00208610	37
38	62.58135477	535.49004150	0.00186745	38
39	69.77821057	598.07139627	0.00167204	39
40	77.80270479	667.84960685	0.00149734	40
41	86.75001584	745.65231163	0.00134111	41
42	96.72626766	832.40232747	0.00120134	42
43	107.84978844	929.12859513	0.00107628	43
44	120.25251411	1036.97838357	0.00096434	44
45	134.08155323	1157.23089768	0.00086413	45
46	149.50093186	1291.31245091	0.00077441	46
47	166.69335902	1440.81338277	0.00069405	47
48	185.86329601	1607.50692179	0.00062208	48
49	207.23757505	1793.37021779	0.00055761	49
50	231.06989618	2000.60779284	0.00049985	50

12.00% Yearly	Present Value of 1	Present Value of 1 per Period	Payment to Pay Off a Loan of 1	
Years				Years
1	0.87719298	0.87719298	1.14000000	1
2	0.76946753	1.64666051	0.60728972	2
3	0.67497152	2.32163203	0.43073148	3
4	0.59208028	2.91371230	0.34320478	4
5	0.51936866	3.43308097	0.29128355	5
6	0.45558655	3.88866752	0.25715750	6
7	0.39963732	4.28830484	0.23319238	7
8	0.35055905	4.63886389	0.21557002	8
9	0.30750794	4.94637184	0.20216838	9
10	0.26974381	5.21611565	0.19171354	10
11	0.23661738	5.45273302	0.18339427	11
12	0.20755910	5.66029213	0.17666933	12
13	0.18206939	5.84236151	0.17116366	13
14	0.15970999	6.00207150	0.16660914	14
15	0.14009648	6.14216799	0.16280896	15
16	0.12289165	6.26505964	0.15961540	16
17	0.10779969	6.37285933	0.15691544	17
18	0.09456113	6.46742046	0.15462115	18
19	0.08294836	6.55036883	0.15266316	19
20	0.07276172	6.62313055	0.15098600	20
21	0.06382607	6.68695662	0.14954486	21
22	0.05598778	6.74294441	0.14830317	22
23	0.04911209	6.79205650	0.14723081	23
24	0.04308078	6.83513728	0.14630284	24
25	0.03779016	6.87292744	0.14549841	25
26	0.03314926	6.90607670	0.14480001	26
27	0.02907830	6.93515500	0.14419288	27
28	0.02550728	6.96066228	0.14366449	28
29	0.02237481	6.98303709	0.14320417	29
30	0.01962702	7.00266411	0.14280279	30
31	0.01721669	7.01988080	0.14245256	31
32	0.01510236	7.03498316	0.14214675	32
33	0.01324768	7.04823084	0.14187958	33
34	0.01162077	7.05985161	0.14164604	34
35	0.01019366	7.07004528	0.14144181	35
36	0.00894181	7.07898708	0.14126315	36
37	0.00784369	7.08683078	0.14110680	37
38	0.00688043	7.09371121	0.14096993	38
39	0.00603547	7.09974667	0.14085010	39
40	0.00529427	7.10504094	0.14074514	40
41	0.00464410	7.10968504	0.14065321	41
42	0.00407377	7.11375880	0.14057266	42
43	0.00357348	7.11733228	0.14050208	43
44	0.00313463	7.12046692	0.14044023	44
45	0.00274968	7.12321659	0.14038602	45
46	0.00241200	7.12562859	0.14033850	46
47	0.00211579	7.12774438	0.14029684	47
48	0.00185595	7.12960033	0.14026032	48
49	0.00162803	7.13122836	0.14022830	49
50	0.00142810	7.13265646	0.14020022	50

	Future Value of 1	Future Value of 1 per Period	Payment for Sinking Fund of 1	**12.00%**
Years				Yearly
				Years
1	1.12000000	1.00000000	1.00000000	1
2	1.25440000	2.12000000	0.47169811	2
3	1.40492800	3.37440000	0.29634898	3
4	1.57351936	4.77932800	0.20923444	4
5	1.76234168	6.35284736	0.15740973	5
6	1.97382269	8.11518904	0.12322572	6
7	2.21068141	10.08901173	0.09911774	7
8	2.47596318	12.29969314	0.08130284	8
9	2.77307876	14.77565631	0.06767889	9
10	3.10584821	17.54873507	0.05698416	10
11	3.47854999	20.65458328	0.04841540	11
12	3.89597599	24.13313327	0.04143681	12
13	4.36349311	28.02910926	0.03567720	13
14	4.88711229	32.39260238	0.03087125	14
15	5.47356576	37.27971466	0.02682424	15
16	6.13039365	42.75328042	0.02339002	16
17	6.86604089	48.88367407	0.02045673	17
18	7.68996580	55.74971496	0.01793731	18
19	8.61276169	63.43968075	0.01576300	19
20	9.64629309	72.05244244	0.01387878	20
21	10.80384826	81.69873554	0.01224009	21
22	12.10031006	92.50258380	0.01081051	22
23	13.55234726	104.60289386	0.00955996	23
24	15.17862893	118.15524112	0.00846344	24
25	17.00006441	133.33387006	0.00749997	25
26	19.04007214	150.33393446	0.00665186	26
27	21.32488079	169.37400660	0.00590409	27
28	23.88386649	190.69888739	0.00524387	28
29	26.74993047	214.58275388	0.00466021	29
30	29.95992212	241.33268434	0.00414366	30
31	33.55511278	271.29260646	0.00368606	31
32	37.58172631	304.84771924	0.00328033	32
33	42.09153347	342.42944555	0.00292031	33
34	47.14251748	384.52097901	0.00260064	34
35	52.79961958	431.66349649	0.00231662	35
36	59.13557393	484.46311607	0.00206414	36
37	66.23184280	543.59869000	0.00183959	37
38	74.17966394	609.83053388	0.00163980	38
39	83.08122361	684.01019674	0.00146197	39
40	93.05097044	767.09142034	0.00130363	40
41	104.21708689	860.14239079	0.00116260	41
42	116.72313732	964.35947768	0.00103696	42
43	130.72991380	1081.08261500	0.00092500	43
44	146.41750346	1211.81252880	0.00082521	44
45	163.98760387	1358.23003226	0.00073625	45
46	183.66611634	1522.21763613	0.00065694	46
47	205.70605030	1705.88375247	0.00058621	47
48	230.39077633	1911.58980276	0.00052312	48
49	258.03766949	2141.98057909	0.00046686	49
50	289.00218983	2400.01824858	0.00041666	50

12.50% Yearly	Present Value of 1	Present Value of 1 per Period	Payment to Pay Off a Loan of 1	
Years				Years
1	0.88888889	0.88888889	1.12500000	1
2	0.79012346	1.67901235	0.59558824	2
3	0.70233196	2.38134431	0.41993088	3
4	0.62429508	3.00563938	0.33270791	4
5	0.55492896	3.56056834	0.28085404	5
6	0.49327018	4.05383853	0.24667978	6
7	0.43846239	4.49230091	0.22260308	7
8	0.38974434	4.88204525	0.20483219	8
9	0.34643942	5.22848467	0.19126000	9
10	0.30794615	5.53643082	0.18062178	10
11	0.27372991	5.81016073	0.17211228	11
12	0.24331547	6.05347620	0.16519434	12
13	0.21628042	6.26975662	0.15949582	13
14	0.19224926	6.46200589	0.15475071	14
15	0.17088823	6.63289412	0.15076375	15
16	0.15190065	6.78479478	0.14738839	16
17	0.13502280	6.91981758	0.14451248	17
18	0.12002027	7.03983785	0.14204873	18
19	0.10668468	7.14652253	0.13992820	19
20	0.09483083	7.24135336	0.13809573	20
21	0.08429407	7.32564743	0.13650671	21
22	0.07492806	7.40057550	0.13512463	22
23	0.06660272	7.46717822	0.13391940	23
24	0.05920242	7.52638064	0.13286599	24
25	0.05262437	7.57900501	0.13194344	25
26	0.04677722	7.62578223	0.13113409	26
27	0.04157975	7.66736198	0.13042295	27
28	0.03695978	7.70432176	0.12979728	28
29	0.03285314	7.73717490	0.12924614	29
30	0.02920279	7.76637769	0.12876016	30
31	0.02595803	7.79233572	0.12833123	31
32	0.02307381	7.81540953	0.12795235	32
33	0.02051005	7.83591958	0.12761744	33
34	0.01823116	7.85415074	0.12732121	34
35	0.01620547	7.87035622	0.12705905	35
36	0.01440486	7.88476108	0.12682692	36
37	0.01280432	7.89756540	0.12662130	37
38	0.01138162	7.90894703	0.12643908	38
39	0.01011700	7.91906402	0.12627755	39
40	0.00899289	7.92805691	0.12613431	40
41	0.00799368	7.93605059	0.12600726	41
42	0.00710549	7.94315608	0.12589454	42
43	0.00631599	7.94947207	0.12579452	43
44	0.00561421	7.95508628	0.12570574	44
45	0.00499041	7.96007670	0.12562693	45
46	0.00443592	7.96451262	0.12555696	46
47	0.00394304	7.96845566	0.12549483	47
48	0.00350493	7.97196059	0.12543966	48
49	0.00311549	7.97507608	0.12539065	49
50	0.00276932	7.97784540	0.12534713	50

	Future Value of 1	Future Value of 1 per Period	Payment for Sinking Fund of 1	**12.50%** Yearly
Years				Years
1	1.12500000	1.00000000	1.00000000	1
2	1.26562500	2.12500000	0.47058824	2
3	1.42382813	3.39062500	0.29493088	3
4	1.60180664	4.81445313	0.20770791	4
5	1.80203247	6.41625977	0.15585404	5
6	2.02728653	8.21829224	0.12167978	6
7	2.28069735	10.24557877	0.09760308	7
8	2.56578451	12.52627611	0.07983219	8
9	2.88650758	15.09206063	0.06626000	9
10	3.24732103	17.97856820	0.05562178	10
11	3.65323615	21.22588923	0.04711228	11
12	4.10989067	24.87912538	0.04019434	12
13	4.62362701	28.98901606	0.03449582	13
14	5.20158038	33.61264306	0.02975071	14
15	5.85177793	38.81422345	0.02576375	15
16	6.58325017	44.66600138	0.02238839	16
17	7.40615644	51.24925155	0.01951248	17
18	8.33192600	58.65540799	0.01704873	18
19	9.37341675	66.98733399	0.01492820	19
20	10.54509384	76.36075074	0.01309573	20
21	11.86323057	86.90584458	0.01150671	21
22	13.34613439	98.76907515	0.01012463	22
23	15.01440119	112.11520955	0.00891940	23
24	16.89120134	127.12961074	0.00786599	24
25	19.00260151	144.02081209	0.00694344	25
26	21.37792670	163.02341360	0.00613409	26
27	24.05016754	184.40134030	0.00542295	27
28	27.05643848	208.45150783	0.00479728	28
29	30.43849329	235.50794631	0.00424614	29
30	34.24330495	265.94643960	0.00376016	30
31	38.52371807	300.18974455	0.00333123	31
32	43.33918283	338.71346262	0.00295235	32
33	48.75658068	382.05264545	0.00261744	33
34	54.85115327	430.80922613	0.00232121	34
35	61.70754742	485.66037939	0.00205905	35
36	69.42099085	547.36792682	0.00182692	36
37	78.09861471	616.78891767	0.00162130	37
38	87.86094155	694.88753238	0.00143908	38
39	98.84355924	782.74847393	0.00127755	39
40	111.19900415	881.59203317	0.00113431	40
41	125.09887966	992.79103731	0.00100726	41
42	140.73623962	1117.88991698	0.00089454	42
43	158.32826958	1258.62615660	0.00079452	43
44	178.11930327	1416.95442618	0.00070574	44
45	200.38421618	1595.07372945	0.00062693	45
46	225.43224320	1795.45794563	0.00055696	46
47	253.61127360	2020.89018883	0.00049483	47
48	285.31268280	2274.50146244	0.00043966	48
49	320.97676816	2559.81414524	0.00039065	49
50	361.09886417	2880.79091340	0.00034713	50

13.00% Yearly	Present Value of 1	Present Value of 1 per Period	Payment to Pay Off a Loan of 1	
Years				Years
1	0.88495575	0.88495575	1.13000000	1
2	0.78314668	1.66810244	0.59948357	2
3	0.69305016	2.36115260	0.42352197	3
4	0.61331873	2.97447133	0.33619420	4
5	0.54275994	3.51723126	0.28431454	5
6	0.48031853	3.99754979	0.25015323	6
7	0.42506064	4.42261043	0.22611080	7
8	0.37615986	4.79877029	0.20838672	8
9	0.33288483	5.13165513	0.19486890	9
10	0.29458835	5.42624348	0.18428956	10
11	0.26069765	5.68694113	0.17584145	11
12	0.23070589	5.91764702	0.16898608	12
13	0.20416450	6.12181152	0.16335034	13
14	0.18067655	6.30248807	0.15866750	14
15	0.15989075	6.46237882	0.15474178	15
16	0.14149624	6.60387506	0.15142624	16
17	0.12521791	6.72909298	0.14860844	17
18	0.11081231	6.83990529	0.14620085	18
19	0.09806399	6.93796928	0.14413439	19
20	0.08678229	7.02475158	0.14235379	20
21	0.07679849	7.10155007	0.14081433	21
22	0.06796327	7.16951334	0.13947948	22
23	0.06014448	7.22965782	0.13831913	23
24	0.05322521	7.28288303	0.13730826	24
25	0.04710195	7.32998498	0.13642593	25
26	0.04168314	7.37166812	0.13565451	26
27	0.03688774	7.40855586	0.13497907	27
28	0.03264402	7.44119988	0.13438693	28
29	0.02888851	7.47008839	0.13386722	29
30	0.02556505	7.49565344	0.13341065	30
31	0.02262394	7.51827738	0.13300919	31
32	0.02002119	7.53829857	0.13265593	32
33	0.01771786	7.55601643	0.13234487	33
34	0.01567953	7.57169596	0.13207081	34
35	0.01387569	7.58557164	0.13182922	35
36	0.01227937	7.59785101	0.13161616	36
37	0.01086670	7.60871771	0.13142819	37
38	0.00961655	7.61833426	0.13126229	38
39	0.00851022	7.62684447	0.13111582	39
40	0.00753117	7.63437564	0.13098648	40
41	0.00666475	7.64104039	0.13087223	41
42	0.00589801	7.64693840	0.13077129	42
43	0.00521948	7.65215787	0.13068209	43
44	0.00461901	7.65677688	0.13060326	44
45	0.00408762	7.66086450	0.13053357	45
46	0.00361736	7.66448185	0.13047196	46
47	0.00320120	7.66768306	0.13041749	47
48	0.00283292	7.67051598	0.13036933	48
49	0.00250701	7.67302299	0.13032673	49
50	0.00221859	7.67524158	0.13028906	50

Years	Future Value of 1	Future Value of 1 per Period	Payment for Sinking Fund of 1	**13.00%** Yearly Years
1	1.13000000	1.00000000	1.00000000	1
2	1.27690000	2.13000000	0.46948357	2
3	1.44289700	3.40690000	0.29352197	3
4	1.63047361	4.84979700	0.20619420	4
5	1.84243518	6.48027061	0.15431454	5
6	2.08195175	8.32270579	0.12015323	6
7	2.35260548	10.40465754	0.09611080	7
8	2.65844419	12.75726302	0.07838672	8
9	3.00404194	15.41570722	0.06486890	9
10	3.39456739	18.41974915	0.05428956	10
11	3.83586115	21.81431654	0.04584145	11
12	4.33452310	25.65017769	0.03898608	12
13	4.89801110	29.98470079	0.03335034	13
14	5.53475255	34.88271190	0.02866750	14
15	6.25427038	40.41746444	0.02474178	15
16	7.06732553	46.67173482	0.02142624	16
17	7.98607785	53.73906035	0.01860844	17
18	9.02426797	61.72513819	0.01620085	18
19	10.19742280	70.74940616	0.01413439	19
20	11.52308776	80.94682896	0.01235379	20
21	13.02108917	92.46991672	0.01081433	21
22	14.71383077	105.49100590	0.00947948	22
23	16.62662877	120.20483667	0.00831913	23
24	18.78809051	136.83146543	0.00730826	24
25	21.23054227	155.61955594	0.00642593	25
26	23.99051277	176.85009821	0.00565451	26
27	27.10927943	200.84061098	0.00497907	27
28	30.63348575	227.94989040	0.00438693	28
29	34.61583890	258.58337616	0.00386722	29
30	39.11589796	293.19921506	0.00341065	30
31	44.20096469	332.31511301	0.00300919	31
32	49.94709010	376.51607771	0.00265593	32
33	56.44021181	426.46316781	0.00234487	33
34	63.77743935	482.90337962	0.00207081	34
35	72.06850647	546.68081897	0.00182922	35
36	81.43741231	618.74932544	0.00161616	36
37	92.02427591	700.18673775	0.00142819	37
38	103.98743178	792.21101365	0.00126229	38
39	117.50579791	896.19844543	0.00111582	39
40	132.78155163	1013.70424333	0.00098648	40
41	150.04315335	1146.48579497	0.00087223	41
42	169.54876328	1296.52894831	0.00077129	42
43	191.59010251	1466.07771159	0.00068209	43
44	216.49681583	1657.66781410	0.00060326	44
45	244.64140189	1874.16462994	0.00053357	45
46	276.44478414	2118.80603183	0.00047196	46
47	312.38260608	2395.25081596	0.00041749	47
48	352.99234487	2707.63342204	0.00036933	48
49	398.88134970	3060.62576691	0.00032673	49
50	450.73592516	3459.50711660	0.00028906	50

14.00% Yearly	Present Value of 1	Present Value of 1 per Period	Payment to Pay Off a Loan of 1	
Years				Years
1	0.87719298	0.87719298	1.14000000	1
2	0.76946753	1.64666051	0.60728972	2
3	0.67497152	2.32163203	0.43073148	3
4	0.59208028	2.91371230	0.34320478	4
5	0.51936866	3.43308097	0.29128355	5
6	0.45558655	3.88866752	0.25715750	6
7	0.39963732	4.28830484	0.23319238	7
8	0.35055905	4.63886389	0.21557002	8
9	0.30750794	4.94637184	0.20216838	9
10	0.26974381	5.21611565	0.19171354	10
11	0.23661738	5.45273302	0.18339427	11
12	0.20755910	5.66029213	0.17666933	12
13	0.18206939	5.84236151	0.17116366	13
14	0.15970999	6.00207150	0.16660914	14
15	0.14009648	6.14216799	0.16280896	15
16	0.12289165	6.26505964	0.15961540	16
17	0.10779969	6.37285933	0.15691544	17
18	0.09456113	6.46742046	0.15462115	18
19	0.08294836	6.55036883	0.15266316	19
20	0.07276172	6.62313055	0.15098600	20
21	0.06382607	6.68695662	0.14954486	21
22	0.05598778	6.74294441	0.14830317	22
23	0.04911209	6.79205650	0.14723081	23
24	0.04308078	6.83513728	0.14630284	24
25	0.03779016	6.87292744	0.14549841	25
26	0.03314926	6.90607670	0.14480001	26
27	0.02907830	6.93515500	0.14419288	27
28	0.02550728	6.96066228	0.14366449	28
29	0.02237481	6.98303709	0.14320417	29
30	0.01962702	7.00266411	0.14280279	30
31	0.01721669	7.01988080	0.14245256	31
32	0.01510236	7.03498316	0.14214675	32
33	0.01324768	7.04823084	0.14187958	33
34	0.01162077	7.05985161	0.14164604	34
35	0.01019366	7.07004528	0.14144181	35
36	0.00894181	7.07898708	0.14126315	36
37	0.00784369	7.08683078	0.14110680	37
38	0.00688043	7.09371121	0.14096993	38
39	0.00603547	7.09974667	0.14085010	39
40	0.00529427	7.10504094	0.14074514	40
41	0.00464410	7.10968504	0.14065321	41
42	0.00407377	7.11375880	0.14057266	42
43	0.00357348	7.11733228	0.14050208	43
44	0.00313463	7.12046692	0.14044023	44
45	0.00274968	7.12321659	0.14038602	45
46	0.00241200	7.12562859	0.14033850	46
47	0.00211579	7.12774438	0.14029684	47
48	0.00185595	7.12960033	0.14026032	48
49	0.00162803	7.13122836	0.14022830	49
50	0.00142810	7.13265646	0.14020022	50

	Future Value of 1	Future Value of 1 per Period	Payment for Sinking Fund of 1	**14.00%** Yearly
Years				Years
1	1.14000000	1.00000000	1.00000000	1
2	1.29960000	2.14000000	0.46728972	2
3	1.48154400	3.43960000	0.29073148	3
4	1.68896016	4.92114400	0.20320478	4
5	1.92541458	6.61010416	0.15128355	5
6	2.19497262	8.53551874	0.11715750	6
7	2.50226879	10.73049137	0.09319238	7
8	2.85258642	13.23276016	0.07557002	8
9	3.25194852	16.08534658	0.06216838	9
10	3.70722131	19.33729510	0.05171354	10
11	4.22623230	23.04451641	0.04339427	11
12	4.81790482	27.27074871	0.03666933	12
13	5.49241149	32.08865353	0.03116366	13
14	6.26134910	37.58106503	0.02660914	14
15	7.13793798	43.84241413	0.02280896	15
16	8.13724930	50.98035211	0.01961540	16
17	9.27646420	59.11760141	0.01691544	17
18	10.57516918	68.39406560	0.01462115	18
19	12.05569287	78.96923479	0.01266316	19
20	13.74348987	91.02492766	0.01098600	20
21	15.66757845	104.76841753	0.00954486	21
22	17.86103944	120.43599598	0.00830317	22
23	20.36158496	138.29703542	0.00723081	23
24	23.21220685	158.65862038	0.00630284	24
25	26.46191581	181.87082723	0.00549841	25
26	30.16658403	208.33274304	0.00480001	26
27	34.38990579	238.49932707	0.00419288	27
28	39.20449260	272.88923286	0.00366449	28
29	44.69312156	312.09372546	0.00320417	29
30	50.95015858	356.78684702	0.00280279	30
31	58.08318078	407.73700561	0.00245256	31
32	66.21482609	465.82018639	0.00214675	32
33	75.48490175	532.03501249	0.00187958	33
34	86.05278799	607.51991423	0.00164604	34
35	98.10017831	693.57270223	0.00144181	35
36	111.83420328	791.67288054	0.00126315	36
37	127.49099173	903.50708382	0.00110680	37
38	145.33973058	1030.99807555	0.00096993	38
39	165.68729286	1176.33780613	0.00085010	39
40	188.88351386	1342.02509898	0.00074514	40
41	215.32720580	1530.90861284	0.00065321	41
42	245.47301461	1746.23581864	0.00057266	42
43	279.83923665	1991.70883325	0.00050208	43
44	319.01672979	2271.54806990	0.00044023	44
45	363.67907196	2590.56479969	0.00038602	45
46	414.59414203	2954.24387165	0.00033850	46
47	472.63732191	3368.83801368	0.00029684	47
48	538.80654698	3841.47533559	0.00026032	48
49	614.23946356	4380.28188258	0.00022830	49
50	700.23298846	4994.52134614	0.00020022	50

15.00% Yearly	Present Value of 1	Present Value of 1 per Period	Payment to Pay Off a Loan of 1	
Years				Years
1	0.86956522	0.86956522	1.15000000	1
2	0.75614367	1.62570888	0.61511628	2
3	0.65751623	2.28322512	0.43797696	3
4	0.57175325	2.85497836	0.35026535	4
5	0.49717674	3.35215510	0.29831555	5
6	0.43232760	3.78448269	0.26423691	6
7	0.37593704	4.16041973	0.24036036	7
8	0.32690177	4.48732151	0.22285009	8
9	0.28426241	4.77158392	0.20957402	9
10	0.24718471	5.01876863	0.19925206	10
11	0.21494322	5.23371185	0.19106898	11
12	0.18690715	5.42061900	0.18448078	12
13	0.16252796	5.58314696	0.17911046	13
14	0.14132866	5.72447561	0.17468849	14
15	0.12289449	5.84737010	0.17101705	15
16	0.10686477	5.95423487	0.16794769	16
17	0.09292589	6.04716076	0.16536686	17
18	0.08080512	6.12796587	0.16318629	18
19	0.07026532	6.19823119	0.16133635	19
20	0.06110028	6.25933147	0.15976147	20
21	0.05313068	6.31246215	0.15841679	21
22	0.04620059	6.35866274	0.15726577	22
23	0.04017443	6.39883717	0.15627839	23
24	0.03493428	6.43377145	0.15542983	24
25	0.03037764	6.46414909	0.15469940	25
26	0.02641534	6.49056442	0.15406981	26
27	0.02296986	6.51353428	0.15352648	27
28	0.01997379	6.53350807	0.15305713	28
29	0.01736851	6.55087658	0.15265133	29
30	0.01510305	6.56597964	0.15230020	30
31	0.01313309	6.57911273	0.15199618	31
32	0.01142008	6.59053281	0.15173280	32
33	0.00993050	6.60046331	0.15150452	33
34	0.00863522	6.60909853	0.15130657	34
35	0.00750889	6.61660742	0.15113485	35
36	0.00652947	6.62313689	0.15098586	36
37	0.00567780	6.62881468	0.15085653	37
38	0.00493722	6.63375190	0.15074426	38
39	0.00429323	6.63804513	0.15064676	39
40	0.00373324	6.64177837	0.15056209	40
41	0.00324630	6.64502467	0.15048853	41
42	0.00282287	6.64784754	0.15042463	42
43	0.00245467	6.65030221	0.15036911	43
44	0.00213449	6.65243670	0.15032086	44
45	0.00185608	6.65429279	0.15027893	45
46	0.00161398	6.65590677	0.15024249	46
47	0.00140346	6.65731024	0.15021082	47
48	0.00122040	6.65853064	0.15018328	48
49	0.00106122	6.65959186	0.15015935	49
50	0.00092280	6.66051466	0.15013855	50

	Future Value of 1	Future Value of 1 per Period	Payment for Sinking Fund of 1	**15.00%**
Years				Yearly Years
1	1.15000000	1.00000000	1.00000000	1
2	1.32250000	2.15000000	0.46511628	2
3	1.52087500	3.47250000	0.28797696	3
4	1.74900625	4.99337500	0.20026535	4
5	2.01135719	6.74238125	0.14831555	5
6	2.31306077	8.75373844	0.11423691	6
7	2.66001988	11.06799920	0.09036036	7
8	3.05902286	13.72681908	0.07285009	8
9	3.51787629	16.78584195	0.05957402	9
10	4.04555774	20.30371824	0.04925206	10
11	4.65239140	24.34927597	0.04106898	11
12	5.35025011	29.00166737	0.03448078	12
13	6.15278762	34.35191748	0.02911046	13
14	7.07570576	40.50470510	0.02468849	14
15	8.13706163	47.58041086	0.02101705	15
16	9.35762087	55.71747249	0.01794769	16
17	10.76126400	65.07509336	0.01536686	17
18	12.37545361	75.83635737	0.01318629	18
19	14.23177165	88.21181097	0.01133635	19
20	16.36653739	102.44358262	0.00976147	20
21	18.82151800	118.81012001	0.00841679	21
22	21.64474570	137.63163801	0.00726577	22
23	24.89145756	159.27638372	0.00627839	23
24	28.62517619	184.16784127	0.00542984	24
25	32.91895262	212.79301747	0.00469940	25
26	37.85679551	245.71197009	0.00406981	26
27	43.53531484	283.56876560	0.00352648	27
28	50.06561207	327.10408044	0.00305713	28
29	57.57545388	377.16969250	0.00265133	29
30	66.21177196	434.74514638	0.00230020	30
31	76.14353775	500.95691834	0.00199618	31
32	87.56506841	577.10045609	0.00173280	32
33	100.69982867	664.66552450	0.00150452	33
34	115.80480298	765.36535317	0.00130657	34
35	133.17552342	881.17015615	0.00113485	35
36	153.15185194	1014.34567957	0.00098586	36
37	176.12462973	1167.49753151	0.00085653	37
38	202.54332419	1343.62216123	0.00074426	38
39	232.92482281	1546.16548542	0.00064676	39
40	267.86354623	1779.09030823	0.00056209	40
41	308.04307817	2046.95385447	0.00048853	41
42	354.24953990	2354.99693264	0.00042463	42
43	407.38697088	2709.24647253	0.00036911	43
44	468.49501651	3116.63344341	0.00032086	44
45	538.76926899	3585.12845992	0.00027893	45
46	619.58465934	4123.89772891	0.00024249	46
47	712.52235824	4743.48238825	0.00021082	47
48	819.40071197	5456.00474648	0.00018328	48
49	942.31081877	6275.40545846	0.00015935	49
50	1083.65744158	7217.71627723	0.00013855	50

16.00% Yearly	Present Value of 1	Present Value of 1 per Period	Payment to Pay Off a Loan of 1	
Years				Years
1	0.86206897	0.86206897	1.16000000	1
2	0.74316290	1.60523187	0.62296296	2
3	0.64065767	2.24588954	0.44525787	3
4	0.55229110	2.79818064	0.35737507	4
5	0.47611302	3.27429365	0.30540938	5
6	0.41044225	3.68473591	0.27138987	6
7	0.35382953	4.03856544	0.24761268	7
8	0.30502546	4.34359090	0.23022426	8
9	0.26295298	4.60654388	0.21708249	9
10	0.22668360	4.83322748	0.20690108	10
11	0.19541690	5.02864438	0.19886075	11
12	0.16846284	5.19710722	0.19241473	12
13	0.14522659	5.34233381	0.18718411	13
14	0.12519534	5.46752915	0.18289797	14
15	0.10792701	5.57545616	0.17935752	15
16	0.09304059	5.66849669	0.17641362	16
17	0.08020735	5.74870404	0.17395225	17
18	0.06914427	5.81784831	0.17188485	18
19	0.05960713	5.87745544	0.17014166	19
20	0.05138546	5.92884090	0.16866703	20
21	0.04429781	5.97313871	0.16741617	21
22	0.03818776	6.01132647	0.16635264	22
23	0.03292049	6.04424696	0.16544658	23
24	0.02837973	6.07262669	0.16467339	24
25	0.02446528	6.09709197	0.16401262	25
26	0.02109076	6.11818273	0.16344723	26
27	0.01818169	6.13636443	0.16296294	27
28	0.01567387	6.15203830	0.16254775	28
29	0.01351196	6.16555026	0.16219153	29
30	0.01164824	6.17719850	0.16188568	30
31	0.01004159	6.18724008	0.16162295	31
32	0.00865654	6.19589662	0.16139714	32
33	0.00746253	6.20335916	0.16120298	33
34	0.00643322	6.20979238	0.16103598	34
35	0.00554588	6.21533826	0.16089229	35
36	0.00478093	6.22011919	0.16076862	36
37	0.00412149	6.22424068	0.16066217	37
38	0.00355301	6.22779369	0.16057051	38
39	0.00306294	6.23085663	0.16049158	39
40	0.00264047	6.23349709	0.16042359	40
41	0.00227626	6.23577336	0.16036503	41
42	0.00196230	6.23773565	0.16031458	42
43	0.00169163	6.23942729	0.16027112	43
44	0.00145831	6.24088559	0.16023367	44
45	0.00125716	6.24214275	0.16020140	45
46	0.00108376	6.24322651	0.16017359	46
47	0.00093427	6.24416078	0.16014962	47
48	0.00080541	6.24496619	0.16012897	48
49	0.00069432	6.24566051	0.16011117	49
50	0.00059855	6.24625906	0.16009583	50

	Future Value of 1	Future Value of 1 per Period	Payment for Sinking Fund of 1	**16.00%** Yearly
Years				Years
1	1.16000000	1.00000000	1.00000000	1
2	1.34560000	2.16000000	0.46296296	2
3	1.56089600	3.50560000	0.28525787	3
4	1.81063936	5.06649600	0.19737507	4
5	2.10034166	6.87713536	0.14540938	5
6	2.43639632	8.97747702	0.11138987	6
7	2.82621973	11.41387334	0.08761268	7
8	3.27841489	14.24009307	0.07022426	8
9	3.80296127	17.51850797	0.05708249	9
10	4.41143508	21.32146924	0.04690108	10
11	5.11726469	25.73290432	0.03886075	11
12	5.93602704	30.85016901	0.03241473	12
13	6.88579137	36.78619605	0.02718411	13
14	7.98751799	43.67198742	0.02289797	14
15	9.26552087	51.65950541	0.01935752	15
16	10.74800420	60.92502627	0.01641362	16
17	12.46768488	71.67303048	0.01395225	17
18	14.46251446	84.14071536	0.01188485	18
19	16.77651677	98.60322981	0.01014166	19
20	19.46075945	115.37974658	0.00866703	20
21	22.57448097	134.84050604	0.00741617	21
22	26.18639792	157.41498700	0.00635264	22
23	30.37622159	183.60138492	0.00544658	23
24	35.23641704	213.97760651	0.00467339	24
25	40.87424377	249.21402355	0.00401262	25
26	47.41412277	290.08826732	0.00344723	26
27	55.00038241	337.50239009	0.00296294	27
28	63.80044360	392.50277250	0.00254775	28
29	74.00851458	456.30321610	0.00219153	29
30	85.84987691	530.31173068	0.00188568	30
31	99.58585721	616.16160759	0.00162295	31
32	115.51959437	715.74746480	0.00139714	32
33	134.00272947	831.26705917	0.00120298	33
34	155.44316618	965.26978864	0.00103598	34
35	180.31407277	1120.71295482	0.00089229	35
36	209.16432441	1301.02702759	0.00076862	36
37	242.63061632	1510.19135201	0.00066217	37
38	281.45151493	1752.82196833	0.00057051	38
39	326.48375732	2034.27348326	0.00049158	39
40	378.72115849	2360.75724058	0.00042359	40
41	439.31654385	2739.47839907	0.00036503	41
42	509.60719087	3178.79494293	0.00031458	42
43	591.14434141	3688.40213380	0.00027112	43
44	685.72743603	4279.54647520	0.00023367	44
45	795.44382580	4965.27391123	0.00020140	45
46	922.71483793	5760.71773703	0.00017359	46
47	1070.34921199	6683.43257496	0.00014962	47
48	1241.60508591	7753.78178695	0.00012897	48
49	1440.26189966	8995.38687286	0.00011117	49
50	1670.70380360	10435.64877252	0.00009583	50

5.00% Daily	Future Value of 1	Future Value of 1 per Period	Payment for Sinking Fund of 1	
Days				Days
1	1.00013889	1.00000000	1.00000000	1
2	1.00027780	2.00013889	0.49996528	2
3	1.00041672	3.00041669	0.33328704	3
4	1.00055567	4.00083341	0.24994792	4
5	1.00069464	5.00138908	0.19994445	5
6	1.00083362	6.00208372	0.16660881	6
7	1.00097263	7.00291734	0.14279763	7
8	1.00111165	8.00388997	0.12493925	8
9	1.00125069	9.00500162	0.11104940	9
10	1.00138976	10.00625232	0.09993752	10
11	1.00152884	11.00764207	0.09084598	11
12	1.00166794	12.00917091	0.08326970	12
13	1.00180706	13.01083885	0.07685900	13
14	1.00194620	14.01264591	0.07136411	14
15	1.00208536	15.01459211	0.06660188	15
16	1.00222454	16.01667747	0.06243492	16
17	1.00236374	17.01890201	0.05875820	17
18	1.00250295	18.02126575	0.05549000	18
19	1.00264219	19.02376870	0.05256582	19
20	1.00278145	20.02641089	0.04993406	20
21	1.00292072	21.02919234	0.04755294	21
22	1.00306002	22.03211306	0.04538829	22
23	1.00319933	23.03517308	0.04341187	23
24	1.00333866	24.03837241	0.04160015	24
25	1.00347802	25.04171107	0.03993337	25
26	1.00361739	26.04518908	0.03839481	26
27	1.00375678	27.04880647	0.03697021	27
28	1.00389619	28.05256325	0.03564737	28
29	1.00403562	29.05645944	0.03441576	29
Months				Months
1	1.00417507	30.06049506	0.03326625	1
2	1.00836757	60.24649475	0.01659848	2
3	1.01257757	90.55852307	0.01104258	3
4	1.01680515	120.99710618	0.00826466	4
5	1.02105039	151.56277248	0.00659793	5
6	1.02531334	182.25605253	0.00548679	6
7	1.02959409	213.07747914	0.00469313	7
8	1.03389272	244.02758733	0.00409790	8
9	1.03820929	275.10691434	0.00363495	9
10	1.04254389	306.31599968	0.00326460	10
11	1.04689658	337.65538510	0.00296160	11
12	1.05126745	369.12561461	0.00270910	12
24	1.10516324	757.17535691	0.00132070	24
36	1.16182214	1165.11941860	0.00085828	36
48	1.22138580	1593.97730063	0.00062726	48
60	1.28400313	2044.82251323	0.00048904	60
72	1.34983069	2518.78095658	0.00039702	72
84	1.41903306	3017.03803906	0.00033145	84
96	1.49178326	3540.83948984	0.00028242	96
108	1.56826318	4091.49490347	0.00024441	108
120	1.64866403	4670.38101404	0.00021412	120
132	1.73318682	5278.94513729	0.00018943	132
144	1.82204289	5918.70878917	0.00016896	144
156	1.91545437	6591.27148982	0.00015172	156
168	2.01365483	7298.31476272	0.00013702	168
180	2.11688977	8041.60633877	0.00012435	180
192	2.22541730	8823.00457592	0.00011334	192
204	2.33950876	9644.46310536	0.00010369	204
216	2.45944940	10508.03571598	0.00009517	216
228	2.58553910	11415.88148920	0.00008760	228
240	2.71809308	12370.27019701	0.00008084	240

	Future Value of 1	Future Value of 1 per Period	Payment for Sinking Fund of 1	**5.50%** Daily
Days				**Days**
1	1.00015278	1.00000000	1.00000000	1
2	1.00030558	2.00015278	0.49996181	2
3	1.00045840	3.00045836	0.33328241	3
4	1.00061125	4.00091676	0.24994272	4
5	1.00076412	5.00152801	0.19993890	5
6	1.00091702	6.00229213	0.16660302	6
7	1.00106993	7.00320915	0.14279168	7
8	1.00122288	8.00427909	0.12493318	8
9	1.00137584	9.00550196	0.11104323	9
10	1.00152883	10.00687780	0.09993127	10
11	1.00168184	11.00840663	0.09083967	11
12	1.00183487	12.01008847	0.08326333	12
13	1.00198793	13.01192334	0.07685259	13
14	1.00214101	14.01391128	0.07135767	14
15	1.00229412	15.01605229	0.06659540	15
16	1.00244725	16.01834641	0.06242842	16
17	1.00260040	17.02079366	0.05875167	17
18	1.00275357	18.02339406	0.05548345	18
19	1.00290677	19.02614763	0.05255925	19
20	1.00305999	20.02905440	0.04992747	20
21	1.00321324	21.03211440	0.04754634	21
22	1.00336651	22.03532764	0.04538167	22
23	1.00351980	23.03869415	0.04340524	23
24	1.00367312	24.04221395	0.04159351	24
25	1.00382645	25.04588706	0.03992672	25
26	1.00397982	26.04971352	0.03838814	26
27	1.00413320	27.05369334	0.03696353	27
28	1.00428661	28.05782654	0.03564068	28
29	1.00444005	29.06211315	0.03440906	29
Months				**Months**
1	1.00459350	30.06655320	0.03325955	1
2	1.00920810	60.27121714	0.01659167	2
3	1.01384390	90.61462624	0.01103575	3
4	1.01850099	121.09741783	0.00825781	4
5	1.02317948	151.72023216	0.00659108	5
6	1.02787946	182.48371242	0.00547994	6
7	1.03260102	213.38850476	0.00468629	7
8	1.03734428	244.43525831	0.00409106	8
9	1.04210932	275.62462155	0.00362812	9
10	1.04689625	306.95726039	0.00325778	10
11	1.05170517	338.43382213	0.00295479	11
12	1.05653618	370.05497148	0.00270230	12
24	1.11626869	761.03143604	0.00131401	24
36	1.17937826	1174.11221488	0.00085171	36
48	1.24605579	1610.54700142	0.00062091	48
60	1.31650302	2071.65614196	0.00048271	60
72	1.39093307	2558.83463011	0.00039080	72
84	1.46957111	3073.55632710	0.00032536	84
96	1.55265504	3617.37842065	0.00027644	96
108	1.64043622	4191.94613590	0.00023855	108
120	1.73318021	4798.99771274	0.00020838	120
132	1.83116759	5440.36966449	0.00018381	132
144	1.93469480	6118.00233391	0.00016345	144
156	2.04407505	6833.94576333	0.00014633	156
168	2.15963923	7590.36589662	0.00013175	168
180	2.28173698	8389.55113185	0.00011920	180
192	2.41073766	9233.91924436	0.00010830	192
204	2.54703155	10126.02470125	0.00009876	204
216	2.69103098	11068.56638943	0.00009035	216
228	2.84317158	12064.39578058	0.00008289	228
240	3.00391363	13116.52555765	0.00007624	240

6.00% Daily	Future Value of 1	Future Value of 1 per Period	Payment for Sinking Fund of 1	
Days				Days
1	1.00016667	1.00000000	1.00000000	1
2	1.00033336	2.00016667	0.49995834	2
3	1.00050008	3.00050056	0.33327778	3
4	1.00066683	4.00100011	0.24993751	4
5	1.00083361	5.00166694	0.19993334	5
6	1.00100042	6.00250056	0.16659724	6
7	1.00116725	7.00350097	0.14278573	7
8	1.00133411	8.00466822	0.12492710	8
9	1.00150100	9.00600233	0.11103706	9
10	1.00166792	10.00750333	0.09992502	10
11	1.00183486	11.00917125	0.09083336	11
12	1.00200183	12.01100611	0.08325697	12
13	1.00216883	13.01300795	0.07684618	13
14	1.00233586	14.01517678	0.07135122	14
15	1.00250292	15.01751265	0.06658892	15
16	1.00267000	16.02001556	0.06242191	16
17	1.00283711	17.02268557	0.05874514	17
18	1.00300425	18.02552268	0.05547689	18
19	1.00317142	19.02852693	0.05255268	19
20	1.00333862	20.03169836	0.04992088	20
21	1.00350584	21.03503697	0.04753973	21
22	1.00367309	22.03854281	0.04537505	22
23	1.00384037	23.04221590	0.04339860	23
24	1.00400768	24.04605627	0.04158686	24
25	1.00417501	25.05006395	0.03992006	25
26	1.00434237	26.05423896	0.03838147	26
27	1.00450976	27.05858133	0.03695685	27
28	1.00467718	28.06309109	0.03563399	28
29	1.00484463	29.06776828	0.03440237	29
Months				Months
1	1.00501210	30.07261290	0.03325285	1
2	1.01004933	60.29595282	0.01658486	2
3	1.01511180	90.67077520	0.01102891	3
4	1.02019964	121.19783929	0.00825097	4
5	1.02531298	151.87790814	0.00658424	5
6	1.03045196	182.71174864	0.00547310	6
7	1.03561669	213.70013149	0.00467945	7
8	1.04080731	244.84383129	0.00408424	8
9	1.04602394	276.14362648	0.00362130	9
10	1.05126672	307.60029945	0.00325097	10
11	1.05653577	339.21463648	0.00294799	11
12	1.06183124	370.98742779	0.00269551	12
24	1.12748558	764.91346752	0.00130734	24
36	1.19719941	1183.19644195	0.00084517	36
48	1.27122373	1627.34237050	0.00061450	48
60	1.34982507	2098.95039166	0.00047645	60
72	1.43328642	2599.71852060	0.00038466	72
84	1.52190829	3131.44976289	0.00031934	84
96	1.61600977	3696.05860615	0.00027056	96
108	1.71592965	4295.57791315	0.00023280	108
120	1.82202771	4932.16624110	0.00020275	120
132	1.93468594	5608.11561343	0.00017831	132
144	2.05430996	6325.85977226	0.00015808	144
156	2.18133049	7087.98294097	0.00014108	156
168	2.31620485	7897.22912868	0.00012663	168
180	2.45941867	8756.51201000	0.00011420	180
192	2.61148757	9668.92541564	0.00010342	192
204	2.77295908	10637.75447168	0.00009400	204
216	2.94441457	11666.48742763	0.00008572	216
228	3.12647137	12758.82821579	0.00007838	228
240	3.31978496	13918.70978716	0.00007185	240

	Future Value of 1	Future Value of 1 per Period	Payment for Sinking Fund of 1	**6.50%**
				Daily
Days				Days
1	1.00018056	1.00000000	1.00000000	1
2	1.00036114	2.00018056	0.49995487	2
3	1.00054176	3.00054170	0.33327316	3
4	1.00072242	4.00108346	0.24993230	4
5	1.00090310	5.00180588	0.19992779	5
6	1.00108382	6.00270899	0.16659145	6
7	1.00126457	7.00379281	0.14277978	7
8	1.00144536	8.00505738	0.12492103	8
9	1.00162617	9.00650274	0.11103089	9
10	1.00180702	10.00812891	0.09991878	10
11	1.00198791	11.00993594	0.09082705	11
12	1.00216882	12.01192384	0.08325061	12
13	1.00234977	13.01409266	0.07683978	13
14	1.00253075	14.01644243	0.07134478	14
15	1.00271176	15.01897317	0.06658245	15
16	1.00289280	16.02168493	0.06241541	16
17	1.00307388	17.02457774	0.05873861	17
18	1.00325499	18.02765162	0.05547034	18
19	1.00343614	19.03090661	0.05254610	19
20	1.00361731	20.03434275	0.04991429	20
21	1.00379852	21.03796006	0.04753313	21
22	1.00397976	22.04175858	0.04536843	22
23	1.00416104	23.04573834	0.04339197	23
24	1.00434234	24.04989938	0.04158022	24
25	1.00452368	25.05424172	0.03991340	25
26	1.00470505	26.05876540	0.03837480	26
27	1.00488646	27.06347046	0.03695018	27
28	1.00506790	28.06835692	0.03562731	28
29	1.00524937	29.07342482	0.03439567	29
Months				Months
1	1.00543087	30.07867419	0.03324615	1
2	1.01089124	60.32070179	0.01657806	2
3	1.01638126	90.72696997	0.01102208	3
4	1.02190109	121.29837069	0.00824413	4
5	1.02745091	152.03580077	0.00657740	5
6	1.03303086	182.94016189	0.00546627	6
7	1.03864112	214.01236063	0.00467263	7
8	1.04428185	245.25330849	0.00407742	8
9	1.04995321	276.66392193	0.00361449	9
10	1.05565537	308.24512239	0.00324417	10
11	1.06138850	339.99783630	0.00294120	11
12	1.06715276	371.92299512	0.00268873	12
24	1.13881502	768.82164699	0.00130069	24
36	1.21528959	1192.37313996	0.00083866	36
48	1.29689965	1644.36728597	0.00060814	48
60	1.38399004	2126.71408774	0.00047021	60
72	1.47692880	2641.45180998	0.00037858	72
84	1.57610865	3190.75559249	0.00031341	84
96	1.68194870	3776.94664173	0.00026476	96
108	1.79489620	4402.50203958	0.00022714	108
120	1.91542844	5070.06521080	0.00019724	120
132	2.04405475	5782.45709346	0.00017294	132
144	2.18131868	6542.68805938	0.00015284	144
156	2.32780025	7353.97063518	0.00013598	156
168	2.48411847	8219.73307753	0.00012166	168
180	2.65093389	9143.63386000	0.00010937	180
192	2.82895143	10129.57713275	0.00009872	192
204	3.01892333	11181.72922043	0.00008943	204
216	3.22165237	12304.53622791	0.00008127	216
228	3.43799523	13502.74282826	0.00007406	228
240	3.66886611	14781.41231248	0.00006765	240

7.00% Daily	Future Value of 1	Future Value of 1 per Period	Payment for Sinking Fund of 1	
Days				Days
1	1.00019444	1.00000000	1.00000000	1
2	1.00038893	2.00019444	0.49995139	2
3	1.00058345	3.00058337	0.33326853	3
4	1.00077800	4.00116682	0.24992710	4
5	1.00097260	5.00194482	0.19992224	5
6	1.00116723	6.00291742	0.16658567	6
7	1.00136191	7.00408466	0.14277383	7
8	1.00155661	8.00544656	0.12491496	8
9	1.00175136	9.00700318	0.11102472	9
10	1.00194615	10.00875454	0.09991253	10
11	1.00214097	11.01070069	0.09082074	11
12	1.00233583	12.01284165	0.08324425	12
13	1.00253073	13.01517749	0.07683337	13
14	1.00272567	14.01770821	0.07133834	14
15	1.00292064	15.02043388	0.06657597	15
16	1.00311565	16.02335452	0.06240890	16
17	1.00331070	17.02647017	0.05873208	17
18	1.00350579	18.02978087	0.05546379	18
19	1.00370092	19.03328667	0.05253953	19
20	1.00389608	20.03698758	0.04990770	20
21	1.00409128	21.04088366	0.04752652	21
22	1.00428652	22.04497495	0.04536181	22
23	1.00448180	23.04926147	0.04338534	23
24	1.00467712	24.05374327	0.04157357	24
25	1.00487247	25.05842039	0.03990675	25
26	1.00506786	26.06329286	0.03836814	26
27	1.00526329	27.06836072	0.03694350	27
28	1.00545876	28.07362401	0.03562062	28
29	1.00565427	29.07908277	0.03438898	29
Months				Months
1	1.00584981	30.08473704	0.03323945	1
2	1.01173384	60.34546407	0.01657125	2
3	1.01765229	90.78321061	0.01101525	3
4	1.02360536	121.39901218	0.00823730	4
5	1.02959326	152.19391037	0.00657057	5
6	1.03561619	183.16895286	0.00545944	6
7	1.04167434	214.32519347	0.00466581	7
8	1.04776794	245.66369216	0.00407061	8
9	1.05389718	277.18651512	0.00360769	9
10	1.06006228	308.89173475	0.00323738	10
11	1.06626344	340.78342974	0.00293441	11
12	1.07250088	372.86168509	0.00268196	12
24	1.15025814	772.75617166	0.00129407	24
36	1.23365288	1201.64336169	0.00083219	36
48	1.32309380	1661.62525181	0.00060182	48
60	1.41901927	2154.95623521	0.00046405	60
72	1.52189942	2684.05415063	0.00037257	72
84	1.63223847	3251.51213222	0.00030755	84
96	1.75057720	3860.11131867	0.00025906	96
108	1.87749559	4512.83448365	0.00022159	108
120	2.01361568	5212.88065459	0.00019183	120
132	2.15960460	5963.68079120	0.00016768	132
144	2.31617784	6768.91460084	0.00014773	144
156	2.48410278	7632.52857287	0.00013102	156
168	2.66420242	8558.75532062	0.00011684	168
180	2.85735945	9552.13432563	0.00010469	180
192	3.06452054	10617.53418588	0.00009418	192
204	3.28670098	11760.11647696	0.00008503	204
216	3.52498971	12985.66134335	0.00007701	216
228	3.78055457	14299.99494491	0.00006993	228
240	4.05464812	15709.61889341	0.00006366	240

	Future Value of 1	Future Value of 1 per Period	Payment for Sinking Fund of 1	**7.50%** Daily
Days				Days
1	1.00020833	1.00000000	1.00000000	1
2	1.00041671	2.00020833	0.49994792	2
3	1.00062513	3.00062504	0.33326390	3
4	1.00083359	4.00125017	0.24992189	4
5	1.00104210	5.00208377	0.19991668	5
6	1.00125065	6.00312587	0.16657988	6
7	1.00145925	7.00437652	0.14276788	7
8	1.00166788	8.00583576	0.12490888	8
9	1.00187656	9.00750365	0.11101855	9
10	1.00208529	10.00938021	0.09990629	10
11	1.00229406	11.01146550	0.09081443	11
12	1.00250287	12.01375955	0.08323789	12
13	1.00271172	13.01626242	0.07682697	13
14	1.00292062	14.01897414	0.07133190	14
15	1.00312956	15.02189476	0.06656950	15
16	1.00333855	16.02502432	0.06240240	16
17	1.00354758	17.02836287	0.05872555	17
18	1.00375665	18.03191044	0.05545724	18
19	1.00396576	19.03566709	0.05253296	19
20	1.00417492	20.03963286	0.04990111	20
21	1.00438413	21.04380778	0.04751992	21
22	1.00459337	22.04819191	0.04535519	22
23	1.00480266	23.05278528	0.04337871	23
24	1.00501200	24.05758794	0.04156693	24
25	1.00522137	25.06259994	0.03990009	25
26	1.00543080	26.06782132	0.03836147	26
27	1.00564026	27.07325211	0.03693683	27
28	1.00584977	28.07889237	0.03561394	28
29	1.00605932	29.08474214	0.03438229	29
Months				Months
1	1.00626892	30.09080146	0.03323275	1
2	1.01257713	60.37023966	0.01656445	2
3	1.01892490	90.83949715	0.01100843	3
4	1.02531245	121.49976387	0.00823047	4
5	1.03174005	152.35223727	0.00656374	5
6	1.03820794	183.39812226	0.00545262	6
7	1.04471638	214.63863132	0.00465899	7
8	1.05126562	246.07498455	0.00406380	8
9	1.05785592	277.72490888	0.00360090	9
10	1.06448753	309.54014208	0.00323060	10
11	1.07116071	341.57142500	0.00292765	11
12	1.07787573	373.80350936	0.00267520	12
24	1.16181609	776.71724031	0.00128747	24
36	1.25229337	1211.00817263	0.00082576	36
48	1.34981663	1679.11982882	0.00059555	48
60	1.45493459	2183.68602249	0.00045794	60
72	1.56823868	2727.54567738	0.00036663	72
84	1.69036642	3313.75880052	0.00030177	84
96	1.82200494	3945.62369922	0.00025345	96
108	1.96389490	4626.69553887	0.00021614	108
120	2.11683466	5360.80634598	0.00018654	120
132	2.28168470	6152.08656891	0.00016255	132
144	2.45937257	7004.98831772	0.00014276	144
156	2.65089800	7924.31041379	0.00012619	156
168	2.85733862	8915.22539022	0.00011217	168
180	3.07985596	9983.30859492	0.00010017	180
192	3.31970199	11134.56956008	0.00008981	192
204	3.57822621	12375.48581461	0.00008080	204
216	3.85688319	13713.03932971	0.00007292	216
228	4.15724079	15154.75580271	0.00006599	228
240	4.48098896	16708.74700010	0.00005985	240

8.00% Daily	Future Value of 1	Future Value of 1 per Period	Payment for Sinking Fund of 1	
Days				Days
1	1.00022222	1.00000000	1.00000000	1
2	1.00044449	2.00022222	0.49994445	2
3	1.00066681	3.00066672	0.33325927	3
4	1.00088919	4.00133353	0.24991668	4
5	1.00111161	5.00222272	0.19991113	5
6	1.00133407	6.00333432	0.16657410	6
7	1.00155659	7.00466840	0.14276193	7
8	1.00177916	8.00622499	0.12490281	8
9	1.00200178	9.00800415	0.11101238	9
10	1.00222445	10.01000593	0.09990004	10
11	1.00244716	11.01223037	0.09080813	11
12	1.00266993	12.01467754	0.08323153	12
13	1.00289274	13.01734746	0.07682057	13
14	1.00311561	14.02024021	0.07132545	14
15	1.00333852	15.02335582	0.06656302	15
16	1.00356149	16.02669434	0.06239590	16
17	1.00378450	17.03025583	0.05871902	17
18	1.00400756	18.03404033	0.05545069	18
19	1.00423068	19.03804789	0.05252639	19
20	1.00445384	20.04227857	0.04989453	20
21	1.00467705	21.04673241	0.04751331	21
22	1.00490031	22.05140946	0.04534858	22
23	1.00512362	23.05630978	0.04337208	23
24	1.00534699	24.06143340	0.04156028	24
25	1.00557040	25.06678039	0.03989344	25
26	1.00579386	26.07235078	0.03835481	26
27	1.00601737	27.07814464	0.03693015	27
28	1.00624092	28.08416200	0.03560726	28
29	1.00646453	29.09040293	0.03437560	29
Months				Months
1	1.00668819	30.09686746	0.03322605	1
2	1.01342112	60.39502857	0.01655765	2
3	1.02019907	90.89582963	0.01100160	3
4	1.02702236	121.60062592	0.00822364	4
5	1.03389128	152.51078181	0.00655691	5
6	1.04080615	183.62767078	0.00544580	6
7	1.04776726	214.95267550	0.00465219	7
8	1.05477493	246.48718789	0.00405701	8
9	1.06182947	278.23260918	0.00359412	9
10	1.06893119	310.19034997	0.00322383	10
11	1.07608041	342.36183029	0.00292089	11
12	1.08327744	374.74847967	0.00266846	12
24	1.17349001	780.70505333	0.00128089	24
36	1.27121526	1220.46865118	0.00081936	36
48	1.37707881	1696.85463562	0.00058933	48
60	1.49175841	2212.91282527	0.00045189	60
72	1.61598823	2771.94701980	0.00036076	72
84	1.75056359	3377.53615089	0.00029607	84
96	1.89634604	4033.55719445	0.00024792	96
108	2.05426889	4744.20999107	0.00021078	108
120	2.22534314	5514.04413326	0.00018136	120
132	2.41066402	6347.98809198	0.00015753	132
144	2.61141795	7251.38076862	0.00013790	144
156	2.82889015	8230.00567463	0.00012151	156
168	3.06447288	9290.12795745	0.00010764	168
180	3.31967434	10438.53450999	0.00009580	180
192	3.59612832	11682.57742023	0.00008560	192
204	3.89560468	13030.22103918	0.00007674	204
216	4.22002066	14490.09296866	0.00006901	216
228	4.57145318	16071.53929504	0.00006222	228
240	4.95215209	17784.68442286	0.00005623	240

	Future Value of 1	Future Value of 1 per Period	Payment for Sinking Fund of 1	**8.50%** Daily
Days				Days
1	1.00023611	1.00000000	1.00000000	1
2	1.00047228	2.00023611	0.49994098	2
3	1.00070850	3.00070839	0.33325464	3
4	1.00094478	4.00141689	0.24991148	4
5	1.00118111	5.00236167	0.19990558	5
6	1.00141750	6.00354278	0.16656831	6
7	1.00165395	7.00496028	0.14275598	7
8	1.00189045	8.00661423	0.12489674	8
9	1.00212701	9.00850468	0.11100621	9
10	1.00236362	10.01063169	0.09989380	10
11	1.00260029	11.01299531	0.09080182	11
12	1.00283702	12.01559560	0.08322517	12
13	1.00307380	13.01843262	0.07681416	13
14	1.00331063	14.02150642	0.07131901	14
15	1.00354753	15.02481705	0.06655655	15
16	1.00378447	16.02836458	0.06238940	16
17	1.00402148	17.03214905	0.05871250	17
18	1.00425854	18.03617053	0.05544414	18
19	1.00449566	19.04042907	0.05251982	19
20	1.00473283	20.04492473	0.04988794	20
21	1.00497006	21.04965756	0.04750671	21
22	1.00520734	22.05462762	0.04534196	22
23	1.00544468	23.05983496	0.04336544	23
24	1.00568208	24.06527964	0.04155364	24
25	1.00591953	25.07096172	0.03988678	25
26	1.00615704	26.07688125	0.03834814	26
27	1.00639461	27.08303830	0.03692348	27
28	1.00663223	28.08943290	0.03560058	28
29	1.00686990	29.09606513	0.03436891	29
Months				Months
1	1.00710764	30.10293503	0.03321935	1
2	1.01426579	60.41983081	0.01655086	2
3	1.02147483	90.95220810	0.01099479	3
4	1.02873510	121.70159845	0.00821682	4
5	1.03604698	152.66954432	0.00655009	5
6	1.04341082	183.85759912	0.00543899	6
7	1.05082701	215.26732731	0.00464539	7
8	1.05829591	246.90030446	0.00405022	8
9	1.06581789	278.75811734	0.00358734	9
10	1.07339334	310.84236401	0.00321706	10
11	1.08102263	343.15465386	0.00291414	11
12	1.08870614	375.69660776	0.00266172	12
24	1.18528107	784.71981272	0.00127434	24
36	1.29042278	1230.02588880	0.00081299	36
48	1.40489121	1714.83334956	0.00058315	48
60	1.52951369	2242.64621050	0.00044590	60
72	1.66519095	2817.27931483	0.00035495	72
84	1.81290362	3442.88590577	0.00029045	84
96	1.97371931	4123.98764474	0.00024248	96
108	2.14880033	4865.50729231	0.00020553	108
120	2.33941212	5672.80428814	0.00017628	120
132	2.54693235	6551.71348713	0.00015263	132
144	2.77286090	7508.58733164	0.00013318	144
156	3.01883069	8550.34176472	0.00011695	156
168	3.28661952	9684.50621603	0.00010326	168
180	3.57816287	10919.27802191	0.00009158	180
192	3.89556789	12263.58167279	0.00008154	192
204	4.24112870	13727.13331623	0.00007285	204
216	4.61734287	15320.51098178	0.00006527	216
228	5.02692955	17055.23103517	0.00005863	228
240	5.47284908	18943.83141455	0.00005279	240

9.00% Daily	Future Value of 1	Future Value of 1 per Period	Payment for Sinking Fund of 1	
Days				Days
1	1.00025000	1.00000000	1.00000000	1
2	1.00050006	2.00025000	0.49993751	2
3	1.00075019	3.00075006	0.33325001	3
4	1.00100038	4.00150025	0.24990627	4
5	1.00125063	5.00250063	0.19990002	5
6	1.00150094	6.00375125	0.16656253	6
7	1.00175131	7.00525219	0.14275004	7
8	1.00200175	8.00700350	0.12489067	8
9	1.00225225	9.00900525	0.11100005	9
10	1.00250281	10.01125750	0.09988755	10
11	1.00275344	11.01376032	0.09079551	11
12	1.00300413	12.01651376	0.08321881	12
13	1.00325488	13.01951789	0.07680718	13
14	1.00350569	14.02277277	0.07131257	14
15	1.00375657	15.02627846	0.06655008	15
16	1.00400751	16.03003503	0.06238290	16
17	1.00425851	17.03404254	0.05870597	17
18	1.00450958	18.03830105	0.05543759	18
19	1.00476070	19.04281062	0.05251326	19
20	1.00501189	20.04757133	0.04988135	20
21	1.00526315	21.05258322	0.04750011	21
22	1.00551446	22.05784636	0.04533534	22
23	1.00576584	23.06336083	0.04335882	23
24	1.00601728	24.06912667	0.04154700	24
25	1.00626879	25.07514395	0.03988013	25
26	1.00652035	26.08141273	0.03834148	26
27	1.00677198	27.08793309	0.03691681	27
28	1.00702368	28.09470507	0.03559390	28
29	1.00727543	29.10172875	0.03436222	29
Months				Months
1	1.00752725	30.10900418	0.03321266	1
2	1.01511116	60.44464639	0.01654406	2
3	1.02275216	91.00863260	0.01098797	3
4	1.03045067	121.80268160	0.00821000	4
5	1.03820713	152.82852514	0.00654328	5
6	1.04602198	184.08790800	0.00543219	6
7	1.05389565	215.58258807	0.00463859	7
8	1.06182858	247.31433651	0.00404344	8
9	1.06982123	279.28493779	0.00358057	9
10	1.07787405	311.49618981	0.00321031	10
11	1.08598748	343.94990401	0.00290740	11
12	1.09416198	376.64790546	0.00265500	12
24	1.19719043	788.76172209	0.00126781	24
36	1.30992025	1239.68099018	0.00080666	36
48	1.43326493	1733.05970774	0.00057701	48
60	1.56822399	2272.89594044	0.00043997	60
72	1.71589105	2863.56421972	0.00034922	72
84	1.87746275	3509.85099156	0.00028491	84
96	2.05424835	4216.99340313	0.00023714	96
108	2.24768044	4990.72174175	0.00020037	108
120	2.45932647	5837.30586990	0.00017131	120
132	2.69090151	6763.60603272	0.00014785	132
144	2.94428211	7777.12844957	0.00012858	144
156	3.22152154	8886.08614028	0.00011254	156
168	3.52486637	10099.46547886	0.00009902	168
180	3.85677475	11427.09901404	0.00008751	180
192	4.21993629	12879.74514678	0.00007764	192
204	4.61729383	14469.17531034	0.00006911	204
216	5.05206734	16208.26935939	0.00006170	216
228	5.52777999	18111.11994118	0.00005521	228
240	6.04828667	20193.14669449	0.00004952	240

Days	Future Value of 1	Future Value of 1 per Period	Payment for Sinking Fund of 1	Daily Days
1	1.00026389	1.00000000	1.00000000	1
2	1.00052785	2.00026389	0.49993404	2
3	1.00079188	3.00079174	0.33324539	3
4	1.00105597	4.00158361	0.24990106	4
5	1.00132014	5.00263959	0.19989447	5
6	1.00158438	6.00395973	0.16655675	6
7	1.00184869	7.00554410	0.14274409	7
8	1.00211306	8.00739279	0.12488459	8
9	1.00237751	9.00950585	0.11099388	9
10	1.00264202	10.01188336	0.09988131	10
11	1.00290661	11.01452539	0.09078920	11
12	1.00317127	12.01743200	0.08321245	12
13	1.00343599	13.02060326	0.07680136	13
14	1.00370079	14.02403926	0.07130613	14
15	1.00396565	15.02774004	0.06654361	15
16	1.00423059	16.03170570	0.06237639	16
17	1.00449559	17.03593629	0.05869944	17
18	1.00476067	18.04043188	0.05543105	18
19	1.00502581	19.04519255	0.05250669	19
20	1.00529103	20.05021836	0.04987477	20
21	1.00555631	21.05550939	0.04749351	21
22	1.00582167	22.06106571	0.04532873	22
23	1.00608710	23.06688738	0.04335219	23
24	1.00635259	24.07297447	0.04154036	24
25	1.00661816	25.07932707	0.03987348	25
26	1.00688379	26.08594522	0.03833462	26
27	1.00714950	27.09282901	0.03691014	27
28	1.00741527	28.09997851	0.03558722	28
29	1.00768112	29.10739378	0.03435553	29

Months				Months
1	1.00794703	30.11507490	0.03320596	1
2	1.01595722	60.46947531	0.01653727	2
3	1.02403107	91.06510316	0.01098115	3
4	1.03216908	121.90387550	0.00820318	4
5	1.04037176	152.98772460	0.00653647	5
6	1.04863963	184.31859810	0.00542539	6
7	1.05697320	215.89845910	0.00463181	7
8	1.06537301	247.72928632	0.00403666	8
9	1.07383956	279.81307419	0.00357381	9
10	1.08237340	312.15183301	0.00320357	10
11	1.09097506	344.74758903	0.00290067	11
12	1.09964507	377.60238462	0.00264829	12
24	1.20921929	792.83098669	0.00126130	24
36	1.32971203	1249.43507342	0.00080036	36
48	1.46221129	1751.53750804	0.00057093	48
60	1.60791344	2303.67197676	0.00043409	60
72	1.76813409	2910.82392533	0.00034355	72
84	1.94431994	3578.47557457	0.00027945	84
96	2.13806185	4312.65542162	0.00023188	96
108	2.35110918	5119.99926734	0.00019531	108
120	2.58538563	6007.77710567	0.00016645	120
132	2.84300657	6984.02488286	0.00014318	132
144	3.12629817	8057.55094179	0.00012411	144
156	3.43781838	9238.04858399	0.00010825	156
168	3.78038004	10536.17700078	0.00009491	168
180	4.15707629	11963.65751935	0.00008359	180
192	4.57130846	13533.37943943	0.00007389	192
204	5.02681683	15259.51641595	0.00006553	204
216	5.52771437	17157.65443875	0.00005828	216
228	6.07852387	19244.93256475	0.00005196	228
240	6.68421883	21540.19767350	0.00004642	240

10.00% Daily	Future Value of 1	Future Value of 1 per Period	Payment for Sinking Fund of 1	
Days				Days
1	1.00027778	1.00000000	1.00000000	1
2	1.00055563	2.00027778	0.49993057	2
3	1.00083356	3.00083341	0.33324076	3
4	1.00111157	4.00166698	0.24989586	4
5	1.00138966	5.00277855	0.19988892	5
6	1.00166782	6.00416821	0.16655096	6
7	1.00194607	7.00583603	0.14273814	7
8	1.00222438	8.00778210	0.12487862	8
9	1.00250278	9.01000648	0.11098771	9
10	1.00278125	10.01250926	0.09987506	10
11	1.00305980	11.01529052	0.09078290	11
12	1.00333843	12.01835032	0.08320610	12
13	1.00361714	13.02168875	0.07679495	13
14	1.00389592	14.02530589	0.07129969	14
15	1.00417478	15.02920180	0.06653713	15
16	1.00445372	16.03337658	0.06236989	16
17	1.00473273	17.03783030	0.05869292	17
18	1.00501182	18.04256303	0.05542450	18
19	1.00529099	19.04757485	0.05250012	19
20	1.00557024	20.05286584	0.04986818	20
21	1.00584957	21.05843609	0.04748691	21
22	1.00612897	22.06428565	0.04532211	22
23	1.00640845	23.07041462	0.04334556	23
24	1.00668801	24.07682307	0.04153372	24
25	1.00696764	25.08351107	0.03986683	25
26	1.00724736	26.09047872	0.03832816	26
27	1.00752715	27.09772607	0.03690347	27
28	1.00780701	28.10525322	0.03558054	28
29	1.00808696	29.11306023	0.03434885	29
Months				Months
1	1.00836699	30.12114719	0.03319527	1
2	1.01680398	60.49431758	0.01653048	2
3	1.02531156	91.12161984	0.01097434	3
4	1.03389033	122.00518029	0.00819637	4
5	1.04254087	153.14714304	0.00652967	5
6	1.05126380	184.54967013	0.00541860	6
7	1.06005971	216.21494171	0.00462503	7
8	1.06892921	248.14515615	0.00402990	8
9	1.07787293	280.34253022	0.00356706	9
10	1.08689147	312.80929925	0.00319684	10
11	1.09598548	345.54771727	0.00289396	11
12	1.10515557	378.56005714	0.00264159	12
24	1.22136884	796.92781341	0.00125485	24
36	1.34980258	1259.28927016	0.00079410	36
48	1.49174184	1770.27061009	0.00056489	48
60	1.64860680	2334.98448482	0.00042827	60
72	1.82196699	2959.08116974	0.00033794	72
84	2.01355697	3648.80509819	0.00027406	84
96	2.22529371	4411.05734046	0.00022670	96
108	2.45929574	5253.46465284	0.00019035	108
120	2.71790439	6184.45578752	0.00016170	120
132	3.00370717	7213.34582697	0.00013863	132
144	3.31956372	8350.42938646	0.00011975	144
156	3.66863434	9607.08361740	0.00010409	156
168	4.05441168	10995.88204209	0.00009094	168
180	4.48075566	12530.72035872	0.00007980	180
192	4.95193208	14226.95547559	0.00007029	192
204	5.47265532	16101.55916544	0.00006211	204
216	6.04813552	18173.28787751	0.00005503	216
228	6.68413067	20462.87040613	0.00004887	228
240	7.38700425	22993.21529389	0.00004349	240

	Future Value of 1	Future Value of 1 per Period	Payment for Sinking Fund of 1	**10.50%** Daily
Days				Days
1	1.00029167	1.00000000	1.00000000	1
2	1.00058342	2.00029167	0.49992709	2
3	1.00087526	3.00087509	0.33323613	3
4	1.00116718	4.00175034	0.24989065	4
5	1.00145918	5.00291752	0.19988337	5
6	1.00175128	6.00437670	0.16654518	6
7	1.00204345	7.00612798	0.14273219	7
8	1.00233572	8.00817143	0.12487245	8
9	1.00262806	9.01050715	0.11098154	9
10	1.00292050	10.01313521	0.09986882	10
11	1.00321302	11.01605571	0.09077659	11
12	1.00350562	12.01926873	0.08319974	12
13	1.00379831	13.02277435	0.07678855	13
14	1.00409108	14.02657266	0.07129325	14
15	1.00438394	15.03066374	0.06653066	15
16	1.00467689	16.03504768	0.06236339	16
17	1.00496992	17.03972457	0.05868639	17
18	1.00526304	18.04469449	0.05541795	18
19	1.00555624	19.04995753	0.05249356	19
20	1.00584952	20.05551377	0.04748160	20
21	1.00614290	21.06136329	0.04748031	21
22	1.00643636	22.06750619	0.04531550	22
23	1.00672990	23.07394254	0.04333893	23
24	1.00702353	24.08067244	0.04152708	24
25	1.00731724	25.08769597	0.03986018	25
26	1.00761105	26.09501322	0.03832150	26
27	1.00790493	27.10262426	0.03689680	27
28	1.00819890	28.11052920	0.03557386	28
29	1.00849296	29.11872810	0.03434216	29
Months				Months
1	1.00878711	30.12722106	0.03319257	1
2	1.01765143	60.51917322	0.01652369	2
3	1.02659364	91.17818268	0.01096754	3
4	1.03561442	122.10659611	0.00818957	4
5	1.04471448	153.30678079	0.00652287	5
6	1.05389449	184.78112481	0.00541181	6
7	1.06315518	216.53203723	0.00461825	7
8	1.07249723	248.56194829	0.00402314	8
9	1.08192138	280.87330957	0.00356032	9
10	1.09142834	313.46859422	0.00319011	10
11	1.10101884	346.35029709	0.00288725	11
12	1.11069361	379.52093498	0.00263490	12
24	1.23364029	801.05241082	0.00124836	24
36	1.37019638	1269.24472578	0.00078787	36
48	1.52186836	1789.26293640	0.00055889	48
60	1.69032945	2366.84383795	0.00042250	60
72	1.87743812	3008.35925228	0.00033241	72
84	2.08525851	3720.86633795	0.00026875	84
96	2.31608329	4512.28558067	0.00022162	96
108	2.57245891	5391.28767804	0.00018548	108
120	2.85721366	6367.58968728	0.00015705	120
132	3.17348894	7451.96208650	0.00013419	132
144	3.52477388	8656.36757688	0.00011552	144
156	3.91494381	9994.09305412	0.00010006	156
168	4.34830305	11479.89618832	0.00008711	168
180	4.82963240	13130.16822930	0.00007616	180
192	5.36424183	14963.11483344	0.00006683	192
204	5.95802910	16998.95690687	0.00005883	204
216	6.61754482	19260.15368072	0.00005192	216
228	7.35006472	21771.65047942	0.00004593	228
240	8.16366989	24561.15391533	0.00004071	240

11.00%

Daily

Days	Future Value of 1	Future Value of 1 per Period	Payment for Sinking Fund of 1	Days
1	1.00030556	1.00000000	1.00000000	1
2	1.00061120	2.00030556	0.49992362	2
3	1.00091695	3.00091676	0.33323150	3
4	1.00122278	4.00183371	0.24988545	4
5	1.00152871	5.00305649	0.19987782	5
6	1.00183473	6.00458520	0.16653940	6
7	1.00214085	7.00641994	0.14272624	7
8	1.00244706	8.00856079	0.12486638	8
9	1.00275336	9.01100785	0.11097538	9
10	1.00305976	10.01376121	0.09986258	10
11	1.00336625	11.01682097	0.09077029	11
12	1.00367283	12.02018722	0.08319338	12
13	1.00397951	13.02386006	0.07678215	13
14	1.00428628	14.02783957	0.07128681	14
15	1.00459315	15.03212585	0.06652419	15
16	1.00490011	16.03671900	0.06235689	16
17	1.00520716	17.04161911	0.05867987	17
18	1.00551431	18.04682627	0.05541141	18
19	1.00582155	19.05234058	0.05248699	19
20	1.00612888	20.05816213	0.04985502	20
21	1.00643631	21.06429101	0.04747371	21
22	1.00674383	22.07072732	0.04530888	22
23	1.00705145	23.07747116	0.04333230	23
24	1.00735916	24.08452261	0.04152044	24
25	1.00766696	25.09188177	0.03985353	25
26	1.00797486	26.09954873	0.03831484	26
27	1.00828285	27.10752359	0.03689013	27
28	1.00859094	28.11580645	0.03556718	28
29	1.00889912	29.12439739	0.03433547	29

Months				Months
1	1.00920740	30.13329651	0.03318588	1
2	1.01849957	60.54404222	0.01651690	2
3	1.02787730	91.23479171	0.01096073	3
4	1.03734137	122.20812308	0.00818276	4
5	1.04689258	153.46663819	0.00651607	5
6	1.05653174	185.01296284	0.00540503	6
7	1.06625964	216.84974699	0.00461149	7
8	1.07607712	248.97966502	0.00401639	8
9	1.08598499	281.40541594	0.00355359	9
10	1.09598408	314.12972360	0.00318340	10
11	1.10607524	347.15533691	0.00288055	11
12	1.11625931	380.48503014	0.00262822	12
24	1.24603486	805.20498915	0.00124192	24
36	1.39089802	1279.30259957	0.00078168	36
48	1.55260287	1808.51847331	0.00055294	48
60	1.73310741	2399.26062189	0.00041680	60
72	1.93459729	3058.68204787	0.00032694	72
84	2.15951225	3794.76735697	0.00026352	84
96	2.41057566	4616.42943972	0.00021662	96
108	2.69082754	5533.61739317	0.00018071	108
120	3.00366130	6557.43698960	0.00015250	120
132	3.35286491	7700.28515076	0.00012987	132
144	3.74266668	8976.00005601	0.00011141	144
156	4.17778655	10400.02870198	0.00009615	156
168	4.66349315	11989.61394253	0.00008341	168
180	5.20566767	13764.00327391	0.00007265	180
192	5.81087502	15744.68189308	0.00006351	192
204	6.48644337	17955.63285128	0.00005569	204
216	7.24055283	20423.62745285	0.00004896	216
228	8.08233454	23178.54941565	0.00004314	228
240	9.02198122	26253.75671807	0.00003809	240

	Future Value of 1	Future Value of 1 per Period	Payment for Sinking Fund of 1	**11.50%**
				Daily
Days				Days
1	1.00031944	1.00000000	1.00000000	1
2	1.00063899	2.00031944	0.49992015	2
3	1.00095864	3.00095844	0.33322687	3
4	1.00127839	4.00191707	0.24988024	4
5	1.00159824	5.00319547	0.19987226	5
6	1.00191820	6.00479371	0.16653361	6
7	1.00223826	7.00671191	0.14272030	7
8	1.00255841	8.00895016	0.12486031	8
9	1.00287868	9.01150858	0.11096921	9
10	1.00319904	10.01438725	0.09985633	10
11	1.00351951	11.01758629	0.09076398	11
12	1.00384008	12.02110580	0.08318702	12
13	1.00416075	13.02494587	0.07677575	13
14	1.00448152	14.02910662	0.07128038	14
15	1.00480240	15.03358814	0.06651772	15
16	1.00512337	16.03839054	0.06235040	16
17	1.00544446	17.04351391	0.05867335	17
18	1.00576564	18.04895837	0.05540486	18
19	1.00608693	19.05472401	0.05248042	19
20	1.00640831	20.06081093	0.04984843	20
21	1.00672981	21.06721925	0.04746711	21
22	1.00705140	22.07394905	0.04530227	22
23	1.00737310	23.08100045	0.04332568	23
24	1.00769490	24.08837355	0.04151380	24
25	1.00801680	25.09606845	0.03984688	25
26	1.00833881	26.10408525	0.03830818	26
27	1.00866091	27.11242405	0.03688346	27
28	1.00898312	28.12108497	0.03556051	28
29	1.00930544	29.13006809	0.03432879	29
Months				Months
1	1.00962786	30.13937353	0.03317919	1
2	1.01934841	60.56892459	0.01651012	2
3	1.02916255	91.29144697	0.01095393	3
4	1.03907117	122.30976135	0.00817596	4
5	1.04907520	153.62671558	0.00650928	5
6	1.05917555	185.24518492	0.00539825	6
7	1.06937313	217.16807231	0.00460473	7
8	1.07966890	249.39830865	0.00400965	8
9	1.09006380	281.93885304	0.00354687	9
10	1.10055878	314.79269309	0.00317669	10
11	1.11115480	347.96284516	0.00287387	11
12	1.12185284	381.45235466	0.00262156	12
24	1.25855378	809.38576034	0.00123550	24
36	1.41191213	1289.46406492	0.00077552	36
48	1.58395763	1828.04127218	0.00054703	48
60	1.77696736	2432.24563929	0.00041114	60
72	1.99349587	3110.07402176	0.00032154	72
84	2.23640899	3870.49771462	0.00025836	84
96	2.50892177	4723.58119066	0.00021170	96
108	2.81464100	5680.61530718	0.00017604	108
120	3.15761299	6754.26674449	0.00014805	120
132	3.54237708	7958.74565378	0.00012565	132
144	3.97402578	9309.99373349	0.00010741	144
156	4.45827209	10825.89522320	0.00009237	156
168	5.00152518	12526.51360779	0.00007983	168
180	5.61097521	14434.35716467	0.00006928	180
192	6.29468844	16574.67686867	0.00006033	192
204	7.06171408	18975.80059752	0.00005270	204
216	7.92220396	21669.50806115	0.00004615	216
228	8.88754698	24691.45141727	0.00004050	228
240	9.97051978	28081.62714009	0.00003561	240

12.00%
Daily

Days	Future Value of 1	Future Value of 1 per Period	Payment for Sinking Fund of 1	Days
1	1.00033333	1.00000000	1.00000000	1
2	1.00066678	2.00033333	0.49991668	2
3	1.00100033	3.00100011	0.33322225	3
4	1.00133400	4.00200044	0.24987503	4
5	1.00166778	5.00333444	0.19986671	5
6	1.00200167	6.00500222	0.16652783	6
7	1.00233567	7.00700389	0.14271435	7
8	1.00266978	8.00933956	0.12485424	8
9	1.00300400	9.01200934	0.11096305	9
10	1.00333834	10.01501334	0.09985009	10
11	1.00367278	11.01835168	0.09075768	11
12	1.00400734	12.02202446	0.08318067	12
13	1.00434201	13.02603180	0.07676935	13
14	1.00467679	14.03037381	0.07127394	14
15	1.00501168	15.03505061	0.06651125	15
16	1.00534669	16.04006229	0.06234390	16
17	1.00568180	17.04540898	0.05866682	17
18	1.00601703	18.05109078	0.05539821	18
19	1.00635237	19.05710781	0.05247386	19
20	1.00668782	20.06346018	0.04984185	20
21	1.00702338	21.07014800	0.04746051	21
22	1.00735906	22.07717138	0.04529566	22
23	1.00769484	23.08453044	0.04331905	23
24	1.00803074	24.09222528	0.04150717	24
25	1.00836675	25.10025602	0.03984023	25
26	1.00870287	26.10862278	0.03830152	26
27	1.00903911	27.11732565	0.03687679	27
28	1.00937545	28.12636476	0.03555383	28
29	1.00971191	29.13574021	0.03432211	29

Months				Months
1	1.01004848	30.14545213	0.03317250	1
2	1.02019794	60.59382035	0.01650333	2
3	1.03044938	91.34814852	0.01094713	3
4	1.04080384	122.41151106	0.00816907	4
5	1.05126234	153.78701330	0.00650250	5
6	1.06182593	185.47779178	0.00539148	6
7	1.07249567	217.48701453	0.00459798	7
8	1.08327263	249.81788146	0.00400292	8
9	1.09415787	282.47362458	0.00354015	9
10	1.10515250	315.45750842	0.00317000	10
11	1.11625761	348.77283029	0.00286720	11
12	1.12747431	382.42292063	0.00261491	12
24	1.27119831	813.59493801	0.00122911	24
36	1.43324344	1299.73030944	0.00076939	36
48	1.61594515	1847.83545040	0.00054117	48
60	1.82193664	2465.80991429	0.00040555	60
72	2.05418675	3162.56024464	0.00031620	72
84	2.31604278	3948.12834042	0.00025328	84
96	2.61127873	4833.83618471	0.00020688	96
108	2.94414967	5832.44902255	0.00017145	108
120	3.31945311	6958.35933973	0.00014371	120
132	3.74259810	8227.79429420	0.00012154	132
144	4.21968320	9659.04958962	0.00010353	144
156	4.75758439	11272.75316179	0.00008871	156
168	5.36405416	13092.16247832	0.00007638	168
180	6.04783325	15143.49973641	0.00006603	180
192	6.81877660	17456.32978964	0.00005729	192
204	7.68799542	20063.98625083	0.00004984	204
216	8.66801730	23004.05191199	0.00004347	216
228	9.77296680	26318.90040548	0.00003800	228
240	11.01876897	30056.30691308	0.00003327	240

	Future Value of 1	Future Value of 1 per Period	Payment for Sinking Fund of 1	**12.50%** Daily
Days				Days
1	1.00034722	1.00000000	1.00000000	1
2	1.00069457	2.00034722	0.49991321	2
3	1.00104203	3.00104179	0.33321762	3
4	1.00138961	4.00208382	0.24986983	4
5	1.00173732	5.00347343	0.19986116	5
6	1.00208514	6.00521075	0.16652205	6
7	1.00243309	7.00729589	0.14270840	7
8	1.00278116	8.00972898	0.12484817	8
9	1.00312934	9.01251013	0.11095688	9
10	1.00347765	10.01563948	0.09984385	10
11	1.00382608	11.01911713	0.09075137	11
12	1.00417463	12.02294321	0.08317431	12
13	1.00452330	13.02711784	0.07676295	13
14	1.00487210	14.03164115	0.07126750	14
15	1.00522101	15.03651325	0.06650478	15
16	1.00557005	16.04173426	0.06233740	16
17	1.00591920	17.04730430	0.05866030	17
18	1.00626848	18.05322351	0.05539177	18
19	1.00661788	19.05949199	0.05246730	19
20	1.00696740	20.06610987	0.04983527	20
21	1.00731704	21.07307727	0.04745391	21
22	1.00766680	22.08039431	0.04528905	22
23	1.00801669	23.08806111	0.04331243	23
24	1.00836669	24.09607780	0.04150053	24
25	1.00871682	25.10444449	0.03983358	25
26	1.00906707	26.11316131	0.03829487	26
27	1.00941744	27.12222838	0.03687013	27
28	1.00976793	28.13164582	0.03554716	28
29	1.01011855	29.14141376	0.03431543	29
Months				Months
1	1.01046928	30.15153230	0.03316581	1
2	1.02104817	60.61872950	0.01649655	2
3	1.03173781	91.40489638	0.01094033	3
4	1.04253937	122.51337232	0.00816237	4
5	1.05345400	153.94753168	0.00649572	5
6	1.06448291	185.71078411	0.00538472	6
7	1.07562728	217.80657499	0.00459123	7
8	1.08688833	250.23838576	0.00399619	8
9	1.09826727	283.00573430	0.00353345	9
10	1.10976534	316.12417534	0.00316331	10
11	1.12138378	349.58530079	0.00286053	11
12	1.13312387	383.39674021	0.00260826	12
24	1.28396970	817.83273751	0.00122274	24
36	1.45489671	1310.10253522	0.00076330	36
48	1.64857819	1867.90519257	0.00053536	48
60	1.86804330	2499.96469731	0.00040001	60
72	2.11672445	3216.16640822	0.00031093	72
84	2.39851099	4027.71166124	0.00024828	84
96	2.71781005	4947.29295750	0.00020213	96
108	3.07961544	5989.29247298	0.00016696	108
120	3.48958576	7170.00699456	0.00013947	120
132	3.95413292	8507.90280040	0.00011754	132
144	4.48052239	10023.90447106	0.00009976	144
156	5.07698686	11741.72214822	0.00008517	156
168	5.75285499	13688.22235930	0.00007306	168
180	6.51869729	15893.84820779	0.00006292	180
192	7.38649149	18393.09550089	0.00005437	192
204	8.36980981	21225.05226104	0.00004711	204
216	9.48403127	24434.01005949	0.00004093	216
228	10.74658220	28070.15673273	0.00003563	228
240	12.17720879	32190.36131619	0.00003107	240

13.00%
Daily

Days	Future Value of 1	Future Value of 1 per Period	Payment for Sinking Fund of 1	Days
1	1.00036111	1.00000000	1.00000000	1
2	1.00072235	2.00036111	0.49990974	2
3	1.00108372	3.00108346	0.33321299	3
4	1.00144523	4.00216719	0.24986462	4
5	1.00180686	5.00361242	0.19985561	5
6	1.00216862	6.00541928	0.16651627	6
7	1.00253052	7.00758790	0.14270246	7
8	1.00289254	8.01011842	0.12484210	8
9	1.00325470	9.01301096	0.11095071	9
10	1.00361698	10.01626566	0.09983761	10
11	1.00397940	11.01988264	0.09074507	11
12	1.00434195	12.02386204	0.08316795	12
13	1.00470463	13.02820400	0.07675655	13
14	1.00506744	14.03290862	0.07126106	14
15	1.00543038	15.03797606	0.06649831	15
16	1.00579345	16.04340644	0.06233090	16
17	1.00615666	17.04919990	0.05865378	17
18	1.00651999	18.05535655	0.05538523	18
19	1.00688346	19.06187654	0.05246073	19
20	1.00724705	20.06876000	0.04982869	20
21	1.00761078	21.07600705	0.04744732	21
22	1.00797464	22.08361783	0.04528244	22
23	1.00833863	23.09159247	0.04330580	23
24	1.00870275	24.09993110	0.04149389	24
25	1.00906701	25.10863385	0.03982694	25
26	1.00943139	26.11770066	0.03828821	26
27	1.00979591	27.12713225	0.03686346	27
28	1.01016056	28.13692816	0.03554048	28
29	1.01052534	29.14708872	0.03430874	29
Months				**Months**
1	1.01089025	30.15761406	0.03315912	1
2	1.02189910	60.64365205	0.01648977	2
3	1.03302783	91.46169061	0.01093354	3
4	1.04427776	122.61534530	0.00815559	4
5	1.05565021	154.10827106	0.00648894	5
6	1.06714650	185.94416264	0.00537796	6
7	1.07876799	218.12675502	0.00458449	7
8	1.09051605	250.65982387	0.00398947	8
9	1.10239204	283.54718595	0.00352675	9
10	1.11439736	316.79269961	0.00315664	10
11	1.12653343	350.40026521	0.00285388	11
12	1.13880166	384.37382558	0.00260163	12
24	1.29686922	822.09937593	0.00121640	24
36	1.47687682	1320.58195895	0.00075724	36
48	1.68186977	1888.25475160	0.00052959	48
60	1.91531609	2534.72146977	0.00039452	60
72	2.18116514	3270.91884106	0.00030572	72
84	2.48391448	4109.30162902	0.00024335	84
96	2.82868593	5064.05333903	0.00019747	96
108	3.22131223	6151.32617054	0.00016257	108
120	3.66843571	7389.51427512	0.00013533	120
132	4.17762067	8799.56494306	0.00011364	132
144	4.75748136	10405.33298332	0.00009610	144
156	5.41782766	12233.98429192	0.00008174	156
168	6.16983113	14316.45543632	0.00006985	168
180	7.02621393	16687.97703089	0.00005992	180
192	8.00146408	19388.66975770	0.00005158	192
204	9.11208057	22464.22311608	0.00004452	204
216	10.37685247	25966.66838369	0.00003851	216
228	11.81717681	29955.25886583	0.00003338	228
240	13.45742056	34497.47232492	0.00002899	240

	Future Value of 1	Future Value of 1 per Period	Payment for Sinking Fund of 1	**14.00%** Daily
Days				Days
1	1.00038889	1.00000000	1.00000000	1
2	1.00077793	2.00038889	0.49990280	2
3	1.00116712	3.00116682	0.33320374	3
4	1.00155646	4.00233394	0.24985421	4
5	1.00194596	5.00389040	0.19984450	5
6	1.00233560	6.00583636	0.16650470	6
7	1.00272540	7.00817196	0.14269056	7
8	1.00311535	8.01089736	0.12482996	8
9	1.00350545	9.01401271	0.11093838	9
10	1.00389570	10.01751816	0.09982512	10
11	1.00428611	11.02141386	0.09073246	11
12	1.00467666	12.02569997	0.08315524	12
13	1.00506737	13.03037663	0.07674315	13
14	1.00545823	14.03544400	0.07124819	14
15	1.00584924	15.04090223	0.06648537	15
16	1.00624040	16.04675147	0.06231791	16
17	1.00663172	17.05299187	0.05864074	17
18	1.00702319	18.05962359	0.05537214	18
19	1.00741481	19.06664677	0.05244761	19
20	1.00780658	20.07406158	0.04981553	20
21	1.00819850	21.08186816	0.04743413	21
22	1.00859058	22.09006667	0.04526922	22
23	1.00898281	23.09865725	0.04329256	23
24	1.00937519	24.10764006	0.04148063	24
25	1.00976773	25.11701525	0.03981365	25
26	1.01016042	26.12678298	0.03827490	26
27	1.01055326	27.13694340	0.03685013	27
28	1.01094625	28.14749665	0.03552714	28
29	1.01133939	29.15844290	0.03429538	29
Months				Months
1	1.01173269	30.16978229	0.03314575	1
2	1.02360304	60.69353739	0.01647622	2
3	1.03561266	91.57541833	0.01091996	3
4	1.04776319	122.81962690	0.00814202	4
5	1.06005627	154.43041419	0.00647541	5
6	1.07249359	186.41208114	0.00536446	6
7	1.08507683	218.76897917	0.00457103	7
8	1.09780770	251.50551076	0.00397606	8
9	1.11068794	284.62613003	0.00351338	9
10	1.12371930	318.13534336	0.00314332	10
11	1.13690355	352.03771001	0.00284060	11
12	1.15024249	386.33784272	0.00258841	12
24	1.32305780	830.72004660	0.00120377	24
36	1.52183730	1341.86734126	0.00074523	36
48	1.75048193	1929.81068047	0.00051819	48
60	2.01347870	2606.08809352	0.00038372	60
72	2.31598877	3383.97111201	0.00029551	72
84	2.66394869	4278.72521554	0.00023371	84
96	3.06418699	5307.90940745	0.00018840	96
108	3.52455809	6491.72079954	0.00015404	108
120	4.05409649	7853.39096806	0.00012733	120
132	4.66319406	9419.64185924	0.00010616	132
144	5.36380396	11221.21019115	0.00008912	144
156	6.16967525	13293.45064306	0.00007523	156
168	7.09662265	15677.02966944	0.00006379	168
180	8.16283694	18418.72355432	0.00005429	180
192	9.38924192	21572.33636732	0.00004636	192
204	10.79990505	25199.75583569	0.00003968	204
216	12.42250972	29372.16785318	0.00003405	216
228	14.28889857	34171.45345980	0.00002926	228
240	16.43569833	39691.79570725	0.00002519	240

	Future Value of 1	Future Value of 1 per Period	Payment for Sinking Fund of 1	
Days				Days
1	1.00041667	1.00000000	1.00000000	1
2	1.00083351	2.00041667	0.49989586	2
3	1.00125052	3.00125017	0.33319448	3
4	1.00166771	4.00250069	0.24984380	4
5	1.00208507	5.00416840	0.19983340	5
6	1.00250261	6.00625347	0.16649314	6
7	1.00292032	7.00875608	0.14267867	7
8	1.00333820	8.01167639	0.12481782	8
9	1.00375626	9.01501459	0.11092605	9
10	1.00417449	10.01877085	0.09981264	10
11	1.00459289	11.02294534	0.09071985	11
12	1.00501147	12.02753823	0.08314253	12
13	1.00543023	13.03254970	0.07673096	13
14	1.00584916	14.03797993	0.07123532	14
15	1.00626826	15.04382909	0.06647244	15
16	1.00668754	16.05009735	0.06230492	16
17	1.00710699	17.05678489	0.05862770	17
18	1.00752662	18.06389189	0.05535906	18
19	1.00794642	19.07141851	0.05243448	19
20	1.00836640	20.07936493	0.04980237	20
21	1.00878655	21.08773134	0.04742094	21
22	1.00920688	22.09651789	0.04525600	22
23	1.00962739	23.10572477	0.04327932	23
24	1.01004806	24.11535216	0.04146736	24
25	1.01046892	25.12540022	0.03980036	25
26	1.01088995	26.13586914	0.03826159	26
27	1.01131115	27.14675908	0.03683681	27
28	1.01173253	28.15807023	0.03551380	28
29	1.01215408	29.16980276	0.03428203	29
Months				Months
1	1.01257582	30.18195685	0.03313238	1
2	1.02530978	60.74347641	0.01646267	2
3	1.03820389	91.68933200	0.01090639	3
4	1.05126015	123.02435696	0.00812847	4
5	1.06448060	154.75344540	0.00646189	5
6	1.07786731	186.88155301	0.00535098	6
7	1.09142237	219.41369776	0.00455760	7
8	1.10514790	252.35496076	0.00396267	8
9	1.11904604	285.71048699	0.00350005	9
10	1.13311895	319.48548617	0.00313003	10
11	1.14736885	353.68523350	0.00282737	11
12	1.16179795	388.31507054	0.00257523	12
24	1.34977447	839.45872191	0.00119124	24
36	1.56816520	1363.59648945	0.00073335	36
48	1.82189111	1972.53867124	0.00050696	48
60	2.11666935	2680.00644730	0.00037313	60
72	2.45914211	3501.94105643	0.00028556	72
84	2.85702625	4456.86299711	0.00022437	84
96	3.31928723	5566.28934644	0.00017965	96
108	3.85634108	6855.21860040	0.00014587	108
120	4.48028915	8352.69396025	0.00011972	120
132	5.20519073	10092.45775761	0.00009908	132
144	6.04737990	12113.71176400	0.00008255	144
156	7.02583355	14462.00051708	0.00006915	156
168	8.16259899	17190.23756716	0.00005817	168
180	9.48329074	20359.89776831	0.00004912	180
192	11.01766770	24042.40247969	0.00004159	192
204	12.80030370	28320.72888973	0.00003531	204
216	14.87136655	33291.27972548	0.00003004	216
228	17.27752312	39066.05547722	0.00002560	228
240	20.07299087	45775.17808454	0.00002185	240

	Future Value of 1	Future Value of 1 per Period	Payment for Sinking Fund of 1	**16.00%** Daily
Days				Days
1	1.00044444	1.00000000	1.00000000	1
2	1.00088909	2.00044444	0.49988891	2
3	1.00133393	3.00133353	0.33318523	3
4	1.00177896	4.00266746	0.24983340	4
5	1.00222420	5.00444642	0.19982230	5
6	1.00266963	6.00667062	0.16648158	6
7	1.00311526	7.00934025	0.14266678	7
8	1.00356109	8.01245551	0.12480569	8
9	1.00400712	9.01601660	0.11091373	9
10	1.00445334	10.02002372	0.09980016	10
11	1.00489977	11.02447707	0.09070725	11
12	1.00534639	12.02937683	0.08312983	12
13	1.00579321	13.03472322	0.07671816	13
14	1.00624023	14.04051643	0.07122245	14
15	1.00668745	15.04675666	0.06645951	15
16	1.00713486	16.05344411	0.06229193	16
17	1.00758248	17.06057897	0.05861466	17
18	1.00803029	18.06816145	0.05534597	18
19	1.00847831	19.07619175	0.05242136	19
20	1.00892652	20.08467006	0.04978922	20
21	1.00937493	21.09359658	0.04740775	21
22	1.00982354	22.10297151	0.04524279	22
23	1.01027235	23.11279505	0.04326608	23
24	1.01072136	24.12306740	0.04145410	24
25	1.01117057	25.13378877	0.03978708	25
26	1.01161998	26.14495934	0.03824829	26
27	1.01206959	27.15657932	0.03682349	27
28	1.01251940	28.16864891	0.03550046	28
29	1.01296941	29.18116831	0.03426868	29
Months				Months
1	1.01341962	30.19413772	0.03311901	1
2	1.02701932	60.79346920	0.01644914	2
3	1.04080153	91.80343199	0.01089284	3
4	1.05476868	123.22953657	0.00811494	4
5	1.06892327	155.07736745	0.00644839	5
6	1.08326782	187.35258401	0.00533753	6
7	1.09780485	220.06092160	0.00454420	7
8	1.11253697	253.20819256	0.00394932	8
9	1.12746679	286.80028718	0.00348675	9
10	1.14259697	320.84317484	0.00311679	10
11	1.15793018	355.34290501	0.00281418	11
12	1.17346916	390.30560834	0.00256209	12
24	1.37702987	848.31720241	0.00117880	24
36	1.61590208	1385.77968263	0.00072162	36
48	1.89621126	2016.47532744	0.00049591	48
60	2.22514543	2756.57721550	0.00036277	60
72	2.61113954	3625.06395584	0.00027586	72
84	3.06409172	4644.20636087	0.00021532	84
96	3.59561713	5840.13854206	0.00017123	96
108	4.21934581	7243.52807325	0.00013805	108
120	4.95127218	8890.36240654	0.00011248	120
132	5.81016520	10822.87170707	0.00009240	132
144	6.81804968	13090.61177122	0.00007639	144
156	8.00077102	15751.73479772	0.00006349	156
168	9.38865804	18874.48059832	0.00005298	168
180	11.01730066	22538.92648753	0.00004437	180
192	12.92846254	26839.04072431	0.00003726	192
204	15.17115207	31885.09216246	0.00003136	204
216	17.80287907	37806.47790118	0.00002645	216
228	20.89112953	44755.04144565	0.00002234	228
240	24.51509621	52908.96646625	0.00001890	240

225

5.00%	Future Value of 1	Future Value of 1 per Period	Payment for Sinking Fund of 1	
Continuous				
Years				Years
1	1.05127110	1.00000000	1.00000000	1
2	1.10517092	2.05127110	0.48750260	2
3	1.16183424	3.15644201	0.31681241	3
4	1.22140276	4.31827626	0.23157388	4
5	1.28402542	5.53967902	0.18051587	5
6	1.34985881	6.82370443	0.14654797	6
7	1.41906755	8.17356324	0.12234566	7
8	1.49182470	9.59263079	0.10424669	8
9	1.56831219	11.08445549	0.09021643	9
10	1.64872127	12.65276767	0.07903409	10
11	1.73325302	14.30148894	0.06992279	11
12	1.82211880	16.03474196	0.06236458	12
13	1.91554083	17.85686076	0.05600088	13
14	2.01375271	19.77240159	0.05057555	14
15	2.11700002	21.78615430	0.04590071	15
16	2.22554093	23.90315431	0.04183548	16
17	2.33964685	26.12869524	0.03827210	17
18	2.45960311	28.46834209	0.03512674	18
19	2.58570966	30.92794520	0.03233322	19
20	2.71828183	33.51365486	0.02983858	20
21	2.85765112	36.23193669	0.02759996	21
22	3.00416602	39.08958781	0.02558226	22
23	3.15819291	42.09375383	0.02375649	23
24	3.32011692	45.25194674	0.02209850	24
25	3.49034296	48.57206367	0.02058797	25
26	3.66929667	52.06240662	0.01920772	26
27	3.85742553	55.73170329	0.01794311	27
28	4.05519997	59.58912882	0.01678158	28
29	4.26311452	63.64432879	0.01571232	29
30	4.48168907	67.90744330	0.01472593	30
31	4.71147018	72.38913238	0.01381423	31
32	4.95303242	77.10060256	0.01297007	32
33	5.20697983	82.05363498	0.01218715	33
34	5.47394739	87.26061481	0.01145992	34
35	5.75460268	92.73456220	0.01078347	35
36	6.04964746	98.48916488	0.01015340	36
37	6.35981952	104.53881234	0.00956583	37
38	6.68589444	110.89863186	0.00901724	38
39	7.02868758	117.58452631	0.00850452	39
40	7.38905610	124.61321389	0.00802483	40
41	7.76790111	132.00226999	0.00757563	41
42	8.16616991	139.77017109	0.00715460	42
43	8.58485840	147.93634100	0.00675966	43
44	9.02501350	156.52119940	0.00638891	44
45	9.48773584	165.54621290	0.00604061	45
46	9.97418245	175.03394874	0.00571318	46
47	10.48556972	185.00813119	0.00540517	47
48	11.02317638	195.49370092	0.00511525	48
49	11.58834672	206.51687730	0.00484222	49
50	12.18249396	218.10522402	0.00458494	50

Years	Future Value of 1	Future Value of 1 per Period	Payment for Sinking Fund of 1	**5.50%** Continuous Years
1	1.05654061	1.00000000	1.00000000	1
2	1.11627807	2.05654061	0.48625347	2
3	1.17939312	3.17281869	0.31517717	3
4	1.24607673	4.35221180	0.22976823	4
5	1.31653067	5.59828853	0.17862602	5
6	1.39096813	6.91481921	0.14461694	6
7	1.46961432	8.30578734	0.12039798	7
8	1.55270722	9.77540166	0.10229759	8
9	1.64049824	11.32810888	0.08827599	9
10	1.73325302	12.96860712	0.07710928	10
11	1.83125221	14.70186013	0.06801860	11
12	1.93479233	16.53311234	0.06048468	12
13	2.04418668	18.46790468	0.05414799	13
14	2.15976625	20.51209136	0.04875173	14
15	2.28188077	22.67185761	0.04410755	15
16	2.41089971	24.95373838	0.04007416	16
17	2.54721346	27.36463809	0.03654351	17
18	2.69123447	29.91185154	0.03343156	18
19	2.84339852	32.60308602	0.03067194	19
20	3.00416602	35.44648454	0.02821154	20
21	3.17402342	38.45065056	0.02600736	21
22	3.35348465	41.62467398	0.02402421	22
23	3.54309274	44.97815863	0.02223301	23
24	3.74342138	48.52125137	0.02060953	24
25	3.95507672	52.26467275	0.01913338	25
26	4.17869919	56.21974947	0.01778734	26
27	4.41496541	60.39844866	0.01655672	27
28	4.66459027	64.81341407	0.01542890	28
29	4.92832907	69.47800435	0.01439304	29
30	5.20697983	74.40633342	0.01343972	30
31	5.50138567	79.61331324	0.01256071	31
32	5.81243739	85.11469891	0.01174885	32
33	6.14107618	90.92713631	0.01099782	33
34	6.48829640	97.06821248	0.01030203	34
35	6.85514867	103.55650888	0.00965656	35
36	7.24274299	110.41165755	0.00905701	36
37	7.65225213	117.65440053	0.00849947	37
38	8.08491516	125.30665266	0.00798042	38
39	8.54204124	133.39156782	0.00749673	39
40	9.02501350	141.93360906	0.00704555	40
41	9.53529331	150.95862256	0.00662433	41
42	10.07442466	160.49391587	0.00623077	42
43	10.64403882	170.56834053	0.00586275	43
44	11.24585931	181.21237934	0.00551839	44
45	11.88170711	192.45823866	0.00519593	45
46	12.55350614	204.33994577	0.00489381	46
47	13.26328909	216.89345191	0.00461056	47
48	14.01320361	230.15674100	0.00434487	48
49	14.80551875	244.16994461	0.00409551	49
50	15.64263188	258.97546336	0.00386137	50

6.00% Continuous	Future Value of 1	Future Value of 1 per Period	Payment for Sinking Fund of 1	
Years				Years
1	1.06183655	1.00000000	1.00000000	1
2	1.12749685	2.06183655	0.48500450	2
3	1.19721736	3.18933340	0.31354514	3
4	1.27124915	4.38655076	0.22796955	4
5	1.34985881	5.65779991	0.17674715	5
6	1.43332941	7.00765872	0.14270101	6
7	1.52196156	8.44098813	0.11846954	7
8	1.61607440	9.96294969	0.10037188	8
9	1.71600686	11.57902409	0.08636306	9
10	1.82211880	13.29503095	0.07521607	10
11	1.93479233	15.11714975	0.06615004	11
12	2.05443321	17.05194209	0.05864435	12
13	2.18147227	19.10637530	0.05233855	13
14	2.31636698	21.28784756	0.04697516	14
15	2.45960311	23.60421454	0.04236532	15
16	2.61169647	26.06381765	0.03836736	16
17	2.77319476	28.67551413	0.03487296	17
18	2.94467955	31.44870889	0.03179781	18
19	3.12676837	34.39338844	0.02907536	19
20	3.32011692	37.52015681	0.02665234	20
21	3.52542149	40.84027373	0.02448563	21
22	3.74342138	44.36569522	0.02253994	22
23	3.97490163	48.10911659	0.02078608	23
24	4.22069582	52.08401822	0.01919975	24
25	4.48168907	56.30471404	0.01776050	25
26	4.75882125	60.78640311	0.01645105	26
27	5.05309032	65.54522435	0.01525664	27
28	5.36555597	70.59831467	0.01416464	28
29	5.69734342	75.96387064	0.01316415	29
30	6.04964746	81.66121406	0.01224572	30
31	6.42373677	87.71086153	0.01140110	31
32	6.82095847	94.13459830	0.01062309	32
33	7.24274299	100.95555677	0.00990535	33
34	7.69060920	108.19829975	0.00924229	34
35	8.16616991	115.88890895	0.00862895	35
36	8.67113766	124.05507887	0.00806094	36
37	9.20733087	132.72621652	0.00753431	37
38	9.77668041	141.93354739	0.00704555	38
39	10.38123656	151.71022780	0.00659151	39
40	11.02317638	162.09146436	0.00616936	40
41	11.70481154	173.11464074	0.00577652	41
42	12.42859666	184.81945228	0.00541069	42
43	13.19713816	197.24804895	0.00506976	43
44	14.01320361	210.44518711	0.00475183	44
45	14.87973172	224.45839071	0.00445517	45
46	15.79984295	239.33812244	0.00417819	46
47	16.77685067	255.13796539	0.00391945	47
48	17.81427318	271.91481606	0.00367762	48
49	18.91584631	289.72908924	0.00345150	49
50	20.08553692	308.64493555	0.00323997	50

	Future Value of 1	Future Value of 1 per Period	Payment for Sinking Fund of 1	**6.50%** Continuous
Years				Years
1	1.06715902	1.00000000	1.00000000	1
2	1.13882838	2.06715902	0.48375572	2
3	1.21531099	3.20598741	0.31191638	3
4	1.29693009	4.42129839	0.22617790	4
5	1.38403065	5.71822848	0.17487934	5
6	1.47698079	7.10225913	0.14080027	6
7	1.57617338	8.57923992	0.11656044	7
8	1.68202765	10.15541330	0.09846965	8
9	1.79499099	11.83744095	0.08447772	9
10	1.91554083	13.63243194	0.07335448	10
11	2.04418668	15.54797277	0.06431707	11
12	2.18147227	17.59215945	0.05684350	12
13	2.32797781	19.77363172	0.05057240	13
14	2.48432253	22.10160953	0.04524557	14
15	2.65116721	24.58593206	0.04067367	15
16	2.82921701	27.23709927	0.03671463	16
17	3.01922447	30.06631629	0.03325981	17
18	3.22199264	33.08554076	0.03022468	18
19	3.43837852	36.30753340	0.02754249	19
20	3.66929667	39.74591192	0.02515982	20
21	3.91572305	43.41520858	0.02303340	21
22	4.17869919	47.33093164	0.02112783	22
23	4.45933655	51.50963083	0.01941385	23
24	4.75882125	55.96896738	0.01786704	24
25	5.07841904	60.72778863	0.01646693	25
26	5.41948071	65.80620766	0.01519613	26
27	5.78344774	71.22568837	0.01403988	27
28	6.17185845	77.00913611	0.01298547	28
29	6.58635444	83.18099456	0.01202198	29
30	7.02868758	89.76734900	0.01113991	30
31	7.50072738	96.79603658	0.01033100	31
32	8.00446891	104.29676396	0.00958803	32
33	8.54204124	112.30123288	0.00890462	33
34	9.11571639	120.84327412	0.00827518	34
35	9.72791901	129.95899051	0.00769474	35
36	10.38123656	139.68690952	0.00715887	36
37	11.07843028	150.06814608	0.00666364	37
38	11.82244685	161.14657637	0.00620553	38
39	12.61643085	172.96902322	0.00578138	39
40	13.46373804	185.58545407	0.00538835	40
41	14.36794955	199.04919210	0.00502388	41
42	15.33288702	213.41714165	0.00468566	42
43	16.36262875	228.75002867	0.00437158	43
44	17.46152694	245.11265742	0.00407976	44
45	18.63422605	262.57418436	0.00380845	45
46	19.88568249	281.20841041	0.00355608	46
47	21.22118553	301.09409290	0.00332122	47
48	22.64637964	322.31527843	0.00310255	48
49	24.16728841	344.96165807	0.00289887	49
50	25.79033992	369.12894647	0.00270908	50

7.00%	Future Value of 1	Future Value of 1 per Period	Payment for Sinking Fund of 1	
Continuous				
Years				Years
1	1.07250818	1.00000000	1.00000000	1
2	1.15027380	2.07250818	0.48250714	2
3	1.23367806	3.22278198	0.31029092	3
4	1.32312981	4.45646004	0.22439335	4
5	1.41906755	5.77958985	0.17302266	5
6	1.52196156	7.19865740	0.13891479	6
7	1.63231622	8.72061896	0.11467076	7
8	1.75067250	10.35293518	0.09659097	8
9	1.87761058	12.10360768	0.08261999	9
10	2.01375271	13.98121826	0.07152453	10
11	2.15976625	15.99497096	0.06251965	11
12	2.31636698	18.15473722	0.05508204	12
13	2.48432253	20.47110419	0.04884934	13
14	2.66445624	22.95542673	0.04356268	14
15	2.85765112	25.61988297	0.03903218	15
16	3.06485420	28.47753409	0.03511540	16
17	3.28708121	31.54238829	0.03170337	17
18	3.52542149	34.82946950	0.02871132	18
19	3.78104339	38.35489099	0.02607229	19
20	4.05519997	42.13593437	0.02373271	20
21	4.34923514	46.19113434	0.02164918	21
22	4.66459027	50.54036948	0.01978616	22
23	5.00281123	55.20495975	0.01811431	23
24	5.36555597	60.20777098	0.01660915	24
25	5.75460268	65.57332695	0.01525010	25
26	6.17185845	71.32792963	0.01401975	26
27	6.61936868	77.49978808	0.01290326	27
28	7.09932707	84.11915676	0.01188790	28
29	7.61408636	91.21848382	0.01096269	29
30	8.16616991	98.83257018	0.01011812	30
31	8.75828404	106.99874009	0.00934590	31
32	9.39333129	115.75702414	0.00863878	32
33	10.07442466	125.15035542	0.00799039	33
34	10.80490286	135.22478008	0.00739509	34
35	11.58834672	146.02968294	0.00684792	35
36	12.42859666	157.61802966	0.00634445	36
37	13.32977160	170.04662632	0.00588074	37
38	14.29628910	183.37639793	0.00545326	38
39	15.33288702	197.67268703	0.00505887	39
40	16.44464677	213.00557405	0.00469471	40
41	17.63701820	229.45022082	0.00435824	41
42	18.91584631	247.08723902	0.00404715	42
43	20.28739993	266.00308533	0.00375935	43
44	21.75840240	286.29048525	0.00349296	44
45	23.33606458	308.04888765	0.00324624	45
46	25.02812018	331.38495223	0.00301764	46
47	26.84286366	356.41307241	0.00280573	47
48	28.78919088	383.25593607	0.00260922	48
49	30.87664275	412.04512695	0.00242692	49
50	33.11545196	442.92176970	0.00225774	50

	Future Value of 1	Future Value of 1 per Period	Payment for Sinking Fund of 1	**7.50%** Continuous
Years				Years
1	1.07788415	1.00000000	1.00000000	1
2	1.16183424	2.07788415	0.48125878	2
3	1.25232272	3.23971839	0.30866880	3
4	1.34985881	4.49204111	0.22261595	4
5	1.45499141	5.84189992	0.17117719	5
6	1.56831219	7.29689133	0.13704466	6
7	1.69045885	8.86520352	0.11280057	7
8	1.82211880	10.55566237	0.09473588	8
9	1.96403298	12.37778117	0.08078992	9
10	2.11700002	14.34181414	0.06972619	10
11	2.28188077	16.45881416	0.06075772	11
12	2.45960311	18.74069492	0.05335981	12
13	2.65116721	21.20029804	0.04716915	13
14	2.85765112	23.85146525	0.04192615	14
15	3.08021685	26.70911636	0.03744040	15
16	3.32011692	29.78933321	0.03356906	16
17	3.57870141	33.10945014	0.03020286	17
18	3.85742553	36.68815155	0.02725676	18
19	4.15785784	40.54557708	0.02466360	19
20	4.48168907	44.70343492	0.02236965	20
21	4.83074162	49.18512399	0.02033135	21
22	5.20697983	54.01586561	0.01851308	22
23	5.61252103	59.22284544	0.01688538	23
24	6.04964746	64.83536646	0.01542368	24
25	6.52081912	70.88501393	0.01410735	25
26	7.02868758	77.40583305	0.01291892	26
27	7.57611094	84.43452063	0.01184350	27
28	8.16616991	92.01063157	0.01086831	28
29	8.80218512	100.17680149	0.00998235	29
30	9.48773584	108.97898661	0.00917608	30
31	10.22668009	118.46672245	0.00844119	31
32	11.02317638	128.69340253	0.00777041	32
33	11.88170711	139.71657891	0.00715735	33
34	12.80710378	151.59828603	0.00659638	34
35	13.80457419	164.40538981	0.00608253	35
36	14.87973172	178.20996399	0.00561136	36
37	16.03862700	193.08969572	0.00517894	37
38	17.28778184	209.12832271	0.00478175	38
39	18.63422605	226.41610456	0.00441665	39
40	20.08553692	245.05033061	0.00408079	40
41	21.64988191	265.13586753	0.00377165	41
42	23.33606458	286.78574944	0.00348692	42
43	25.15357416	310.12181402	0.00322454	43
44	27.11263892	335.27538818	0.00298262	44
45	29.22428378	362.38802710	0.00275947	45
46	31.50039231	391.61231088	0.00255355	46
47	33.95377362	423.11270319	0.00236344	47
48	36.59823444	457.06647680	0.00218787	48
49	39.44865686	493.66471125	0.00202567	49
50	42.52108200	533.11336810	0.00187577	50

8.00%	Future Value of 1	Future Value of 1 per Period	Payment for Sinking Fund of 1	
Continuous				
Years				Years
1	1.08328707	1.00000000	1.00000000	1
2	1.17351087	2.08328707	0.48001066	2
3	1.27124915	3.25679794	0.30705006	3
4	1.37712776	4.52804709	0.22084576	4
5	1.49182470	5.90517485	0.16934300	5
6	1.61607440	7.39699955	0.13518995	6
7	1.75067250	9.01307395	0.11094994	7
8	1.89648088	10.76374645	0.09290446	8
9	2.05443321	12.66022733	0.07898752	9
10	2.22554093	14.71466054	0.06795943	10
11	2.41089971	16.94020147	0.05903118	11
12	2.61169647	19.35110118	0.05167665	12
13	2.82921701	21.96279765	0.04553154	13
14	3.06485420	24.79201467	0.04033557	14
15	3.32011692	27.85686887	0.03589779	15
16	3.59663973	31.17698579	0.03207494	16
17	3.89619330	34.77362552	0.02875743	17
18	4.22069582	38.66981882	0.02585996	18
19	4.57222520	42.89051464	0.02331518	19
20	4.95303242	47.46273983	0.02106916	20
21	5.36555597	52.41577226	0.01907823	21
22	5.81243739	57.78132823	0.01730663	22
23	6.29653826	63.59376562	0.01572481	23
24	6.82095847	69.89030388	0.01430814	24
25	7.38905610	76.71126235	0.01303590	25
26	8.00446891	84.10031845	0.01189056	26
27	8.67113766	92.10478737	0.01085720	27
28	9.39333129	100.77592502	0.00992300	28
29	10.17567431	110.16925631	0.00907694	29
30	11.02317638	120.34493062	0.00830945	30
31	11.94126442	131.36810700	0.00761220	31
32	12.93581732	143.30937142	0.00697791	32
33	14.01320361	156.24518873	0.00640020	33
34	15.18032224	170.25839234	0.00587343	34
35	16.44464677	185.43871458	0.00539262	35
36	17.81427318	201.88336135	0.00495336	36
37	19.29797176	219.69763453	0.00455171	37
38	20.90524324	238.99560629	0.00418418	38
39	22.64637964	259.90084953	0.00384762	39
40	24.53253020	282.54722917	0.00353923	40
41	26.57577270	307.07975937	0.00325648	41
42	28.78919088	333.65553207	0.00299710	42
43	31.18695817	362.44472294	0.00275904	43
44	33.78442846	393.63168111	0.00254045	44
45	36.59823444	427.41610958	0.00233964	45
46	39.64639407	464.01434402	0.00215511	46
47	42.94842598	503.66073809	0.00198546	47
48	46.52547444	546.60916407	0.00182946	48
49	50.40044478	593.13463851	0.00168596	49
50	54.59815003	643.53508329	0.00155392	50

Years	Future Value of 1	Future Value of 1 per Period	Payment for Sinking Fund of 1	**8.50%** Continuous Years
1	1.08871707	1.00000000	1.00000000	1
2	1.18530485	2.08871707	0.47876279	2
3	1.29046162	3.27402192	0.30543473	3
4	1.40494759	4.56448354	0.21908284	4
5	1.52959042	5.96943113	0.16752015	5
6	1.66529119	7.49902155	0.13335073	6
7	1.81303094	9.16431274	0.10911893	7
8	1.97387773	10.97734369	0.09109672	8
9	2.14899437	12.95122142	0.07721279	9
10	2.33964685	15.10021580	0.06622422	10
11	2.54721346	17.43986265	0.05733990	11
12	2.77319476	19.98707611	0.05003233	12
13	3.01922447	22.76027087	0.04393621	13
14	3.28708121	25.77949534	0.03879052	14
15	3.57870141	29.06657655	0.03440378	15
16	3.89619330	32.64527796	0.03063230	16
17	4.24185214	36.54147126	0.02736617	17
18	4.61817682	40.78332340	0.02451983	18
19	5.02788792	45.40150022	0.02202570	19
20	5.47394739	50.42938815	0.01982971	20
21	5.95957995	55.90333554	0.01788802	21
22	6.48829640	61.86291549	0.01616477	22
23	7.06391902	68.35121188	0.01463032	23
24	7.69060920	75.41513091	0.01325994	24
25	8.37289749	83.10574011	0.01203286	25
26	9.11571639	91.47863760	0.01093151	26
27	9.92443601	100.59435399	0.00994092	27
28	10.80490286	110.51879000	0.00904824	28
29	11.76348215	121.32369286	0.00824241	29
30	12.80710378	133.08717502	0.00751387	30
31	13.94331246	145.89427880	0.00685428	31
32	15.18032224	159.83759126	0.00625635	32
33	16.52707591	175.01791351	0.00571370	33
34	17.99330960	191.54498941	0.00522071	34
35	19.58962325	209.53829902	0.00477240	35
36	21.32755716	229.12792226	0.00436437	36
37	23.21967547	250.45547943	0.00399273	37
38	25.27965697	273.67515490	0.00365397	38
39	27.52239398	298.95481187	0.00334499	39
40	29.96410005	326.47720586	0.00306300	40
41	32.62242711	356.44130590	0.00280551	41
42	35.51659315	389.06373301	0.00257027	42
43	38.66752112	424.58032616	0.00235527	43
44	42.09799016	463.24784728	0.00215867	44
45	45.83280037	505.34583744	0.00197884	45
46	49.89895197	551.17863781	0.00181429	46
47	54.32584062	601.07758978	0.00166368	47
48	59.14546985	655.40343041	0.00152578	48
49	64.39268244	714.54890026	0.00139948	49
50	70.10541235	778.94158270	0.00128379	50

9.00%	Future Value of 1	Future Value of 1 per Period	Payment for Sinking Fund of 1	
Continuous				
Years				Years
1	1.09417428	1.00000000	1.00000000	1
2	1.19721736	2.09417428	0.47751518	2
3	1.30996445	3.29139165	0.30382285	3
4	1.43332941	4.60135610	0.21732724	4
5	1.56831219	6.03468551	0.16570872	5
6	1.71600686	7.60299770	0.13152707	6
7	1.87761058	9.31900456	0.10730760	7
8	2.05443321	11.19661514	0.08931271	8
9	2.24790799	13.25104835	0.07546573	9
10	2.45960311	15.49895634	0.06452047	10
11	2.69123447	17.95855945	0.05568375	11
12	2.94467955	20.64979392	0.04842663	12
13	3.22199264	23.59447347	0.04238281	13
14	3.52542149	26.81646611	0.03729052	14
15	3.85742553	30.34188760	0.03295774	15
16	4.22069582	34.19931313	0.02924035	16
17	4.61817682	38.42000894	0.02602810	17
18	5.05309032	43.03818577	0.02323518	18
19	5.52896148	48.09127608	0.02079379	19
20	6.04964746	53.62023756	0.01864967	20
21	6.61936868	59.66988503	0.01675887	21
22	7.24274299	66.28925371	0.01508540	22
23	7.92482312	73.53199669	0.01359952	23
24	8.67113766	81.45681981	0.01227644	24
25	9.48773584	90.12795747	0.01109534	25
26	10.38123656	99.61569330	0.01003858	26
27	11.35888208	109.99692987	0.00909116	27
28	12.42859666	121.35581195	0.00824023	28
29	13.59905085	133.78440861	0.00747471	29
30	14.87973172	147.38345946	0.00678502	30
31	16.28101980	162.26319119	0.00616283	31
32	17.81427318	178.54421099	0.00560085	32
33	19.49191960	196.35848417	0.00509273	33
34	21.32755716	215.85040376	0.00463284	34
35	23.33606458	237.17796093	0.00421624	35
36	25.53372175	260.51402551	0.00383856	36
37	27.93834170	286.04774726	0.00349592	37
38	30.56941502	313.98608896	0.00318485	38
39	33.44826778	344.55550398	0.00290229	39
40	36.59823444	378.00377176	0.00264548	40
41	40.04484696	414.60200621	0.00241195	41
42	43.81604174	454.64685316	0.00219951	42
43	47.94238608	498.46289490	0.00200617	43
44	52.45732595	546.40528098	0.00183014	44
45	57.39745705	598.86260693	0.00166983	45
46	62.80282145	656.26006398	0.00152379	46
47	68.71723217	719.06288542	0.00139070	47
48	75.18862829	787.78011760	0.00126939	48
49	82.26946350	862.96874589	0.00115879	49
50	90.01713130	945.23820939	0.00105793	50

	Future Value of 1	Future Value of 1 per Period	Payment for Sinking Fund of 1	**9.50%** Continuous
Years				Years
1	1.09965886	1.00000000	1.00000000	1
2	1.20924960	2.09965886	0.47626785	2
3	1.32976203	3.30890845	0.30221447	3
4	1.46228459	4.63867048	0.21557901	4
5	1.60801420	6.10095507	0.16390876	5
6	1.76826705	7.70896927	0.12971903	6
7	1.94449052	9.47723632	0.10551599	7
8	2.13827622	11.42172684	0.08755244	8
9	2.35137438	13.56000306	0.07374630	9
10	2.58570966	15.91137744	0.06284811	10
11	2.84339852	18.49708710	0.05406257	11
12	3.12676837	21.34048562	0.04685929	12
13	3.43837852	24.46725399	0.04087095	13
14	3.78104339	27.90563251	0.03583506	14
15	4.15785784	31.68667590	0.03155901	15
16	4.57222520	35.84453374	0.02789826	16
17	5.02788792	40.41675894	0.02474221	17
18	5.52896148	45.44464686	0.02200479	18
19	6.07997145	50.97360834	0.01961800	19
20	6.68589444	57.05357979	0.01752738	20
21	7.35220303	63.73947423	0.01568886	21
22	8.08491516	71.09167726	0.01406634	22
23	8.89064855	79.17659242	0.01263000	23
24	9.77668041	88.06724097	0.01135496	24
25	10.75101319	97.84392138	0.01022036	25
26	11.82244685	108.59493457	0.00920853	26
27	13.00056837	120.41738142	0.00830445	27
28	14.29628910	133.41803979	0.00749524	28
29	15.72104090	147.71432889	0.00676982	29
30	17.28778184	163.43536979	0.00611863	30
31	19.01066239	180.72315163	0.00553333	31
32	20.90524324	199.73381402	0.00500666	32
33	22.98863584	220.63905725	0.00453229	33
34	25.27965697	243.62769310	0.00410462	34
35	27.79899864	268.90735007	0.00371875	35
36	30.56941502	296.70634871	0.00337034	36
37	33.61592792	327.27576373	0.00305553	37
38	36.96605281	360.89169165	0.00277091	38
39	40.65004732	397.85774447	0.00251346	39
40	44.70118449	438.50779179	0.00228046	40
41	49.15605336	483.20897628	0.00206950	41
42	54.05488936	532.36502964	0.00187841	42
43	59.44193775	586.41991901	0.00170526	43
44	65.36585321	645.86185676	0.00154832	44
45	71.88013931	711.22770997	0.00140602	45
46	79.04363170	783.10784928	0.00127696	46
47	86.92102954	862.15148098	0.00115989	47
48	95.58347983	949.07251052	0.00105366	48
49	105.10922000	1044.65599035	0.00095725	49
50	115.58428453	1149.76521035	0.00086974	50

10.00% Continuous	Future Value of 1	Future Value of 1 per Period	Payment for Sinking Fund of 1	
Years				Years
1	1.10517092	1.00000000	1.00000000	1
2	1.22140276	2.10517092	0.47502081	2
3	1.34985881	3.32657368	0.30060961	3
4	1.49182470	4.67643248	0.21383822	4
5	1.64872127	6.16825718	0.16212035	5
6	1.82211880	7.81697845	0.12792667	6
7	2.01375271	9.63909725	0.10374416	7
8	2.22554093	11.65284996	0.08581592	8
9	2.45960311	13.87839089	0.07205446	9
10	2.71828183	16.33799400	0.06120702	10
11	3.00416602	19.05627583	0.05247615	11
12	3.32011692	22.06044185	0.04533001	12
13	3.66929667	25.38055877	0.03940024	13
14	4.05519997	29.04985544	0.03442358	14
15	4.48168907	33.10505541	0.03020687	15
16	4.95303242	37.58674448	0.02660512	16
17	5.47394739	42.53977690	0.02350741	17
18	6.04964746	48.01372430	0.02082738	18
19	6.68589444	54.06337176	0.01849681	19
20	7.38905610	60.74926620	0.01646110	20
21	8.16616991	68.13832230	0.01467603	21
22	9.02501350	76.30449221	0.01310539	22
23	9.97418245	85.32950571	0.01171928	23
24	11.02317638	95.30368817	0.01049277	24
25	12.18249396	106.32686455	0.00940496	25
26	13.46373804	118.50935851	0.00843815	26
27	14.87973172	131.97309654	0.00757730	27
28	16.44464677	146.85282827	0.00680954	28
29	18.17414537	163.29747504	0.00612379	29
30	20.08553692	181.47162041	0.00551050	30
31	22.19795128	201.55715733	0.00496137	31
32	24.53253020	223.75510861	0.00446917	32
33	27.11263892	248.28763881	0.00402759	33
34	29.96410005	275.40027773	0.00363108	34
35	33.11545196	305.36437778	0.00327478	35
36	36.59823444	338.47982974	0.00295439	36
37	40.44730436	375.07806418	0.00266611	37
38	44.70118449	415.52536854	0.00240659	38
39	49.40244911	460.22655304	0.00217284	39
40	54.59815003	509.62900214	0.00196221	40
41	60.34028760	564.22715217	0.00177234	41
42	66.68633104	624.56743977	0.00160111	42
43	73.69979370	691.25377081	0.00144665	43
44	81.45086866	764.95356451	0.00130727	44
45	90.01713130	846.40443318	0.00118147	45
46	99.48431564	936.42156448	0.00106790	46
47	109.94717245	1035.90588012	0.00096534	47
48	121.51041752	1145.85305257	0.00087271	48
49	134.28977968	1267.36347009	0.00078904	49
50	148.41315910	1401.65324978	0.00071344	50

	Future Value of 1	Future Value of 1 per Period	Payment for Sinking Fund of 1	**10.50%** Continuous
Years				Years
1	1.11071061	1.00000000	1.00000000	1
2	1.23367806	2.11071061	0.47377409	2
3	1.37025931	3.34438867	0.29900831	3
4	1.52196156	4.71464798	0.21210491	4
5	1.69045885	6.23660954	0.16034353	5
6	1.87761058	7.92706839	0.12615004	6
7	2.08548199	9.80467896	0.10199212	7
8	2.31636698	11.89016096	0.08410315	8
9	2.57281338	14.20652793	0.07039018	9
10	2.85765112	16.77934131	0.05959710	10
11	3.17402342	19.63699243	0.05092430	11
12	3.52542149	22.81101585	0.04383847	12
13	3.91572305	26.33643734	0.03797021	13
14	4.34923514	30.25216039	0.03305549	14
15	4.83074162	34.60139553	0.02890057	15
16	5.36555597	39.43213715	0.02536003	16
17	5.95957995	44.79769312	0.02232258	17
18	6.61936868	50.75727307	0.01970161	18
19	7.35220303	57.37664175	0.01742870	19
20	8.16616991	64.72884477	0.01544906	20
21	9.07025157	72.89501469	0.01371836	21
22	10.07442466	81.96526625	0.01220029	22
23	11.18977036	92.03969091	0.01086488	23
24	12.42859666	103.22946127	0.00968716	24
25	13.80457419	115.65805793	0.00864618	25
26	15.33288702	129.46263212	0.00772424	26
27	17.03040030	144.79551914	0.00690629	27
28	18.91584631	161.82591944	0.00617948	28
29	21.01003120	180.74176575	0.00553276	29
30	23.33606458	201.75179695	0.00495659	30
31	25.91961453	225.08786153	0.00444271	31
32	28.78919088	251.00747607	0.00398395	32
33	31.97645977	279.79666695	0.00357402	33
34	35.51659315	311.77312672	0.00320746	34
35	39.44865686	347.28971987	0.00287944	35
36	43.81604174	386.73837673	0.00258573	36
37	48.66694246	430.55441846	0.00232259	37
38	54.05488936	479.22136092	0.00208672	38
39	60.03933916	533.27625029	0.00187520	39
40	66.68633104	593.31558944	0.00168544	40
41	74.06921545	660.00192049	0.00151515	41
42	82.26946350	734.07113594	0.00136227	42
43	91.37756602	816.34059944	0.00122498	43
44	101.49403213	907.71816546	0.00110166	44
45	112.73049837	1009.21219759	0.00099087	45
46	125.21096065	1121.94269597	0.00089131	46
47	139.07314253	1247.15365662	0.00080183	47
48	154.47001503	1386.22679916	0.00072138	48
49	171.57148467	1540.69681418	0.00064906	49
50	190.56626846	1712.26829885	0.00058402	50

11.00% Continuous	Future Value of 1	Future Value of 1 per Period	Payment for Sinking Fund of 1	
Years				Years
1	1.11627807	1.00000000	1.00000000	1
2	1.24607673	2.11627807	0.47252770	2
3	1.39096813	3.36235480	0.29741061	3
4	1.55270722	4.75332293	0.21037914	4
5	1.73325302	6.30603015	0.15857837	5
6	1.93479233	8.03928317	0.12438920	6
7	2.15976625	9.97407550	0.10025992	7
8	2.41089971	12.13384175	0.08241413	8
9	2.69123447	14.54474146	0.06875337	9
10	3.00416602	17.23597593	0.05801818	10
11	3.35348465	20.24014196	0.04940677	11
12	3.74342138	23.59362661	0.04238433	12
13	4.17869919	27.33704799	0.03658039	13
14	4.66459027	31.51574718	0.03173017	14
15	5.20697983	36.18033745	0.02763932	15
16	5.81243739	41.38731728	0.02416199	16
17	6.48829640	47.19975467	0.02118655	17
18	7.24274299	53.68805107	0.01862612	18
19	8.08491516	60.93079406	0.01641206	19
20	9.02501350	69.01570922	0.01448945	20
21	10.07442466	78.04072272	0.01281382	21
22	11.24585931	88.11514737	0.01134809	22
23	12.55350614	99.36100669	0.01006431	23
24	14.01320361	111.91451283	0.00893539	24
25	15.64263188	125.92771643	0.00794106	25
26	17.46152694	141.57034832	0.00706363	26
27	19.49191960	159.03187525	0.00628805	27
28	21.75840240	178.52379485	0.00560149	28
29	24.28842744	200.28219725	0.00499296	29
30	27.11263892	224.57062469	0.00445294	30
31	30.26524426	251.68326361	0.00397325	31
32	33.78442846	281.94850787	0.00354675	32
33	37.71281662	315.73293633	0.00316723	33
34	42.09799016	353.44575295	0.00282929	34
35	46.99306323	395.54374312	0.00252817	35
36	52.45732595	442.53680635	0.00225970	36
37	58.55696259	494.99413230	0.00202023	37
38	65.36585321	553.55109489	0.00180652	38
39	72.96646850	618.91694810	0.00161573	39
40	81.45086866	691.88341660	0.00144533	40
41	90.92181851	773.33428527	0.00129310	41
42	101.49403213	864.25610378	0.00115706	42
43	113.29556235	965.75013591	0.00103546	43
44	126.46935173	1079.04569826	0.00092674	44
45	141.17496392	1205.51504999	0.00082952	45
46	157.59051632	1346.69001391	0.00074256	46
47	175.91483748	1504.28053023	0.00066477	47
48	196.36987535	1680.19536771	0.00059517	48
49	219.20338555	1876.56524307	0.00053289	49
50	244.69193226	2095.76862862	0.00047715	50

Years	Future Value of 1	Future Value of 1 per Period	Payment for Sinking Fund of 1	Years
1	1.12187344	1.00000000	1.00000000	1
2	1.25860001	2.12187344	0.47128164	2
3	1.41198992	3.38047345	0.29581655	3
4	1.58407398	4.79246337	0.20866096	4
5	1.77713053	6.37653735	0.15682493	5
6	1.99371553	8.15366788	0.12264419	6
7	2.23669650	10.14738341	0.09854757	7
8	2.50929039	12.38407991	0.08074883	8
9	2.81510624	14.89337030	0.06714397	9
10	3.15819291	17.70847654	0.05647013	10
11	3.54309274	20.86666945	0.04792332	11
12	3.97490163	24.40976218	0.04096722	12
13	4.45933655	28.38466381	0.03523029	13
14	5.00281123	32.84400036	0.03044696	14
15	5.61252103	37.84681159	0.02642231	15
16	6.29653826	43.45933262	0.02301002	16
17	7.06391902	49.75587088	0.02009813	17
18	7.92482312	56.81978991	0.01759950	18
19	8.89064855	64.74461302	0.01544530	19
20	9.97418245	73.63526158	0.01358045	20
21	11.18977036	83.60944403	0.01196037	21
22	12.55350614	94.79921439	0.01054861	22
23	14.08344508	107.35272053	0.00931509	23
24	15.79984295	121.43616561	0.00823478	24
25	17.72542412	137.23600856	0.00728672	25
26	19.88568249	154.96143268	0.00645322	26
27	22.30921898	174.84711517	0.00571928	27
28	25.02812018	197.15633415	0.00507212	28
29	28.07838322	222.18445433	0.00450076	29
30	31.50039231	250.26283755	0.00399580	30
31	35.33945340	281.76322986	0.00354908	31
32	39.64639407	317.10268326	0.00315355	32
33	44.47823641	356.74907734	0.00280309	33
34	49.89895197	401.22731374	0.00249235	34
35	55.98030878	451.12626571	0.00221667	35
36	62.80282145	507.10657450	0.00197197	36
37	70.45681719	569.90939595	0.00175466	37
38	79.04363170	640.36621313	0.00156161	38
39	88.67695081	719.40984483	0.00139003	39
40	99.48431564	808.08679565	0.00123749	40
41	111.60881117	907.57111129	0.00110184	41
42	125.21096065	1019.17992246	0.00098118	42
43	140.47085085	1144.39088312	0.00087383	43
44	157.59051632	1284.86173397	0.00077829	44
45	176.79661428	1442.45225029	0.00069326	45
46	198.34342541	1619.24886457	0.00061757	46
47	222.51622048	1817.59228998	0.00055018	47
48	249.63503719	2040.10851046	0.00049017	48
49	280.05891731	2289.74354765	0.00043673	49
50	314.19066029	2569.80246496	0.00038913	50

12.00%	Future Value of 1	Future Value of 1 per Period	Payment for Sinking Fund of 1	
Continuous				
Years				Years
1	1.12749685	1.00000000	1.00000000	1
2	1.27124915	2.12749685	0.47003595	2
3	1.43332941	3.39874600	0.29422616	3
4	1.61607440	4.83207542	0.20695041	4
5	1.82211880	6.44814982	0.15508325	5
6	2.05443321	8.27026862	0.12091506	6
7	2.31636698	10.32470183	0.09685510	7
8	2.61169647	12.64106881	0.07910723	8
9	2.94467955	15.25276508	0.06556188	9
10	3.32011692	18.19744483	0.05495277	10
11	3.74342138	21.51756175	0.04647367	11
12	4.22069582	25.26098313	0.03958674	12
13	4.75882125	29.48167895	0.03391937	13
14	5.36555597	34.24050019	0.02920518	14
15	6.04964746	39.60605616	0.02524866	15
16	6.82095847	45.65570363	0.02190307	16
17	7.69060920	52.47666210	0.01905609	17
18	8.67113766	60.16727130	0.01662033	18
19	9.77668041	68.83840896	0.01452677	19
20	11.02317638	78.61508936	0.01272020	20
21	12.42859666	89.63826575	0.01115595	21
22	14.01320361	102.06686241	0.00979750	22
23	15.79984295	116.08006602	0.00861474	23
24	17.81427318	131.87990897	0.00758266	24
25	20.08553692	149.69418214	0.00668029	25
26	22.64637964	169.77971907	0.00588999	26
27	25.53372175	192.42609871	0.00519680	27
28	28.78919088	217.95982046	0.00458800	28
29	32.45972208	246.74901134	0.00405270	29
30	36.59823444	279.20873341	0.00358155	30
31	41.26439411	315.80696786	0.00316649	31
32	46.52547444	357.07136197	0.00280056	32
33	52.45732595	403.59683641	0.00247772	33
34	59.14546985	456.05416235	0.00219272	34
35	66.68633104	515.19963220	0.00194100	35
36	75.18862829	581.88596625	0.00171855	36
37	84.77494167	657.07459154	0.00152190	37
38	95.58347983	741.84953321	0.00134798	38
39	107.77007257	837.43301304	0.00119413	39
40	121.51041752	945.20308561	0.00105797	40
41	137.00261319	1066.71350313	0.00093746	41
42	154.47001503	1203.71611632	0.00083076	42
43	174.16445561	1358.18613134	0.00073628	43
44	196.36987535	1532.35058695	0.00065259	44
45	221.40641620	1728.72046230	0.00057846	45
46	249.63503719	1950.12687850	0.00051279	46
47	281.46271848	2199.76191569	0.00045459	47
48	317.34832892	2481.22463417	0.00040303	48
49	357.80924171	2798.57296309	0.00035732	49
50	403.42879349	3156.38220480	0.00031682	50

	Future Value of 1	Future Value of 1 per Period	Payment for Sinking Fund of 1	**12.50%** Continuous
Years				Years
1	1.13314845	1.00000000	1.00000000	1
2	1.28402542	2.13314845	0.46879063	2
3	1.45499141	3.41717387	0.29263948	3
4	1.64872127	4.87216528	0.20524755	4
5	1.86824596	6.52088656	0.15335338	5
6	2.11700002	8.38913251	0.11920184	6
7	2.39887529	10.50613253	0.09518250	7
8	2.71828183	12.90500782	0.07748930	8
9	3.08021685	15.62328965	0.06400701	9
10	3.49034296	18.70350650	0.05346591	10
11	3.95507672	22.19384946	0.04505753	11
12	4.48168907	26.14892618	0.03824249	12
13	5.07841904	30.63061525	0.03264708	13
14	5.75460268	35.70903429	0.02800412	14
15	6.52081912	41.46363696	0.02411752	15
16	7.38905610	47.98445608	0.02084008	16
17	8.37289749	55.37351218	0.01805918	17
18	9.48773584	63.74640967	0.01568716	18
19	10.75101319	73.23414551	0.01365483	19
20	12.18249396	83.98515869	0.01190687	20
21	13.80457419	96.16765265	0.01039851	21
22	15.64263188	109.97222684	0.00909320	22
23	17.72542412	125.61485873	0.00796084	23
24	20.08553692	143.34028285	0.00697641	24
25	22.75989509	163.42581977	0.00611898	25
26	25.79033992	186.18571486	0.00537098	26
27	29.22428378	211.97605478	0.00471751	27
28	33.11545196	241.20033856	0.00414593	28
29	37.52472316	274.31579052	0.00364543	29
30	42.52108200	311.84051368	0.00320677	30
31	48.18269829	354.36159568	0.00282198	31
32	54.59815003	402.54429397	0.00248420	32
33	61.86780925	457.14244400	0.00218750	33
34	70.10541235	519.01025325	0.00192674	34
35	79.43983955	589.11566560	0.00169746	35
36	90.01713130	668.55550515	0.00149576	36
37	102.00277308	758.57263645	0.00131827	37
38	115.58428453	860.57540954	0.00116201	38
39	130.97415321	976.15969406	0.00102442	39
40	148.41315910	1107.13384727	0.00090323	40
41	168.17414165	1255.54700638	0.00079647	41
42	190.56626846	1423.72114803	0.00070238	42
43	215.93987231	1614.28741649	0.00061947	43
44	244.69193226	1830.22728880	0.00054638	44
45	277.27228452	2074.91922106	0.00048195	45
46	314.19066029	2352.19150559	0.00042514	46
47	356.02466067	2666.38216587	0.00037504	47
48	403.42879349	3022.40682654	0.00033086	48
49	457.14471327	3425.83562004	0.00029190	49
50	518.01282467	3882.98033330	0.00025753	50

13.00%
Continuous

Years	Future Value of 1	Future Value of 1 per Period	Payment for Sinking Fund of 1	Years
1	1.13882838	1.00000000	1.00000000	1
2	1.29693009	2.13882838	0.46754569	2
3	1.47698079	3.43575847	0.29105655	3
4	1.68202765	4.91273926	0.20355243	4
5	1.91554083	6.59476691	0.15163538	5
6	2.18147227	8.51030774	0.11750456	6
7	2.48432253	10.69178001	0.09352980	7
8	2.82921701	13.17610254	0.07589498	8
9	3.22199264	16.00531956	0.06247923	9
10	3.66929667	19.22731219	0.05200935	10
11	4.17869919	22.89660886	0.04367459	11
12	4.75882125	27.07530805	0.03693402	12
13	5.41948071	31.83412930	0.03141283	13
14	6.17185845	37.25361000	0.02684304	14
15	7.02868758	43.42546845	0.02302796	15
16	8.00446891	50.45415603	0.01901997	16
17	9.11571639	58.45862495	0.01710612	17
18	10.38123656	67.57434134	0.01479852	18
19	11.82244685	77.95557790	0.01282782	19
20	13.46373804	89.77802476	0.01113858	20
21	15.33288702	103.24176279	0.00968600	21
22	17.46152694	118.57464981	0.00843351	22
23	19.88568249	136.03617675	0.00735099	23
24	22.64637964	155.92185924	0.00641347	24
25	25.79033992	178.56823888	0.00560010	25
26	29.37077111	204.35857880	0.00489336	26
27	33.44826778	233.72934991	0.00427845	27
28	38.09183673	267.17761770	0.00374283	28
29	43.38006484	305.26945442	0.00327579	29
30	49.40244911	348.64951926	0.00286821	30
31	56.26091125	398.05196836	0.00251223	31
32	64.07152260	454.31287961	0.00220113	32
33	72.96646850	518.38440221	0.00192907	33
34	83.09628536	591.35087071	0.00169104	34
35	94.63240831	674.44715607	0.00148270	35
36	107.77007257	769.07956438	0.00130026	36
37	122.73161752	876.84963696	0.00114045	37
38	139.77024956	999.58125447	0.00100042	38
39	159.17432734	1139.35150403	0.00087769	39
40	181.27224188	1298.52583138	0.00077010	40
41	206.43797416	1479.79807325	0.00067577	41
42	235.09742437	1686.23604741	0.00059304	42
43	267.73561971	1921.33347177	0.00052047	43
44	304.90492296	2189.06909149	0.00045682	44
45	347.23438048	2493.97401444	0.00040097	45
46	395.44036816	2841.20839492	0.00035196	46
47	450.33871517	3236.64876308	0.00030896	47
48	512.85851094	3686.98747824	0.00027122	48
49	584.05782889	4199.84598919	0.00023810	49
50	665.14163304	4783.90381808	0.00020903	50

	Future Value of 1	Future Value of 1 per Period	Payment for Sinking Fund of 1	**14.00%** Continuous
Years				Years
1	1.15027380	1.00000000	1.00000000	1
2	1.32312981	2.15027380	0.46505705	2
3	1.52196156	3.47340361	0.28790204	3
4	1.75067250	4.99536517	0.20018557	4
5	2.01375271	6.74603767	0.14823516	5
6	2.31636698	8.75979037	0.11415798	6
7	2.66445624	11.07615735	0.09028402	7
8	3.06485420	13.74061359	0.07277695	8
9	3.52542149	16.80546780	0.05950444	9
10	4.05519997	20.33088928	0.04918624	10
11	4.66459027	24.38608925	0.04100699	11
12	5.36555597	29.05067952	0.03442260	12
13	6.17185845	34.41623549	0.02905605	13
14	7.09932707	40.58809394	0.02463777	14
15	8.16616991	47.68742101	0.02096989	15
16	9.39333129	55.85359092	0.01790395	16
17	10.80490286	65.24692221	0.01532639	17
18	12.42859666	76.05182507	0.01314893	18
19	14.29628910	88.48042174	0.01130194	19
20	16.44464677	102.77671083	0.00972983	20
21	18.91584631	119.22135761	0.00838776	21
22	21.75840240	138.13720392	0.00723918	22
23	25.02812018	159.89560631	0.00625408	23
24	28.78919088	184.92372650	0.00540763	24
25	33.11545196	213.71291737	0.00467917	25
26	38.09183673	246.82836933	0.00405140	26
27	43.81604174	284.92020606	0.00350975	27
28	50.40044478	328.73624779	0.00304195	28
29	57.97431108	379.13669257	0.00263757	29
30	66.68633104	437.11100365	0.00228775	30
31	76.70753934	503.79733469	0.00198493	31
32	88.23467268	580.50487403	0.00172264	32
33	101.49403213	668.73954671	0.00149535	33
34	116.74592590	770.23357884	0.00129831	34
35	134.28977968	886.97950473	0.00112742	35
36	154.47001503	1021.26928442	0.00097917	36
37	177.68281099	1175.73929945	0.00085053	37
38	204.38388199	1353.42211044	0.00073887	38
39	235.09742437	1557.80599243	0.00064193	39
40	270.42640743	1792.90341680	0.00055775	40
41	311.06441098	2063.32982422	0.00048465	41
42	357.80924171	2374.39423520	0.00042116	42
43	411.57859573	2732.20347691	0.00036600	43
44	473.42807483	3143.78207264	0.00031809	44
45	544.57191013	3617.21014747	0.00027646	45
46	626.40679981	4161.78205760	0.00024028	46
47	720.53932925	4788.18885741	0.00020885	47
48	828.81751148	5508.72818666	0.00018153	48
49	953.36706749	6337.54569814	0.00015779	49
50	1096.63315843	7290.91276563	0.00013716	50

15.00% **Continuous**	Future Value of 1	Future Value of 1 per Period	Payment for Sinking Fund of 1	
Years				Years
1	1.16183424	1.00000000	1.00000000	1
2	1.34985881	2.16183424	0.46257015	2
3	1.56831219	3.51169305	0.28476293	3
4	1.82211880	5.08000524	0.19685019	4
5	2.11700002	6.90212404	0.14488294	5
6	2.45960311	9.01912405	0.11087551	6
7	2.85765112	11.47872716	0.08711767	7
8	3.32011692	14.33637828	0.06975262	8
9	3.85742553	17.65649520	0.05663638	9
10	4.48168907	21.51392074	0.04648153	10
11	5.20697983	25.99560981	0.03846803	11
12	6.04964746	31.20258963	0.03204862	12
13	7.02868758	37.25223710	0.02684403	13
14	8.16616991	44.28092468	0.02258309	14
15	9.48773584	52.44709459	0.01906683	15
16	11.02317638	61.93483043	0.01614600	16
17	12.80710378	72.95800681	0.01370651	17
18	14.87973172	85.76511059	0.01165975	18
19	17.28778184	100.64484232	0.00993593	19
20	20.08553692	117.93262416	0.00847942	20
21	23.33606458	138.01816108	0.00724542	21
22	27.11263892	161.35422566	0.00619754	22
23	31.50039231	188.46686458	0.00530597	23
24	36.59823444	219.96725689	0.00454613	24
25	42.52108200	256.56549133	0.00389764	25
26	49.40244911	299.08657333	0.00334351	26
27	57.39745705	348.48902244	0.00286953	27
28	66.68633104	405.88647948	0.00246374	28
29	77.47846293	472.57281052	0.00211608	29
30	90.01713130	550.05127345	0.00181801	30
31	104.58498558	640.06840475	0.00156233	31
32	121.51041752	744.65339033	0.00134291	32
33	141.17496392	866.16380785	0.00115452	33
34	164.02190730	1007.33872177	0.00099271	34
35	190.56626846	1171.36067907	0.00085371	35
36	221.40641620	1361.92694753	0.00073425	36
37	257.23755591	1583.33336373	0.00063158	37
38	298.86740097	1840.57091964	0.00054331	38
39	347.23438048	2139.43832060	0.00046741	39
40	403.42879349	2486.67270108	0.00040214	40
41	468.71738678	2890.10149457	0.00034601	41
42	544.57191013	3358.81888136	0.00029772	42
43	632.70229281	3903.39079148	0.00025619	43
44	735.09518924	4536.09308430	0.00022045	44
45	854.05876253	5271.18827354	0.00018971	45
46	992.27471561	6125.24703606	0.00016326	46
47	1152.85874278	7117.52175167	0.00014050	47
48	1339.43076439	8270.38049445	0.00012091	48
49	1556.19652784	9609.81125885	0.00010406	49
50	1808.04241446	11166.00778668	0.00008956	50

	Future Value of 1	Future Value of 1 per Period	Payment for Sinking Fund of 1	**16.00%** Continuous
Years				Years
1	1.17351087	1.00000000	1.00000000	1
2	1.37712776	2.17351087	0.46008512	2
3	1.61607440	3.55063864	0.28163947	3
4	1.89648088	5.16671304	0.19354665	4
5	2.22554093	7.06319392	0.14157901	5
6	2.61169647	9.28873485	0.10765729	6
7	3.06485420	11.90043132	0.08403057	7
8	3.59663973	14.96528552	0.06682131	8
9	4.22069582	18.56192525	0.05387372	9
10	4.95303242	22.78262106	0.04389311	10
11	5.81243739	27.73565349	0.03605468	11
12	6.82095847	33.54809088	0.02980796	12
13	8.00446891	40.36904935	0.02477145	13
14	9.39333129	48.37351827	0.02067247	14
15	11.02317638	57.76684955	0.01731097	15
16	12.93581732	68.79002594	0.01453699	16
17	15.18032224	81.72584325	0.01223603	17
18	17.81427318	96.90616550	0.01031926	18
19	20.90524324	114.72043868	0.00871684	19
20	24.53253020	135.62568191	0.00737323	20
21	28.78919088	160.15821211	0.00624383	21
22	33.78442846	188.94740299	0.00529248	22
23	39.64639407	222.73183145	0.00448970	23
24	46.52547444	262.37822552	0.00381129	24
25	54.59815003	308.90369996	0.00323725	25
26	64.07152260	363.50185000	0.00275102	26
27	75.18862829	427.57337260	0.00233878	27
28	88.23467268	502.76200089	0.00198901	28
29	103.54434758	590.99667356	0.00169206	29
30	121.51041752	694.54102115	0.00143980	30
31	142.59379590	816.05143867	0.00122541	31
32	167.33536962	958.64523456	0.00104314	32
33	196.36987535	1125.98060418	0.00088811	33
34	230.44218346	1322.35047954	0.00075623	34
35	270.42640743	1552.79266300	0.00064400	35
36	317.34832892	1823.21907042	0.00054848	36
37	372.41171388	2140.56739934	0.00046717	37
38	437.02919472	2512.97911322	0.00039793	38
39	512.85851094	2950.00830793	0.00033898	39
40	601.84503787	3462.86681888	0.00028878	40
41	706.27169460	4064.71185675	0.00024602	41
42	828.81751148	4770.98355134	0.00020960	42
43	972.62635979	5599.80106283	0.00017858	43
44	1141.38760663	6572.42742262	0.00015215	44
45	1339.43076439	7713.81502925	0.00012964	45
46	1571.83656296	9053.24579364	0.00011046	46
47	1844.56729405	10625.08235660	0.00009412	47
48	2164.61977185	12469.64965065	0.00008019	48
49	2540.20483383	14634.26942250	0.00006833	49
50	2980.95798704	17174.47425633	0.00005823	50

Glossary

amortization   reduction of a loan by periodic payments; sum of repayments in a given period

annual mortgage constant   quotient of one year's loan payments divided by the loan amount

Annual Percentage Rate (APR)   effective yield to a lender from interest, points and certain fees

annuity   any stream of periodic payments or an agreement to pay stated sums at certain dates

appraisal   estimate of the value of property at a certain date, prepared according to standard principles; see also **fair market value**

capitalization   process of estimating value by reference to current and projected future income; most often, this is current income divided by a cap rate   **capitalization rate** or **cap rate**   rate of return <u>on</u> and <u>of</u> a real estate investment

discount   to calculate the present value of a sum to be received in future; **discount rate**   interest rate at which a present value is estimated

equity   that form of capital not entitled to be repaid at a specific time; the value of real property minus the current balance of debt on it

fair market value (FMV)   price for property that a buyer would pay a seller, both of them willing, informed, and acting without undue pressures

future value   sum of a deposit and interest on it

income stream   periodic revenues promised or received from a lease or property; an annuity

leased fee   interest of a landlord in property leased to a tenant, especially for a long term

leasehold   interest a tenant holds in property by means of a lease, especially a long-term lease

net   after deduction of all charges;   **net operating income**   result after deducting operating expenses from total income;   **net present value** sum of future economic benefits discounted to the present minus the initial cost or price;   **net rent** rent free of all real estate taxes and operating costs

point   one percent of a loan; points are paid by a borrower or loan seller to increase loan yield

present value   value in terms of money today of payments or a lease reversion to be received in the future, discounted at a market rate of return

rent   payment for the right to use property for a term;   **contract rent**   rent fixed by lease or other contract, especially as distinguished from market rent;   **market rent**   rent that is or would be paid under open market conditions

recapture   the portion of overall property yield used to retire an investment

reversion   return to the landlord of the use of a leased property at the end of the lease term

sinking fund   accumulation of deposits and interest on them, held to meet future obligations

time value of money   weighting money transactions by the market discount rate for investments

value   measure of transferable utility in an asset or property right; see **fair market value**

About the Authors

JACK C. ESTES (deceased) was owner and manager of Century 21-Estes, Inc., Realtors in Falls Church, Virginia. He was also president and director of his own real estate school, a real estate appraiser, and lecturer. Mr. Estes was the author of *Real Estate License Preparation Course for the Uniform Examinations* and the *Handbook of Loan Payment Tables*.

DENNIS R. KELLEY has 28 years of experience in investment, financing, appraising and management. He is head of the real estate advisory division of LaSalle National Trust. He is the author of *The McGraw-Hill Handbook of Financial Tables for Real Estate*.